ALSO BY WILLIAM DIETRICH

The Final Forest

NORTHWEST PASSAGE

THE GREAT COLUMBIA RIVER

William Dietrich

by

William Dietrich

SIMON & SCHUSTER

New York   London   Toronto   Sydney   Tokyo   Singapore

SIMON & SCHUSTER
Rockefeller Center
1230 Avenue of the Americas
New York, New York 10020

SIMON & SCHUSTER and colophon are registered
trademarks of Simon & Schuster Inc.

Designed by Hyun Joo Kim

Manufactured in the United States of America

1   3   5   7   9   10   8   6   4   2

Library of Congress Cataloging-in-Publication Data
Dietrich, William, date.
Northwest passage : the great Columbia River / by William Dietrich.
p.   cm.
Includes bibliographical references and index.
1. Columbia River—History. 2. Columbia River Region—History.
I. Title.
F853.D54   1995
979.7—dc20   94-41920
CIP

ISBN 0-671-79650-X

The author is grateful for permission to reprint the following copyrighted material:
Excerpted lines from "Roll On, Columbia," words by Woody Guthrie, music based on
"Goodnight, Irene" by Huddie Ledbetter and John A. Lomax, TRO © Copyright 1936
(Renewed) 1957 (Renewed) and 1963 (Renewed) Ludlow Music, Inc., New York.
Excerpted lines from "Talking Columbia," words and music by Woody Guthrie TRO ©
Copyright 1961 (Renewed) 1963 (Renewed) Ludlow Music, Inc., New York.
Excerpted lines from "The Grand Coulee Dam," words and music by Woody Guthrie TRO
© Copyright 1958 (Renewed) 1963 (Renewed) 1976 Ludlow Music, Inc., New York.
Excerpted lines from "Pastures of Plenty," words and music by Woody Guthrie TRO ©
Copyright 1960 (Renewed) 1963 (Renewed) Ludlow Music, Inc., New York.

ACKNOWLEDGMENTS

This book benefited from the contributions of a large number of people who share my love of the Columbia River. To those quoted in the text and cited in the bibliography, I am in obvious debt. At the risk of unintentional omissions, many others deserve to be thanked.

Besides his own published work, Gene Tollefson at the Bonneville Power Administration shared three volumes of additional material. The University of Washington's Sandra Hines, Marion Marts, Bill Beyers, John Skalski, and Richard Morrill are among those who shared their thoughts; many others are cited in the text. Bill Lang and his staff at the Center for Columbia River History, located in Vancouver, provided a superb introduction to both the subject and to people such as Hobe Kytr at the Maritime History Museum in Astoria. Energy consultant Jim Lazar provided valuable material on the river's electricity tradeoffs. Don Moos, a former Washington director of agriculture and fisheries, shared his insights in a daylong tour and introduced me to Hu Blonk. Army Corps of Engineers historian Bill Willingham and Corps historical consultant Lisa Mighetto lent their expertise. The Wenatchee *World's* Wilfred Woods provided insight and valuable publications from his newspaper. The Grays Harbor Historical Seaport provided two voyages on the *Lady Washington;* Ray Hickey and Pat Jensen of Tidewater Barge Lines, a trip on their tugs.

A large number of government agencies provided invaluable help. A partial listing includes John Harrison, Linda Gist, John Volkman, Jim Ruff, and Peter Paquet of the Northwest Power Planning Council; Dulcy Mahar and Bill Murlin of the Bonneville Power Administration; Art Carroll of the U.S. Forest Service; Dexter Pitman and Steve Pettit of Idaho Fish and Game; Donald McIssac, Doug DeHart, Frank Young, and Steve King of the Oregon Department of Fish and Wildlife; Tom Flag of the National Marine Fisheries Service; Tony Floor and Wes Ebel (retired) of the Washington Department of Fish and Wildlife; Bill Gray, John Keys, and Marjo Richards of the Bureau of Reclamation; John McKearn, Kyle Schilling, and Sarah Wick of the Corps of Engineers; Lionel Boyer of the Shoshone-Bannock tribe; and the staff of Idaho governor Cecil Andrus. The U.S. Geological Survey, U.S. Coast Guard, National Park Service, Environmental Protection Agency, Washington Department of Ecology, Washington Public Power Supply System, B.C. Ministry of the Environment, B.C. Hydro, Washington State Parks, Washington Water Power, Idaho Power, and Douglas, Chelan, and Grant PUDs all provided information and aid.

I have always been extended courtesy and help on periodic trips to Hanford from the staffs of the Department of Energy, Westinghouse Hanford, and Battelle Pacific Northwest Labs. Insight has also been offered by the Yakima, Colville, and Warm Springs confederated tribes, and I benefited from collections developed by the Wanapum and Nez Perce. Northwest Indian historian Robert Ruby gave help and advice, attorney Tom Keefe, Jr., was unflagging in his support of David Sohappy and Indian rights, and Native Americans have long provided patient help; Wilbur Slockish is one of the latest to whom I am indebted.

In no particular order I must also thank Nancy Russell of Friends of the Columbia Gorge; fish biologists Tony Nigro, Willa Nehlsen, Harry Wagner, and John Skidmore; Les Dewey at Columbia Aluminum; Chuck Brendecke of Hydrosphere of Boulder, Colorado; Willard Fields of Chelan PUD; the staff at Cominco; Lori Bodi of American Rivers; Margie Sproat at Mica Dam; Bob Jackman of Citizens for a Clean Columbia; and representatives of the Columbia River Alliance, Direct Service Industries, Citizens for a Clean Columbia, and Riverwatch.

I learned about the Columbia while in the employ of two newspapers, the Vancouver *Columbian* and *Seattle Times.* Of the many fine people at the former I must cite former city editor Gregg Herrington for the opportunities he provided. I am indebted to the *Times* for time to work on this book and support from Mark Watanabe, Alex McLeod, Ross Anderson, Eric Nalder, and Marla Williams, to name just a few. I am grateful for the insights of Columbia River students Wayne Davis, Amy Hagstrom, Paul Jacobson, Karen Keith, Hilary Lorenz, Teresa Mitchell, Carole Teshima Morris, Dian Million, Jim Smith, and Aimee Trebon. I owe special thanks to teacher, mentor, and editor Robert Keller of Fairhaven College and his wife, Pat Karlberg.

Agent Kris Dahl of ICM provided the idea and impetus for this book. Editors Alice Mayhew and Sarah Baker at Simon & Schuster provided skill, sage advice, and encouragement. Finally I must thank the most remarkable woman I know, my wife, Holly, who has been unfailingly supportive in the long, difficult process of writing books.

To my daughters, Lisa and Heidi

In the end, we will conserve only what we love, we will love only what we understand, and we will understand only what we are taught.

—*Baba Dioum, Senegalese conservationist*

Boundary of
Columbia Basin

N

ROCKY MOUNTAIN

KOOTENAY
Columbia
Lake
Kootenay
SHUSWAP
SELKIRK MTS.
PURCELL MTS.
Kootenay R.
Columbia R.
LAKES
OKANOGAN
Kettle
Falls
COLVILLE
METHOW
Okanogan R.
CASCADE MTS.
CHELAN
WENATCHI
Columbia
Yakima
WANA
COWL
CHEHALIS
SANPOIL
PEND D'OREILLE
KALISPELL
Clark Fork R.
COEUR D'ALENE
SPOKANE
COLUMBIA
FLATHEAD
R.
atwater R.
OUSE
R.

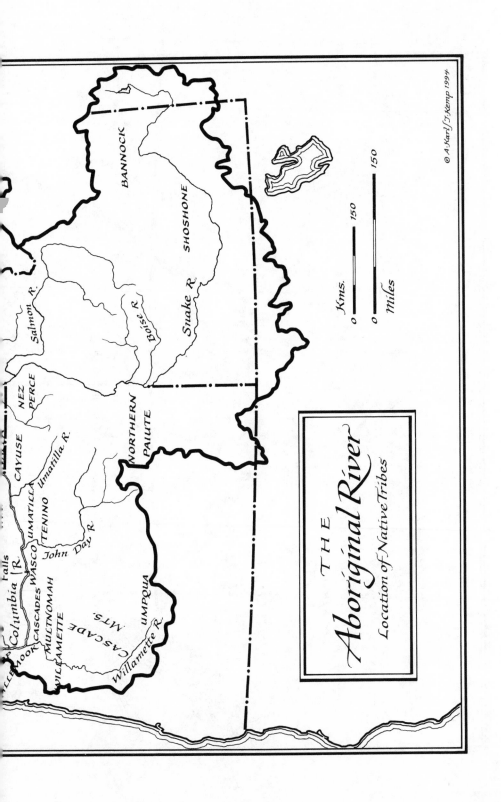

THE
Aboriginal River
Location of Native Tribes

BANNOCK

SHOSHONE

Boise R.

Snake R.

Salmon R.

NEZ PERCE

Umatilla R.

CAYUSE

UMATILLA

WASCO

CASCADES

TENINO

John Day R.

MULTNOMAH

WILLAMETTE

CASCADE MTS.

UMPQUA

Willamette R.

NORTHERN PAIUTE

Columbia R.

Falls

Kms.

0   150

Miles

0   150

© A.Karl/J.Kemp 1994

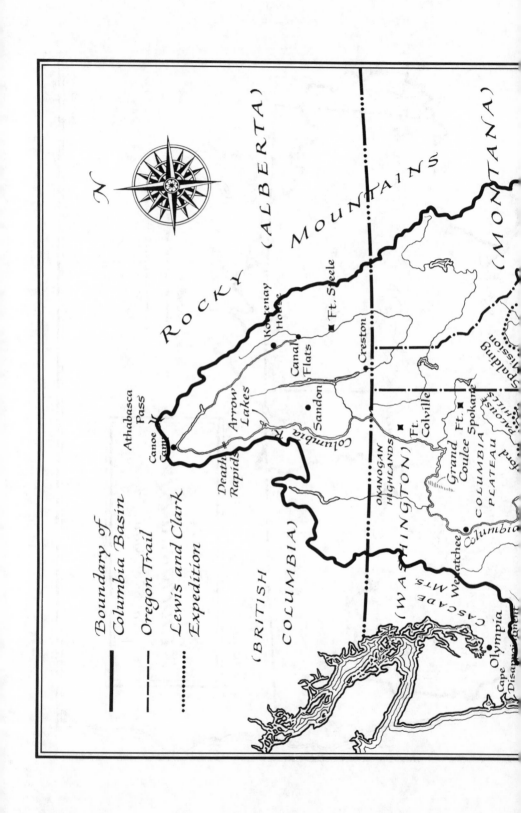

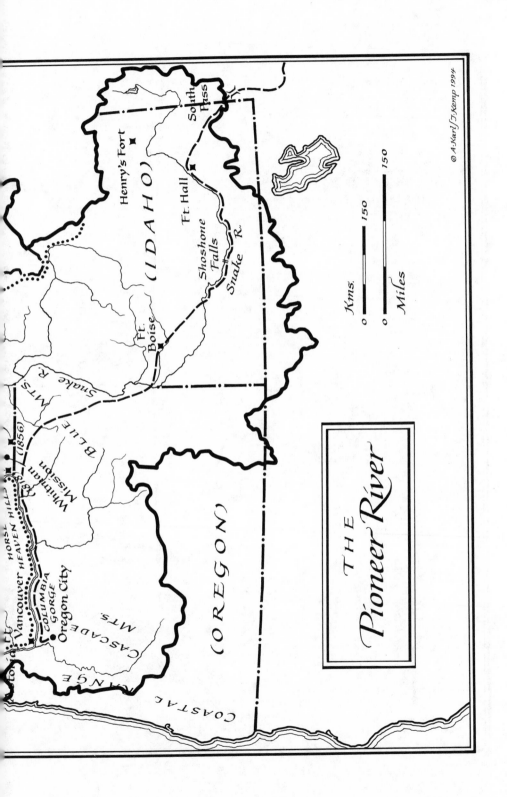

THE
Pioneer River

© A.Karl/J.Kemp 1994

Kms. 0 ⊢——⊣ 150

Miles 0 ⊢——⊣ 150

(IDAHO)

Henry's Fort

Ft. Hall

South Pass

Shoshone Falls

Snake R.

Ft. Boise

Snake R.

BLUE MTS.

Whitman Mission

(1856)

(1843)

HORSE HEAVEN HILLS

Vancouver

COLUMBIA GORGE

Oregon City

CASCADE MTS.

COASTAL RANGE

(OREGON)

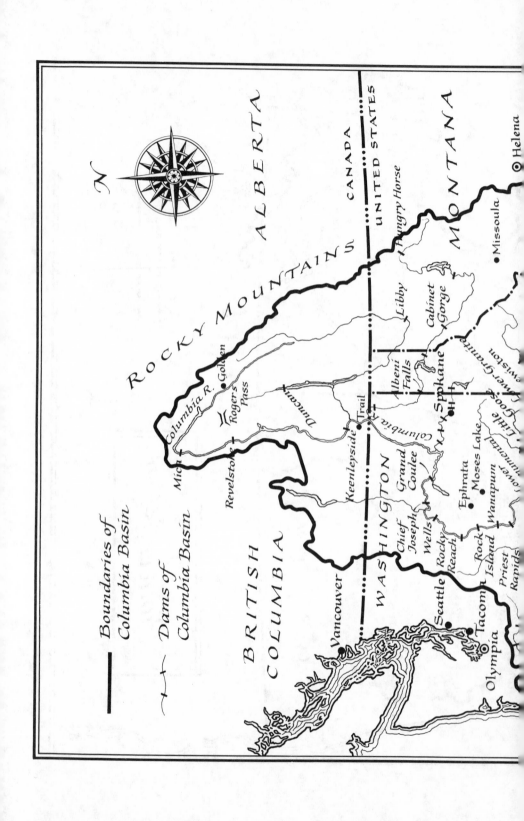

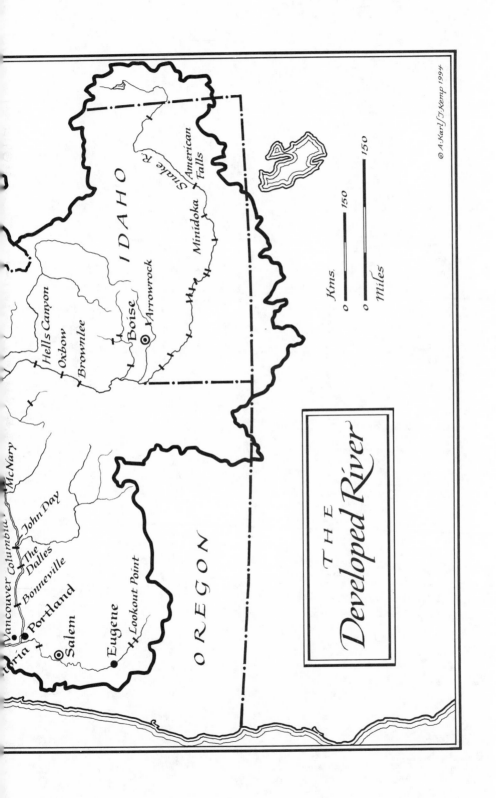

THE
Developed River

Kms. 0 ———— 150
Miles 0 ———— 150

© A. Karl / J. Kemp 1994

CONTENTS

Introduction

It was a fine dam. Scrap lumber was used to represent its concrete and a patching compound called Fixall formed the brown desert hills it nestled between. The Columbia River was plywood, painted blue and coated with varnish to produce a wet sheen. My grade-school model of Grand Coulee Dam was probably a bit *too* good, betraying my father's help, but it got a top grade anyway. Even in miniature, the world's biggest concrete structure drew the eye. There was a geometric boldness to it. The straight wedge was in such sharp contrast to the irregular canyon, and the elevation difference between the river below and the reservoir behind was testimony to the dam's strength and power. The assignment had been to model something of the Pacific Northwest. Grand Coulee was the most obvious subject I could think of.

I liked dams. I've since learned of their steep environmental costs, but my admiration for the sheer cockiness of the human achievement they represent has not disappeared. To hold back the huge, cold, powerful Columbia River! They are not just dead concrete but a human artifact, as evocative as a Paleolithic carving or soaring rocket: the product of thousands of people working millions of hours to make something lasting. After Grand Coulee Dam was dedicated, one of its most tireless proponents, a newspaper publisher named Rufus Woods, distilled its allure in a 1942 speech to assembled high school students. "Could you come back here a thousand years hence, or could your spirit hover around this place ten thousand years hence," Woods predicted, "you would hear the sojourners talking as they beheld this slab of concrete, and you would hear them say, 'Here, in 1942, indeed there once lived a great people.' "

I grew up in Washington State and the dams of the Columbia were a part of the region's mythology. I sang "Roll On, Columbia" with my fourth-grade choir at the Puyallup County Fair. I accompanied my parents when they journeyed to Chief Joseph Dam to bid on painting the interior of its powerhouse. The building is the longest in-line generator structure in the world, nearly half a mile in extent, and the twenty-seven generators that march down its beige concrete interior run on so far that they become difficult to count in the distance. Chief Joseph was grander than any cathedral I had ever seen, a place that throbbed to the churn of turbine blades and hummed to the buzz of electricity. It also seemed utterly empty of people. Here was something heroic in scale, coldly imposing in its robotic grandeur, as tireless as running water. Who could help but be impressed?

My attitude was typical of the era. About the same time I was being enthralled by dams, author Allan Cullen, in his 1962 book, *Rivers in Harness*, described his thoughts when riding an elevator down the interior of Hoover Dam near Las Vegas: "The elevator ride is somehow a disturbing one, for you know that leaping, straining masses of water are only a matter of yards from you. You feel a sense of apprehension at the fragility of man and his works. But it gives way, as you continue to descend, to a new feeling of exhilaration and confidence, as you realize that the dam will protect you after all. You feel sudden wonder at the knowledge that small weak creatures very much like yourself somehow succeeded in damming this potent river. By the time you reach the bottom of the shaft, you feel like a giant, holding back the rush of water yourself with one contemptuously outstretched hand."

This romance could not last. In a frenzied burst of construction after World War II, the dam builders overreached themselves. In a generation America went from too many floods to too many flooded reservoirs. Hydroelectricity went from miracle to status quo. Undeveloped rivers went from something useless to something precious in their rarity. Irrigation projects struggled to justify their rising costs to farmers and taxpayers. It has been two decades now since Congress last authorized a major reclamation project.

By the 1980s, some social critics saw the river culture of the western United States as a disaster instead of a triumph. "Accepting the authority of engineers, scientists, economists and bureaucrats along with the power of capital, the common people have become a herd," historian Donald Worster caustically charged in his 1985 book, *Rivers of Empire*. "They live as docile masses governed by clocks. More and more of their needs are attended to by others, even their leisure time is organized for them. Someone decides what they should want, what will keep them amused and uncomplaining, and what they must accept as reality."

The Columbia, boasting the second-largest flow in the United States, once seemed the most inexhaustible of rivers: able to produce more fish than anyone could eat, more power than anyone could use, and more water than anyone could pump. By 1968, however, Washington senator Henry Jackson wrote into law a prohibition against even *studying* the export of its water to other regions of the nation. In the quarter century since, the Columbia seemed increasingly inadequate to serve even the Pacific Northwest. A struggle between competing river users became acrimonious and bitter. By 1990 petitions were filed to put some of its salmon runs on the endangered species list.

To a Pacific Northwest journalist such as myself, the river was inescapable as a subject. Its energy powered the region and its history dictated the region's history. Stories took me to the Columbia and its tributaries again and again. Many of the people I encountered, however, looked at the river from the narrow perspective of their own experience. One colleague said it was as if everyone looked at the Columbia through a pipe. Many of those who lived on its banks had only the vaguest idea of where the river originated in Canada, how it was run by engineers each day, or what happened to the water downstream. I was reminded of the poem about the blind men and the elephant, in which one feels the beast's leg and concludes it is a tree, another holds its tail and believes it a rope, and so on. Each interest group looked at the Columbia and saw a different river.

That experience dictated the approach of this book. I had lived and reported on the Columbia myself—in Vancouver, Washington—yet knew relatively little about it. My work as a writer on environmental issues, particularly the old-growth forests of the Pacific Northwest, had introduced me to the idea of ecosystems and the interrelationship of many parts to a greater whole. I wanted a comprehensive understanding of the river embracing history, geology, biology, hydrology, economics, and contemporary politics and management.

Readers familiar with the complexity of the Columbia River will recognize the resulting ambition of this book. Its subject is huge. Sections of its chapters could be, and in some cases have been, books in themselves. I have unavoidably had to summarize points that could be, and have been, examined in excruciatingly technical detail.

One of the mistakes of the past, however, has been our tendency to focus narrowly on development of some part of a river without considering consequences for the whole. "When we [whites] are confronted by a complex problem, we want to take a part of the complexity and deal with that," remarked Steve Parker, a fish biologist hired by the Yakima Indian tribe. The Henry Ford assembly line is an example of this kind of specialization, Parker said. Its economic success is why narrow focus and admiration of specialists became ingrained in American culture. The river's first human inhabitants, however, thought differently. To them, time was more a cycle than a progressive arrow, and as a result they exhibited more caution about what might be and displayed more respect for what was. I hope this book will encourage readers to ponder the advantages and disadvantages of each approach.

The desire to examine the Columbia from a variety of perspectives suggested the structure of the book. While the first twelve chapters dwell primarily on the natural and human history of the river and the last five primarily on the contemporary river, past and present are entwined throughout the text. The Columbia today is the product of its yesterdays.

Similarly, the book does not follow the river from source to mouth but skips and hops around its basin, moving from subject to subject rather than place to place. The Columbia River cannot be understood as a thread of water alone. It is the product of a huge watershed in which each action reverberates with every other action. I have attempted in the book's organization to give a sense of that. I hope the reader's journey will prove smooth enough, but maps and a chronology have been included to aid orientation.

Finally, this book relies heavily on personal observations, my own and many others. This, too, is deliberate. The Columbia River is not just an economic resource. It is an emotional and spiritual one. I am not as interested in dictating how readers should feel and think about the river as in persuading them that it is a subject to be felt and thought about—not taken for granted. For too long the Columbia has been left to the experts. The one thing America's most beautiful river cannot endure is our indifference.

What happens to the Columbia, after all, is what happens to us. The Yakimas say that when the salmon are gone, they will be gone.

1

The Picnic in the Coulee

Grand Coulee Dam with Banks Lake
Reservoir and Steamboat Rock in the
background. *(Bureau of Reclamation)*

When seen from the reservoir it rises from, Steamboat Rock does indeed appear to be steaming toward Grand Coulee Dam. Flat and elongated, the basalt mesa looks like a giant stern-wheeler superstructure on a deck of sagebrush desert. The deck, in turn, seems to be floating on top of Banks Lake, which fills about half of that fifty-mile-long geologic scar across central Washington State known as the Grand Coulee. It is the rock's ruddy summit, however, not the artificial lake, that provides the best vantage point to begin an understanding of the Columbia River's history. There one can see the geographic logic of an idea that utterly changed the Pacific Northwest.

The mesa is the kind of attention-getting monolith that almost demands to be climbed to its hurricane deck, but instead of a boat stair there is a steep, crumbling trail up a draw in the volcanic cliffs to the eight-hundred-foot-high plateau on top. This table is about a square mile in area. Paths wind away through bunch grass to its abrupt cliffs, giving grand views of the Coulee, the reservoir, the blue bluffs of the distant Okanogan Highlands, and in spring a pencil line of green wheat along the Coulee's rim.

I cannot see the Columbia at all. The river and its famous dam are ten miles to the north, tucked down in a canyon more than a thousand feet below me. Only silver power pylons on the Coulee horizon, looking like the stiff stick figures of Native American petroglyphs, point to where generators hum. The river used to flow around this point, however. Steamboat Rock is a stubbornly uneroded piece of volcanic plateau that cleaved the Columbia in two, back when the river was an Ice Age torrent excavating the Grand Coulee. After the glaciers retreated and the prehistoric riverbed went dry, the rock sat for ten thousand years like a sternwheeler grounded by a departed tide, silent and evocative as an old wreck. Now it crowns a peninsula in a lake named for the man who oversaw construction of Grand Coulee Dam, a reservoir that once more has filled the old river channel with water.

The view seems vaguely disorienting. Steamboat Rock is in the Evergreen State, but Grand Coulee is mostly treeless and raw in the rain shadow of the Cascade Mountains. The view is of rock ramparts and wrung-out sky. A state park at the rock's base uses sprinklers to maintain an oasis of lawn with a metronomic *whick-whick* that keeps time with the insects, the green only emphasizing the long reach of the surrounding desert. I am looking at a Pacific Northwest that is a rusty brown, a desert canyon with a floor of water.

Grand Coulee roughly marks the northernmost extent of that region of desert and basin that occupies most of the West between the Pacific Coast ranges and the Rocky Mountains. From where I am standing, this arid domain runs for two thousand miles south into central Mexico. I drove this long dryness once when coming out of the Yucatan, and was at first awed and then bored and finally just anxiously impatient by the endless miles of sage and cactus and sunburnt mountains, the hard peaks rising like islands from evaporated seas. When I finally turned west from this sere monotony I pierced the Cascades where the Columbia does and ran into a cool marine storm in its gorge. A hundred waterfalls braided the Oregon cliffs and rain dimpled the pewter surface of Bonneville Pool. My mind relaxed, finally, as if visually slaking a great thirst. I had seen the true nature of the West, a region where history is to a large extent the history of water. At traditional meals of the Yakima Indian Tribe southwest of Grand Coulee a glass of water is served at the start of any feast and at its end, a reminder of the centrality of water to this land, the Creator's gift never to be taken for granted.

Oregon senator Mark Hatfield once put it differently. "I am convinced it was not the six-gun that won the West," he told a conference audience, "but water impounded that won the West."

Steamboat Rock can be as hot and hard as an anvil in high summer. But on the day I remember, at the end of a wet spring, its tabletop summit was muggy warm and still bloomed lushly with yellow arrow-leaf balsam and purple lupine and pink phlox. An apple farmer had pointed out purple sage to me and I marveled at it. I had always assumed this Zane Grey botany to be a descriptive figure of language, but it is in fact a figwort that blooms a bold, beautiful purple. The air smelled of sage and dust and artificial lake, that jarring combination our civilization has created in the dry country.

Steamboat Rock is anchored within the confines of one of the most dramatic features of the Pacific Northwest. The word "coulee" comes from the French verb *couler*, "to flow," and has become western vernacular for a dry watercourse. Down this huge channel the swollen waters of the Columbia poured when its normal path was blocked by an Ice Age glacier half a mile high. Had I been standing on Steamboat then, the ice would have been a white-gray wall to the north higher than the Manhattan skyline, grinding at the edge of the Columbia Plateau. A wet, cold wind would have blown off the sheet across a bitter landscape of tundra. Below me the river would have roared with a volume up to fifty times its present flow, milky with glacial flour, and the spray where it broke around Steamboat would have coated the rock's lava prow with frost. The prehistoric river chewed through the Columbia Plateau for almost thirty miles, plunged four hundred feet down basalt cliffs in what was the greatest waterfall in the world, and then carved the lower Grand Coulee for another fifteen miles. The result is a channel two to five miles wide and up to a thousand feet deep, running southwest with oxidized red walls of such sheer and even height that it brings to mind science fiction paintings of the imagined canals of Mars. Basalt rubble covers the base of the cliffs like a skirt. Talus that once spilled onto a flat pan of desert sand is now lapped by water.

The coulee is somber, eerie, and magnificent at the same time. Early fur trader Alexander Ross anticipated the typical mixed reaction of the modern visitor. "While in one place the solemn gloom forbids the wanderer to advance," he described, "in another the prospect is lively and inviting, the ground being thickly studded with ranges of columns, pillars, battlements, turrets, and steps above steps, in every variety of shade and color." Parts of the coulee are indeed so sculpted and other sections, now under seventy feet of stored water, were as smooth as a causeway. "Thunder and lightning are known to be more frequent here than in other parts," Ross goes on in his colorful fashion, "and a rumbling in the earth is sometimes heard. According to Indian tradition, it is the abode of evil spirits." I remembered that line when I awoke late one night while camped by Steamboat's flank, my tent suddenly shaken by a high, howling wind that sent other campers stumbling out in the dark to secure their powerboats to the shoreline. There was no rumbling in the earth, but the strange tempest died as quickly and mysteriously as it came.

The coulee walls present a cross-section of one of the greatest basalt flows on the earth's surface, a hot flood of magma that ran over the interior Pacific Northwest like crusted syrup in waves more than one hundred feet high. As the lava cooled it fractured vertically into polygons. When the cliffs erode they break at these joints to form a wall of connected columns, leaving a corrugated face like the brooding palisade of a log fort or the pipes on an endless organ. The effect is beautiful without being pretty. The dull volcanic rock has a coarseness that seems to swallow light, and there is a majestic grim confinement to the coulee reminiscent of a prison yard. Yet the disquieting effect of this geology is relieved by the bright splotches of orange and mustard-green lichen splashed along the cliffs as if from a rain of paint. Life has made its own tenacious treaty here. On Steamboat's summit birds chatter and flit over its meadow, and a large herd of apparently literate deer have taken refuge around posted "no hunting" signs.

• • •

I've come to this point to reimagine a picnic in the coulee. Sunday, June 28, 1931, was bright but blessedly cool here, a perfect day for a rally—which was fortunate since this was to prove the biggest such gathering in local memory. An auto caravan of farmers and shopkeepers and small-town lawyers wound down the dry coulee that day past Steamboat Rock, a long plume of dust pointing toward the gathering point where, once more, they would hear of a fantastic plan to fill this country with water.

For three decades before this picnic, the western half of the Columbia Plateau had been emptying of people. The initial wave of hopeful settlers brought by the railroads had given up; the region's seven to ten inches of annual rainfall had proven inadequate for farming. Since 1910 the population of the area had dropped 40 percent, and abandoned fields were being recolonized by cheat grass and sagebrush. Hot winds banged the doors of deserted farmhouses, and rusting windmills squealed as they tried in futility to raise water from wells run dry. Drought had come to the Northwest along with the Crash in 1929, and vast dust clouds more than a thousand miles long blew off the arid plateau. Dust had engulfed an ocean liner six hundred miles off the Pacific Northwest coast just two months before the 1931 rally. Even today a hard summer wind across the fields of eastern Washington can turn the sky an eerie yellow-brown: one navigates with headlights, and traffic signals and the neon beer signs in the windows of farm-town taverns glow like lighthouse beacons. In lesser breezes dust devils as high as a Douglas fir spin lazily over the furrows under a broad blue sky, dancing a minuet with plowing tractors.

As the region's topsoil blew away, hope went with it. A half century of overgrazing and ill-advised plowing had caught up with the so-called Inland Empire. Half the farms in Franklin County were foreclosed or abandoned in the first years of the Great Depression.

Now a handful of dreamers from places most Americans had never heard of—Wenatchee and Ephrata and Brewster and Waterville—proposed a solution as grand as the coulee they gathered in. The federal government, they contended, should construct the biggest dam ever built, a dam that would plug the nation's second-biggest river and water an area twice the size of Rhode Island. The dam would create the world's longest artificial lake, require the world's largest concrete mixing plant, pour water down the world's biggest spillway, and lift water into the coulee with the world's most powerful pumps. It would be three times more massive than Boulder Dam (later renamed Hoover) rising on the Colorado River near Las Vegas. It would have three times the mass of the Great Pyramid of Cheops.

The rally was in direct response to a rival one the day before. If there was public unanimity that the arid interior of the Pacific Northwest needed water, there was no consensus on how to supply it. For thirteen years residents argued whether a government dam or private canal was the most practicable scheme. On the side of the canal proposal was the Columbia Basin Irrigation League, a business coalition that had the backing of the Spokane establishment and Washington Water Power, the powerful private electric utility based in that city. On Saturday the Irrigation League had held a rally of one thousand people in nearby Lind to urge the digging of a one-hundred-and-thirty-mile canal from Pend Oreille Lake in northern Idaho to the rain-starved plateau. This scheme required no big dam or pumps, and thus needed no generators that would compete with Washington Water Power. Not incidentally, the "gravity plan," as it was known, would feed water to the Spokane River and thus the utility's turbines, strengthening its monopoly in the region.

This group seemed to have the upper hand. The eminent George Goethals, engineer of the Panama Canal, visited the area for just six days in 1922 and gave his support to the canal, a recommendation that killed serious public discussion of a dam at Grand Coulee for the next seven years. The Bureau of Reclamation, which was already directing construction of Boulder Dam, was intrigued by Grand Coulee but still a bit overwhelmed by a dam that, if built, would generate sixteen times as much electricity as everything the Bureau had built since 1902. The Army Corps of Engineers, which was examining the entire Columbia River, had yet to issue its recommendation, and attempts to enlist President Hoover behind a dam at Grand Coulee were rebuffed. "We do not need further additions to our agricultural lands at present," Hoover said. Many Americans elsewhere thought a dam was absurd. "Up in the Grand Coulee area there is no one to sell the power to except the jackrabbits and rattlesnakes," Republican congressman Francis Culkin of New York would warn his House colleagues.

Promoting the dam was another league, the Columbia River Development League, a grassroots coalition powered not by money but by the tireless enthusiasm of Ephrata lawyers and a boosterish Wenatchee newspaper publisher. This league hoped their Sunday picnic and rally would visibly demonstrate that as the depression deepened, sentiment was swinging behind government intervention to build the dam. Certainly after years of derision toward the idea the tide now seemed to be turning. In 1927 the Idaho legislature passed a law attempting to reserve would-be canal water from its panhandle. In 1929 the Grange, which was worried about farm surpluses if the government irrigated new western lands, was won over by promises of cheap electricity to farms from a dam at Grand Coulee. Half the rural households in Washington, and two-thirds in Oregon, were still without power half a century after Thomas Edison invented an effective lightbulb. As the drought worsened, Pacific Northwest streams that supplied hydropower to the cities west of the Cascades ran so low that the city of Tacoma had to borrow power from the aircraft carrier *Lexington*, rekindling interest in tapping the mighty Columbia. And in 1930, Washington voters had reacted to scandal that rocked the nation's private utilities in the wake of the stock market crash by approving a law allowing creation of public power districts. Public utilities needed a source of public power, and a government dam on the Columbia could provide it. Finally, if Hoover remained reluctant to back Grand Coulee Dam, a new administration might be persuaded. New York governor Franklin Delano Roosevelt had won decisive reelection in 1930 after creating a public utility there. Might he run for President?

At issue was not just an engineering dispute of dam versus canal. It was, in the minds of many farmers and merchants, a battle between public versus private power, government development versus the abuses of free enterprise, the common versus an elite, and small town versus big city. Grand Coulee Dam would be cited as an argument for the democratic potential of physical and social engineering, the ability of big government to harness nature for the benefit of the little man. As such, it was a micro-cosm of the philosophic struggle over the proper role of the state and proper scale of human development that was to occupy much of the twentieth century. Here was the promise that modern tech-nology could not only remake the landscape, but society itself.

In the Soviet Union, Lenin had proclaimed, "Communism is Soviet government plus electrification of the whole country." Here in America, visionaries were proposing that harnessed wa-ter would make economically feasible family-sized forty-acre farms, "land for the landless," and a new generation of agricul-tural pioneers in central Washington four hundred thousand strong. Damming rivers for water and power would free agricul-ture in the West from monopolization by huge ranches and big business, giving new life to Thomas Jefferson's dream of a democ-racy grounded on the values of yeoman farmers. Electricity would also bring to rural America the labor-saving machines al-ready enjoyed by the city, and would allow the dispersal of indus-try to smaller towns, reducing pollution and crowding. Not incidentally, a dam would resuscitate the parched economy of those locals still hanging on to farms and stores around Grand Coulee. After irrigation, land prices in the irrigated flats to the south would soar more than a hundred times above their depres-sion value.

The picnic and rally began with an 8:30 A.M. visit to the dam site itself. To an untrained eye the location was unremarkable. The Columbia, with a general course to the south and west, twisted to run north here for a few miles. Flush with rain and snow melt from Canada, the powerful river ran in a steep valley of barren, rounded hills about one thousand feet deep and two thousand feet wide at river level. The canyon broadened to more than a mile wide at its top, requiring a long, high, fat, and intimi-datingly expensive dam.

The site's advantages were twofold. First, the river had cut through fractured basalt and glacial till down close to the granite bedrock that could serve as an adequate foundation. Second, and most important, the site was at the lip of the neighboring Grand Coulee, the key to the whole scheme in this otherwise mystify-ingly remote spot.

The picnic caravan wound down a gravel road to the river-bank, and people got out of their cars for a few minutes to look around at the emptiness. At most two dozen people lived in the canyon here, running a cable ferry where the dam would go and trying to eke out a marginal living on bench land a few miles downstream. An Indian called One-Eyed-Charlie occupied the east bank, and across the river the Nat Washington family had tried and failed to farm three thousand acres of scrubland bought from two black families for nine hundred gold dollars in 1909. A proud family descended from George Washington's younger brother, the Washingtons had lost a southern estate called Claymont Court after the Civil War. Starting over out West, they had tried to go it alone without the government. To bring water to his eighty-foot-high benchland, Washington used a "current pump." This was a Rube Goldberg contraption in which the current would push a giant oar downstream, pumping water, and then the board would spring clear of the river and lurch back. It could be moved up and down on wooden rails to follow the water level of the wildly fluctuating Columbia.

The river proved not so easily tapped. The first year, June snowmelt required that the pump be pulled off the rails to keep it from being swept away and a young orchard of apple trees died of thirst. The next year a new set of trees survived the summer only to be gnawed off by rabbits that could reach their branches on deep snow. With that kind of experience the Washingtons dreamed of government help. Scott McCann, an amateur geologist who ran a grocery store in Coulee City, convinced Nat of the feasibility of the dam proposed by Ephrata lawyer Billy Clapp and the flamboyant publisher of the Wenatchee *World*, Rufus Woods. Washington was a rising star in the Democratic Party, and during the 1920 national convention he got the chance to describe the dam idea to vice-presidential candidate Franklin Roosevelt. Roosevelt listened: Washington was not just a farmer but smooth, personable, a potential candidate someday for governor. "He had glamour," his son, Nat, Jr., remembers. "He spoke with a soft southern accent. If he had been alive during the Roosevelt years, there is no telling how far he might have gone."

The river struck first, on July 10, 1926. Nat, Jr., a retired state senator who lives next door to the Bureau of Reclamation headquarters in Ephrata, vividly remembered the trauma more than sixty years later. "There was a warm pool behind a sandbar," he described. "I was twelve years old. My dad was teaching me to swim. I had no idea what my uncle was doing. Somehow he got on the river side of the sandbar and began to be swept away. My dad, who was an excellent swimmer, dived in. I remember shouting, waving my arm: 'Come on in, come on in, come on in!' He just wouldn't do it. He wouldn't do it. My aunt had gone in as well to help, and both were taken by the current. My uncle had already disappeared." He paused a moment, remembering that day with a grim, awful clarity. "I went to get some horses to ride for help. I dreaded seeing my grandmother, and having to tell her what had happened. Aunt Pearl dived in, and I didn't. Every complex I have, I blame on that."

A month later, the river gave up the bodies at Brewster. Such stories were not uncommon. The Columbia was big, cold, rock-studded, erratic. Damned useless if you were a farmer, damned dangerous if you had to cross it. Even today, ask longtime river residents what they remember about the river before the dams, and one of the commonest recollections was the admonition not to swim in it. The Columbia killed. "Thought the old Columbia would never amount to much," folk hero Woody Guthrie would later sing.

On the Sunday of the picnic the assembled dam enthusiasts remembered Washington and his dream. They listened while a lawyer and contractor named James O'Sullivan stood on the Columbia's shore and pointed out to the crowd exactly where the structure would go. Then the group dispersed to their cars and farm trucks and wound back up the thousand-foot bluff and over a divide down into Grand Coulee. The coulee floor was about six hundred feet higher than the bed of the nearby river.

The route was deliberately symbolic. The Columbia Plateau is scarred by coulees, gouged out by Ice Age floods greater than any others known to have occurred on earth: Moses Coulee, French Coulee, Black Rock Coulee, Dry Coulee, Lynch Coulee, Rocky Coulee, Bauer Coulee, Washtucna Coulee, Old Maid Coulee, and so on, one after another writhing across a scabland of washes and broad sandy plains, where occasional knobs of lava poke above the surface like the conning towers of submarines. Grand Coulee dwarfs them all, and no place better illustrates the potential power of water. Big rivers are usually opaque, a rumpled two-dimensional sheet of swirling liquid with only the boils and eddies giving a clue to the depth underneath. Here in Grand Coulee was the bottom of a vanished flood where a person could get a sense of depth as well as width, a notion of just what rivers can do. And the Coulee pointed to what Bureau of Reclamation commissioner Elmore Mead called "the largest and finest compact body of land feasible of irrigation remaining in the United States."

The idea was daringly simple. The dominant geographic feature in eastern Washington, eastern Oregon, and southern Idaho is a broad basalt plateau more than 100,000 square miles in extent. In central Washington this high rolling landscape is ringed by the Cascade Mountains to the west, the Okanogan Highlands to the north, the Rockies to the east, and the Blue Mountains to the south, explaining the confusing appellation of Columbia "Basin" to the plateau even though much of the basin is far above the level of the Columbia and Snake rivers.

The plateau is not really flat. It is rumpled by rolling hills and cut by coulees. But on the broadest scale it is like a vast plate tilted from northeast to southwest, its upper rim as much as twenty-seven hundred feet above sea level and the southwest apron only three hundred and seventy feet high, ending at Pasco, Washington. Bending around the northern and western fringe of this plateau is the Columbia River. If the river's water could somehow be lifted to the plateau's northern rim, it would run by gravity southward for two hundred miles before rejoining the Columbia, irrigating up to a million acres of farmland. Accordingly, these farmers wanted to duplicate what the Ice Age had done: to dam the Columbia until it spilled south through the Grand Coulee to plateau farmland. The initial proposal by Billy Clapp had called for a titanic structure eight hundred feet high to bring the reservoir level nearly up to the summit of the lip of land between the Columbia and the coulee. That, however, would back the river more than a hundred miles into Canada. The proposal had been scaled back to a dam five hundred and fifty feet high above bedrock, creating a reservoir that reached to the border. This would generate more than enough electricity to pump river water up and over the rest of the way: enough electricity, promoters promised, to pay for the dam; enough electricity, detractors scoffed, that the region couldn't use it all for the next one hundred and fifty years. The adjacent Upper Coulee would be turned into a natural reservoir, a basalt bathtub, with a low dam twenty-seven miles to the south to hold irrigation water in place until farmers needed it.

The Pacific Northwest's reputation as a wet place—based on the heavily populated green trough that runs from Vancouver, British Columbia, past Seattle and Portland to Eugene, Oregon— is misleading. The Cascade Mountains block much of this moisture from reaching the interior of the region, leaving desert and prairie in their eastern shadow. Lewis and Clark called the resulting landscape "the Great Columbia Plain." The resulting landscape is so confusingly varied, so rich and poor in soils, so wet and dry depending on site and elevation, that it baffled some of the settlers looking for a homestead. Many early explorers misjudged the agricultural potential of what are now some of the richest wheat-growing lands of the United States, mistakenly dismissing them as too dry. Yet after pioneers plowed these areas and raised record harvests of dryland wheat, later homesteaders trying to imitate their success learned the hard way just where the limits of feasible rainfall lay. A distance of ten miles east or west or a few hundred feet in elevation could mean an inch difference in rainfall and success or failure in farming. The Pacific Northwest, which receives up to two hundred inches of precipitation in its rain forests, can get as little as five inches in the deserts next to stretches of the Columbia River. The plateau was at the boundary of arable land and waste, and accordingly is bisected by the longest creek in America. In any other place a watercourse like Crab Creek would either develop into a proper river or evaporate in the desert sun. Here it just crawled across the scablands, neither accumulating any appreciable flow nor disappearing, until it finally drizzled into the Columbia.

The dream was not new. Northwest irrigation dated back to Marcus Whitman's first ditch in the Walla Walla Valley in 1837. Later, private irrigation companies both failed and flourished, and by 1910, 2.3 million acres were watered in the region, twothirds in Idaho. Several abortive private irrigation schemes for the Columbia Plateau were attempted using windmills, a steam-fired coal plant, and gasoline engines, but high cost and disappointing crops bankrupted all of them. Schemes drew con men and hucksters. Near the agriculturally tempting Wahluke Slope, the body of one promoter of an irrigation scheme was dragged from the Columbia. His partner had disappeared with a million dollars in invested funds before a drop of water was pumped.

So the land stayed dry while the nation's second biggest river, fourth largest in North America, roared and foamed just beyond the coulee's northern lip. It might as well have been on the moon. The Columbia had dug itself one to two thousand feet below the level of the Columbia Plateau, and up on top abandoned farms were pitted by blowing sand.

This, then, was a rally for water. Grand Coulee Dam would ultimately prove far more significant to the nation as a generator of electricity, but the initial scheme was simply to use the power to pay for pumps. While there were a few shiny Cadillacs in the procession motoring down Grand Coulee, many more were open-top Model T Fords or wheezing farm trucks. These were mostly ordinary people, small-town folks ground down by the depression and dreaming of a big government project that could economically rescue where fate had happened to drop them.

The monied utilities had looked at the Columbia already. Seattle's powerful private utility, Puget Sound Power & Light, was already constructing the first low dam on the river, at Rock Island seventy-five miles to the southwest. This more modest effort, however, would not create the vast reservoir storage, irrigation network, or enormous electric generation of a Grand Coulee. Seven years earlier a subsidiary of General Electric had proposed a private $100 million dam and industrial complex at Priest Rapids, one hundred miles to the southwest, but that scheme had been killed by the 1929 Crash.

The Columbia River Development League, in contrast, had big dreams and empty pockets. O'Sullivan was probably one of the worst-compensated lobbyists in the country. In 1909 he had purchased farm land on the Columbia Plateau that remained distressingly, pointedly dry. When Billy Clapp got a story on his dam idea into the Wenatchee *World,* development-happy publisher Rufus Woods persuaded O'Sullivan to look at the site. Drawing on his experience as an engineer, O'Sullivan had written a series of articles in 1920 supporting the proposal. Experts and agencies scoffed, however, and he soon retreated to Port Huron, Michigan, to take over his family's contracting business. Then the Crash came in 1929, souring construction and improving the political climate for the dam. O'Sullivan left his family in Michigan and came back west as the Development League's chief lobbyist and spokesman. Promised a salary of two hundred dollars a month, in reality he was paid so infrequently by his depression-battered constituents that he had to cash a life-insurance policy to provide money for his family. When the league managed to scrape together $129 in donations and deposited it in a local bank, the bank closed its doors and froze all accounts the next day. When O'Sullivan set out to make speeches at forty towns in sub-zero weather, dam enthusiast Roxie Thorsen replaced her promised five-dollar donation with shaving cream and a razor. At Almira, the hotel manager donated a room and bath. Others shared meals.

Just why O'Sullivan so doggedly pursued this dam has never been adequately explained. In 1983 his daughter recalled to the Wenatchee *World* that O'Sullivan was a lover of history. At Grand Coulee, perhaps, he saw an opportunity to make it.

So down the coulee the auto caravan rolled, their imagination jogged even more by Dry Falls. Here the Upper Coulee opened and flattened for several miles and then dropped down a four-hundred-foot cliff to become the Lower Coulee. When the Columbia poured down this course it created a waterfall greater than any in existence today, a cataract more than twice the height of Niagara and three and a half times as wide. Its roar shook the land for miles. The cars crawled down to the base of these silent cliffs and proceeded on a few miles to a pleasant oasis called Park Lake. Sun Lakes State Park occupies the site today.

The assembly grew swiftly after church that morning as more people congregated from Wilbur and Almira, Davenport and Odessa, Coulee City and Soap Lake. Numbers were politically important so an obliging Washington State patrolman assigned two Boy Scouts to count the vehicles filing into the park. They tallied 2,160, most packed with people, lending credence to an estimate in the Grant County *Journal* that more than eight thousand gathered to hear the speeches and honk horns in approval of statements they liked.

A few orchard trees grew next to Park Lake, visible proof of the soil's fertility if it could just get water. Nearby the league promoters had set up a stage. At its rear was a map of the proposed project, on either side were large signs giving salient facts, and just behind the microphone American flags were planted as exclamation points to the day's emotion. While the assembled families unpacked their lunch baskets, Congressman Ralph Horr of Seattle seized the opportunity to give a forty-five-minute harangue against Prohibition. Bored, the crowd wryly muttered, "He's just wet—all wet," as Horr rambled on.

At 1:30 P.M.—the fried chicken, sandwiches, and Horr's interminable address all having been disposed of—Rufus Woods called the meeting to order. O'Sullivan got up to once more recite the facts in favor of a dam, convincing another one hundred and fifty-nine people to pay the dollar required for membership in the Development League. Other politicians rebuked Horr for ignoring the day's subject, but Congressman Sam B. Hill joked that Horr had not really wandered far afield, for he spent most of his time "damning certain laws."

Clarence Dill rose to speak. He had won narrow election to the U.S. Senate by four thousand votes, and attributed his margin to the residents of central Washington who liked his open-mindedness toward a dam. Still, he expressed caution. A big dam was a hard sell in Washington, D.C., he warned.

More enthusiastically, Congressman Hill told them the rolling plateau of abandoned homesteads and grit-pitted barns could become a "garden of Eden." Later he marveled at the size of the congregation. "I never saw such a crowd in that country," he remarked.

Dill's caution was sensible. What the crowd was asking for was construction of the biggest dam on earth, probably costing more than all previous federal public works projects combined. It would have to be built in the midst of the Great Depression for a five-state region with only 3.5 million people, about 3 percent of the nation's population. The dam would generate enough power to light several large cities in a landscape where there were none, water farms where there was no one to eat the food, and create a lake one hundred and fifty miles long. The whole idea struck many people as ludicrously fantastic, even after Grand Coulee construction began. Writer Herbert Corey wrote in a 1934 article for *Public Utilities Fortnightly* that Grand Coulee Dam was "the most colossally humorous stunt of our notably funny generation," and in a 1937 issue of *Collier's* magazine, Jim Marshall predicted that the big new federal dams would prove to be "enormous white elephants about as useful as the pyramids."

The Grand Coulee rally, however, ultimately proved a success beyond the wildest dreams of its organizers. Grand Coulee and Bonneville Dam, near Portland, became major public works projects of the Roosevelt administration that would be elected the following year. By 1934, seven thousand people were living at Grand Coulee to build the dam. It took another twenty years for the water to flow south as promised, but by 1963 the population of Grant County to the south, which would receive much of the water, had grown eight times to fifty thousand people.

This was just the beginning. In 1932 the Army Corps of Engineers completed a massive study proposing a network of ten dams between Bonneville and the Canadian border, a blueprint later expanded into Canada. In the next forty years, engineers would construct fourteen huge dams on the Columbia River itself, twenty on its major tributary, the Snake, and bring the number of significant power and irrigation dams in the Columbia River Basin as a whole to more than five hundred, two hundred and eleven of them classified as "major" by utility statisticians. The mighty Columbia was not just harnessed, it was utterly transformed from an unruly river into a series of placid pools: the most heavily dammed river system and the greatest producer of hydroelectricity in the world. As such, Grand Coulee and its cousins became a model of technological mastery. In Russia, India, China, Latin America, and Africa, dams became synonymous with progress. Delegations from these areas regularly make pilgrimages to Grand Coulee today, less to learn from the half-century-old wonder than to pay homage.

The Columbia River in its natural state was a miserable waterway for navigation but a potentially superb resource for hydroelectricity. Its fall of half a mile in elevation from its source—four times that of the Mississippi, in half the distance—meant it and its tributaries represented more than 40 percent of the hydroelectric potential in the nation.

The depression-era promises made for the river initially seemed extravagant. It would power factories for more than 200,000 new industrial workers. It would water enough land for 100,000 farms. It would increase the region's overall population by 2.5 million and create a water highway for commercial river traffic from the Pacific Ocean to Idaho. It would tap hydroelectricity, which electric visionary J. D. Ross of Seattle called "a coal mine that never gives out, an oil well that never runs dry." It would remake the Pacific Northwest, the final frontier in the Lower Forty-eight states, to conform to the most idealistic visions of the mid-twentieth century. The Columbia would demonstrate what science, engineering, and political reform could accomplish. "Thomas Jefferson's dream of a great, free and independent empire on the banks of the Columbia can come true!" Ross enthused.

In many ways those promises were fulfilled. Irrigation created entirely new towns in the Columbia Basin. Columbia River barges did reach Idaho and proved so cost-effective they now pick up wheat railroaded from the Dakotas. The river's electricity powered a dozen new aluminum plants and the Hanford atomic weapons complex. Basin population more than doubled, from 2.8 million in 1933 to more than 7 million today. Disastrous floods that wreaked havoc as late as 1948 were tamed. The rural poor not only got power with the new dams, but at rates half the national average. The electricity proved crucial to the development of World War II industries, providing the energy to make the aluminum for a third of America's warplanes. If the Columbia and tributary Snake River did not exist, neither to a large extent would Seattle and Portland, or Spokane and Boise, at their present scale.

Still, speeches are as important for what they omit as for what they say. In all the talk that summer picnic day in Grand Coulee—and indeed, in all the years when the fate of the Columbia was decided—its most obvious historic use was seldom mentioned. The Columbia River boasted the greatest chinook salmon and steelhead trout runs in the world. For thousands of years the region's native inhabitants had used the fish as a primary source of food and the foundation of their wealth and culture. Pacific salmon, which died as they spawned, also fed a complex ecosystem with nutrients and energy imported from the ocean. Creatures ranging from bears to bugs depended on the annual cycle. Today, those runs have declined an estimated 85 percent, despite the production of more than 170 million young fish each year by artificial hatcheries. Half of the original salmon and steelhead habitat in the basin is gone. A third of all stream miles in the basin have been blocked by dams with no means of fish passage. Scores of individual salmon runs are extinct. As the fish runs approach collapse, so do the cultures built around them, from tribal reservation economies to Scandinavian gillnetters at the river's mouth. Ephrata's gain in vegetables is Astoria's loss in fish.

Nor would the great dam create quite the political utopia that the picnicking farmers envisioned. By the time Grand Coulee was completed, agriculture was being transformed by mechanization, fertilizers, and pesticides. Farm labor shrank, farm size grew, and productivity soared. The dam ultimately watered just two thousand farms, not one hundred thousand. Moreover, the government built Grand Coulee and other western irrigation projects at the same time it took surplus agricultural lands out of production in the East. By the 1990s, the biggest crop in the Columbia Basin Irrigation Project would not be apples or potatoes or beans or beets or anything humans directly consume. It would be alfalfa. Nitrogen-fixing dairy feed.

There was even less thought at that rally of changing the nature of the river itself. Nch'i-Wana, or Big River, as some tribes called the Columbia, was central to the region's self-image. The Pacific Northwest celebrated an identity as distinct as that of New York or Miami or Las Vegas. It was an outsized place, virgin and untamed, always a region of imminent "empire" shaped by a tumultuous geography ranging from titanic trees to glaciered volcanic peaks. The Columbia's size and cussed unruliness were a part of this, and people first cheered and then began to have misgivings as the rapids and falls were stilled: the Cascades, The Dalles, Celilo Falls, Priest Rapids, Kettle Falls, Devil's Canyon, Death Rapids, Surprise Rapids. The river of legend and pioneer lore eventually would be regulated by computer. Historian Richard White called the result "part plumbing, half-machine. The Columbia has become a robo-river, a cyborg of sorts." The river became polluted by pulp mill discharges, tailings dumped from smelters, radioactivity from Hanford, pesticides from farm fields, eroded sediment from tilling and logging, heat from reactors and power plants. It became a disturbing model not just of engineering achievement but of environmental cost. In the 1980s and early 1990s, Northwest utilities spent an estimated $1.3 billion in direct payments and lost power revenues—more than Grand Coulee and all its irrigation works initially cost—trying to double remaining fish runs. The effort failed.

In 1990 the Shoshone-Bannock tribe of Idaho—the tribe of Sacajawea, who helped guide Lewis and Clark to this country—filed suit under the Endangered Species Act to protect rapidly dwindling salmon that once swam to their ancestral territory. With that petition, control of the river began to pass from the engineers to the biologists and lawyers, with consequences still unknown at this writing. Initially, confusion reigned. Two months after the petition was filed, Idaho Fish and Game Department officials were still trying to poison lakes where sockeye had once spawned in order to clear them for trout, the rotenone dribbling into the Salmon River and killing fifty to one hundred adult Chinook and thousands of young salmon. Agencies on the Columbia have a long history of working at cross-purposes, in ignorance of each other's goals and data. They still do.

This is not a book to either glorify or condemn what has happened to the Columbia River. Each generation that approached the river was a product of its time, necessarily captive to the assumptions and necessities of that moment. Yet examination of the Columbia's past and troubled present is instructive. Serious thought about what we've done provides perspective for future management decisions. It can allow us to question our own assumptions and look at the river through different eyes. No major American river has been transformed quite so grandly, quickly, and completely as the Columbia. In microcosm it tells the story of American civilization itself, our proudest achievements and most dubious legacies.

The Columbia and its tributaries, reaching and snaking through canyons and around glaciered peaks in a thousand tortured courses, collect water from a quarter-million-square-mile basin, an area bigger than France. By the time it reaches the sea the river has gathered moisture from an atlas of geographical extremes, ranging from ice fields in the Canadian Rockies to American sagebrush desert. Its basin runs from the hamlet of Canoe River, halfway up British Columbia, to Tuscarora, Nevada. It extends from Astoria, near the Pacific coast of Oregon, to Yellowstone National Park in Wyoming. Plateau and canyon, mountain and dune, rain forest and bunch-grass steppe: all contribute to the gathering waters. The Columbia has seven times the flow of the longer Colorado and two hundred times that of the even longer Rio Grande. Though half of the Columbia basin is desert, it gathers two and a half times as much water per square mile of its drainage area as does the Mississippi-Missouri system. It is the biggest river in the American West, and the only major one to pierce the rampart of the Cascades and the Sierra Nevadas.

Simple size does not fully convey the Columbia's significance. It is a river that elicits emotion, that tells us stories about ourselves. It is the most beautiful big American river in the grandeur and variety of its landscape, the most daring in its engineering, and the most disturbing in its capture. Its final glorious gorge is a National Scenic Area where the surface of the Columbia is scoured by wind-surfer sails as colorful as a convention of butterflies. But the same river winds through the industrial valley of Trail, British Columbia, which was so polluted earlier in this century that its champion hockey team is called the Smoke Eaters. It flows past the nation's biggest collection of radioactive waste, a former nuclear weapons fuel complex where one of the high school football teams is called the Bombers. In its scenery and modification, the Columbia is a river of jarring contrast, like some kind of object lesson laid down by God and man.

The beauty is still there. Few rivers wind through such a dramatic, primeval, and raw landscape. It runs from canyon to broad lake and back again, from wet forest to dry desert and once more to forest. High waterfalls fall off the sheer side of its windswept final gorge like music from the sky. In Canada glaciers color the river aqua with their ground flour. The Columbia is in a landscape so epic as to almost be swallowed up by it. If the sawing of the Colorado into the depths of the Grand Canyon reminds us of the planet's age, the Columbia's course through a geologically young landscape reminds us how many times the earth has remade itself.

Still, the primary lesson of the Columbia is of people. The Mississippi, I suspect, will always remain in the American imagination a nineteenth-century river. It will forever be the place of Tom and Huck, of sternwheeler and flatboat, of the siege of Vicksburg and the Battle of New Orleans. The Columbia, in contrast, is our twentieth-century river. Its dams represent the optimistic faith in technology of the century's beginning, and the restless misgivings about large-scale engineering at the century's end. It is the river of the turbine, the dynamo, the reactor, and the airplane. It is the river of Tom Swift, Franklin D. Roosevelt, *Popular Mechanics*, and Nagasaki. In the first three decades after World War II, major dams were completed in the Columbia Basin at a pace faster than one per year. It is a river so transformed as seemingly invented. If you want to see how America dreamed at the height of the American Century, come to the Columbia.

It is a river of imagination. People imagined a great western river had to exist before the Columbia was explored, and once found, how it could be remodeled into something useful. Now they imagine, wistfully, what the great falls and fish runs and thunder of its floods must have been like. The Columbia today is a technocratic battleground, a river turned on and off by valves and switches to please the competing needs of irrigators and shippers and power users and fishermen and Indian tribes and environmentalists. In its rare free-flowing stretches it can rise and fall six to eight feet per day as dams push water through their turbines to match the rhythm of daily electricity demand by urban residents hundreds of miles away. A female salmon, who has fought past the dams and in her final shuddering lays her eggs on a drowned gravel bar upriver, dies not knowing her eggs may be dry and dead twelve hours later because of the rhythm of light switches flicking on and off in an arc of cities from Vancouver, Canada, to Los Angeles. The Columbia is that cruelest of all stories: a thing changed into exactly what Americans wanted, and, once changed, proving to be a disappointment of an entirely different sort.

There is precedent for this.

In 1831 the Nez Perce and Flathead nations in the Columbia Basin sent a delegation of seven tribesmen two thousand miles east to St. Louis, reportedly seeking the "white man's Book of Heaven" in order to acquire the spirit power of the trappers and traders beginning to crisscross the region.

This was not the first time the Nez Perce had shown such initiative. They had swiftly become preeminent horse breeders on the Columbia Plateau after acquiring that animal about 1720, developing the famed Appaloosa. In the summer of 1805 they sent a delegation of three young men to trade with the Crow tribe for six guns and swiftly used them to defeat a Shoshone raiding party. They were not afraid of the newcomers, and sought to learn their secrets.

The Nez Perce befriended Lewis and Clark when the explorers traversed the tribe's territory. In 1831 the natives learned William Clark still served as superintendent of Indian Affairs in St. Louis and apparently assumed he could help them gain the book that perhaps explained the white man's power. Joining the trade expedition returning across the Great Plains from the annual fur rendezvous at Wyoming's Green River, the Indians accompanied it to the bustling frontier city. Exactly what Native Americans such as No-Horns-on-His-Head and Rabbit-Skin-Leggings thought they would acquire remains unclear, since they could find no one who could speak Salish or Shahaptin and had to communicate by sign language. Certainly their personal fate was unhappy. Three turned back, two died of disease in St. Louis, one died at Fort Union on the way home in 1832, and the last was killed by Blackfoot Indians in Montana that fall. Still, a garbled version of their visit was printed in a New England Christian newspaper, and it inspired the arrival of a number of Protestant missionaries in the Columbia River Basin. These idealistic and well-intentioned saviors brought farming, education, disease, and a wave of new immigration that completely changed Native American life in ways those seven Nez Perce delegates would no doubt have deemed disastrous.

The Indians sought power, and received it, but at a cost they never anticipated. Their innocent journey is a useful metaphor for the journey our civilization has made in its pursuit of power from the Columbia River.

2

The River of Imagination

The *Columbia Redidiva* at the mouth of the Columbia River.
(*Washington State Historical Museum*)

Prepare to unfurl the main tops'l and fore tops'l!

A dozen volunteers monkey into the bewildering rigging of the brig *Lady Washington*, leaning from the tarred shrouds to embrace a yardarm and then sidestepping carefully, almost mincing, along a rope foot-rest to unknot the sail ties. The resulting blossoms of white canvas are like the opening of a flower.

The command comes as a relief after a long, windless day of puttering down the Washington coast accompanied by the monotonous rumbling of a diesel engine, a concession to modern clocks. The ship will keep its scheduled appointment at a Portland shipyard, but only at the cost of obnoxious noise. Now an evening breeze is blowing into the mouth of the Columbia and the sailors seize the opportunity to enter the river as it was entered two centered two centuries ago. To a sea chantey and the squeak of blocks the deckhands have hauled the yards up the stout Douglas fir masts. The canvas is first loosened; then the sails are trimmed at an angle to catch the wind. They pop and fill and the engine is cut. It is quiet at last, the absence of noise more evocative of the past than the ship's ten miles of standing and running rigging or its simple wooden tiller. We can hear a soft hiss of spray as the blunt hull moves in the evening's easy swell. The lines creak as they are tugged by the zephyr. So often on the Columbia I am surrounded by machine noise: the ceaseless rumble of a tug, the vibration of slightly misaligned hydroelectric turbines, the shriek of practicing navy jets slaloming down a canyon, the hollow metal thump of cars boarding a ferry. The river has been purged of rapids and yet its waters throb with sound. If the animals have named us, it must be as the Noisemakers. We have lost the art of listening. Now, with the sails filled, we can hear. No one talks much.

It is high summer but there is a brisk chill that is typical of the water at the Columbia's mouth. Less typically, the last of a floodtide on a calm day has made the river's notorious bar lie down like a welcoming carpet and we sweep in with a gentle bob. As we approached the Columbia from the sea the day's last light had picked its way through chinks in a wall of cloud out on the Pacific horizon, the rays spotlighting the modern, slowly regreening clearcuts on the Willapa Hills. Now, as we ghost into the river and the light fails, a half moon rises to complement other signs of dramatic change on the river: the long, foam-trimmed jetties, the red and green navigation lights rocking on the buoys, the electric glow of Astoria. There is a juxtaposition of ships to further jumble time. A pleasure sloop points out to sea, the lateness of her departure making us speculate she is starting a long passage, perhaps to Hawaii. The inward-bound log export ship *Tan Noble* rides high and empty as she steams past us and on upriver, the rusting red wall of her steel hull towering over our *Lady*. We are on a sixty-eight-foot replica of the first American ship to round the Horn into the Pacific Ocean and reach the Northwest coast and Hawaii. This was the ship first commanded by Captain Robert Gray, the Boston merchant captain and fur trader. Gray later swapped the *Lady Washington* for the *Columbia Rediviva* and went on to discover this huge river, naming it for that larger ship. The state centennial organizers, however, chose the smaller, more maneuverable *Lady*—named in honor of General Washington's wife, Martha—as a more practical candidate for replication in 1989. It could be built for the budgeted $2 million and could poke into the Northwest's smaller harbors for celebratory visits. The modest brig is impressive enough. It has eleven sails and one hundred and seven different "sail stations," or work positions, that volunteers must memorize in order to respond correctly to commands. Apparently this is not intimidating. There is a waiting list of modern Americans wishing to learn the arcane web of rope and tackle.

"It's like a missing link that people have been seeking for a long time," said Mick, a first mate at the Gray's Harbor Historical Seaport at Aberdeen.

I am impressed by the compactness of this ocean-girdling voyager, its stoutness, the accumulation of hard-won experience its complex rigging represents, and the long, long track of its explorations. This was the spaceship of the eighteenth century, a vessel that could cruise longer than a nuclear submarine, be repaired with wood obtainable on almost any shore, and which sailed to the Northwest coast in voyages that took three years, longer than a modern mission to Mars. The director of the seaport is Les Bolton, a blond, bearded, former Puget Sound Sea Scout who decided he'd been born a century too late. He has spent fifteen years sailing square-rigged ships from various nations. "There are more astronauts in America than people who get paid to do what I do," Bolton says.

The halo of light marking Astoria makes it difficult to imagine what the Columbia must have seemed like to the first explorers. They battled growling surf at the entrance bar to enter a broad estuary eight to twelve miles wide: gray, the sky typically wet, the banks shrouded with dark fir, the bottom a shifting arabesque of sand bars on which Gray grounded, discouraging him from probing very far upriver.

More evident, perhaps, is what an apparition these ships must have seemed to the natives, the *Lady* sweeping in from the sea without sound or paddle. "She was brilliantly colored," Bolton describes, his eyes leaving this century as he focuses on that past. "She had red, blue, and yellow trim. The sails were like square clouds. There was nothing white on the coast, no way to make white cloth, and yet here came this thing as white as clouds.

The masts were like trees, the hull as big as a small island. These dead eyes"—he grasps the tarred dual sockets holding the shrouds—"were called that because they looked to some like skulls. And the men aboard were white. They had the pallor of death."

Native Americans lived on the Columbia for at least eleven thousand years before European discovery. When it was drowned by The Dalles Dam in 1957, the Indian fishing community at the river's Celilo Falls, two hundred and fifty miles upstream, dated back eight millennia and was the oldest continuously inhabited community on the continent. Whites came to the Columbia very, very late. This book will discuss the natural river and the aboriginal river in some detail, but because this is the story of the river's development it must first explain how the Columbia entered modern consciousness. Its Euro-American exploration set attitudes for all that was to follow.

The European tardiness in finding the Columbia was not for want of seeking it. It was a river expected to exist long before it was actually seen by whites, a river wished for before it was discovered. "Destiny's river was there because it had to be there," historian James Ronda has observed. "Europeans invented the Columbia before they saw it."

Sheer distance from Europe made the Northwest coast of North America one of the last to be charted. Its rocks and inlets and rivers were a mystery for three centuries after Columbus's first discovery. But common sense suggested to speculative geographers and dreaming merchants that the great rivers of the New World pouring their waters into the Atlantic would have a counterpart somewhere on the Pacific coast. Providence would provide a quick portage across the Continental Divide to a watery highway. The "Great River of the West" waited only to be found: this last great hope for a Northwest Passage.

Common sense was very nearly wrong. The network of river routes that accommodated explorers and pioneers in the Mississippi basin and Canadian Plains does not, for the most part, exist in the West. The mountain ranges are too near the coast, meaning there is no room for vast, unified drainage basins comparable to the Mississippi or Amazon. The mountain backbone of the Western Hemisphere runs nearly unbroken from Tierra del Fuego at South America's tip to the Alaska Range and Mount McKinley.

On all that long Pacific coast of eleven thousand miles, the Columbia is not just the largest river, it is the only navigable river that permits penetration of the interior.

Rivers were key to the exploration and settlement of North America. Here was a landmass nearly three times the size of Europe, stretching from the Arctic to the tropics, and covered, from east to west in turn, by primeval forest, vast windswept plains, and the Rockies, the longest single mountain chain in the world. The most efficient way of penetrating such a huge area was by boat, and the continent's eastern two-thirds seemed designed to encourage water travel. From the St. Lawrence and Great Lakes, portages led to the Mississippi, the Missouri, the Saskatchewan, the Athabasca, the Mackenzie, and so on. "The waterways were almost miraculous in their range and intricacy," historian Chester Martin has noted, "and the birch bark canoe a miracle of efficiency. A trader could embark at Cumberland House [a Hudson's Bay Company trading post on Canada's Saskatchewan River not far west of Lake Winnipeg] and, with no portage longer than a single day, could reach the Arctic Ocean, the Pacific, the Atlantic, or the Gulf of Mexico."

Canadians reached the Rocky Mountains a generation before Daniel Boone led the first American settlers across the Appalachian Mountains into Kentucky, and the reason was in large part the birch bark canoe. These craft were typically thirty-two feet long, five feet wide, and weighed only three hundred pounds when dry. Yet they could carry eight thousand pounds of crew and freight and had a draft of only eighteen inches. Driven by the forty-five-stroke-per-minute pace of the French-Canadian *voyageurs*, the canoes averaged four miles per hour during days eighteen hours long in the northern summer. Despite frequent rapids and distances the equivalent of an Atlantic crossing, average cargo losses for Montreal's North West Company were as low as one half of 1 percent. The craft were fragile—it was not difficult to put a foot through one—but easily repaired with fresh bark and tallow. So enamored were the Canadians of yellow birch bark that when they came to the Pacific coast to trade they were reluctant to adopt the Indians' cedar log canoes on the lower Columbia River. The fur-trading North West Company had a supply of birch bark shipped from eastern Canada to London and then around Cape Horn to the mouth of the river.

The efficiency and ease of water transport in an age before

paved roads, railroads, or airplanes is hard to exaggerate. In 1826 it took just nine canoes to carry seventy people and fourteen tons of freight from Fort Vancouver up the Columbia to its junction with the Snake River. When these goods were transferred to land it took seventy horses, even though the humans for the most part walked. Horses had to be bought, fed, controlled, and rested, skills that did not come naturally to the *voyageurs*. An account of a typical early pack trip up the Okanogan Trail records that the party did not start moving until 9:00 or 10:00 A.M. because of the laborious loading of the animals. Actual travel time was limited to three or four hours to provide time to rest, to unload, to water and picket the animals, and to camp.

It is indicative of the difficulty of canoe travel on the steep rivers of the Columbia River Basin that fur traders routinely used horses anyway. Indians east of the Cascades got most of their wealth from selling the whites their horses, not furs. Not only did the animals provide overland transport away from the difficult rivers, but in winter it was not uncommon for the trappers to eat their pack string to survive: Fort Colville was moved to more suitable agricultural land because fur company bookkeepers protested the cost of buying, and eating, up to two hundred horses each winter. Another example of the high cost of land transport was the experience of an 1831–32 trapping party into the bleak Snake River country. It lost one hundred and fourteen of three hundred and twenty-nine horses to disease, falls, theft, or the need for meat. "What cursed country is this!" wrote its leader, Peter Skene Ogden.

The American reliance on rivers was similar to the Canadian, though in the United States the vessels of choice were the bateau and flatboat and steamboat more than the canoe. The first steamer ran from Pittsburgh to New Orleans in 1811. Missouri steamboats would later carry two hundred tons across waist-deep water, and some Columbia River boats drew only a foot. People boasted they could steam across fresh dew. The ability of steamboats to negotiate rivers was remarkable. It was a steamboat that supplied Custer's last ill-fated foray in Montana against the Plains Indians, the *Far West* poking within eleven miles of the remote Little Bighorn battlefield to take off the wounded. In the nineteenth century, boats were built to negotiate rivers as they were. Not until the twentieth century were rivers rebuilt to accommodate boats.

So, even as hopes dimmed for finding a saltwater Northwest Passage, they persisted for its river equivalent. Where sailing ships could not go, perhaps the canoe could. In 1673, Louis Joliet and Jacques Marquette discovered the Missouri River at its junction with the Mississippi and proposed that by ascending that stream, one might reach a portage with a west-flowing river to the Pacific. The French began putting a "Great River of the West" on their maps, even though none had ever seen it. French officials began using the word "Ouragan," picked up from the Plains Indians, as a name for this imagined passage. The British, meanwhile, introduced in the 1720s the idea of symmetrical geography. The eastern half of the continent had narrow, ridgelike mountain ranges that separated navigable drainages by only a short portage. Why not the West?

In 1765, two years after the English conquest of Canada, famed colonial ranger leader Robert Rogers sought permission from the "Right Honourable the Lords Committee of His Majesty's Council" to send an expedition west from Lake Superior to seek the continent's summit and the great river "Ourigan" he surmised had to be just on the other side. He envisioned a pyramidal height of land in the continent's center from which major rivers radiated in all directions. (Rogers was not completely wrong: Triple Divide in Montana's Glacier National Park sends water to the Arctic, Pacific, and Gulf.) The resulting expedition by Jonathan Carver foundered on the forbidding vastness of the Great Plains, but Indians confirmed to the *voyageurs* the story of a great river somewhere beyond the mountains, a river Carver called "Oregan" in a 1778 book on his travels. The name has never been confirmed as a Plains Indian word for the Columbia, but it carried its romantic ring into the language. In 1810, William Cullen Bryant extolled the distant Northwest in his "Thanatopsis," evoking "the continuous woods/Where rolls the Oregon, and hears no sound, save his own dashings."

The precise location of this noble river was an utter mystery that led to the wildest guesses. Yankee-born fur trader Peter Pond pushed into Canada's Athabasca Country for the North West Company. In the winter of 1787–88 he sketched a map speculating that a great river led west from Great Slave Lake to Cook Inlet in Alaska, which sea explorer James Cook had found a decade earlier. The connection does not exist, but Alexander Mackenzie later set out to find it.

The same speculation occurred for lands to the south. At the end of the 1780s, Boston physician Thomas Bulfinch (who would later help organize the financing of Gray's fur trade voyage that would discover the mouth of the Columbia) wrote in *Oregon and Eldorado* that there had to be a connection between the Mississippi-Missouri system and the Great River of the West, stating, "A few hundred miles of land carriage will complete the travel from ocean to ocean." As late as 1795, Aaron Arrowsmith's map of North America concluded that the Rocky Mountains were only 3,250 feet high from their base, underestimating reality by more than half.

The easiest way to first discover the Columbia, geographers agreed, would be by sea, and indeed the river's entrance today can make it seem the most apparent of Pacific Coast rivers. The Columbia's gray-green snout, tonguing its way into the cold blue of the North Pacific, can be distinctive as spilled paint on a sunny day. It is a river alive with life, where millions of fish funnel to spawn. Colonies of seabirds float a few miles offshore, rising and falling on swells like mattresses of brown and white. At the mouth proper, gulls wheel and squabble in funneled concentration. The bar that marks the river's entrance is a picket fence of breaking surf that marks the shore like a scrawl of chalk. From a ship at sea on a clear day the presence of the Columbia seems obvious. It parts the rolling hills of the Coast Range like a Moses, the resulting gap leading the eye into a green, clouded interior.

In the fogs and tides of cautious coastal exploration, however, before jetties and buoys and lighthouses, the Columbia River was not obvious at all. The river tricked its would-be discoverers with embarrassing regularity. It was missed by Spain's surveying Juan Perez in 1774. Bruno Heceta failed to enter it the next year, though the latter suspected from currents and water color that he had found the mouth of a great river or passage and optimistically named it Rio San Roque. His crew was too weakened by scurvy to man a longboat to investigate.

British explorer James Cook, one of history's greatest navigators, missed the river completely in 1778, sailing past it in the dark. Ten years later, British trader John Meares was so discouraged by the line of unbroken surf across the Columbia's mouth that he concluded, "Disappointment continues to accompany us. We can now with safety assert that . . . no such river as that of Saint Roc exists, as laid down in the Spanish charts." He named the apparent bay Deception and its rocky northern cape Disappointment.

In 1792, British captain George Vancouver spotted the Columbia's distinctive color off Meares's Cape Disappointment but, "not considering this opening worthy of more attention," as he wrote, the explorer sailed on.

A few weeks later the pugnacious, risk-taking, curious Boston merchant captain Robert Gray rode his *Columbia Rediviva* over the bar and into history.

The Great River of the West proved maddeningly hard to reach from the landward side as well. The width of the Rockies and the steep fall of the westward rivers proved as much a disappointment as Meares's Cape. Lewis and Clark were sent west by President Jefferson to find a route of commerce, but their report about the sea of mountains in central Idaho was hardly encouraging. Lewis described "one range above another as they recede from the river until the most distant and lofty have their tops clad with snow." Five years later, financier John Jacob Astor tried to send a party overland toward the Columbia's mouth by a more southerly route, seeking an easier trail. Its members nearly starved.

In Canada where the Columbia begins, it enters recorded history as a river of confusion. At its source the river flows north, not south or west. Accordingly, when the upper Columbia was first encountered in 1801 by two scouting French-Canadians, it seemed to have no connection with the swollen estuary Gray had discovered hundreds of miles to the southwest, nine years before. Fur company explorer David Thompson established a trading post near the Columbia's beginning in 1807, but thought he was on the nearby Kootenay River. Mackenzie was puzzled enough to propose that it was the upper Fraser River that was part of the Columbia. When finally mapped in 1811, the Columbia proved to be a river of disappointing course, terrifying rapids, and unpredictable flows. From its first locks and breakwaters to its last dams, it would take the newcomers about a century to transform it.

From its earliest entry into European and American history, the Columbia was seen as a highway to wealth, an avenue of empire and a resource to be exploited. None of the newcomers were terribly interested in whatever beauties or curiosities or intricate ecosystems the Columbia possessed as a river. It was a strategic asset. Possession of the Great River of the West would confer geographic advantage in monopolizing the fur trade that was key to the Spanish, Russian, British, and American rivals who were closing in from all directions.

"Whatever course may be taken from the Atlantic, the Columbia is the line of communication from the Pacific Ocean," wrote Alexander Mackenzie in 1801, "as it is the only navigable river in the whole extent of Vancouver's minute survey of the coast. Its banks also form the first level country in all the southern extent of continental coast from Cook's entry, and, consequently, the most northern situation fit for colonization, and suitable to the residence of a civilized people."

The Columbia's colonization, however, would not really get under way until the Oregon Trail was developed in the 1840s. For the first half century after Gray's discovery the river's history is that of furs, from the sea otter used to fringe Chinese cloaks to the beaver. The fur of the latter could be processed into a durable, water-shedding felt for European hats, ranging from the tricorner to the naval cocked hat to the high helmet of Napoleonic-era infantry to the stovepipe. It is useful to examine the Columbia's exploration by these fur traders and empire seekers in some detail, because it both demonstrates the river's importance in breaching the Cascade Mountains and the difficulties that led to dreams of harnessing it.

For more than two hundred years the Spanish had considered the Pacific their private lake, but by 1770 their grip began to weaken. The Russians had conquered Siberia and explored Alaska by 1741, built a permanent settlement in the Aleutian Islands by 1773, and constructed a post just one hundred miles north of San Francisco in 1812 before deciding they were overextended and retreating.

Britain's Cook established British and American interest with his detailed exploration of the Northwest coast in his last voyage of 1778–80. After Cook was killed by natives in Hawaii, his surviving crew went on and were astounded that the Chinese would pay the equivalent of a hundred dollars for a single North Coast sea otter fur that the English had obtained for nails and trinkets. Cook's journal extolling the fur trade was not published until 1784, but in 1783 an American named John Ledyard—who had served as a corporal of marines on the British voyage—broke the Admiralty's publishing embargo with his own account. He emphasized the fortune to be made in a wet, cold, and distant part of the globe.

The news intrigued America. The Revolution had just been won and the young nation was anxious for its share of global commerce. Three years later Ledyard met Thomas Jefferson in Paris, when the latter was minister to France, and proposed finding the Great River of the West by an unusual route. Ledyard planned to cross Siberia, take a Russian ship to the Northwest coast, find the river leading into the interior, ascend it to the Missouri, and then float down to the United States. He actually set out to accomplish this fantastic plan but was arrested by Catherine the Great in Russia and expelled to Europe. Ledyard later died of fever in Cairo while planning an expedition to discover the source of the Nile.

Seaports were buzzing, however, with the fur reports of Cook and Ledyard. Charles Bulfinch, son of the Thomas who had speculated on a Rocky Mountain portage, returned to Boston from London in 1787 with word that English merchant captains were preparing to retrace Cook's path. They would sell trade goods to the Indians, Indian furs to the Chinese, and Chinese tea, clothing, and dinnerware to Europe and America in a grand global triangle. The New Englanders decided to do no less. For a century the Americans had been outflanked from access to the North American fur trade by French and British forts on the frontier. Going by water, they could make a neat end run not only around the continent but also their continental rivals.

While Americans prepared to go by sea, the British in Canada pressed ahead on land. The Hudson's Bay Company had been chartered by the British Crown in 1670 and from its bases on that chill body of water had launched a careful and conservative fur trade with the Cree Indians of northern Canada. Meanwhile, the French launched a fur trade of their own from the St. Lawrence, using the network of waterways reached via the Great Lakes. They formed alliances with tribes that tormented the English through four North American wars until Britain finally conquered Canada. The French *voyageurs* and fur traders were subsequently reorganized under enterprising Scot entrepreneurs as the North West Company in the same year that Ledyard's fur report was published. The Nor'Westers and the Bay men were soon locked in a race across Canada to control the industry, a struggle that ultimately led to pitched battles and didn't end until the British Crown ordered the two companies consolidated under Bay leadership in 1821. Meanwhile, Canadians would dominate the early exploration and settlement history of the Pacific Northwest. Until 1840 or so, the most commonly spoken European language in the "Columbia Department" was French.

In its heyday, the North West Company was a brilliantly adventuresome firm, pushing to the Rockies and then mapping most of what lay on the other side. It roamed from the Arctic to the Columbia Basin. While an American ship discovered the Columbia and Lewis and Clark would first descend its lower reaches, the initial penetration of the interior Northwest with a network of fur posts was a Nor'Wester accomplishment. The muscle behind this was the French-Canadian *voyageur*, physically screened in the communities around Montreal for the broad shoulders and short legs needed to tolerate exhausting days of driving a canoe. Singing songs as they paddled and portaging canoe and freight across rugged trails, *the voyageurs* shared endurance and discipline unmatched by Americans. Each portaged bundle always weighed ninety pounds so that supervisors could tell by its heft if anything had been pilfered. A black *voyageur* named Pierre Bonga was recorded as carrying five bundles at once.

"These people are indispensable to the prosecution of the trade," said American Ramsay Crooks in explaining why the Pacific Fur Company organized by John Jacob Astor hired so many Canadian *voyageurs*. "Their places cannot be supplied by Americans, who are for the most part too independent to submit quietly to control. 'Tis only in the Canadian that we find the temper of mind to render him patient, docile and persevering."

The *voyageurs* took Indian wives, dressed flamboyantly with feathers and plumes in their caps, partied with legendary drunken vigor in the Great Halls of the fur headquarters, submitted to a grinding discipline, and thrived on a bland diet of game and pemmican. The latter was a mixture of dried buffalo meat and berries with something of the consistency of dehydrated dog food. It proved remarkably free of spoilage; one eighty-year-old cache unearthed in Manitoba in 1934 was still edible. The *voyageurs* consumed a pound and a half per day.

French *voyageurs* were completely at home in a wilderness of stunning distance and brutal winters. In 1822 a *voyageur* in his seventies boasted of his life to Alexander Ross: "I have now been forty-two years in this country. For twenty-four I was a light canoeman; I required but little sleep, but sometimes got less than I required. No portage was too long for me. Fifty songs a day were nothing to me. I could carry, paddle, walk and sing with any man I ever saw. . . . I had twelve wives in the country, and was once possessed of fifty horses, and six running dogs, trimmed in the first style. I wanted for nothing, and I spent all my earnings in the enjoyment of pleasure. Yet, were I young again, I would glory in commencing the same career. There is no life as happy as a *voyageur*'s life; none so independent; no place where a man enjoys so much variety and freedom as in the Indian country!"

Ultimately the North West Company was at a crippling disadvantage to its Bay rival and to American ships. Its canoe-serviced supply lines from Montreal were up to forty-three hundred miles long, across sixty lakes and three hundred and thirty portages. That was twice the distance faced by the Hudson's Bay Company, which used the bay to reach far into the Canadian interior by sea. Accordingly, North West Company furs generally took months or even a year longer to reach market and earn a return, a geographic handicap that sheer aggressiveness could not overcome. At its height, however, the North West Company swept westward to the longitude of Washington and Oregon at a time when Americans had little idea what lay more than a few miles west of the Mississippi River. Even as the Boston sea merchants laid their plans, Nor'Wester Alexander Mackenzie was setting out in 1789 to discover the Great River of the West.

Mackenzie was a great explorer with terrible luck. He set out to find Peter Pond's fabled river, which did not exist, and thus missed the Columbia, which did. Had he crossed the Rockies at a more southerly point his incredible determination would likely have brought him down the Columbia before any rival, staking a claim that might have resulted in the Canadian flag flying over Washington, Oregon, and Idaho today. It was not to be. He was just twenty-five years old when he set out and discovered the great Arctic river that bears his name, and thirty, exhausted, and depressed when, after being the first white man to cross the continent north of Mexico, he left the Northwest forever. "I am fully bent on going," he wrote on January 13, 1794, after his two epic explorations. "I am more anxious now than ever. For I think it unpardonable in any man to remain in this country who can afford to leave it." Among his discoveries was devil's club, that fearsome nettle of wet Northwest forests.

Mackenzie's youth and exhaustion are typical of the first travelers to the steep and hard Columbia country. Simon Fraser was twenty-eight when he set out to explore the Fraser River (which he thought might be the Columbia), David Thompson was thirty-one when he made his first abortive attempt to cross the Rockies, Robert Gray was thirty-two when he first sailed for the Northwest Coast, Meriwether Lewis was twenty-nine and William Clark thirty-three when they set out West. None followed their greatest discoveries with subsequent trips. Fraser, Thompson, and Lewis died poor, Lewis a probable suicide. Their discoveries were carried out in the so-called Little Ice Age that ran from 1350 to about 1870 and produced more severe winters and cooler summers than experienced before or since. The cooling drove the Vikings out of Greenland, ended corn agriculture among the ancestors of the Cree Indians of Canada, and hampered western exploration with deep mountain snows that were a constant complaint in journals.

Mackenzie set out from Lake Athabasca with a party of *voyageurs* on June 3, 1789, enlisting a Dogrib Indian guide by threatening to cut the native's throat if he didn't help guide the expedition. The Indian was so terrified of supposed monsters that the explorer had to sleep on the native's vermin-infested coat to prevent him from running off. The Scot found and followed the huge river that bears his name to the Arctic Ocean but realized, as he viewed the pack ice, that this was not the Great River of the West proposed by Peter Pond. He was back by fall, having covered three thousand miles in one hundred and two days of hard canoeing.

Undaunted, Mackenzie again set out to find the Northwest Passage. In 1793 he crossed the Rockies by struggling up the Peace River to a portage that indeed, as long promised, was only eight hundred and seventeen paces across a ridge to a tributary of the Fraser. Could this be the fabled River Oregon? The Fraser, alas, became impassible in precipitous canyons. Mackenzie gambled and took native advice to cache his canoe and follow a faint trail overland toward the "stinking lake," or Pacific Ocean. Once more he enlisted a native guide and once more the Indian threatened to desert, so once more Mackenzie shared his bed with him. "My companion's hair being greased with fish oil, and his body smeared with red earth, my sense of smelling threatened to interrupt my rest," the Scot recorded in his journal, "but these inconveniences yielded to my fatigue, and I passed a night of sound repose." The Nor'Westers crossed the Coast Range into temperate rain forest and descended into the Bella Coola country of present-day central British Columbia. They were befriended by one group of natives and threatened by another: the latter apparently had already had one clash with ship-borne white men. The explorer marked a rock with the statement, "Alex Mackenzie. From Canada By Land. 22nd July 1793." Then he went home. The route proved no more useful than the Mackenzie River and only contributed to growing confusion about the location of the Columbia. Nor was the detail of his geographic information as useful as that which would later be gathered by Lewis and Clark. "I could not stop to dig into the earth," he complained, "over whose surface I was compelled to pass with rapid steps; nor could I turn aside to collect the plants which nature might have scattered on the way." Unlike Meriwether Lewis, he was not equipped to make a methodical survey.

Mackenzie's timing was unfortunate. He did not know that Robert Gray had discovered the mouth of the Columbia the year before. He did learn that explorer George Vancouver had visited the Bella Coola inlet by ship just forty-nine days before his own arrival by land. Mackenzie's misfortune was typical of the geographic hard luck of the Canadians: Simon Fraser would find a huge Pacific river to which he would give his name but discover it was so dangerous as to be unnavigable. David Thompson contributed more to early knowledge of Pacific Northwest geography than any other explorer but failed again and again to exploit the route of the Columbia he kept stumbling on. Mackenzie proposed a trading post at the Columbia's mouth nine years before Astoria was built there by Americans, but the Colonial Office in London ignored him.

While the Canadians pushed overland, a group of Boston merchants and sea captains met in the elder Bulfinch's Boston mansion and pooled $49,000 to outfit the first American ship for the Northwest fur trade. She was the square-rigged *Columbia Rediviva,* or Columbia Reborn, a reconditioned three-hundred-ton craft 83.5 feet long and twenty-three feet wide with three masts, two decks, and ten cannon. The group recruited as master a Massachusetts captain named John Kendrick, forty-seven, who had commanded privateers during the Revolution. Accompanying Kendrick would be the more maneuverable *Lady Washington*, captained by Revolutionary War veteran Gray. Trade cargo included hoes, axes, hammers, knives, combs, mirrors, and glass beads. The ensuing adventures that led to discovery of the Columbia illustrate three early trends: a complex and uneasy relationship with Northwest natives, the international rivalry for the remote coast, and the advent of global trade that continues to be critical to the river to this day. The distance was epic. The Americans suffered from scurvy on the long passage out, some dying of the disease on the *Columbia*, and when that ship returned to Boston Harbor as the first American vessel to circumnavigate the globe, it had traveled, by the estimate of its log, some 48,889 miles.

The two ships set out from Boston on September 30, 1787. After a difficult passage around Cape Horn in which the vessels became separated by storms, Gray sailed on ahead in the smaller *Lady Washington*. He made landfall at southern Oregon on August 14, 1788, nearly a year after leaving Boston. The Americans observed large number of campfires along the coast and concluded, correctly, that this meant a heavily inhabited area. Near Tillamook Head the current from the Columbia and a rising wind kept the sloop from making northward progress, so Gray put into what is today known as Tillamook Bay, south of the river mouth. It was the first of several instances of Gray entering a harbor that other captains would not try; Englishman John Meares had sailed by a few weeks before and considered it too hazardous, just as he had missed the mouth of the Columbia.

The Tillamook Indians had to be coaxed to approach the ship, but the berries they offered were gratefully gobbled as an antidote to scurvy. The reception encouraged a small, poorly armed party of Americans to go onto the beach. The cautious friendliness soon evaporated. A native snatched the cutlass left unattended in the sand by a black named Marcus Lopez, who had shipped as Gray's servant when the ships paused in the Cape Verde Islands. Lopez gave chase, was killed, and other crewmen got caught up in a running fight back to their longboat. Three sailors were wounded, one seriously, and the longboat escaped being cut off by native canoes only when Gray opened fire with cannons. This tragic first clash resulted in Gray giving the bay the name "Murderer's Harbor," after the first recorded death from a native clash in Oregon, that of a black man. While Gray would trade peacefully and successfully with the natives on many other occasions, this skirmish left him quick to open fire if threatened.

Other conflicts accompanied the American venture. Three years later, in June 1791, Captain Kendrick—who had by that time swapped ships with Gray and commanded the *Lady*—fought off an Indian attack in Canada's Barell's Sound, killing as many as fifty natives. A song celebrating the successful defense, called "Ballad of the Bold Northwestmen," became one of the popular tunes of nineteenth-century seaports. Its lyrics were a warning that reflected a growing hostility between two cultures:

> *I'll have you take warning and always ready be,*
> *For to suppress those savages of Northwest America,*
> *For they are so desirous some vessel for to gain*
> *That they will never leave off, till most of them are slain.*

Gray sailed on to Nootka Sound on the west coast of Vancouver Island, at the time the maritime headquarters of the Pacific Northwest. Here American, English, Spanish, and Portuguese ships could be found anchored side by side. On September 23 Kendrick's *Columbia* arrived and the Americans spent the winter at Nootka, recovering from the long passage and repairing their ships. The following spring the *Lady Washington* set out under Gray's command to trade along the Washington coast. He found that iron chisels were in particularly high demand: they started a "golden age" of Native American carving along the coast that produced the totem poles and other art that would enchant later anthropologists and decorate today's museums. The Americans also regretted they had not brought more copper, a trade item the British used with great success.

Gray next sailed north to the Queen Charlotte Islands. At one point he poked so close to land that his bowsprit broke against the rocks, the crew escaping destruction only by warping the ship away from the surf with ropes and longboats. He returned to Nootka Sound to find Kendrick still at anchor in the *Columbia*, having accomplished nothing. More ominously, two Spanish warships were at hand to drive off any English.

Here was the first dramatic showdown for possession of the Northwest. Spain regarded this rush for furs with alarm, and had decided to confront her most powerful rival with force. While the Americans stayed on the sidelines, the Spaniards seized several British ships and crews. The bluster was short-lived. Spain was unwilling to go to war with a burgeoning Britain for such a remote prize, and negotiation in Europe the following year led to the crews' release and the ships' return. Spain's concession of the right of other nations to have access to the Northwest coast was the first significant act that would help extend the United States to the Pacific. The subsequent retreat of the Russians would leave the Americans and English as the chief rivals, with the U.S.-Canada boundary not set until 1846.

Such geopolitics did not immediately concern the Americans, however. Kendrick surprised Gray by proposing they swap ships and that Gray take their furs to China, sell them, and return to Boston while Kendrick continued trading in the Pacific. Gray left Vancouver Island with the *Columbia* on July 30, 1789, and became the first American captain to reach Hawaii. There he took on board two high-ranking Hawaiian youths named Attoo and Opie and proceeded on to China. Gray's stop in Hawaii foreshadowed the islands' importance in subsequent Columbia River history. The islands had become a replenishing point and Hawaiians, called Kanakas, later proved willing to hire on as laborers for fur posts.

At Canton, Gray sold the ship's approximately one thousand furs for $21,404, spent $10,163 on supplies and repairs, and purchased a cargo of six hundred chests of Bohea tea for $11,241. (By 1805 the Chinese would be importing almost two hundred thousand skins of otter, seal, and beaver a year.) Then he set sail for Boston around Africa, completing the circumnavigation on August 9, 1790, almost three years after leaving. His return created a sensation in the young Republic, Attoo parading down Boston's streets in his feather cloak of brilliant tropic red and yellow. Seawater had spoiled half the tea and thus the voyage's profit, however. Gray was ordered to return to the Northwest coast as soon as possible. He left in less than two months, on October 2, 1790.

The trip around the Horn was repeated with more pleasant weather this time, though scurvy reappeared by the time the *Co-*

lumbia reached the equator in the Pacific. The trip from Boston to Nootka was cut from the first voyage's twelve months to eight. Yet Gray was not all business: he had a merchant's assignment but an explorer's curiosity, and he continued probing the coastline. The captain again wintered over at Vancouver Island, where he reencountered Kendrick and the *Lady Washington.*

Kendrick sailed for China in September with a load of furs, converted the *Lady Washington* to a square-rigged brig, sold himself the ship, and apparently had no intention of ever returning to his employers in Boston. He was later killed in a bizarre accident in Hawaii when a gun fired from an English ship in friendly salute proved to be accidentally loaded with a cannon ball. The *Lady Washington* was later wrecked in Southeast Asia, leaving Gray's *Columbia* to find the West's greatest river.

In the spring of 1792, Gray left Nootka and cruised down the Oregon coast in search of more furs, then turned north again, noticing the Columbia's powerful current. Near the Strait of Juan de Fuca he met Britain's George Vancouver, a former lieutenant of Cook who was now mapping the Northwest coast for the British Admiralty. Gray told Vancouver about the current but the English captain said he doubted a river could exist there because of the solid line of powerful surf between the two capes. Instead, Vancouver pointed his vessels into the strait, where he discovered Puget Sound and circled the large island that bears his name. Gray, meanwhile, pointed his ship back south.

By this time the Boston men were wary of Indians. Attoo, who had returned from Boston to the Northwest coast with Gray, had already narrowly saved the *Columbia* from destruction by the natives. The Hawaiian, apparently unhappy with his long stay with the white men, had fled the ship and sought shelter with the Indians on Vancouver Island. To force his return Gray seized a Nootka chief, and when Attoo was brought back he was beaten by his captain. Assuming the Hawaiian was now thoroughly disaffected, the Indians subsequently took him into their confidence about their plans to attack Gray, promising him a reward of furs if he would wet the sailor's muskets. At the last minute, the boy warned the captain and forestalled an attack.

This incident was freshly in mind on May 7, when Gray entered the large harbor on Washington's coast that bears his name. He anchored in five fathoms and the Indians of what were probably the Chehalis tribe came out in canoes. "They appeared to be a savage sett and was well armed," crewman John Boit wrote, "every man having his Quiver and Bow slung over his shoulder— Without doubt we are the first Civilized people that ever visited this port, & these poor fellows view'd us & the Ship with the greatest astonishment—their language was different from any we have yet heard. . . . they are stout made and very ugly." Curiosity turned to violence on the night of May 8, when the natives approached in canoes and the nervous Americans fired their cannon, destroying one canoe bearing twenty men and driving the others off. Boit said the Indians probably had no idea of the power of artillery, "But they was too near us for to admit any hesitation in how to proceed. . . . I am very sorry we was oblig'd to Kill the poor divells but it cou'd not with safety be avoided."

After this clash the natives still showed a willingness to trade, but a now nervous Gray raised anchor and sailed south to explore at last that powerful, mysterious current. Most of Gray's own log has been lost and we are left only with accounts by crewmen to shed light on the captain's thinking. Was he hoping to discover the legendary river, or simply poking into every inlet that offered furs? We don't know. On May 12, 1792, three hundred years after Columbus voyaged to America, Gray took advantage of a calm sea to slip over the breakers at the Columbia's bar.

The river was huge. It poured down with such volume in the spring that its taste was fresh virtually to the bar itself, and the Americans noted that entire trees floated down with the current. About twenty canoes approached, offering furs and salmon with a familiarity that suggested the natives had received word of coastal trading. The salmon were sold two for a nail. "They appear'd to view the Ship with the greatest astonishment & no doubt we was the first Civiliz'd people that they ever saw," Boit wrote again. The ship proceeded to a village on the north shore where the estuary was still four miles wide. Here the Indians traded four otter skins for a sheet of copper, a beaver skin for two spikes, and other furs for one spike. The natives reported there were fifty villages on the banks of the river, and on May 15 the *Columbia* sailed a short distance upstream, halting when it grounded on sand in the upper estuary. Gray and Boit went ashore and walked in awe under the huge trees of the coastal mainland. Whether they made formal claim is disputed—Boit's entry "& take possession" was added to his log later, in a different ink— but at a time when American settlement hardly extended beyond the Appalachians, there could have been no thought of overland settlement anyway. "This river in my opinion, wou'd be a fine place for to sett up a Factory," Boit wrote, meaning a fur trading post. "The Men at Columbia's River are strait limb'd, fine looking fellows & the women are very pretty."

Gray called his river "Columbia's River," after his ship. The British later accepted his name when they dominated the river, and the Hudson's Bay Company called the Pacific Northwest its "Columbia District." The Americans in contrast adopted for the region the supposed Plains Indian name: Oregon. The "Oregon Country" initially referred to the entire Northwest, including British Columbia. In 1848, two years after the international boundary was set at the Forty-ninth Parallel, Oregon Territory was created and included the future states of Oregon, Washington, Idaho, and western Montana.

Within five years, settlers north of the Columbia River wanted a separate territory not dominated by the older settlements to the south, and in 1853 petitioned for creation of Columbia Territory. Congressman Richard Stanton of Kentucky inexplicably proposed Washington instead "as we already have a territory [District] of Columbia . . . but we have never yet dignified a territory with the name of [George] Washington." Within five minutes the House had agreed to a name that has created far worse confusion with the capital than Columbia would have.

The Hudson's Bay Company meanwhile moved its headquarters from the Columbia River to Victoria on Vancouver Island, but retained the name Columbia District. When a mainland colony was established in 1858, the name on the only map Queen Victoria consulted referred to the area as Columbia, and she simply insisted the new addition to the empire be known as "British" Columbia to avoid a mixup with the South American country Colombia.

Thus Oregon was named for a Plains Indian rumor, Washington by a Congress that in trying to avoid confusion instead compounded it, and British Columbia for an American ship. The origin of "Idaho" is even more obscure: varying accounts propose different translations of an Indian word that may have come not from the state's natives but the linguistically related Comanche or even the Kiowa Apache. A long-standing joke is that when Idaho schoolchildren are quizzed on the origin of their state's name they answer it is named after the Idaho Power Company.

Gray stayed in the Columbia's mouth for eight days, trading for one hundred and fifty otter, three hundred beaver, and six hundred other land furs. Then he sailed for Nootka. He gave a chart he made of the estuary to the Spanish commander, Bodega y Quadra, who in turn gave it to a chagrined Vancouver, the Briton disappointed he had missed his chance at the great river's discovery. In October, Vancouver sent Lieutenant William Broughton in the brig *Chatham* into the Columbia, who dutifully claimed it for Britain and charted the first one hundred miles to the Washougal River. Broughton sailed and rowed upriver in seasonal low water and his soundings were so different from Gray's that he assumed the American was incompetent. It actually was the first evidence of how erratic Columbia flows could be. Based on Broughton's figures, the Hudson's Bay Company later founded Fort Vancouver about one hundred miles from the Columbia's mouth; however, the river's annual rise of up to twenty feet kept flooding half the post's cultivated fields.

What an oversized, intimidating landscape Broughton's men experienced! The river was immense, green, and must have been choked with salmon. On either shore was a wall of alder, cottonwood, and maple, backed by fir and hemlock forest two hundred to three hundred feet high. The snowy white cones of Mounts Hood and St. Helens would have been glimpsed from various bends, and at the farthest British penetration the river would have seemed to disappear into the looming Cascade Mountains toward an interior that could only be guessed at. The banks of the river were already thickly populated by a people who lived in plank houses, carved swift cedar canoes, and feasted on the fat, silvery fish. Fifty war canoes put out from one village, only to put down their bows in amazement when one of the seamen demonstrated a musket.

It would be thirteen years before Lewis and Clark led the first whites to paddle down the Columbia from the interior. By that time more than a hundred American ships would have entered the dangerous mouth of the Columbia to trade. Taking advantage of cumbersome Crown regulations that attempted to maintain the East India Company's monopoly of the Chinese trade, Americans quickly seized most of the Northwest coast fur business. They even carried Russian furs in return for supplying the Russian posts with food. When the Chinese market slumped and English regulations were modified, however, Americans lost their dominance. Eventually it would be British ships that would transport most Columbia Basin furs to Europe. Still, Gray's river discovery would prove momentous in the later debate between Britain and the United States as to who deserved to control the Oregon Country. Negotiators need look no further than the river's name to confirm which white captain had sighted it first.

In Boston the discovery was received with relative indifference. The profits were still disappointing and the joint venture was disbanded. The river had been found as a by-product of trade, not of exploration. There was no suggestion to follow up the discovery with a permanent post on the river's mouth, and no interest yet in lands around the river. The *Columbia* was sold and served in the transatlantic trade until it was wrecked in 1801, "ript to pieces," as its decommissioning papers stated. Gray continued at sea as a merchant captain but never returned to the Northwest coast. He died of yellow fever on a voyage to South Carolina in 1806. Congress later rejected the plea of his widow for compensation for his discovery.

The long-imagined river had been found, but geographers' assertions that the Great River must have its origin near the headwaters of the Missouri were yet to be tested. The map of the western United States between the foothills of the Cascade Mountains and the Mississippi remained largely a blank. The Columbia's significance could not be determined until the map was filled in.

3

Vagrant and Most Dangerous

The blockhouse at Fort Rains, attacked by Indians in the 1856 battle at The Cascades of the Columbia. *(University of Washington Library)*

The Columbia is a river that does not go anywhere.

Oh, it is more than twelve hundred miles in length all right—long enough to reach halfway across the United States if straightened—but it twists like a garden hose toward a source high in the rugged mountains of Canada. While geographers hoped for a passage linking east with west, the Columbia runs more miles north and south. Its course is so confusing that it took explorers from the North West Company eleven years to realize they had found the fabled Great River of the West after they first stumbled upon it. Remote, steep-banked, too wet here and too dry there, hot, cold, and windy, the Columbia's shoreline remains relatively unpopulated even today. The Mississippi can claim at least five major American cities on its banks. The Columbia can boast just one, Portland, and even Portland is centered on the adjacent Willamette, not the main river. The Columbia is omnipresent in the psychology of the Pacific Northwest: it powers the region and from my home in Seattle I must cross it to reach any of the other forty-seven contiguous states. By the same token, Americans can travel almost everywhere in this country without physically encountering the nation's second-biggest river at all.

The Columbia's failure to point to a clear destination is the first and most basic fact about understanding what has happened to it. The river did not conveniently lead, it did not easily haul, and it had no large riverside constituency besides its Native Americans. When found by Europeans it was a cataract of wildly seasonal flows, impassable falls and rapids, deep canyons, desolate desert terrain, and Canadian mountains with incredible winter snows. It had a dangerous entrance and a remote origin. The most physically risky and frustrating part of the Oregon Trail was the final raft or canoe passage down the Columbia River Gorge, a route so dangerous that a majority of pioneers paid tolls to take an exhausting alternate route across the shoulder of Mount Hood. It took two decades of exploration after Robert Gray's discovery to recognize that the Great River of the West was not the imperial highway that was dreamed of. If the natives had adapted to the river as it was, the newcomers mused about adapting the river to themselves. First, of course, they had to complete their geographic understanding of it.

After Robert Gray's entry into the Columbia's mouth, the river's origin was the next portion to be discovered by whites. The source was not immediately recognized, however, and the initial encounter was accidental.

By 1799, seven years after Gray's entry, both the North West Company and the Hudson's Bay Company had responded to Indian invitations and established trading posts on the western Canadian plains. The forts were at the junction of the Saskatchewan and Clearwater rivers, just one hundred miles from the Continental Divide and due east of today's Jasper National Park. Penetration of the Rockies at this latitude soon followed, an effort to match Mackenzie's earlier crossing of the mountains farther north. The first whites to see the upper Columbia were probably two French-Canadian employees of the North West Company named La Gasse and Le Blanc. At the direction of company clerk David Thompson, the pair accompanied a party of friendly Kootenay Indians across the Rockies to a large, north-flowing river (the Columbia) in 1800. They followed it upstream to a flat gravel divide about a mile and half wide that separated the Columbia's source lake from another large river (the Kootenay) and then followed this second river south to what is now the international boundary. The pair wintered there with the natives. Little is known of the Canadians' eight-month winter journey except that it remained historically insignificant, resulting in no further penetration of the Pacific Northwest. The first river they encountered pointed north while the mouth of Gray's river was far to the southwest, so no connection was made between the two. The pair returned to the plains fur posts the next year, but were not used as guides in an abortive attempt by Thompson in 1801 to reach the Pacific Ocean, an expedition that stalled without crossing the Rockies.

With travel across the rugged mountains of future British Columbia so difficult, the fur companies temporarily lost interest in reaching by land a coast that was already being exploited by sea. This provided the opening for the Americans and the most famous, fascinating, and momentous of all Columbia River explorations, the expedition of Meriwether Lewis and William Clark. The route their "Corps of Discovery" found proved disappointing in its difficulty, but the trek was enormously important.

First, it further staked American claim to the region. Just as the British narrowly missed being the first to enter the river's mouth, they failed to be first to explore the Pacific Northwest interior. While the Hudson's Bay Company would later dominate the Columbia Basin for almost three decades, the Lewis and Clark expedition, coupled with the later flood of pioneers, meant that most of the basin would eventually be recognized as part of the United States.

Lewis and Clark also transformed the Pacific Northwest to a place of reality instead of fantasy, a destination that could demonstrably be reached and someday developed. At the time President Thomas Jefferson dispatched the expedition, he and other scholars speculated the mastodon might still roam the West. The adventurers found no elephants, but in contrast to Mackenzie's quick dashes they collected specimens and artifacts, drew careful maps, and recorded tribes and populations. With the unknown partially vanquished, the crossing and settlement of the continent became only a matter of time.

The Lewis and Clark journey was very much Thomas Jefferson's expedition. It was a quest conceived long before the Louisiana Purchase in order to fill in the frustrating blanks of the North American maps that the statesman collected to hang in the foyer of Monticello. Jefferson may have dreamed of exploring the West since he was six years old. It was then, in 1749, that his father, Peter, and other gentlemen of Albemarle County, Virginia, chartered the Loyal Land Company. Its purpose was to map and market the West, and the founders speculated about following the distant Missouri River and seeing if it somehow connected to the Pacific. Jefferson later collected the best library in North America of published material on the far Northwest.

In his lifetime the Virginian would never venture west of the Shenandoah River, and he initially believed the Blue Ridge Mountains were probably higher than the Rockies. But Jefferson's brilliant curiosity extended the reach of the United States across the continent. He solicited advice from experts on making astronomical measurements to determine location, on writing secret codes, and on the best possible list of expeditionary supplies. His personal secretary, Meriwether Lewis, was sent to Philadelphia to learn new techniques for surveying, for the preservation of biological specimens, and for the sustenance of the expedition's health. Jefferson then sent a confidential message to Congress on January 18, 1803, proposing the journey. Before the Louisiana Purchase had even been made, he wanted to cross the continent.

Coincidental events leading to the trek had been set in motion three years before. Spain had ceded "Louisiana" to France in 1800, that name representing a vast territory that stretched from the Gulf of Mexico to the crest of the Rockies in Montana. With France and England engaged in the Napoleonic Wars, Jefferson became worried that either the French would launch a military expedition up the Mississippi toward British Canada or that the English would attack the other way to seize New Orleans. Either campaign could threaten American security. In response, the

President ordered a garrisoning of western outposts and proposed a secret reconnaissance by Lewis and Clark of the upper Missouri.

Enter Napoleon Bonaparte, connected in two intriguing ways to the history of the Columbia River. His competition for a means to preserve food for his armies led to the invention of canning in 1807, a technology that eventually made possible the huge salmon harvests on the Columbia more than half a century later. More significantly, Napoleon found himself at war with Britain again by 1803, and in strategic difficulty. His grand scheme to reestablish the French empire in North America and overawe the United States by sending an army up the Mississippi River had collapsed. The intended force was destroyed along the way on the island of Hispaniola (now Haiti and the Dominican Republic) by yellow fever, contracted while putting down a black slave rebellion. Left with no army in America, Napoleon decided in April that Louisiana had become a New World distraction he could do without, but one that England must be forestalled from seizing. He offered to sell the tract to the neutral United States for $15 million, $3.75 million of the price to be paid by settlement of American claims against France. It was the biggest real estate bargain in history, doubling the size of the young nation with an 800,000-square-mile tract of land that ran to the eastern edge of the Columbia drainage but did not include the Pacific Northwest. The surprise offer coincided neatly with the secret expedition Jefferson was already planning.

Here at last was the opportunity to find a riverine Northwest Passage across American territory. Jefferson's letter to Meriwether Lewis on June 20, 1803, stated that it was the mission of the "Corps of Discovery of the Northwest to explore the Missouri river, & such principal stream of it, as, by it's course and communication with the waters of the Pacific ocean, whether the Columbia, Oregon, Colorado or any other river, may offer the most direct and practicable water communication across this continent for the purposes of commerce." Jefferson wanted a river that led somewhere, that allowed goods and people and furs to move across the continent.

The resulting Lewis and Clark expedition is famous because it was so successful, and successful because it was well-led, carefully planned, and quite lucky.

The leadership was superb. Meriwether Lewis, a family friend of Jefferson, had become the President's private secretary a month before the inauguration in 1801. Jefferson probably made the choice specifically to prepare for his long-dreamed-of western mission of exploration. Lewis had impressive experience, having served in the militia and army since the Whisky Rebellion. At one point he had also reported to the equally able William Clark, the brother of famed Revolutionary War hero George Rogers Clark and an experienced Indian fighter in his own right. Lewis urged the appointment of his former colleague as the other expedition leader. The respect the two had developed for each other while in the army persisted during the long, difficult expedition, a cooperation and friendship virtually unmatched in exploration history. While Clark was technically a lieutenant and Lewis a captain at the time of the trek, they effectively shared command. They also managed to instill in their Corps of Discovery a strict military discipline and high morale that persisted over the 4,150 miles they traveled to reach the Pacific.

One example of the careful planning was the explorers' decision to seal their powder in lead canisters, keeping it dry even when dumped into rugged, canoe-tossing rivers. Without this precaution, "we should not have a single charge of powder at this time," Lewis wrote at the Columbia's mouth.

The Corps of Discovery also enjoyed extraordinary luck in not encountering crippling storms, falls, disease, or battle. They were mostly helped rather than hindered by the Native Americans they encountered, obtaining food, horses, and canoes.

Finally, its members exercised good judgment. The explorers brilliantly maintained peaceful relations with most tribes. They struck a shrewd balance between carrying supplies, trading with Indians for others, and living off the land. They drilled the Corps members and trained them. Rural Americans were not necessarily natural marksmen, but conscious practice before leaving St. Louis and necessary hunting along the way meant that by the time the party reached the Columbia's mouth, virtually all its members were crack shots. Lewis and Clark also made a number of astute deductions, such as realizing that the presence of salmon in the Clearwater River meant that there could be no truly immense falls between that stream and the sea and that it could probably be navigated safely.

The expedition failed, of course, to find the water route sought for Jefferson's "commerce." There was no eight-hundred-and-seventeen-pace portage such as Mackenzie had found far to the north. Instead, Lewis and Clark overcame a gap of three hundred and fifty miles from the Missouri to the Clearwater River in Idaho. For three hundred years, Europeans had sought an easy water route across North America. Lewis and Clark established that it did not exist. But in turning the nation's interior from a place of speculation to a real geography, they changed the infant nation's view of itself as powerfully as the photographs of a marbled blue earth taken from the moon have influenced the environmental movement in our own time.

Lewis and Clark were not particularly entranced with the Columbia River country. They set out in 1804, wintered with the Mandan Indians on the Plains, ascended the Missouri and crossed the Rockies during the spring and summer of 1805, and reached the mouth of the Columbia in the fall. Wintering on the Oregon shore at rudely built Fort Clatsop, they returned to St. Louis in 1806. Thus they ascended the Missouri River when the river was full and the plains green and alluring. They descended the Snake and Columbia when water was low, rapids plentiful, and the plateau brown. They quickly tired of the camas root they found west of the Continental Divide. Salmon runs were at a peak but many in the expedition preferred boiled dog to the fish. Early white reaction to salmon was definitely mixed, some praising the flavor and abundance of the fish and others suffering from diarrhea or other distress from its oily flesh.

After building canoes on Idaho's Clearwater River the explorers began the five-hundred-mile water descent to the sea. They were not encouraged by what they found. They passed thirty rapids on the lower Snake River alone, upsetting two canoes. Its canyon was deep and so treeless that they had difficulty finding sufficient firewood. When they struggled the one to two thousand feet up the enclosing grassy bluffs to examine the country they were floating through, they found a vast rolling plain, cut by coulees of gnarled basalt. The Snake's junction with the Columbia was a desert.

On the Columbia River itself the explorers encountered Celilo Falls and the Cascades of the Columbia. The natives were astounded when the explorers rode their canoes through The

Dalles, where a river that was frequently a mile in width squeezed down to forty-five yards and was "swelling and boiling in a most tremendious manner." Lewis and Clark noted with disappointment that the Columbia fell the same altitude as the Missouri in a much shorter distance, producing much more difficult rapids. The Indians who controlled these checkpoints were, in Lewis's words, "poor, dirty, proud, haughty, inhospitable, parsimonious and faithless in every respect." There were so many fleas at The Dalles that the expedition members shed their clothes to avoid infestation.

When the explorers returned the next spring, the river was so swollen and rough that they lost a dearly purchased Indian canoe just trying to tow it by rope along the rocky shore of the Cascades. Once they reached the Snake they elected not to try to paddle upstream on that rapids-plagued river, instead buying horses and following an overland trail.

The expedition leaders did correctly deduce on their return trip that, near the western foothills of Idaho, rainfall was adequate for farming. This Palouse country would eventually become the most productive wheatland in the nation. The pair also predicted that Oregon's Willamette Valley south of Portland would become heavily populated farm country. But their overall impression was cautious and unflattering. They had an eye for beauty on the trip, remarking on the grand display of sunset color in the skies above the plains, or how a field of Idaho wildflowers shimmered like water. But many of their Columbia River entries depict the current as difficult, the weather unappealing, and the Indians as thievish.

They reached the ocean in November at the beginning of what appears to have been a wet winter even by coastal Pacific Northwest standards. Clark wrote, "The emmence Seas and waves which breake on the rocks & Coasts to the S.W. & N.W. roars like an emence fall at a distance, and this roaring has continued ever Since our arrival in the neighborhood of the Sea Coast, which has been 24 days since we arrived in Sight of the Great Western (for I cannot say Pacific) Ocian, as I have not seen one pacific day since my arrival in its vicinity, and its waters which are forming perpetually breake with emence waves on the Sands and rockey coasts, tempestuous and horiable." The weather did not improve his mood. On December 16, 1805, he wrote, "The rain continues, with Tremendous gusts of wind, which is Tremendious. The winds violent. Trees falling in every direction, whorl winds, with gusts of rain. Hail & Thunder, This kind of weather lasts all day, Certainly one of the worst days that ever was!" Their winter at Fort Clatsop continued wet and largely unpleasant, with only twelve rainless days and only six with sunshine. They left earlier than originally planned, on March 23, 1806, in part to escape dreary coastal storms, and as a result arrived back at the Rockies before the snow had sufficiently melted. Yet before leaving they marveled: at a whale thrown up on an Oregon beach, trees twelve feet in diameter, sea otter fur that exceeded in quality anything they had seen to the east.

Lewis and Clark had followed only the lower quarter of the Columbia River. It turned north near its junction with the Snake, pointing through desert toward country they could only guess at. The explorers regarded the Snake as essentially the Columbia's southern fork, but it appeared impractical to ascend as it turned south into the depths of Hells Canyon.

Jefferson's dream of an easy water route across the continent did not appear to be practical.

While Lewis and Clark descended the lower Columbia, Canadian fur trappers searched for its upper reaches, hoping that if the Great River of the West did not connect with the Missouri then it might instead be an easy portage from more northern rivers. By now sea exploration was suggesting that however difficult the Columbia was to enter and ascend, it appeared to be the only feasible route from the coast to the interior. Every alternative looked worse. The exploration that followed in the maze of mountains produced epic confusion.

Which brings us once more to David Thompson, one of the most important, celebrated, confused, and tardy explorers in Pacific Northwest history. Born in England in 1770 and orphaned at the age of two, Thompson was apprenticed to the Hudson's Bay Company shortly after his fourteenth birthday. He arrived at remote Fort Churchill on Hudson Bay in September 1784. By age sixteen he was helping build Manchester House at the western extremity of Canadian penetration onto the Great Plains, and two years later had an accident that changed his life. Thompson broke his leg badly and, while recovering, was taught surveying by an experienced hand named Philip Turnor. In the years to follow

Thompson often didn't seem to know where he was going, but his skill with the sextant and compass let him know exactly where he was. His maps of the Northwest were so precise that the final compilation that hung in Fort William's Great Hall guided cartographers for the next seventy years. Thompson walked and paddled fifty-five thousand miles and left thirty-nine volumes of journals. Yet again and again he turned the wrong way in the hunt for the Columbia, giving Americans time to strengthen their claim to the river country. Tireless, methodical, and a bit priggish, he didn't smoke, drink, or swear. He stayed faithful to his part-Indian wife for sixty years, had thirteen children, and spent evenings subjecting his frequently profane French *voyageurs* to readings from the Bible.

As stated before, with trade ships already plying the Northwest coast the need to penetrate the Rockies from the east was not altogether clear to the Canadian fur companies. Then, in 1804, the North West Company learned that the Americans were dispatching Lewis and Clark. The same year saw the death of Simon McTavish, a company partner who had opposed ventures west of the Rockies because he feared it would lessen the influence of headquarters in Montreal and his own power. The Canadians decided to act. The Nor'Westers ordered Simon Fraser to establish trading posts west of the Continental Divide. In the winter of 1805–1806, while Lewis and Clark were camped at Fort Clatsop at the Columbia's mouth, Fraser followed Alexander Mackenzie's old route across the mountains and established the first trading post west of the Rockies at McLeod Lake. It was more than a hundred miles north of present-day Prince George, British Columbia, and seven hundred straight-line miles northeast of the Columbia's mouth. Fraser built two more posts in 1807, both far north of the Columbia.

Thompson, meanwhile, had initially done little to impress the Hudson's Bay Company with his ability as an explorer. He led expeditions that failed to find a direct water route from Hudson Bay to the Athabasca fur country. Still, he used his newfound expertise with surveying instruments to begin an accurate mapping of the north country. While Gray was a merchant captain with an explorer's heart, Thompson was an explorer who barely tolerated the need to justify his calling by fur trading. When the Bay Company ordered him to spend less time on surveys and more on business, Thompson simply walked seventy-five miles from a Bay post on Reindeer Lake to a North West Company post on the Reindeer River and joined the competition.

He eventually rose to partner and in 1807 was chosen to cross the Rockies farther south than Fraser. Thompson was to establish a post on that mysterious north-flowing river that La Gasse and Le Blanc had encountered seven years before. This, of course, was the Columbia, but the fur traders did not realize that. Thompson called it the Kootenae River, after the name the inhabitants called themselves, and built Kootenae House a mile north of Lake Windermere, near the Columbia's source. (This tribe and the accompanying river were spelled both Kootenay and Kootenai—the first version used today in Canada, the second in the United States—plus Kootenae, Coutanie, Kootonay, Cotonai, Kootana, Kutanas, Kootanas, Kutnehas, Kutonas, Kitunaha, and Kootenuha by various pioneers. The name comes from *ko*, meaning water, and *tinneh*, meaning people.)

Continuing the confusion, Fraser in 1808 set off down the perilous river that bears his name. He believed this was the Columbia and that he would come out at the same point as Lewis and Clark, but the voyage was a nightmare of white water and sheer cliffs. "We had to pass where no human being should venture," the explorer wrote of his trip. After an immensely perilous journey he realized his mistake, but was still confused enough to name the nearby Thompson River for his colleague under the assumption that this was part of the stream on which Kootenae House had been built.

As Fraser followed his river down to the future site of Vancouver, British Columbia, Thompson left Kootenae House, paddled upstream (south) to the Columbia's source at Columbia Lake, portaged a mile and a half across the gravel plain that would later be known as Canal Flats, and entered the real Kootenay River. Thompson thought perhaps *this* south-flowing river was the Columbia, though he named it the McGillivray for a senior partner in the fur company. He followed the Kootenay's long, weirdly looping course south into Montana and then northwest past Bonners Ferry, Idaho, back into British Columbia, and finally to Kootenay Lake. At this point there were only twenty-five miles to go before the Kootenay finally joined the Columbia, but Thompson instead broke off this seemingly circular trip. He paddled back to Bonners Ferry, obtained horses, rode back to Kootenae House and then east across the Continental Divide.

The next year Thompson returned and completed a similar exercise, this time finding the Pend Oreille River in northern Idaho and northeast Washington and following it until he was again twenty-five miles from the Columbia River. Once more he turned back. Thompson seemed to have an almost instinctual aversion to the river his company so desperately wanted him to find.

As a result, the complicated geography of the mountainous Pacific Northwest had still not been sorted out. The Canadians by now thought the Fraser was the Columbia, the Thompson was the Columbia, and the Kootenay was the Columbia, while thinking the Columbia was the Kootenay.

By 1810, Thompson was due a year's leave and was planning to return to eastern Canada. Instead, the Canadians again reacted to American competition, this time word that New York financier John Jacob Astor was dispatching both land and sea expeditions to establish a post at the mouth of the Columbia. A message caught up with Thompson at Rainy Lake to turn around and find the elusive river once and for all. By now North West Company geographers had deduced it must be the river that the Kootenay-mistaken-for-the-McGillivray and the Pend Oreille were flowing toward. Thompson's start was delayed by fear of a battle with the aggressive Piegan Indians, so in midwinter the explorer took a more northerly route up the Athabasca and Whirlpool rivers and found Athabasca Pass. This brought him down to the Columbia at its most northerly point, where it is joined by the Canoe River. Here it made its great bend south.

It was January 18, 1811. Astor's ship the *Tonquin* was already on its way to the Columbia around the Horn, and an overland Astorian expedition led by Wilson Price Hunt was wintering on the Great Plains. The clock of competition was ticking.

Instead of following orders and racing down the Columbia, Thompson wanted to go back up the Columbia to Kootenae House for the winter. His men were exhausted, however. They rebelled and all but three deserted, recrossing the Rocky Mountains. Thompson and the remaining trio lived out the winter in a snow cave lined with wood at the Columbia's junction with the Canoe River, spending their time at "Canoe Camp" building a boat of cedar boards. Then, once more declining to venture down the unknown Columbia with its reports of fearsome rapids and unknown Indians, Thompson finally ascended to Kootenae House in April. By this time Astor's sea expedition had reached the Columbia's mouth.

Unaware of this, Thompson traveled on upriver to the Columbia's source, portaged to the Kootenay River again, and followed a complex route down into Montana and across the Idaho panhandle to Spokane House on the Spokane River. This fur outpost had been built by the North West Company's Finan McDonald the previous year. From there, Thompson took a trail that led northwest and on June 19 finally struck the Columbia again at Kettle Falls, 40 percent of the way down its length. At last the explorer firmly recognized that the river he had mistaken as the Kootenay was in fact the Columbia. He instructed McDonald to explore back upriver to the Big Bend and Canoe Camp and to prepare to move trade goods down this new route. But in his "race" with the Astorians to the mouth of the Columbia, Thompson had gone at least twice as far as would have been necessary had he simply followed the main river.

It took Thompson until July 3 to find a suitable cedar tree to build another boat, but then only eleven days to dash nearly the Columbia's entire length within the United States to the ocean. He paused at the treeless, dusty junction of the Snake and Columbia (where he knew Lewis and Clark had passed six years before) to claim the country. "Know hereby that this country is claimed by Great Britain as part of its territories," his sign read, "and that the North West Company of Merchants from Canada, finding the factory [trading post] for this people [local natives] inconvenient for them, do hereby intend to erect a factory in this place for the commerce of the country around." He came to the mouth of the Columbia on July 15, where he found the Stars and Stripes flying over a rude collection of log huts built by the Astorians.

Had England lost the contest for the Great River of the West? Not really. Most of those manning the American fort were Canadians hired by Astor for their experience in the fur trade. Some historians contend Thompson was in no hurry because he was under the impression that a partnership between the two companies was imminent. Certainly he was allowed to roam the new post at will. He gave the Americans advice on setting up an inland fort up the Columbia and yet at the same time tried to discourage them about the possibilities of upriver trade, a competitive ruse that fooled no one. Whatever Thompson's thinking, he left Astoria in a week.

Traveling upstream he found the Columbia a difficult river. Portages were required around the Cascades, The Dalles, and Celilo Falls. Indians who took just a day or two to canoe downriver from Priest Rapids to the junction with the Snake required a week of backbreaking labor to pole back up. (In coming years the natives would trade two dollars' worth of salmon for a steamboat ride.) To avoid this spot, Thompson departed from the river near present-day Pasco and rode overland to Spokane House with horses purchased from native tribes. From there he went again to Kettle Falls, built still another boat, and on September 2, 1811, prepared to ascend the Columbia and explore the remainder of its length. McDonald had already tried but turned back at Devil's Canyon near Revelstoke. Thompson had more determination, finally reaching the site of his winter's hut at the Big Bend on September 18: the first white to have confirmed and completely followed the Columbia's circuitous route.

While hardly the easy water route the Canadians had dreamed of, the river had two compelling advantages. It led inland through the Cascade Mountains from the sea, allowing sea supply and transport for the western extremity of the fur trade. It would be far easier to ship supplies to the mouth of the Columbia and distribute them upriver than to carry them overland from Montreal or Hudson Bay. And if the Columbia failed to point east-west as Jefferson had hoped, it did promise a rugged highway toward the northern posts of Britain in Canada.

Still, the mouth of this seemingly strategic river was already occupied by the Americans. How had the Astorians beaten the long head start of the Canadian fur trappers? Their bold arrival can be credited to the visionary, ambitious, ill-led, and unlucky grasp for empire by New York financier John Jacob Astor. A destitute German immigrant who had entered the fur trade in the Northeast and made a fortune in just six years, Astor was one of the first great American capitalists, seeking to build with furs what later businessmen would build in rail, oil, automobiles, or computers.

His merchant's world was one to inspire the imagination. During business trips to Montreal, Astor would dine at the North

West Company's Beaver Room, hearing tales of the fur trade, Indians, and an exotic geography that stretched thousands of miles out across the North American continent. On the docks of New York or at the city's Tontine Coffee House, Astor could get firsthand information on foreign ports and barely charted coasts from visiting sea captains. It is as if one could drop into a tavern and chat with astronauts today. The fur trade at the time had the same strategic significance as oil did later, back in an age when Indian tribes were still militarily powerful and furs represented a commodity of high value throughout the northern hemisphere. "British and American diplomats believed that the fur trade was the foundation for both national power and frontier peace," historian James Ronda has noted.

Using as his model the Hudson's Bay and North West Companies, Astor envisioned a global trade network. Goods from America would be used to purchase furs from the Indians on the Northwest coast. These furs would be transported by American ship to China and Europe and be sold for tea, silk, dining ware, and other products that could be marketed in America. An annual supply ship to the Columbia's mouth would sail on to sell the gathered furs in China and finally return to New York with an Asian cargo in a yearly circumnavigation of the planet. At a time when the American frontier was in today's Midwest, Astor was plotting globally.

The North West Company had considered a similar venture the same year Gray discovered the Columbia. Because of English regulations seeking to preserve a monopoly for the East India Company, the Nor'Westers even proposed to use American ships to transport Canadian furs. However, the initial huge profits in the China trade briefly declined as the market became temporarily saturated, while a change in American law made it more difficult to use U.S. ships. The idea of international cooperation never quite came off. Now, in 1810, Astor was revising the scheme, with American ownership but inclusion of Canadian partners to tap their expertise.

The key to his vision would be a post at the mouth of the Columbia. Astoria, as it would be called, would be established by a two-pronged expedition. One would go by sea around the Horn, the other overland.

It was a bold plan, but it foundered on a poor choice of men to lead it and miserable timing. Astoria was launched on the eve of the War of 1812. By the time it was sold to the British, sixty-one of its employees had died in the Pacific Northwest from drownings, disease, and combat with the natives.

For his sea captain Astor chose Jonathan Thorn, a former naval officer who had served with distinction during the war with Tripoli but who was an inflexibly strict disciplinarian. Thorn proved unable to form a cooperative partnership with the mostly Scottish and French fur traders Astor recruited from Canada to accompany him. A description of the captain from French-Canadian fur trader Gabriel Franchere: "A precise and rigid man, naturally hot-tempered, expecting instant obedience at the slightest sign, considering only his duty and caring nothing else for the discontented mutterings of his crew, asking advice of no man and following to the letter the instructions that he received from Mr. Astor—such, approximately, was the man who had been appointed to command our ship."

To lead the land party Astor picked Wilson Price Hunt, a St. Louis merchant with limited frontier experience. He would prove to have neither the skill nor the luck of Lewis and Clark in finding a path across the continent.

Thorn was given command of the *Tonquin*, a ninety-four-foot-long ship of two hundred and sixty-nine tons burden that carried ten guns, a ton of gunpowder, and trade goods worth $54,263.37. Some of the merchandise was cheap baubles the cost-shaving Astor hoped to unload on gullible natives, but the Columbia tribes proved too sophisticated to have much interest in them. Looking for fur trade experience, Astor became partners with three Scottish veterans from Canada. He also recruited fourteen Canadians for the sea journey and fourteen for the land trek to supplement his Americans.

Those going by ship portaged and paddled from Montreal to New York. As the plumed and feathered Canadians swept down the Hudson in their birch bark canoes, singing gaily in French, New York residents hurried to the docks to watch this apparition from the storied western frontier. American sea captains had already made an end run around the Canadian fur empires; now Astor was challenging their dominance head-on. The scheme was thrilling in its vision.

Trouble began immediately, however. The small *Tonquin* was to carry twenty-nine besides its normal crew (typical of the racial diversity of western expeditions, two of the Astorians were free blacks), plus pigs, goats, sheep, and chickens. A quarrel broke out immediately between the fur traders and Thorn on the location of their quarters in the crowded vessel, launching a simmering feud that lasted the rest of the long voyage.

The *Tonquin* slipped out of New York Harbor on September 8, 1810. War was looming with Britain, and Thorn irritated his passengers by refusing to replenish at the Cape Verde Islands because he feared interception by English warships. After stopping instead at the bleak Falkland Islands, he became impatient when some of the passengers stretching their legs ashore failed to return at the announced sailing time. Rather than wait for the fur traders, Thorn simply hoisted anchor and put to sea. The alarmed Canadians ran down to the shore, leaped into their longboat, and pulled hard in pursuit. Thorn didn't come about to wait until one of the Canadians who had stayed aboard, Robert Stuart, pulled two pistols and warned that unless Thorn paused, "You are a dead man this instant." From that point on the ship was firmly split between the Canadian trappers and Thorn loyalists, and the two groups scarcely spoke to each other.

The *Tonquin* hired two dozen Hawaiians as laborers in Honolulu and then sailed for the Columbia in chill March weather, Thorn mulishly forbidding his passengers to break out the cold weather gear. Most of the chickens on deck were swept overboard in storms, and the two sheep died. Wet, shivering, crammed like sardines, and seasick, the ship's passengers regarded the final leg of the passage as a nightmare.

When they reached the river's mouth on the blustery day of March 22, 1811, the bar was far more menacing than when Robert Gray had crossed. Although braved by a hundred ships, the angry entrance was acquiring an evil reputation in the world's seaports. Huge waves as high as a masthead broke across the bar with a thunderous roar and the water was a cold boil of gray water, roiled sand, and ragged foam. Rather than wait for calmer weather, however, Thorn ordered a popular young crewman named John Fox and an inexperienced crew of landsmen into a longboat to find a channel. Fox protested.

"Mr. Fox, if you are afraid of water you should have remained in Boston," Thorn replied. Stung by this rebuke, Fox numbly assented, but as the longboat was being lowered he turned to fur clerk Alexander Ross and confided, "My uncle was drowned here not many years ago, and now I am going to lay my bones with his." As he cast off, Fox shouted, "Farewell my friends, we will perhaps meet again in the next world!" The long-boat vanished in the mountainous breakers only a hundred yards away. The five on board disappeared.

The next day the now-shaken Thorn ordered a second boat to probe. This was seized by the tide, carried inside the river, and wrecked, two drowning and a third dying of hypothermia on shore. By now the passengers regarded Thorn as little more than a murderer. He finally ordered the *Tonquin* itself to try the passage, and the ship pointed its nose into the Columbia. As it passed between the two capes the ship began to pitch wildly, wallowing in the white rollers. Then it struck sand, lurched, and stuck. Breakers began crashing over the side and the ship swung dangerously broadside to the waves, the masts leaning ominously. Anchors were set but wouldn't hold. The ship began jolting from sand bar to sand bar, the sea foaming across its decks, the seamen clutching the rigging in wet panic. Many were convinced they were lost. Then the *Tonquin* broke free a final time and drifted into the estuary. After a voyage of six and a half months, Astor's sea expedition was inside the Columbia—at a cost of eight dead.

The worst was still to come.

Thorn wanted to unload the unhappy fur partners and some of the trade goods as desperately as they wanted to get off his ship. After scouting the estuary they chose a location for a post on the Oregon shore at the present site of Astoria. The landscape seemed more intimidating than welcoming. "The impervious and magnificent forest darkened the landscape as far as the eye could reach," Ross wrote. It was "studded with trees of almost incredible size, many of them measuring fifty feet in girth." Most of the men were neither experienced woodsmen nor hunters. They depended on the Indians to bring salmon for food (trader Robert Stuart called them "by far the finest fish I ever beheld"), were constantly fearful of attack, and were baffled by the huge trees. No one knew exactly how to cut them down, and it often took two days to chop through a single trunk. Even then they would often hang up on other trees rather than topple to earth. Much of the timber cleared for the post site was too huge to be handled easily, and the Astorians had to search for trees small enough to carry and stack to build their fort.

The *Tonquin*, meanwhile, sailed on June 1 for Vancouver Island to trade for furs. Those left behind felt isolated and exposed at its temporary absence, and then even more so after it became overdue. Weeks went by, then months. The Astorians picked up alarming rumors from the coastal tribes that their ship was never coming back.

At Clayoquot Sound on Vancouver Island, Thorn's temper finally sealed his doom. Exploding in a rage when one chief complained at the price paid for furs, he rubbed the headman's face in the skins. This was an insult that would not go unavenged. Some days later the Indian appeared alongside with twenty companions, waving furs and seeking to come on board. Thorn, who apparently viewed the natives with contempt, assented. Despite Astor's warnings about past attacks on ships, the captain had not bothered to rig the overhanging boarding nets along the ship's side, which would have restricted access to a narrow, easily defended entrance. The Indians clambered aboard. Then another canoe appeared and more warriors swarmed up the side. Finally worried, Thorn decided to get his ship under way. As the crew began raising anchor and climbing the rigging, the Indians drew knives, clubs, and hatchets hidden beneath their furs and attacked. Partner Alexander McKay was clubbed to death first. Thorn went down trying to defend himself with a small knife. The rest of the crew was quickly massacred. One exception was a half-Indian interpreter named Jack Ramsay, who leaped overboard and was rescued by some Indian women. It was he, after living with the natives, who would carry the full tale to Astoria two years later. According to Ramsay, the next day a large number of Indians clambered aboard the *Tonquin* to celebrate their victory. Apparently at least one crewman was still alive in the hold. One can imagine his state of mind: his mates dead and the ship captive on a hostile coast, thousands of miles from home. The survivor apparently set off Astor's ton of gunpowder. The ship blew up, killing nearly two hundred Indians by Ramsay's estimate.

The overland Astorian expedition fared little better. In 1810, Wilson Price Hunt went to Lachine, near Montreal, to recruit experienced *voyageurs*. He had little success luring Canadians for an overland journey that had not been made since Lewis and Clark—until he allowed those already hired to parade with feathers in their caps, a sign of status and success in the North. Instantly the Astorian expedition became an elite and sought-after company, and the ranks filled. The combined group of Canadians and Americans journeyed down the Mississippi to St. Louis and then went up the Missouri five hundred miles where they wintered. On April 21, 1811, about a month after the *Tonquin* reached the Columbia, Hunt set out across the continent with sixty men, one Indian woman (Marie Dorion, wife of a French-Canadian named Pierre), and the couple's two children. He struck out on a more southerly route in hope of avoiding the difficult mountains that Lewis and Clark had encountered.

The trip became as disastrous as the *Tonquin's*. Hunt got caught up in a distracting race with another fur group and failed to discover South Pass, the gradual route across the Continental Divide that would later be used by wagon trains on the Oregon Trail. After struggling across the steep ranges of western Wyoming the Astorians did not reach Henry's Fort, a tiny post on Henry's Fork of the Snake River, until October. With the season getting late, Hunt made his most serious mistake, deciding to leave his horses at the fort and to descend the Snake in canoes. The river proved unnavigable. The party encountered Idaho Falls, American Falls, Twin Falls, and then Shoshone Falls in canyons cutting steadily deeper into the cold, hostile, treeless Snake River basalt plateau. At Caldron Linn, Twin Falls was one hundred and eighty-two feet high. Shoshone Falls was two hundred and twelve feet, higher than Niagara, and a thousand feet wide. Canoes abandoned, the party continued on foot along the rugged Snake.

Deciding to split up in hopes one party would find a feasible route out of the hellish country, Hunt followed the left bank and Ramsay Crooks the right. The canyons grew so steep that the Astorians traveling on the rim couldn't descend for drinking water, and the Canadians with Crooks were forced to drink their own urine. At the end of November they encountered the upper end of Hells Canyon, the continent's deepest gorge. Hunt's party turned back. On the other side of the river, Crooks was too sick to go farther. He stayed on the Snake with John Day and a Canadian *voyageur.* The remainder of his group, eleven men led by Donald Mackenzie, struggled on through Hells Canyon. They came out at the Snake's junction with the Clearwater River, the point at which

Lewis and Clark had emerged from the Bitterroot Mountains. Following the explorers' earlier route, they went down the Snake and Columbia to Astoria, arriving on January 18, 1812.

Hunt's group had meanwhile retreated to take shelter with some friendly Shoshone. They set out again on December 21, the shortest day of the year, to struggle across the snowy Blue Mountains of northeastern Oregon. By this time Marie Dorion was eight months pregnant, and at the end of December she gave birth in eastern Oregon's Grande Ronde River valley. The baby died a week later. On January 8 the exhausted, starving party stumbled into a Cayuse Indian camp and again was saved by the natives. After resting a week they set out once more, finally reaching Astoria on February 15.

Meanwhile, Crooks recovered enough to travel, and he and his two companions finally followed. After a terrible journey across the desert of eastern Oregon that drove Day insane, they reached Astoria on May 11.

The Astorian position was now precarious. The *Tonquin* was lost, along with many of the trading supplies. Casualties totaled sixty-one. David Thompson had appeared after canoeing down the Columbia from Kettle Falls, reminding the Americans of the competition they faced from the North West Company. Then came word of war with Great Britain. Meanwhile, Astor's attempts to send relief were failing. A second Astorian ship called the *Beaver* was damaged in a storm before it could complete a mission to set up trade with the Russians, and a third, the *Lark*, sank off Maui. By the end of 1813, the partners at Astoria, many of them Canadians anyway, decided to sell out to the Nor'Westers rather than lose everything to conquest.

The transaction was no sooner agreed to than the British warship *Racoon* showed up to capture the place. Captain William Black was disappointed it had been sold, robbing the crew of any opportunity of prize money. "What, is this the fort I have heard so much of?" he exclaimed when he saw the rude stockade hacked out of the forest. "Great God, I could batter it down with a four-pounder in two hours!" Astoria was renamed Fort George. The Americans, it seemed, had reached too far, too fast.

Ironically, the United States would recover Astoria in name. Despite the British having bought it, Captain Black decided to claim the post for Britain anyway. The Treaty of Ghent that later ended the War of 1812 specified the return of captured possessions, meaning that the Americans could reclaim Astoria, something they could not have done had Black left well enough alone. Accordingly, in 1818 the American flag was dutifully hoisted over the post. The symbolism was meaningless, however. The North West Company remained in charge because Americans were unprepared to make an investment to follow Astor's disastrous example. The war had assured that first the Nor'Westers and then the company they were absorbed by, Hudson's Bay, would dominate the Columbia until the 1840s. The treaty left the ultimate ownership of the Oregon or Columbia country unresolved until 1846, with both Britain and the United States allowed access in the meantime. American fur trade activity, however, focused on the Great Plains and the Rockies, a region within easier reach of cities such as St. Louis.

Astoria turned out to be a poor location to anchor an empire. The site had little farmland. After the Hudson's Bay Company absorbed the North West Company in 1821, the governor of its Columbia division, the energetic and hard-headed George Simpson, decided to move the Columbia River post one hundred miles upriver to a site of open benchland on the north bank. Christened Fort Vancouver in 1824, it eventually became Vancouver, Washington.

Simpson had another reason for abandoning Fort George at the Astoria site. He reasoned it was likely the Columbia would eventually form the international boundary and that Astoria, being on the south bank, would wind up in American possession anyway. The new Fort Vancouver, he bet, would remain in British territory.

He also hoped the change would produce more profit. "Everything appears to me on the Columbia as too extended a scale except *the trade*," he reported caustically, "and when I say that it is confined to four permanent establishments the returns of which do not amount to 20,000 beaver and otters altho the country has been occupied upward of fourteen years, I feel that a very severe reflection is cast on those who had the management of the business. . . ."

Fort Vancouver would grow enough food to supply an expanding network of Bay Company posts. From this center the company's manpower doubled in just ten years, building a solar system of twenty-two fur posts that occupied the Columbia River Basin and upper British Columbia and employed four hundred and fifty people. While Fort Vancouver was too far south of the heart of the Hudson's Bay Company empire for Simpson's tastes, it couldn't be helped. Three decades of exploration had established the Columbia's importance as the most practical sea shipment point in the Pacific Northwest because it formed a corridor through the Cascade Mountains.

It was not that the Columbia was so good: by 1832, Bay man Archibald McDonald would report that a "man's life in the Columbia is become mere lottery" because of drownings, shipwrecks on the bar, rapids, disease, failures of salmon runs, and attacks by Native Americans. However, every alternative was worse. After a terrifying voyage down the Fraser, the energetic Simpson conceded that only the Columbia offered any kind of feasible water highway. From this point on, the development of the Columbia directed the development of the region.

As a water highway comparable to the great rivers of the East, however, the Columbia remained a frustration. The river was navigable, but barely, and experience did not eliminate the hazard. In 1829 nine men drowned and five hundred beaver skins were lost when Bay employees tried to run The Dalles. In 1830 seven drowned in The Little Dalles to the north. In 1838 a dozen died trying to run Death Rapids, and in the five years leading up to 1843, thirty people drowned in the lower Columbia and Willamette. By 1846, the Hudson's Bay Company had calculated that sixty-eight of its employees had drowned traversing the river, a journey that took two weeks downstream but four months up. A Catholic missionary, the Reverend Pierre DeSmet, said the Columbia "in its vagrant course is undoubtedly the most dangerous river on the western side of the American hemisphere." Missionary Henry Spalding considered "the Columbia . . . the most frightful river I ever saw navigated by any craft." Bay employee John Tod described the surrounding country "vile" and John Work called it "wretched." Missionary Mary Walker said that "there is probably more danger in going down the River Columbia to Vancouver than in the whole journey across the [Rocky] Mountains."

This was the fabled river Oregon all right, but the Columbia as found was a cruel joke of irksome course, frequent rapids, and uneven flows. Meares's naming of Cape Disappointment, it seemed, was not entirely inaccurate.

4

Beginning and End

The wreck of the Navy ship *Peacock* at the mouth of the
Columbia River, 1841. *(Washington State Historical Museum)*

Cape Disappointment is a brown basaltic hump of rock that
pokes into the Pacific Ocean like the blunt bow of a container
ship, stained white on its steep flanks by seabird guano. This two-
hundred-and-forty-foot promontory, which marks the entrance to
the Columbia River, is reputed to be the foggiest place in the
United States. It overlooks what navigational charts rank as the
third most dangerous river entrance on earth, and the only one in
the United States that requires the use of river bar pilots. Approximately two thousand vessels, more than one hundred of them
major ships, have sunk here. An estimated seven hundred people
have drowned. As warning the Cape sprouts a white lighthouse
like a horn on its forehead, but even the establishment of this
rudimentary warning beacon was difficult. In 1853, when the bark
Oriole sailed to the river with a construction crew and materials

to build the tower, it grounded on the Columbia bar and was battered to pieces. Another ship followed and the lighthouse was constructed three years later, but that just started the dogged campaign to tame the river. Construction of jetties began in 1885 but it took five decades of improvements to establish them with some permanence in the teeth of winter storms.

Despite the Columbia's violence the river remains a major sea channel. It is traversed by freighters sailing its lower hundred miles to call at Longview, Kalama, Vancouver, and Portland. Barges travel another three hundred sixty miles upstream to Idaho. The pilots who guide modern freighters over the bar where Thorn almost wrecked the *Tonquin* direct an average of eleven ships a day, and they are quick to note that they haven't lost one since the 1950s. The river has lost little of its power to intimidate, however. When pilot Bill Worth directed one Russian ship over the bar in rough weather, he observed the skipper working prayer beads.

Worth spent twenty years at sea before winning admittance to the tight, highly paid fraternity of twenty-two bar pilots who master the Columbia's mouth. A native chief named Comcomly was the first river pilot here, paddling out in a cedar canoe to guide fur-trade ships. The modern organization traces its direct lineage back to George Flavell, who began piloting ships in 1846. Entry is by election from other pilots. Applicants are judged on both competence and personality, the association seeking a combination of unflappability and good humor. Worth laughs easily: an instantly likable mariner who displays the self-assurance of someone who repeatedly does a difficult thing with aplomb.

Still, the glory can seem elusive. Upon his election Worth stepped from being captain of a huge oil tanker to ferried passenger on a German-built pilot boat that bears the name *Peacock* but is more popularly known as "Hitler's Revenge." This steel, round-hulled craft makes rendezvous with freighters as far as seventeen miles out to sea. Almost unsinkable, its sloping sides and sturdy hatches are reminiscent of the U-boats the German yard used to build. But if the *Peacock* is as buoyant as a sea duck, it also rolls miserably with each bar crossing. Pilots jostle for the right to board the day's first freighter and get off the heaving boat, more than willing to leap to a ship's rope ladder despite the possibility of a chill dunking in the swells. "Nobody has fun on the *Peacock*,"

Worth explained cheerily. "You don't live on the *Peacock*, you survive."

About once a year a pilot is crushed between the *Peacock* and a freighter hull, an accident that can stun, cripple, or even kill. Seasickness for those aboard is frequent since the entrance is kept open in all but the most extreme conditions: the Columbia today is closed to shipping only about one week per year, on average. Of course it is the discomfort and danger of the Columbia that in part make it attractive, explained Worth. "We went to a maritime meeting and everyone was asking what you did and I said 'Columbia River Bar pilot' and they said '*Wowwwww*,' " he recounted with a laugh. "So it's partly an ego thing."

Even with jetties and dams and dredging at its mouth, pilots are still necessary. The channel of the Columbia prefers to shift, the flat southern Oregon shore of dunes and grass and wind-twisted pine a reminder that the interstate boundary here is migratory. When the state line was first set the river channel was north of aptly named Sand Island, putting the treeless islet firmly in Oregon. Storms and current have subsequently shoved that piece of geography around like a hockey puck. After migrating several miles across the broad estuary, the island today hugs the Washington shore, only a dredged channel preventing it from tying up to the fishing port of Ilwaco. If it does, "That will be one hell of a boundary dispute," joked a chief of the Coast Guard, Richard Helt.

The mouth is rough because of colliding energy. Pacific swells butt a river that pours down with an average of 150 billion gallons of water a day. When these two forces meet over shallow sand, waves mound like corrugated cardboard. Worth has seen currents so strong that navigational buoys have been sucked under water. Dams have eliminated the worst of the spring floods and dredging has reduced the height of waves that in the nineteenth century routinely reached one hundred feet, but modern ships can still pitch so steeply that their bow or stern scrape the bottom of the channel.

The estuary where these energies play out is a wide brackish bay capable of confusing its first explorers. Its width is so great that the British questioned whether Robert Gray ever got into the river proper. And when William Clark wrote, "Ocian in view! O! The joy," in his journal on November 7, 1805, the expedition was still at Pillar Rock, fifteen miles from the river's mouth. The whitecapped waters of the estuary and the long carry of the sound of booming surf fooled them into thinking they had reached the Pacific. Heavy storms, incessant rain, and seemingly impenetrable dense forest kept them pinned to the riverbank, soaked and miserable, for ten more days before Clark finally saw the true Pacific.

At its source, twelve hundred miles upriver in Canada, the Columbia is also confusingly broad—if one accepts as its source ten-mile-long, reed-fringed Columbia Lake, cupped between the Rocky and Purcell mountains. (The river issuing from the lake, however, is not broad at all: it forms a clear, merry, seventy-five-foot-wide scenic water hazard at the Fairmont Hot Springs golf course. But the point here is geographic similarities.) When lit by the sun the lake is breathtaking in the purity of its birth, a sapphire and emerald gem hugged between two mountain ranges cloaked with forest.

The Columbia's source is the location of one of the stranger relationships in the river's geography. It has a hesitant brush with the Kootenay River but won't marry that stream until the two rivers have completed a huge loop totaling eight hundred miles. Columbia Lake is separated from the Kootenay by that mile-and-a-half-wide patch of forest and meadow called Canal Flats that explorer David Thompson kept portaging across. The infant river drains out of the lake to the north and the Kootenay, at that point the larger river, runs south. At one time in prehistory the rivers were probably linked at Canal Flats, and the close pass of this sister river today sheds light on a question that arouses genial debate among Northwesterners: just what is the ultimate source of the Columbia River?

The entire idea of "sources" of rivers misrepresents their true nature as a hydrological loop, a cycle fed by evaporation from the sea and precipitation from the atmosphere. Still, it would unquestioningly be appealing to straddle a rivulet and know that it, and it alone, could claim to grow into the mighty Columbia. The source lake is too big and vague for some people's tastes, and a few have pointed to a boggy spring on the lake's southern shore as a more dramatically tiny birthplace. The seep's contribution is negligible, however, and one could just as strongly make a case for one or another of the creeks that pour into Columbia Lake, such as Lansdowne, Warspite, Marion, Sun, or Dutch. Unfortunately, there is no reason to choose one of these creeks over another. A popular but erroneous claim made to tourists is that the river rises in the Columbia Ice Field of Banff National Park. While the river and ice field may share a name, the glacial melt water actually enters the river one hundred and fifty miles downstream from Columbia Lake. Thus by default the lake is the source of general geographic consensus.

However, if one insists on a point south of Columbia Lake itself, then perhaps the ultimate source is the Kootenay River. Geologists believe ground water from the Kootenay almost certainly migrates through the gravel of Canal Flats to feed the northern end of Columbia Lake, and so the origin of one river is in part the borrowed flow of another. Why the two rivers are separated or joined at any one point in geologic history is due to deposits of Kootenay sediment that over a period of centuries or millennia marries and later divorces it from the sluggish Columbia. Thus we have here a river so broad at its mouth as to confuse Lewis and Clark, and so imprecise at its beginning as to defeat attempts to pinpoint an initial rivulet. A damned difficult stream.

The cradle of the Columbia is a surprisingly gentle place, however. The river will fall half a mile in its journey to the sea, but for its first one hundred miles it drops a leisurely fifty feet in a meandering course of sloughs, lakes, and marshes that resembles the bucolic lower river west of the Cascade foothills. Near its beginning and just before its end, the Columbia has a similar broad, lazy character.

Between these two points the river once roared down scores of rapids, but now it is as prim and controlled as an English butler as it steps down its staircase of dams. In the process the river crosses an international boundary, and the fact that it does so without breaking its mannered character is as remarkable as the engineering of its dams. Fifteen percent of the Columbia's watershed, 30 to 40 percent of its flow, and 38 percent of its length are in Canada. This required a river treaty of joint cooperation and development unprecedented in the world.

The river's long reach does create jurisdictional tangles, however. Once in the United States, the Columbia gathers water from Washington, Oregon, Idaho, Montana, and small corners of Wyoming and Nevada. The Columbia markets power as far as

Texas and ships wheat from the Dakotas. Californians throwing switches on air conditioners can indirectly cause generators to hum at British Columbia's remote Mica Dam, and Canadians seining Columbia salmon off the coast of Vancouver Island start a ripple of trouble that results in water spillage from dams to help fish that can leave reservoir boat ramps dry near Orofino, Idaho.

Between beginning and end the Columbia gathers water from several dozen major tributary rivers, runs through fourteen huge dams, directly waters nearly a million acres of farmland, generates enough electricity to power a score of major cities, supports a dwindling but still significant fishery, and displays one of the most varied catalogues of scenery on the continent. It bursts through a Cascade mountain gorge so beautiful that some residents are still heartbroken it did not become a national park. The Columbia's terrain along different parts of its course mimics Switzerland, Germany, Italy, Nevada, Nebraska, and New Zealand. Taken as a whole, however, it has a geography unique to itself.

It can be a place of postcard perfection. The view in the eastern gorge around Sam Hill's lonely desert mansion at Maryhill, looking west down a brilliantly blue river toward the dark nest of forest surmounted by the icy egg of Mount Hood, is rousing in its magnificence. But the river also has quieter, subtler beauties that take you by surprise: the olive shadow of a salmon gliding through river murk behind a fish-counting window at McNary Dam, the surprisingly intricate natural garden of grass and flowers the desert can produce on the lonely shore of the Hanford nuclear reservation, the awe-inspiring sixty-story-high caramel-colored rock wall of Mica Dam, the stately silvery march of transmission towers across sagebrush desert, the startling red wink of a distant barn across an ocean of young green wheat, the crystal forest created by a treacherous ice storm near Cape Horn, the wide, solemn eyes of an Indian pictograph staring across the river at a passing Amtrak train.

The Columbia rises in this continent's Switzerland, that corner of steep glaciered mountains and achingly green valleys that is southeastern British Columbia. It gathers itself together in an emerald trench between the Rocky Mountains and the Columbia Mountains, the latter a block of rugged ranges that include the Purcells, the Selkirks, and the Monashees. The river is drip-fed from hundreds of glaciers (by official count, four hundred and twelve in the Selkirks alone) and makes a hairpin turn in Canada, wrapping around its namesake mountains to run back south again through narrow reservoirs and glacier-carved lakes toward the American border.

The Columbia is an important river not because of its twelve-hundred-mile length but because of its volume and fall. With its tributaries, it represents about 40 percent of the potential hydroelectric capacity of the United States.

As it falls the Columbia digs, and while its rocky course keeps it from being a particularly silty river, before the dams it carried 7.5 million tons of sediment to the sea every year. One of the interesting features of the Columbia is the way its colors change like a mood ring as it comes down through the mountains, dropping sediment here and picking it up there: going from glacial milk to aqua, blue, green, browner with the addition of the muddier Snake, and finally a pewter in its lower stretches, opaque and reflective enough to take on the colors of the sky.

The Columbia is a developed river. What this means is that from Donald Station, British Columbia, to Bonneville Dam, near Portland, Oregon—a distance of about nine hundred miles—the Columbia for the most part is a series of computer-regulated hydroelectric pools, filling and falling to the rhythm of political storms as much as meteorological ones. Where possible, each reservoir backs up to the lip of the dam above it, ensuring there is no wasted energy in the river's long run. There are fourteen dams in all—Mica, Revelstoke, and Keenleyside in Canada; Grand Coulee, Chief Joseph, Wells, Rocky Reach, Rock Island, Wanapum, Priest Rapids, McNary, John Day, The Dalles, and Bonneville in the United States—dams so geometric and austere that they seem to hum along on their own like an alien space station.

The powerhouses tremble from the volume of water the Columbia can muster. Craig Sprankle, the Bureau of Reclamation spokesman at Grand Coulee Dam, took me down flights of concrete stairs into the basement of the dam's third powerhouse. We stepped into a dimly lit side corridor with a wet, musty smell far earthier than the faint technological odor of oil and ozone that pervaded the antiseptic main gallery above. Rusty water dribbled into a drain, and the concrete shaft ended in a short flight of stairs leading up to a white-painted steel wall. In the center of the wall was a thick bulkhead door fastened with fat, sweating bolts. We put our hands on the steel and felt its vibration. On the other side was the curving penstock feeding water to just one of Grand Coulee's turbines, energy enough behind just this one wall to light a city nearly the size of Seattle. "Each penstock," Sprankle told me, "carries more water than the entire Colorado River."

The dam highest on the Columbia River is Mica, arguably the most beautiful, surprising, and arrogant on the entire river. It seems as remote as a Guatemalan jungle ruin, rudely intrusive in the pyramidal solidity with which it backs up huge Kinbasket Reservoir: a lake so vast that the timber cleared from its bottom was enough for one hundred thousand homes. Mica is more than one hundred and twenty miles from the nearest town, Revelstoke, and a would-be visitor drives more than two hours up a wild mountain valley with only a few logging trucks and a chain of snow-capped peaks for company. The forested valley tightens and tightens and at last becomes a steep rock-walled canyon and still there is no dam, and then you turn a last corner and there it is: boulders stacked eight hundred feet high from bedrock, or more than six hundred feet above the river surface. This is the tallest earth-fill dam in North America. It is built in a canyon so narrow and absent of level ground that its powerhouse is built in a huge cave blasted out of Mica Mountain, like the secret headquarters of a villain in a James Bond movie. The elevator that rises seven hundred and fifty feet is the highest in Canada west of Toronto, in a location so remote the dam has its own underground sewage treatment plant. The engineering that goes into a structure like this seems fantastic. Excavation in winter was done under a vast tent to keep out the relentless snow. The truck that delivered key equipment had forty-two tires and a second driver at the rear to steer around the mountain curves. The generators were floated into place on a cushion of air.

A wooden stairway climbs the face of the dam like a zipper up its middle. Perspective is so impossible around such a colossal structure that I decided to climb the 1,057 stairs for a sense of scale. (They are numbered so workers can turn off at the correct level and enter access tunnels into the dam. Most big dams are honeycombed with passageways, penstocks, and shafts.) Climbing upward, I began to get a sense of the depth of the turquoise sea Mica holds back, measuring the human triumph of this plug with my own sweat. Panting at the top, I cooled in the chill breeze off a reservoir which curved far out of sight. So grand, so isolated, so indicative of the restless reach of modern technology.

The dam is built on a fault fracture zone with a history of earthquakes and landslides. Accordingly, laser beams measure the precise distance between mountains, giving an alarm at the slightest sign of deformation and thus providing warning for possible evacuation downstreams. American engineers who have run what-if scenarios have determined that if Mica ever failed, every Columbia River dam downstream except the concrete monolith that is Grand Coulee would wash out.

From Mica the river runs south through Canada in a thickly forested landscape, on past parks and pulp mills and the biggest smelter of its kind in the world, then south across the American border into the Okanogan pine hills. On it leads past Grand Coulee, out of the trees now and into an irrigated desert of orchards and vineyards backed by brooding desert cliffs. The Columbia has come to that great interior arid basin, the "Inland Empire" of dams and farms.

At Chief Joseph Dam, a bit more than half the distance from the Columbia's source to its mouth, Native American fishermen cast from a concrete causeway at the base of the dam and try to snag the few salmon that still mill in confusion here. Salmon once swam all the way to Columbia Lake, but first Grand Coulee and then this dam were built without fish ladders. That corked the runs from more than a thousand miles of spawning habitat. Dale Clark is a forty-six-year-old Colville Reservation Indian of Lakes ancestry from Canada who had quit his job at a fast-declining lumber mill to get a degree in public administration. While waiting for classes to start one September, he studied the water for salmon, something he has been periodically doing at this spot for twenty years. Wearing wraparound sunglasses to cut the water glare and an army camouflage jacket to ward off the coolness of the morning, he waited for the telltale shadow of confused fish, stumped by a fortress of concrete. Spotting their dark forms in the river below, he judged their true position by subtracting for the illusionary refraction of the water and hurled a treble-hooked line out beyond. Then he reeled across their backs. Migrating salmon swimming upriver don't feed and usually won't take a lure, so Clark has to snag them, play them to exhaustion, and then haul them up a thirty-foot concrete bulkhead with a gaff hook. On a good day he can catch half a dozen, giving many away to tribal elders. How long does he patiently study the water? "Pretty much all day," he said. "It took a few years to get the hang of it, how to snag them. I learned by watching."

Down, down steps the river, in desert country now, the old petroglyph sites mostly buried under water, the river stilled into obedient discipline. Below Priest Rapids Dam the river enjoys a rare free-flowing stretch and its most productive remaining salmon spawning area. The reason for this remnant natural flow, ironically, is the Hanford nuclear reservation. Here, where the plutonium for the world's first nuclear test at Alamogordo was produced, the hulking obsolete reactors that line the riverbank helped dissuade a start of the proposed Ben Franklin Dam because it would have backed up water over their radioactive remains. Hanford is arguably the single most polluted place in the Western world, but it is also so big, and has been kept free of people for so long, that it is one of the most important wildlife and ecological refuges left in eastern Washington.

Past Hanford the Columbia continues south to join with the Snake River and then bends west through a break in the Horse Heaven Hills called Wallula Gap, its southern bank now in Oregon. The country remains dry and sparsely settled along the pools of McNary and John Day dams, although the aridity is in part an illusion: drive to the top of the bluffs lining the river and you will find farms irrigated with free Columbia water pumped from the reservoirs, vegetables rolling across terrain where wild ponies once roamed.

Shortly before John Day Dam the land begins to rise around the Columbia as it enters the eastern Cascade Mountains. The man-made artifacts along the river become curious: seemingly isolated aluminum smelters, a replica of Stonehenge, the lonely mansion at Maryhill on a bluff so off the beaten track that the woman the mansion was named for refused to ever consider living there. The river enters the boundaries of the Columbia River Gorge National Scenic Area, and the land changes in one of the most sudden and dramatic transitions in the United States: from treeless and arid to forested and wet. Rainfall increases from fourteen inches a year at The Dalles to seventy-five inches at Cascade Locks, fifty miles downriver. Cliffs on the Oregon shore spout seventy waterfalls. On the Washington side the land is more sloping. Table Mountain sheared off near Bonneville Dam eight hundred years ago and slid into the river to create the six-mile-long Cascades of the Columbia, the roaring rapids that halted easy navigation just one hundred and fifty miles from the sea. Indian legend holds that it was not a mountain slope that slid to make the Cascades but a rock arch across the Columbia that broke in a war between jealous volcanoes: the Bridge of the Gods. A silver highway bridge built over the spot today has the same name.

The Gorge comes to a climactic end at the sheer cliffs of Cape Horn and the spectacular promontory of Crown Point. The river empties onto a green, rolling landscape of farm and forest and sprawling subdivision, threading past long sand islands of cottonwood and alder. There is a phallic monolith called Rooster Rock by the proper Oregon State Parks Department and Cock Rock by the pioneers. It is this gentle portion of the Columbia, crossing the trough between the Cascades and coast ranges, that passes Portland and the docks of neighboring Vancouver. The stockade of the reconstructed Hudson's Bay headquarters and the Northwest's oldest apple tree are just a mile from where Interstate 5 crosses the river. The Columbia swings north after that, looking for an opening in the coast range, and finally turns west at Longview for a final surge through the hills. The old fishing villages and mill towns on its tide-influenced final miles have names with a pleasant roll: Clatskanie, Skamokawa, Cathlamet, Altoona, Ilwaco. Then the last long bridge at Astoria, the Capes, the Pacific. Beginning and end.

The first explorers to approach this extraordinary place came by sea, and the bar they met was in many ways the river's most fearsome and unwelcoming part. The land flanking the river's mouth appears lopsided. Oregon's Point Adams is flat, the solidest piece of its dune-grass landscape being the abandoned concrete bunkers of Fort Stevens that took a few shells from a Japanese submarine during World War II. On the Washington shore is Cape Disappointment, its crest of fir and spruce trees bristling like a military haircut. Fort Canby was built in its lee, cannon having been stationed at the Columbia's mouth since the Confederate raider *Alabama* prowled into the North Pacific and sank much of the nation's whaling fleet.

Cape Disappointment is made of lava that boiled up on the sea floor, solidified, was eventually lifted above the waves, and then was rasped by wind and water until rounded. Long rollers crash directly onto its cliffs, the angriest storms throwing spray two hundred feet high. Evidence of the ocean's power comes at the Cape's base, which is pierced by a row of sea caves like an arched colonnade. Right below the lighthouse is a narrow slot in the rock marking the entrance of Dead Man's Cove.

The cove is a particularly pretty spot. The swells surge in past the entrance, water humping in the slot, then divide around an obstruction that looks like a bonsai arrangement that has drifted from Japan, a rock topped by small, wind-twisted trees. The waves finally break on a gray crescent of sand beach backed by a wall of spruce forest. Dead Man's Cove is an idyllic spot for a picnic on a sunny day: a sheltered hole in a wider, windier landscape. The name, however, helps explain Cape Disappointment's appropriate name, the melancholy toll of shipping the mouth of the Columbia has destroyed, and the bodies that have washed ashore. "Perhaps there have been more lives lost here, in proportion to the number of those who have entered this river, than in entering almost any harbor in the world," the Reverend Samuel Parker observed in the 1830s.

When the American steamer *General Warren* grounded in 1852, forty-two people were drowned when, trying to gain the river in a January storm after the crew and passengers taunted a cautious pilot, the ship was destroyed by the monstrous swells. One newly married couple were found on the beach with their hands still locked, her new wedding ring still on her finger.

When the *Laurel* grounded off the Cape in 1929, Captain Louis Johnson stayed on the broken stern for fifty-four hours to fend off salvors. After the fore section was shoved eight hundred feet away by the surf and was pounded to bits, he finally raised a white flag for evacuation. A year later the *Admiral Benson* mistook the wreck of the *Laurel*'s stern for a range buoy and went aground nearby. Captain C. C. Graham stayed on board ten days before agreeing to abandon the wreck, watching a continuous bonfire kept aflame on Cape Disappointment as a sign he was not forgotten.

Some were not so ultimately fortunate. When the American motor vessel *Pescawha* struck the north jetty off Cape Disappointment in 1933, her skipper was crushed trying to launch a lifeboat. The body of Captain Victor H. Riley was retrieved in this cove.

Nearby is Waikiki Beach, named for a drowned Hawaiian Kanaka who washed ashore there.

The treacherous nature of the Columbia's mouth is one reason a majority of its length is in American possession. The Hudson's Bay Company supply ships dreaded the bar: two of thirty-five that journeyed there were lost, twenty-six sailors were drowned, and the bark *Cowlitz* had to wait eighty days off the mouth for water calm enough to enter. "The sea at all times breaks furiously," described American ornithologist John Townsend on an early visit, "the surges dashing to the height of the mast head of a ship, and with the most terrific roaring. Vessels have not infrequently had to stand off shore until the crews have suffered extremely for food and water. This circumstance must ever form a barrier to a permanent settlement here. . . ."

American explorer Lieutenant Charles Wilkes came to much the same opinion. The U.S. Navy lost the *Peacock* on the bar in 1841 and the *Shark* in 1846. "The entrance to the Columbia is impractical two-thirds of the year, and the difficulty of leaving is equally great," Wilkes reported. It was essential, he said, that the navy secure seaports on Puget Sound to the north. Britain's frustration with the Columbia as a highway for its fur empire and American insistence at getting access to the Sound was one reason both nations agreed to a border at the Forty-ninth Parallel, three hundred miles north of the Columbia's mouth. Britain saw little value in the Columbia as a port, while Americans were determined to get a border that provided better harbors. There are four major U.S. Navy bases on Puget Sound today and none on the Columbia.

A trail leads up from Dead Man's Cove into the forest and over the neck of the cape to a Coast Guard station tucked onto a shelf behind the blunt rock, shielded from the pounding ocean. The station buildings are painted white and have red gabled roofs, exhibiting the trim military utility produced by government specifications. The place smells of salt water and mud and moist wetland. On the August day that I visit the morning begins with a gray overcast and light drizzle, the fifty-three-degree ocean firmly limiting how close to summer the mouth of the Columbia can get. The sports fishermen on the river remain bundled, wearing the utilitarian and fashionless shroud of wool and Gore-Tex and slicker and boot that is part of the webbed-foot character of the coastal Pacific Northwest. When the sun breaks through it is bright but teasingly heatless, its warmth sucked away by the moist air. The water stays a somber green-gray.

I am here to see the annual Buoy 10 sports fishery. Each summer until the collapsing salmon fishery was closed in 1994, fishing officials brought the charter and pleasure boat fishery off the open ocean and into the river. Like a funnel, the Columbia begins to concentrate a tide of silver arriving to spawn. A line of buoys marks the river channel into the ocean, and the tenth buoy in from the sea marks the westernmost boundary of where this particular fishery is allowed. On average the Columbia carries enough water down here to easily fill fifty thousand bathtubs each second, yet the competing incoming tide is so strong that Buoy 10 can lean landward like a water skier: the ocean breathes 22 billion cubic feet of water in and out of the estuary each cycle, exerting a tidal influence one hundred and fifty miles upriver to Bonneville Dam. Navigational river buoys are typically anchored with six-ton blocks in the United States. The Coast Guard uses nine tons on the Columbia, and attaches two blocks to each buoy below Astoria.

The sportsmen like to crowd the marker to intercept the salmon and so about six hundred vessels are jammed onto a square mile of choppy water. Nobody except myself seems very impressed. "This is a real mellow day," says Ralph Gilbert, a civilian volunteer in the Coast Guard Auxiliary. "We have days with three thousand boats."

It is an odd conglomeration, this trolling navy. It looks like some kind of Dunkirk rehearsal. There are cabin cruisers and ski boats, aluminum skiffs and high-prowed rapids-runners, sailboats, runabouts, picnic rafts on pontoons, and even a camouflaged duck hunter boat. In one skiff, three fat sportsmen hunch over their trolling poles as a six-pack of beer slides rhythmically from the motion of the waves across the boat bottom. They have six inches of freeboard above the water in a place where waves can quickly mound to thirty feet. The Coast Guard has its national lifeboat school at this spot, and the station's nickname for the Columbia's mouth is "Graveyard of the Pacific." Its motto is "You have to go out." Not posted on the wall, but drilled into every crewman, is the motto's postscript: "You don't have to come back." The deaths of Coast Guardsmen stationed here are marked by engraved nameplates, some of them drowned trying to rescue fools.

The boat names speak of hopeful optimism and short memories of disaster. There are the *Easy Times, Summer Fun, All Weekend, Halcyon, Hot Tub, Foreplay,* and *Gusto.* From each juts a number of poles. As they inch over the invisible Buoy 10 line the wearily patient Coast Guard shoos them back. The salmon, tens of thousands of them, are riding the floodtide into the river. As an introduction to fresh water they confront a wriggling school of lures, a flashing temptation of bait as bright as neon. It must seem like some kind of underwater Las Vegas. Periodically a pole bends, a net is readied, and a silver salmon more than two feet long and brighter than an ingot is hoisted aboard and smacked with a club into immobility.

The limit is two fish per person per day, a quota that probably puts the actual investment per landing at several hundred dollars, if obeyed. This makes no economic sense, but little about Columbia River salmon does. They are a living artifact of a paved-over past, and one upriver hatchery spends an estimated three thousand dollars for every adult salmon it gets back to the natal stream. Call it a tax on progress. People care about the fish that much.

I join the Cape Disappointment station commander, Lieutenant Greg Blandford, on board a new forty-four-foot aluminum patrol craft and we head straight out into the ocean to check on commercial fishermen not restricted by Buoy 10. The world opens and flattens as the boat pulls away from the land, the hills on shore losing their height. My perspective is reversed. It is the land that begins to seem the aberration, the edge. I am reminded that we live on a water planet.

Oceans and lakes cover 71 percent of the earth's surface with 326 million cubic miles of water. All but 1 percent of this is in the sea or frozen. Rivers are one of the rarest manifestations of water; the three hundred cubic miles of water they contain represents just one-millionth of the earth's supply. By comparison, there is ten times as much water suspended as vapor in the atmosphere. There are 2 million cubic miles of groundwater, also flowing, but out of sight and mostly out of mind until it reemerges; half the flow of the Mississippi comes from groundwater seeping into the Big Muddy. Taken together, the world's rivers are so feeble it would take them 34,700 years to fill the ocean. We are drawn to rivers not just by their power and beauty, but by their relative rarity. The continents are drier than we like to think.

As I look down into the speckle of dust motes and plankton caught by light in the opaque Pacific, it seems to make sense that this dark liquid envelope was once our ancestral home, and probably a far more sheltering one than the hard and thin land our distant amphibian ancestors crawled onto, suddenly naked to the sun and stars.

Our affinity for water is a part of our biology. We need to drink at least a quart of water a day because the chemistry of our bodies is based on water. It is a good solvent. A water molecule is shaped a bit like the head of Mickey Mouse, with two of the smallest and simplest atoms in nature, hydrogen, attached like ears to a larger atom of oxygen. The result is a simple molecule small enough to squeeze between bigger ones, fracturing their bonds with each other. Given time and energy, water can dissolve rock. While a water molecule as a whole is electrically neutral, there is a slight negative charge at the oxygen end balanced by a slight positive charge at the two hydrogen ears. This allows water to bond easily with other elements and compounds, forming solutions. If you want a medium that both breaks down matter and then transports the debris, water is ideal. It carries food energy to our cells and removes waste.

Accordingly, two-thirds of our weight is water and we carry a rough replica of the sea inside us. We are walking pink and brown canteens, liable with a false step to breach our skin and lose our ocean. We drink a ton of water a year. In fact, there is almost as much water stored in plants and animals as flows in the planet's rivers: a single Douglas fir tree can hold up to five thousand gallons of water, a human several pails full.

Water has other interesting properties.

It is ubiquitous. Hydrogen is the most abundant element in the universe. Some of the solar system's moons have volcanoes of erupting water that freeze like our own basalt, and the lava that boils out of the earth contains about 5 percent water. Volcanoes are the source of the vapor that eventually condensed in the atmosphere and rained out into the oceans.

If rock can produce water, water carries rock. Rivers are mineral water. The ocean has 47 trillion tons of suspended minerals, and just the world's sixteen largest rivers pour in fifty-six additional tons every second. Only a small part of a river's erosive power comes from chemical dissolution of rock; most comes from the abrasion of transported sediment like liquid sandpaper. Precipitation and rivers wear down North America at an average rate of about a foot every ten thousand years. The Colorado carried enough silt before it was dammed to make a mound one hundred feet square and as high as a twenty-story building every day. The Missouri was so dirty that its steamboat boilers had to be cleaned of mud each evening. Rock in the Columbia Basin is relatively hard and its grinding is slower: Columbia River water has less than half the salts and minerals of the Mississippi and an eighth of the Colorado. Yet just since 1868, the river is estimated to have carried 400 million to 500 million cubic meters of sediment into its estuary. Today such erosion is trapped behind dams, slowly silting over former salmon spawning beds.

Rivers represent dissipated energy. Every day the sun evaporates as much water as is contained in all the world's rivers. Most of this rains back into the sea, but some is lifted and blows over the continents as rain and snow. The vast majority of this potential energy is wasted. Rivers can lose up to 97 percent of it from friction with their beds. Upstream paddlers learn to hug the banks where friction slows the current. The current a few millimeters off the bottom of a river is slower than the flow above, giving rock-dwelling insects and mollusks a relatively sheltered place from the howling hurricane of current overhead. Rivers also spend energy by carrying sediment, like a freight train consuming diesel fuel. When Hoover Dam's reservoir captured Colorado River sediment and the water pouring out of the powerhouse suddenly became relatively clean, it carried so much extra energy downstream that it rapidly sawed down through rock and sediment, leaving irrigation intakes below the dam high and dry.

One way rivers dissipate energy is by meandering across the land, building and dismantling curves in a complex, continuing process. If a river is artificially straightened, it can bring unexpected results. In 1817 the Germans decided to improve the Rhine and keep it from flooding by straightening and shortening its course to hurry flood waters downstream. The bed between Basel and Mannheim was shortened by a third. The sudden excess energy, however, quickly dug the Rhine's channel twenty feet deeper, dropped the water table, killed the roots of orchards, and caused wells to go dry. Again and again, what seems like a simple river engineering problem has turned out not simple at all.

By the late nineteenth century, the federal government decided to try to harness similar energies to fix the mouth of the Columbia. As the Coast Guard boat swings back toward shore I study the first evidence of the engineered river: the long black fingers of the Columbia jetties. When started in the late 1800s, these rock break- waters were one of the largest and most difficult U.S. government building projects yet attempted.

Their purpose was simple enough. It was not just that the river entrance was shallow and rough; it was also unpredictable. The vast river and tides shifted sand around like a fleet of bull- dozers, assuring shipwrecks would lend their vessel's names to such features as Desdemona Shoals and Peacock Spit. (The *Desde- mona* was wrecked when Captain Francis Williams bet the price of a new Sunday suit he could get her inside the bar by New Year's Day, 1857, and didn't wait for a river pilot.) For pilots and captains approaching the Columbia, it was not just a question of keeping to the channel, but finding where it was.

As a solution the Army Corps of Engineers proposed jetties. They would form twin walls jutting out into the ocean to stop the casual slop of sand north and south across the river entrance. Ad- ditionally, by squeezing the river's current at its mouth into a nar- rower passage, they would speed its flow. As a river collides with the ocean it tends to halt and dump its load of sediment, creating a hazardous bar. The fallout is a result of both the slower speed of the water and the tendency of the particles and salt in the sea to combine in a process known as flocculation, gaining weight and settling to the bottom. Accordingly, any restriction that sped the Columbia's punch into deeper water and concentrated the fresh- ness of its waters would force the river to do the work of main- taining its own channel: properly constricted and directed, the Columbia was expected to clean itself.

Actually building the jetties became a formidable challenge. The initial $100,000 appropriated for the South Jetty in 1885 was eaten up by the first thousand feet across a tidewater bay. Its nec- essary width and depth were continually upgraded as winter storms washed or sucked under much of a summer's work. Engineers would ultimately determine that the jetty had to be seven miles long and required 8.2 million tons of stone. The cost eventually exceeded $10 million, a breathtaking sum at the time.

To get rocks of a size large enough to resist battering by the waves, they had to be quarried upstream and barged down. It is illustrative of the different attitudes of the time that the Corps seriously considered blowing up eight-hundred-and-forty-eight-foot-high Beacon Rock, a spectacularly sheer monolith in the Columbia River Gorge a few miles below Bonneville Dam. Dynamite holes were drilled in the famous landmark and only the intervention of private investor Henry Biddle saved it from destruction. He bought the rock and then donated it to Washington State for a park.

Other cliffs and quarries were dynamited, however. Down at the Columbia's mouth a new dock was built at the head of the jetty to unload the automobile-sized boulders by crane onto one of sixty-five waiting railroad dump cars. A railroad trestle was built atop the new jetty, extending on piers to jut over the water beyond the latest rock work. Five locomotives pulled the rock to where it could be dumped. The trestle pilings had to be pounded into deeper and deeper water as the jetty proceeded.

The Columbia and the ocean did not submit easily. "The difficulties that have beset the work accomplished during the past three years cannot be overstated," an officer of the Army Corps of Engineers complained in 1906. "Gale after gale has driven mountainous seas against the outer two miles of jetty and trestle, tumbling down the crest of a finished but too narrow section and carrying out at different times miles of the pile trestle over which the rock is conveyed. No language can adequately describe the fierceness of this onslaught. The place must be seen to be understood and appreciated. It is perhaps no exaggeration to say that there is no work in progress in the United States today at all comparable to this one in the difficulties, uncertainties, and dangers that arise at every stage of its construction."

To cope with such forces, the jetty crest was widened from a planned ten feet to forty. When that proved inadequate, it was broadened to seventy feet in places to deal with the waves, and the height from the sea bottom to the crest grew taller than a five-story building. The base broadened to a width greater than a football field to gain stability. Most of the wooden trestle the tracks ran on was washed out in the winter of 1904 and had to be replaced. In 1906 another mile of track was destroyed in a storm. Not until 1936 when a massive concrete terminal was poured thirty-nine hundred feet from the jetty's seaward end did it finally stop disintegrating. Today the tracks have disappeared but the rock rampart remains as a ruled black line against the foggy softness of the landscape. Breakers frost them white, then pull back. The jetties' rigid defiance is our welcome to the Columbia, announcing that here you are entering something tamed.

The goal to make the river self-cleaning was only briefly successful, however. For a decade or so it seemed to work. Then the scouring action faltered as sand began to accumulate. The old pattern was reestablishing itself.

As we knife back in toward the dissipating armada of fishing boats at Buoy 10, we pass the red-painted dredge kept on station here every summer by the Corps. Its diesel exhaust smudges the air with a puff of black as it sucks at the Columbia, vacuuming the bottom. Periodically it dumps its spoils behind the South Jetty. Appropriately, the Corps' acting chief of navigation in charge of out-bulldozing the Columbia when I inquired was named Dave Beach. "What we do is create a hole in that pile of sand," he said. It is a modest goal, and an endless one. The Corps spends about $5 million a year doing this, or roughly a dollar for every cubic yard of sand laboriously moved elsewhere. The river has proven stubborn; the Corps remains determined.

"We haven't figured nature out yet," acknowledged Beach.

5

The Sculpted River

Cascades of the Columbia, later drowned by Bonneville Dam.
(*Washington State Historical Museum*)

A river appeals to the senses because of its beauty, its smell, its sound, and its ability to slake our thirst, but it captures our imagination because it moves. In a seemingly static landscape of rock and range and tree, a river travels. Its riffles and rapids lead the mind's eye past sunburnt hills glowing pink with prairie grass, into canyons dark under a roof of towering fir, to falls lost at their bottom in a pillow of spray, and across gravel bars of bright stones lacquered by current. When we say a river is alive, we mean it is an embodiment of energy: an animated thing flowing toward us and past us, beckoning us to seek with it, to coast with its current or struggle to its source.

This powerful sense of direction tends to influence any narrative about a river. One way to tell the story of the Columbia is to let its current sweep the tale along with the direction of an aimed arrow, from source to mouth, beginning to end. This book takes the reader up and down the Columbia River, but not in such a lineal fashion.

One reason is that most of the present-day Columbia doesn't seem to move. It betrays our sense of what a river is supposed to be like. The river still flows through its fourteen dams and their fourteen pools, but about as sluggishly as an anaconda that has swallowed fourteen hamsters. The photographs of dams in government brochures usually show the structures with spillways wide open, the river plunging down their face in a spectacular falls. Such sights are a rarity. Any spillage over dams is economically wasteful because it does not turn a turbine. For three-quarters of the Columbia's length, only its regulated and metered boil-up from the penstocks of a powerhouse gives the casual observer much hint of energy or thrust. Still big and windswept in a landscape of epic proportions, the Columbia has nonetheless lost the Pied Piper lure of a free-flowing river. It is not dead, but it is confined, as immobile as a beetle thrown on its back. Having been hobbled and harnessed, the Columbia forces us to study megawatts and acre feet to understand its power.

A second problem with a lineal ascent or descent of the Columbia is that it misleads us as to the true nature of the river, and the true nature of its problems. We are naturally drawn to any river's narrow ribbon of silver winding through a landscape, that concentrated band of water and energy and noise and reflected light. But a river is much more than, well, a river. It is the product of a huge basin. The Columbia is the distillation of 166 million acres of snow and rain and eroded dirt, of nutrients swimming in from the sea and carried down as detritus from the headwaters, of ten thousand decisions on irrigation diversion, pesticide application, fertilizing, pumping, and deciding whether to allow cattle to graze, wade, and defecate in a thousand creeks. To manage a river as a narrow corridor is to fundamentally misunderstand it.

The Columbia is, for example, the product of its tributaries. Naturalist John Muir compared the Columbia to "a rugged, broad-topped picturesque old oak about six hundred miles long and nearly two thousand miles wide measured across the spread of its upper boughs, the main limbs gnarled and swollen with lakes and lake-like expansions, while innumerable smaller lakes shine like fruit among the smaller branches." It is a web of water. The Snake River is only two hundred miles shorter than the entire Columbia and falls nearly four times as much, or ninety-five hundred feet, and so is big and powerful enough in its own right—the nation's tenth largest river—that the early explorers called it the South Fork. To think of the Columbia without thinking of the Snake leaves one captive to arbitrary geographic naming; the Great River of the West is better understood as splitting at Pasco into two halves in which the policies toward one inevitably affect the other.

Nor can we ignore other tributaries: the Kicking Horse, the Illiciliwaet, the Kootenay, the Clark Fork, the Flathead, the Pend Oreille, the Spokane, the Okanogan, the Wenatchee, the Yakima, the Walla Walla, the Umatilla, the John Day, the Deschutes, the Willamette, and the Cowlitz are some that pour their waters into the Columbia proper; Henry's Fork, the Bruneau, the Owyhee, the Malheur, the Grande Ronde, the Salmon, the Clearwater, and the Palouse are a partial roll of those joining the Snake. The fate of tributary rivers dictates in large part the water volume, temperature, sediment, pollution, and fish of the Columbia. So much irrigation water is sucked out of the Umatilla and Yakima rivers each summer that they sometimes run dry.

The sum of all tributary influences is so complex as to almost defy quantification. The head of the Yakima River Canyon is about seventy-five miles from the Columbia itself. This desert canyon, pocketed with pine, is a lovely favorite for fly fishermen and recreationists, but its gravel bars are not nearly as productive of fish as one might expect. Migrating salmon have to squeeze past a hurdle of irrigation dams on the lower Yakima, but this does not fully explain its problem. Understanding comes at the canyon's head, where Wilson Creek returns irrigation water from central Washington's Kittitas Valley as a greasy gout of mud and pesticides and fertilizers, helping explain why what should be one of the prime salmon spawning rivers in the Pacific Northwest sadly is not. The creek looks like an open sewer. Similarly, a pump at an Idaho aquifer, an irrigation circle in eastern Washington, a pulp mill in British Columbia, and a dairy herd in Oregon's Willamette Valley all influence what the Columbia becomes.

Thinking of rivers in terms of their entire basin is a very new idea. Early humans were puzzled by the origin of rivers but assumed their lineal geometry dictated a pinpointable source. In Egypt the Nile runs for its last eighteen hundred miles without tributary or rainfall, seemingly rising and falling to the whim of the gods. Where did the water come from? The Greeks were equally puzzled by the unceasing flow of their rivers. Precipitation seemed inadequate to account for it. Plato proposed that rivers were maintained by underground sources. He postulated that the oceans were filtered of their salt in subterranean systems that included the River Styx, and that these in turn fed underground springs.

Marcus Vitruvius Pollo, a Roman engineer who invented the vertical waterwheel to replace the Greek horizontal one, correctly proposed that groundwater originates as rain or snow that filters through the soil. His view never gained wide currency, however. Well into the seventeenth century, scientists thought that seawater was somehow filtered underground, or perhaps turned to steam by the earth's heat, and thus distilled for rivers. Salt caverns could be explained as the remains of this purification. Finally, in 1674, French scientist Claude Perrault measured precipitation in the upper Seine basin and found it equaled six times the upper river's flow, more than enough to account for the Seine's unceasing vigor. French scientist Edme Mariotte resurrected Vitruvius's idea that rain fed groundwater and springs, explaining why rivers and streams ran even during long periods of drought.

The origin of the Columbia is the sea. If you want to understand the river, understand that the clouds scudding overhead are as important to its life as the actual cold water you dip with your hand. Perturbations in global climate may ultimately prove as important to the Columbia as a dam. The 1980s campaign to double the basin's salmon runs foundered in part because of persistent drought; it, in turn, was probably tied to warming of the distant equatorial Pacific in a phenomenon known as El Niño, yet to be adequately explained by science.

The age of the Columbia River is not known, but the landscape through which it flows and which directs its passage is relatively young. The Colorado has cut Grand Canyon rock that dates back nearly two billion years. Some of the Columbia's volcanic landscape can be measured in a few centuries or millennia, and the great floods that modified its landscape ended just twelve thousand and eight hundred years ago. The oldest rocks in the Columbia River Gorge date back just 50 million years, and far younger volcanic craters, some still barren and others only slowly being recolonized by trees, dot the river basin. Twenty-two dormant volcanoes and two hundred and twenty-five basalt vents have been counted around the gorge. Lava beds pocketed with craters, fissures, and caves pock the forest north of the river.

Not only is the Columbia in a young part of the world; it occupies a stage of geologic drama so extreme that for fifty years it defied belief. Here were mountains such as Oregon's Mazama that blew up like hydrogen bombs, sending hot gases rolling across the landscape for hundreds of miles and leaving behind Crater Lake. Here were eruptions of molten rock that rolled up to four hundred miles across the landscape, pooling like hot pudding into vast basins that eventually covered an area almost as big as New England and New York State combined. Here were water floods so vast they contained ten times the flow of all today's rivers taken together, or the equivalent of sixty Amazon Rivers roaring across the landscape at once. On the Snake River plain were shield volcanoes so numerous they overlapped each other like a pile of coins, and along the Columbia rock slides so big that they briefly dammed the river. This is geologic history as grand opera, with smoke, cymbals, and kettle drums. No—this is geologic history as MTV, all quick cuts and dizzying flicker. Compared to the Columbia, much of the rest of the continent is a stately nineteenth-century novel. When the early Appalachians were 600 million years old, the Pacific Ocean still covered the Columbia's future course.

Coming to grips with the fluidity and violence of this geological landscape was not easy, even for scientists. Two twentieth-century geological theories that are central to the Columbia's story took a half century to be fully accepted by the profession. The first was the idea of continental drift, proposed by the German Alfred Wegener in 1912. He theorized that the continents are moving, and that the collision of continental and oceanic plates could explain much of the world's topography. But while Benjamin Franklin had speculated as early as 1792 that parts of the surface were floating on a liquid interior, Wegener proposed that the continents somehow plowed across solid basalt. This was too much for most geologists to accept. Ridiculed for years, the German explorer died of exposure on Greenland's Ice Cap in 1930 long before his theory was fully accepted.

Continental drift explained too much, however, particularly the jigsaw puzzle fit between Africa and South America. Oceanographers found a mid-Atlantic ridge like a seam between the two hemispheres, and Wegener's idea was slowly modified to include a mantle that was solid but plastic and mobile enough to account for the motion of continents. In the 1960s it was refined to the theory of plate tectonics. Two hundred million years ago, most of the Columbia Basin was underwater. The collision of western North America with Pacific Ocean plates shoved up the land that the Columbia would subsequently traverse.

A second heretical idea was proposed in 1923 by J. Harlen Bretz, a Seattle high school biology teacher turned amateur geologist during the summer. Bretz became so enamored of earth science that he returned to the University of Chicago to earn a doctorate in geology and eventually become a professor there. Subsequent summer exploration of Columbia Plateau scablands made him both famous and controversial. In the previous century geologists and much of the general public had come to embrace one revolutionary proposal, that the earth was not created a biblical six thousand years before (the vice-chancellor of Cambridge University had more precisely determined the moment to be 9:00 A.M. on October 26, 4004 B.C.) but was instead staggeringly, unimaginably old, with 4.6 billion years the current estimate. With this realization came the theory that much of the planet's land was shaped slowly and uniformly by erosion and mountain building: time enough for the Grand Canyon to be carved, Mount Everest raised, and all the diversity of life produced by the patient tinkering of evolution. "Gradualism" replaced Genesis and Noah's Flood, and any hint that sudden catastrophe had also shaped our world smacked of biblical literalism. Then came Bretz, hiking out of the hot coulees with his notebook full of curious observations. He proposed that much of the Columbia Plateau and the river's downstream drainage had been carved and formed in days or weeks by titanic Ice Age floods greater than any the world has since seen.

Geologists scoffed. None had seen the ravaged ground Bretz explored, and Bretz himself could not explain where such volumes of water came from. As an alternative, many scientists proposed gouging of the plateau by glaciers. Then, at the 1940 meeting of the American Association for the Advancement of Science, Joseph Thomas Pardee announced he had found the water Bretz needed. A lake with half the volume of Lake Michigan had formed over western Montana when a glacier had dammed Ice Age rivers. The collapse of the glacier, Pardee quietly noted, could have provided the flood to accomplish the destruction Bretz had found. In 1952, Bretz led a scientific expedition with several sympathetic geologists across the scablands, and they concluded that not only was there abundant geologic evidence for a single great flood, but for more than forty, possibly as many as one hundred. Acceptance still came slowly. One basic geology textbook was not revised to include mention of the Bretz or Spokane floods until 1971, and not until 1979—when he was ninety-six years old—did Bretz finally receive the nation's highest geological award, the Penrose Medal of the Geologic Society of America. In this case, his profession progressed considerably more slowly than a Spokane flood.

Keep in mind, then, that the geologic story of the Columbia is new, recently evolved, and will no doubt continue to be refined. Both plate tectonics and Bretz floods, however, help to explain the geographic drama seen in the Columbia Basin, and thus its subsequent human history.

For example, the most obvious peculiarity about the Columbia is its contorted course. The river is beset with a basic topographical dilemma. It must reach the sea, but plate tectonics pushed up mountain ranges that run primarily north and south, forming a series of walls in its path. The Columbia threads its way up and down until it finds weak points in these ranges to pierce. This serpentine persistence makes the Columbia influence a huge area. It also dashed hopes that the Great River of the West would be a straightforward highway of commerce.

About 200 million years ago, when the great age of the dinosaurs was just getting under way, the earth's land was joined into a single supercontinent geologists have named Pangea. South America and Africa were welded together along the lines still clearly visible today, and North America and Europe were tilted and linked. The western shore of North America was roughly where the Idaho border with Washington and Oregon is today, though the future site of Spokane in Washington was dry and the shore cut back to the east to leave southwestern Idaho under water. Farther north in British Columbia, the coastline ran slightly west of today's continental divide. Washington's Steptoe Butte near Colfax, called Eomoshtoss by the natives, is a remnant of this ancient shoreline. One can drive to its top, look out across rolling wheat fields, and imagine the swells of the ancient ocean.

If we consider the Columbia the sum of a mountain basin and not just a channel of water, its story begins when Pangea began breaking apart. The giant landmass first fractured into two supercontinents geologists call Gondwanaland and Laurasia and then fragmented into roughly the present continents. The Atlantic Ocean began to grow at the stately rate of two to three inches per year that it continues to broaden by today. At the same time the western shore of North America rode up and over the Pacific plate. The thick mountain belt of western North America seems a reasonable result of this collision when we understand that the continent has overridden fifteen hundred miles of the Pacific Ocean floor since Pangea broke up.

Not all of the melted oceanic plate broke clear to the surface. Sometimes the magma crystallized into granite without erupting, creating huge "batholiths" that make up the mass of much of Idaho and western Montana. Other mountains formed when the top of the sea floor diving under the continental edge was scraped off in the collision and mounded at the coastal fringe. This formed part of today's Wallowa and Blue mountains in eastern Washington and Oregon, plus the Klamath Mountains in southwestern Oregon.

In Canada ancient sea floor was being heaved up to make more sedimentary mountains, shoving Cambrian sea fossils and reefs half a billion years old some eight thousand feet into the air. Meanwhile, large offshore islands similar in size to the main islands of Japan docked with northeast Washington and southeast British Columbia, forming the Okanogan Highlands and the Columbia Mountains the river winds around. At least three more of these additions occurred, including one 50 million years ago to form the base of today's North Cascade Mountains and British Columbia's Coast Range. University of British Columbia geologist Bill Matthews jokes that a proper name for our continent might be "the United Plates of America."

Behind the docking of the Okanogan microcontinent developed the Rocky Mountain Trench, believed to be the product of mountain fractures and glacial gouging. This is the longest valley of its kind in the world. It runs from Montana to the Yukon-Alaska border, a distance of twenty-one hundred miles, and is the birthplace of the Columbia, Fraser, and Yukon rivers.

As the new island microcontinents welded to North America's western shore, the ocean trench where sea floor was shoved under the continental plate jumped westward: first to the site of today's Okanogan Valley, and then to a point off the present-day coast. As the ocean bottom descended under the continent it melted, some of the magma floated upward, and volcanoes erupted to form the Cascade Mountains. This continued until about 25 million years ago, when the volcanoes mysteriously snuffed out.

Even at this relatively late date, much of eastern Washington and Oregon—and almost all the western half of those states—remained under water. A vast bay occupied what is much of the Columbia Basin today. As the Cascades quieted, volcanic activity shifted eastward two hundred miles to the Idaho border region again. Huge cracks split the crust and magma poured out in volumes possibly matched only by India's Deccan Plain. The magma filled this bay with what is today called Columbia River basalt, creating the Columbia River Plateau.

The new lava flows ultimately covered one hundred thousand square miles to an average depth of nearly a mile. This outpouring consisted of flows spaced over 12 million years and separated by centuries or even millennia. The climate of the interior Northwest was much wetter then, giving sufficient time for lakes and rivers to form on the cooled and hardened basalt surface. Sometimes plants recolonized and animals browsed before the next magma flood came. This deceptive pause must have made the next eruption all the more awesome and catastrophic. The molten basalt had the plasticity of molasses and ran across the landscape at speeds that are currently in dispute: initial estimates pegged them as fast as thirty to fifty miles per hour while more recent studies have suggested a pace ranging from a walk to a slow crawl. In any event the advancing wave would carry a skin of cooling basalt like elephant hide. Some of this would slide forward and fall in front of the flood, and contemporary observation has suggested that unless the flow is at least fifty feet high, this "clinker dam" would eventually build to the point where it would stop the flow. The typical Columbia basalt flood, however, was one hundred feet high and some exceeded two hundred feet. One eruption, the Roza Basalt Member, covered twenty thousand square miles in an area that extends from the vicinity of Grand Coulee Dam to Pendleton, Oregon, a distance of one hundred and fifty miles. The molten basalt entombed everything in its path. Near Park Lake, where Grand Coulee Dam enthusiasts held their 1931 rally, a rhinoceros—probably already dead and lying in the mud of a pond—was swallowed by the red-hot tide. The rhino left a cast of its body, later discovered by young boys playing in a cave.

Near Vantage, not far from where Interstate 90 crosses the Columbia River, the flows entombed a swampy hardwood forest of elm, maple, gingko, Douglas fir, walnut, and spruce. The trees, deprived of oxygen, did not rot quickly, giving time for silicon to invade their cells and replicate their structure. The result was petrified wood. Glaciers later scraped away enough rock to expose this time capsule, and in the 1930s the Civilian Conservation Corps dug pits to expose various trunks and built a winding trail. There are iron bars over the pits so souvenir-hunting humans won't peck apart in a few years what nature preserved for a million generations.

The bemusing thing about the site is not just the preservation of ancient trees but the topography of Gingko Petrified Forest itself. What was once a flat swamp is now desert hills. A plateau has risen like bread over the swamp and then been eroded into ridges rounded like melons. This is what time can do, and relatively brief geologic time at that. Towering Mount Rainier, nearly three miles high, may be less than a million years old: a blink, by geologic standards.

These basalt flows pushed the river west toward the eastern Cascade foothills. There it was confined, between new rock and a high place. The Columbia chewed down through the basalt even as new flows added to the plateau's height. Between Wenatchee and Chelan the river seems almost hurled against the foothill bluffs, pinned there by a wall of lava that in places still seems to bear down on the Columbia.

About 12 million years ago the great basalt flows ceased and volcanic action once more shifted back to the Cascades. The Columbia did not so much carve a path through these rising mountains as maintain one. It had flowed south along the mountains until it found their lowest point and turned west, and as the Cascades rose, the river cut to maintain its own level. This process was uneven, and at today's Wallula Gap southwest of the Tri-Cities the river ponded behind a barrier of basalt and formed a huge lake. Sediment fell out and when the river finally broke through at Wallula and the lake emptied, centuries of sediment from the dry lakebed blew back over eastern Washington, the loess creating rolling hills hundreds of feet deep in rich soil. Without the Columbia's net of rivers to carry down glacial flour, pond it, settle it, and finally drain away to allow the wind to redeposit it, the rich Palouse country might be stony basalt.

North America continued its westward march. The Oregon coast range, Willapa Hills and Olympic Mountains began to rise above the sea as scrapings from the Pacific plate. The Willamette Valley, which began its existence as a vast saltwater bay, slowly began to fill with eroded sediment and lava flows from surrounding mountains. The new coast range, for reasons not entirely clear, migrated north about fifty miles. That pushed the Columbia River's estuary with it, producing the northward bend of the river past Portland and Vancouver that is still seen today.

The Snake River had an equally troubled history. Rising in the Rockies, it initially may have flowed out of southern Idaho and across southeastern Oregon to empty into the huge interior bay west of the Cascades. The uplift of the Blue Mountains, however, barred this straightforward path. The Snake bent north to eventually link with the Columbia. As the land continued to rise, the river continued to cut. The Snake had chosen a difficult course through the new Seven Devils Mountains, a path that forced it to saw a canyon up to a mile and a half deep. "A lesser river might have given up," noted Bates McKee in his geology text *Cascadia*, "but the Snake had no place to go. It had to cut the deepest canyon in North America, Hells Canyon, and not through sedimentary strata like those found in the Grand Canyon but through hard, massive greenstone."

Even while the lower Snake underwent this heroic excavation, the upper Snake was besieged by volcanoes breaking out like acne on the Snake River plain. As volcanoes rose the Snake twisted between them, skirting first this fresh lava flow, then that, so that one wall of its canyon is often distinct in geology from the rock on the other side, each having come from a different vent. The resulting mass of basalt from all this volcanism is so fractured that for two hundred and sixty-eight miles, from Henry's Fork down to lower Salmon Falls, the north bank of the Snake receives no tributaries. The rivers that pour down from the snowy mountains of central Idaho, such as the Big Lost River, disappear into cracks in the earth to form one of the nation's greatest aquifers, the water continuing to migrate until it reappears as springs on the canyon wall below Milner Dam. The springs pump 200 billion cubic feet of water a year into the river.

By the arrival of the Ice Ages of the last few million years, then, the general course for the great rivers of the Columbia Basin has been set. The most dramatic scene, the real show-stopper of this geologic extravaganza, was about to begin. Enter the glaciers.

What a stark and magnificently hostile landscape the great ice sheets must have produced! The Selkirks and Purcells and Monashees and Cariboos were buried by ice, their summits poking into the air like treading swimmers. At the glacial edge the ice wall ground and growled against the tundra-covered basalt of the Great Columbia Plain. Each rhythmic glaciation tended to obliterate the effects of the one before, but when the ice came down from Canada the last time, beginning about eighteen thousand years ago, it set the stage for the greatest known flood in geologic history.

The edge of the ice sheet was twenty-five hundred feet high when it bulldozed down the Okanogan Valley and crossed the canyon of the Columbia River at the site of Grand Coulee Dam. When it struck the Columbia Plateau on the other side, the glacier peeled off house-size chunks of basalt and carried them south toward Waterville, dropping the boulders into future wheat fields. There they sit squat and immovable to this day, forcing tractors to detour around monoliths the farmers call "haystacks."

The Columbia was unable to quickly push past this glacial dam. It backed up to form Glacial Lake Columbia and then spilled southward to begin carving the Grand Coulee. Another lobe of the Wisconsin glaciation formed an ice dam in the middle of Idaho's panhandle, backing water up over much of western Montana. Lake Missoula covered the site of the future city of Missoula with water a thousand feet deep. About sixteen thousand years ago, the ice dam failed when the water floated the barrier off its rock base. Five hundred cubic miles of water roared toward eastern Washington in a wall a thousand feet high, moving as fast as fifty-eight miles per hour. The flood contained ten times the volume of all the rivers in the world, and pushed before it a shock wave of air and sound that must have broken over the Columbia Plateau like a thunderclap. Icebergs carrying boulders rode the flood like bobbing container ships, some of them not stopping until they reached western Oregon, four hundred miles away. The Columbia Basin's most spectacular sculpting had begun.

The water scoured the land like a sandblaster across old paint. When the velocity of a stream doubles, its ability to move material increases up to sixty-four times. Here was a flood with speeds as much as ten times an ordinary river, scraping new coulees with a slurry of rock, sand, and ice. In Grand Coulee it ripped apart basalt at the lava fractures and began eating backwards, the lip of Dry Falls marching back up the canyon. It created today's Palouse River canyon and falls. It gouged out the Marmes Rock Shelter, where the earliest evidence of humans in the basin would later be found shortly before the site was drowned by Ice Harbor Dam. The flood fanned over the Columbia Plateau in a branching pattern that produced the scablands of the basin, ponded to a depth of twelve hundred feet at Wallula Gap, and then broke through again to crash toward and through the Columbia Gorge. At the future site of Bonneville Dam the flood ran more than eight hundred feet high. Its energy was so great that near John Day River it gouged out a pothole one hundred and sixty-four feet deep, or a few feet below sea level—the home, Native Americans later believed, of a monster called the Swallower who kept an armored sturgeon as a pet. The water's fury pounded the gorge to create Celilo Falls, sheered off abrupt cliffs to create Oregon's series of lovely waterfalls, and foamed onward to flood much of the Willamette Valley. As valley water receded, icebergs settled and left behind rounded granite boulders that would puzzle Oregon pioneers sixteen millennia later.

As unbelievably violent as this flood was, it did not just happen once. The glacier pushed a new ice lobe into Idaho's panhandle, and a new Lake Missoula quickly formed. Then the dam broke again. And again. And again. Each time another five hundred cubic miles of water came roaring down, in cycles estimated to have averaged fifty-five years. Geologists John Elliot Allen and

Sam C. Sargent have calculated that the combined energy of these forty to one hundred floods may have been double that of the asteroid impact of 65 million years ago suspected of wiping out the dinosaurs.

For more than three thousand years this cyclic flooding went on. Finally, 12,800 years ago, the great ice sheet began to retreat for the last time. First Lake Missoula failed to reform. Then Glacial Lake Columbia broke through the Okanogan ice lobe and the Columbia returned to its present-day channel, cutting back down through hundreds of feet of glacial till to its present bed. Dry Falls was silenced. Grand Coulee went dry. The weather warmed and got drier. Humans appeared about two thousand years after the last flood and crept into the Marmes Rock Shelter. As the glaciers receded the Columbia slowly cleared itself of glacial silt, washing its gravel beds clean and producing ideal habitat for spawning salmon. By four thousand years ago the runs were probably reaching the huge numbers that awed the explorers and pioneers.

What happened when this water and debris reached the sea? It was used to build the estuary and beaches and spits on either side of the river mouth. Gravel from Oregon's Blue Mountains has been found in sediments near Astoria. The Columbia's power also formed an underwater canyon that descends from the six-hundred-foot depth of the continental shelf to the abyssal plain two miles below. It is here that the remnants of mountains in Canada, Montana, Wyoming, and Idaho finally come.

A cubic foot of water with sediment weighs more than a cubic foot of clear water; so it tends to sink along an underwater slope, causing what oceanographers call a turbidity current. The pattern has been for Columbia River sediment to slowly migrate down the Pacific shelf, accumulate, and then be jarred loose by an earthquake every five or six centuries. As it slides into the abyss the turbidity current can reach speeds of sixty miles per hour. One underwater avalanche stretched four hundred miles across the ocean bottom, transporting 600 million cubic yards of sediment. These flows have filled the trench off the Pacific Northwest coast where the oceanic plate dives under the continent.

Is the story finished there? No. Eventually this dirt and sand will form sedimentary rock such as shale and be transported by the expanding sea floor back toward the land. There it will either be scraped off to form new coastal mountains or sucked under the floating continent to melt, mix, and perhaps rise again through new volcanoes. The cycle of the Columbia's water is matched by the cycle of its land, ever-eroding, ever-rebuilding, on a scale and time span that mocks everything we have done to the river.

CHAPTER

6

Comcomly's Head

A view of Fort Vancouver on the Columbia at present-day Vancouver, Washington, the headquarters of the Hudson's Bay Company in the Pacific Northwest. *(University of Washington Library)*

In 1835 a young British physician named Meredith Gairdner, frustrated by his confinement as a Hudson's Bay Company clerk on the Columbia and weakening from tuberculosis, decided to become a grave robber.

Gairdner, sent to Fort Vancouver to help combat Indian epidemics, had found it impossible to stem the catastrophic course of disease and suffered the deterioration of his own lungs in the rain. He was equally frustrated that his dream of using time in the West to make new discoveries in the natural sciences had been thwarted by the demands of the trading post. After two years of unhappiness and bad health, the physician was leaving for Hawaii in hopes a warmer climate would save his life. Before he went, however, he was determined to accomplish something of lasting importance. Gairdner wanted to send to England the skull of the greatest chief on the lower Columbia, a Chinook named

Comcomly, who had died in a measles epidemic at the age of sixty-six five years before.

The nineteenth century saw intense interest in craniometry, the measurement of heads, as a possible explanation for the apparent differences between the races and social classes. Many thinkers believed that Indians and Africans were separate, inferior species, and that a smaller brain cavity or more apelike shape of the skull could establish this prejudice mathematically. Harvard paleontologist Stephen Jay Gould has since shown that these researchers misinterpreted their own data to get the result they expected. But to Europeans fascinated, mystified, and repelled by the cultural differences encountered in their surge across the planet, a biological explanation had a commonsense appeal. Skulls might be able to justify slavery or colonialism or the displacement of the Native American if it could establish the natural superiority of one race over another. If so, no specimens were likely to prove more fascinating than those of the Chinook and Clatsop Indians on the lower Columbia.

These tribes had the custom of compressing their babies' foreheads for about a year after birth, producing a sloping "flathead" forehead. (The Flathead tribe of western Montana, incidentally, did not practice this, just as the Nez Perce, meaning "Pierced Nose," did not in the main pierce their noses. Both of these customs were practiced on the coast, however, and confused reports from the frontier probably resulted in the misnaming.) This flattening disgusted many whites: fur company clerk Ross Cox called it an "abominable custom," though he admitted it "is not, I believe, attended with much pain." To the coastal tribes that practiced head flattening, however, the resulting slope of the forehead was a mark of beauty and dignity visibly separating noble from slave. A young Indian who traveled east with missionary Jason Lee found it no stranger than the Euro-American practice of cinching in women's waists to waspish dimensions. When white trappers refused to let their Indian brides flatten the heads of their mixed-blood children, some squaws reportedly resorted to infanticide rather than let their children bear the stigma of a normally rounded head.

This practice also posed an interesting problem to European racial theories. Flattening their skulls did not seem to cost the Chinooks any intelligence. In fact, they had a reputation as being clever, hard-bargaining traders who used their role of middlemen after the arrival of Europeans to elevate themselves to new positions of power. Meriwether Lewis called them "close dealers" who would "stickle for very little, never close a bargain except they think they have the advantage." Comcomly in particular was admired for his adroit political ability at monopolizing the trade and shifting allegiance from Americans to British as circumstance dictated. In his book *Astoria*, Washington Irving described Comcomly as "a shrewd old savage with but one eye." Did head flattening somehow improve mental ability, or at least cast doubt on the notion that head shape dictated intelligence? Here was a question for European science.

Gairdner's curiosity anticipates our own curiosity about Native American culture as a whole. When we consider the enormous transformation of the river in the last two hundred years, an obvious question is whether its damming and diversion was an inevitable by-product of human existence. Clearly, the answer is no. Anthropologists have established that Indians lived on the river for at least eleven thousand years, and benefited from the rhythm of large salmon runs for at least four thousand years, almost as long as Western civilization's history. And while they did not exist in a utopia, neither were they rescued by civilization. "The people appear to live in a State of comparative happiness," observed William Clark after an encounter on the lower Snake River with a tribe believed to be Yakimas, a judgment echoed by others.

Fur trader Alexander Ross had this description of a Chinook village: "On a fine day, it is amusing to see a whole camp or village, both men and women, here and there in numerous little bands, gambling, jeering, and laughing at one another, while groups of children keep in constant motion, either in the water or practicing the bow and arrow, and even the aged take a lively interest in what is passing, and there appears a degree of happiness among them which civilized man, wearied with care and anxious pursuits, perhaps seldom enjoys."

Ross continued in this wistful vein while describing the Okanogan Indians east of the Cascades. "The Indian in his natural state is happy, with his trader he is happy, but the moment he begins to walk in the path of the white man his happiness is at an end. Like a wild animal in a cage, his luster is gone."

The contentment baffled whites conditioned to equate material possessions with happiness. "Although living in a state of the most abject poverty," mused naturalist John Townsend in 1838, "deprived of most of the absolute necessaries of life, and frequently enduring the pangs of protracted starvation, yet these poor people appear happy and contented."

One of the most evocative sites I encountered on the Columbia River is the bar and beach below Hanford's abandoned K Reactor, which manufactured plutonium for atomic bombs. Circular depressions in the desert soil marked the site of native pit houses. I landed by jet boat at this site with archaeologist Jim Chatters of Battelle's Pacific Northwest Laboratories, listened to his account of ancient people, and asked finally which culture was superior: the ingenious modern one that had built the hulking reactor, or the aboriginal village?

Chatters smiled at a question with no easy answer. He pointed out that the reactor operated just fifteen years before becoming obsolete. "Folks have lived here an awful lot longer than it was a reactor site," he said. "They had a nice life. They didn't live as long as we do, but they didn't have nearly as much stress. Their life was much more predictable. It was based on a very intimate understanding of their surroundings."

Gairdner's quest for Comcomly's head was a risky task. Chinook custom was to place the dead body with prized possessions in a cedar canoe and elevate it in the trees above the reach of animals. Memaloose Island, now drowned by Bonneville Dam, was one site used for this purpose. Another was a bluff and islet near the junction of the Cowlitz and Columbia rivers known respectively as Mount Coffin and Coffin Rock. The caching of prized possessions in the death canoes was an obvious temptation to thieves, and disturbance of the burial grounds was regarded by Indians as the most serious of sins. In 1825 a Hudson's Bay surgeon named John Scouler was spotted prowling Mount Coffin and natives set out in enraged pursuit, Scouler barely reaching the safety of his ship *William and Anne.*

While the Indians made no special preservation of the bodies, the death canoes sometimes allowed bodies to dry into a kind of natural mummy that aroused scientific curiosity. In 1834 naturalist John Townsend, a trained physician, discovered the body of a young woman so preserved, crept back in the middle of the night to the canoe that held her corpse, climbed a tree to reach the vessel, and lowered her to the ground with a rope. "Taking the body upon my shoulders," he related, "[I] bore it to my canoe and pushed off into the stream. On arriving at the fort [Williams, on Sauvie Island near present-day Portland] I deposited my prize in the store house and sewed around it a large Indian mat, to give it the appearance of a bale of guns." He left the mummy at the fort until he could safely stow it on board a supply schooner.

This theft did not go unnoticed: the brother of the dead woman appeared at the store. Distraught, the native explained that he had visited her canoe and found it empty. The tracks on the beach showed the toes did not point inward in the Indian manner, meaning a white man must have been the trespasser. Confronted with this deduction, the storekeeper gave the body back, plus several blankets to assuage the insult. He wrote to Townsend that "the poor Indian took the body of his sister upon his shoulders and, as he walked away, grief got the better of his stoicism and the sound of his weeping was heard long after he had entered the forest."

In 1846 artist Paul Kane also robbed one of the canoes of its skulls. He later admitted he "ran no small risk not only in getting it but in having it in my possession afterwards; even the *voyageurs* would have refused to travel with me had they known that I had it among my collections, not only on account of the superstitious dread in which they hold these burial places, but also on account of the danger arising from a discovery, which might cost the lives of the whole party."

Sneaking into the burial grounds at night, Gairdner found that Comcomly's body had been buried in a forest grave to prevent just this kind of desecration. Determined to accomplish at least this goal, however, the coughing, tubercular doctor began to dig. After considerable work he excavated the box that contained the chief's body, pried off the lid, and stared at a skeleton with hair and skin still on the flattened skull. Forced to pause often from coughing spasms that spit up his own blood, Gairdner decapitated the corpse and stole away to a ship bound for Honolulu. From the islands he sent Comcomly's boxed skull on to a friend in England, physician and naturalist John Richardson. In a letter of explanation Gairdner wrote of Comcomly, "By his ability? cunning? or what you please to call it, he raised himself and family to a power and influence which no Indian has since possessed in the districts of the Columbia below the first rapids one hundred and fifty miles from the sea. When the phrenologists look at this frontal development, what will they say to this?! If I return to the Columbia I will endeavor to procure you the whole skeleton. . . ." Gairdner died in Hawaii of tuberculosis the following year.

This bizarre story illustrates the combination of curiosity, respect, callousness, and arrogance with which newcomers regarded the native inhabitants of the Columbia River. Whites had been fascinated and fearful of Indians since their arrival in the Western Hemisphere, and the tribes beyond the Mississippi were the subject of wild speculation well into the nineteenth century. Even after Lewis and Clark, authorities theorized that some western tribes might be descended from the Norse, the Irish, the Welsh, or the Lost Tribes of Israel. Reports described white Indians, black Indians, bearded Indians, dwarf Indians, and Indians living in cities of gold. Reality proved even stranger as Europeans struggled to come to terms with customs and expectations different from their own.

Few tribes in America elicited such a mixed reaction as did those between the Cascades and the sea. They were variously described as smart traders and frustrating hagglers, kind and thievish, developed and dirty, repulsive and yet the source of wives, mistresses, and prostitutes that made transmission of European venereal diseases rampant and gave Fort Vancouver a French-Catholic choir of mixed-blood children.

Maybe what so disturbed the whites who encountered these Indians was not the differences but the similarities between the two cultures. These natives lived in settled communities in wooden houses, preferred trade to war, were proud, self-assured, materialistic, adaptive, artistic, spiritual, and practiced slavery. White traders and natives quickly became mutually dependent and interrelated: four of Comcomly's daughters were married to the partners of Fort Astoria, a political and economic as well as sexual alliance. Ranald McDonald, the son of Archibald McDonald and Comcomly's youngest daughter, Raven (who died in childbirth), recorded that his mother walked three hundred yards from the chief's lodge to a waiting canoe on a carpet of furs at her marriage; the furs were then bundled as a dowry to the traders. The whites in return showered the chief with trade goods.

Not only were Euro-American attitudes mixed, but the natives' demise was tied directly to the arrival of traders and trappers. The grief of the young Indian retrieving the body of his sister may have been for more than her desecration by a grave robber; by that year of 1834 about 90 percent of the once-powerful Chinook were already dead from European diseases. The white invasion had turned from economic opportunity to health catastrophe. In 1844 missionary Jason Lee, after being ordered to close his failed mission in the nearby Willamette Valley, wrote that "when I left the country there were more Indian children in the mission graveyard than alive and in the manual labor school."

The quick decline of this culture in the face of European disease and weaponry is stunning. Just as remarkable has been Native American resilience in spite of it. The Indians on the Columbia today, still burdened with immense and persistent social problems, have nonetheless managed to endure an onslaught of disease, war, dispossession, and cultural assault that staggers the imagination. The survival of their ethnic identity, parts of their culture, and tribal government is evidence of their aboriginal strength.

The collision between native and newcomer eventually became ugly. When the Ward wagon train was destroyed by Indians near Boise in 1854, many bodies were mutilated and some young girls allegedly were burned alive. Conversely, when Oregon militia captured Walla Walla chief Peopeomoxmox by seizing him under a flag of truce in an unrelated conflict two years later, they carved his skull into buttons, and cut off his ears and fingers and displayed them in a jar.

Such tales, and decades of Hollywood movies, have conditioned us to look for heroes and villains in this saga, and to divide it neatly into a conflict of one race versus another. In reality what happened was an enormously complex story of mutual dependence and exploitation, shifting strategies, chronic misunderstandings, bitter ruthlessness, and generous aid by all sides. Oregon militia burned a white Catholic mission in the Yakima Valley they suspected of aiding the natives. The Nez Perce scouted for whites against the Yakima and Spokane in the wars of the 1850s.

While hundreds died during a century of armed conflict in the Columbia Basin, the battles obscure how necessary Native Americans were to the newcomers. Indians fed the Europeans, did the trapping that made the Pacific Northwest economically al-

luring, guided them, rescued them, and supplied them with canoes and horses. The early exploration expeditions, fur posts,
missions, and immigrant caravans simply could not have survived without native help.

Lewis and Clark, for example, relied on tribes along the way
for food, guidance, canoes, and horses. While Sacajawea did not
really guide the expedition, she was invaluable for helping gather
food, making friends with her own Shoshone tribe, and reassur-
ing other tribes by her presence as a female that the explorers
were not leading a war party.

The Wilson Price Hunt expedition was saved several times
by Indian aid. Comcomly's personal rescue of Astorian traders
who had capsized at the Columbia's mouth in 1811 is only one example of repeated rescues of whites by natives. When Marcus
Whitman led the first large wagon train over the Oregon Trail, he
left it at the Snake River to the able care of a Cayuse guide named
Stickus while he rode to a medical emergency at the Spalding
mission. The Cayuse subsequently built a route over the Blue
Mountains that the pioneers considered equal or superior to what
immigrants had been using, gladly paying the fifty cents per
wagon the tribe charged.

Immigrant guidebooks recommended the use of Indian pilots on the Columbia. "It requires the most dexterous management," Overton Johnson and William Winter wrote, "which these
wild navigators are masters of, to pass the dreadful chasm in
safety. A single stroke amiss would be inevitable destruction."
Many Oregon Trail diarists praised the help they got from Indians at the Columbia rapids through the Cascades. Mary Jane
Long recorded in 1852 how the hired natives caught fish, built
fires, brought water, and even went back to a previous encampment to retrieve her father's forgotten gun. They brought it back
before he missed it.

Native Americans successfully tried farming. The Haida and
Tlingits of British Columbia's coast were skilled potato growers
after the tuber's introduction by sea captains, and the crop spread
to Puget Sound and the Columbia. The Cayuse and Walla Walla
tried a variety of crops around the Whitman Mission, the Nez
Perce quickly built a cattle herd of four hundred to five hundred
head, and the Yakima experimented with irrigation. The tribes
sold food to the arriving immigrants.

Our judgment of the white-native collision on the Columbia is hampered by at least three problems.

First, we have only one side of the story. Pioneers recorded impressions on paper while the natives relied on oral tradition that died with the tellers as disease took its toll.

Second, we usually address Native Americans as a group, and this obscures cultural variety and individual personalities. Tribes varied enormously. The Nez Perce scorned the fur trade as "fit for only women and slaves." The Cayuse in the main refused to work at the mission Whitman established in their midst; the neighboring Walla Walla, in contrast, did hire on. Individuals were equally diverse: some kind, some cruel, some wise, some foolish, some pragmatic, some idealistic. "Their noted stoic apathy is more assumed than real," wrote Canadian explorer David Thompson. "In public the Indian wishes it to appear that nothing affects him. But in private, he feels and expresses himself sensitive to everything that happens to him or his family. On becoming acquainted with the Indians I found almost every character in civilized society can be traced among them—from the gravity of a judge to a merry jester, from open-hearted generosity to the avaricious miser."

An example of their diversity was the appearance of an apparently lesbian Indian couple at Fort Astoria. A female dressed up in male clothing, Ko-come-ne-pe-ca, told David Thompson she had experienced a powerful dream and "declared her sex changed, that she was now a Man, dressed and armed herself as such, and also took a young woman to wife."

A third difficulty is that Native Americans changed in the face of invading technology and disease. For example, England's Captain Cook found the women of Vancouver Island's Nootka Sound modest and chaste when he arrived in 1778; after a number of European ship visits George Vancouver found them freely offering sex when he returned in 1792. Such rapid change hinders assessment of precontact native mores.

Lewis and Clark did not travel through an undisturbed, pristine aboriginal culture. The Shoshone they met in Idaho's inhospitable mountains had been recently driven from their traditional western Montana territory by Blackfeet. That tribe, in turn, had been victorious because it was armed with weapons obtained in trade with the Hudson's Bay Company. The horse had reached the Columbia Plateau about eighty years before the explorers, becoming as thoroughly integrated in plateau culture as the automobile in America today. Far from being chained to tradition and resistant to change, tribes quickly recognized the benefits of new technology and traded for it avidly.

Moreover, when the explorers came down the Columbia in 1805, Indian populations had already suffered losses to European smallpox estimated at from 33 to 50 percent over the previous thirty years. While disease had not yet destroyed native culture, one must wonder what effects such a high, sudden mortality had, equal in proportion to the toll of the bubonic plague in Europe. "The small pox has destroyed a great number of the natives in this quarter," Lewis wrote. "It prevailed about 4 years since among the Clatsops and destroyed several hundred of them, four of their chiefs fell victyms to it's ravages. Those Clatsops are deposited in their canoes on the bay a few miles below us. I think the late ravages of the small pox may well account for the number of remains of vilages which we find deserted on the river and sea coast [in] this quarter."

Lewis and Clark saw an Indian in a sailor's jacket at The Dalles, more than two hundred miles from the sea, and they found frequent evidence of European and American goods the rest of the way down the river. More than a hundred American trading ships had already visited the mouth: Clatsops and Chinooks gave the explorers the names of a dozen specific captains and when they might return, impressing the explorers with the power of oral memory. Natives had already picked up English phrases such as "son of a bitch," were disappointed at the paucity and inferiority of trade goods brought overland, and yet were not adverse to providing women, both slave and noble, for sex in exchange for goods. One woman even had the name of a ship's captain, "J. Bowman," tattooed on her arm. Whereas the first ships in 1792 had been able to trade cheap rings or necklaces profitably, just three years later the Chinooks were firmly demanding blankets, cloth, metal, and guns.

Nor was this solely an Anglo-native meeting. Since Gray's discovery the Columbia had been a meeting place of native, French-Canadian, Asian, Pacific Islanders, black, and Hispanic, plus Iroquois, Delaware, and other eastern Indians imported for trapping. By 1820, about twenty Catholic Iroquois trappers had married into Flathead society and given the eastern Plateau Indians their first introduction to Christian ritual. Another group of that tribe almost touched off a war with native bands in the Willamette Valley. Ship crews along the Northwest coast included not just Americans, British, Spanish, French, and Russians, but Mexicans, Filipinos, Hawaiians, and Chinese. A group of fifty Chinese laborers imported by Britain had built the first ship constructed in the Northwest, the schooner *Felice,* in 1788, four years before the Columbia was even discovered.

Indians of the Columbia River formed two broad cultural groups. West of the Cascade Mountains along the lower river were the tribes of the Northwest coastal culture, a fishing people of stable settlements where dense forests did not permit much use of the horse. East of the Cascades and across to the Bitterroots lived the Plateau Indians who had adopted the horse and had a culture similar to Plains tribes. In the Columbia River Gorge between the Cascades and The Dalles, the two cultures came together in congregations of three thousand or more to trade, gamble, gossip, feast, and cavort. The river's piercing of the Cascades made it the trade thoroughfare for tribes who lived hundreds of miles in every direction. Here they exchanged food, fish oil, obsidian, baskets, buffalo hides, and dentalium shells. Smaller but similar gatherings occurred at the Columbia's Kettle Falls and at Fraser and Iron canyons on Canada's Fraser River.

Anthropologists estimate that perhaps fifty thousand to seventy thousand Native Americans lived in the river basin: approximately fifteen thousand on the lower river, thirty thousand on the broad plateau across eastern Washington and Oregon, and the remainder on the Snake plateau and in the mountains of Idaho and British Columbia. The non-Indian immigrant population would not reach that level until the Civil War.

The densest concentration of Native Americans was on the lower river, represented by tribes such as the Chinook, Clatsop, Multnomah, and Willamette. The coastal Indians, confined mostly to the beaches by dense rain forest and thus oriented to the region's immense salmon runs, made up the greatest concentration of Native Americans north of Mexico. Approximately two hundred thousand inhabited the coast and rivers from the California border to southern Alaska. "The native population on the banks of the Columbia is much greater than in any other part of North America I have visited," noted the Bay Company's Simpson. These bands and clans usually spent winters in permanent villages of cedar plank houses and developed a complex culture of art, story, trade, material wealth, regulated war, class, and slavery.

Until large numbers of immigrants began arriving in the 1840s, the newcomers made little physical impact on the land. And until disease devastated their ranks, these Indians considered themselves a military and political match for the newcomers. By 1792 virtually all the warriors at the trading crossroads of Nootka Sound on Vancouver Island owned muskets. They outnumbered the newcomers and so skillfully played the rival ships and nations off against one another that much of the early profit from the China trade evaporated. "A nation of traders and not of hunters," Simpson assessed. Yet when aroused they were fully capable of war. To the north they attacked and destroyed the ships *Boston* in 1803, *Atahualpa* in 1805, and *Tonquin* in 1811, twice assaulted the Russian settlement at Sitka, and otherwise demonstrated that they were not to be trifled with.

Stocky and powerful, the coastal Indians were a canoe people who used six different models on the Columbia alone, driving craft up to fifty feet in length through rough ocean seas, plunging their paddle arms up to their armpits to maintain balance and momentum. They raided and traded for slaves. Sometimes treated with kindness and at other times with indifferent cruelty, slaves were occasionally killed to demonstrate a chief's wealth and power or to accompany a dead noble into the next world. Oregon settlers bought slaves from the Chinook for farm work in the 1840s, and early white accounts contain little outrage over the practice.

Europeans had a varied reaction to the lower Columbia inhabitants. Fur trader Ross Cox complained that their flathead "deformity is unredeemed by any peculiar beauty in features or person. . . . The good qualities of these Indians are few, their vices many. In the latter may be classed thieving, lying, incontinence, gambling and cruelty."

The initial impression of Lewis and Clark was hardly better. While the faces of the women were judged attractive, Lewis wrote of both sexes, "They are low in stature, rather diminutive and illy shapen; possessing thick broad flat feet, thick ankles, crooked legs, wide mouths, thick lips, nose moderately large, fleshy, wide at the extremity with large nostrils, black eyes and coarse black hair."

Yet familiarity changed the explorers' initial judgment. Lewis called them "mild, inoffensive people," and Clark encountered an "extraordinary friendship" at a Clatsop house. Trapper Gabriel Franchere judged: "With all their faults, they seem to me more amenable to civilization than most Indians living east of the mountains. . . . They possess to an eminent degree those qualities opposed to idleness, improvidence and stupidity. The chiefs, in particular, distinguish themselves by their good judgment and intelligence. Generally speaking, they have good minds and tenacious memories."

The whites seemed a bit taken aback by the bare-breasted women and frequent total nudity of the men, who wore a cloak and conical hat only in particularly cold or wet weather. Native reaction to the cold intrigued observers. "I have often seen [lower Columbia Indians] going about, half naked, when the thermometer ranged between thirty and forty degrees," noted the Reverend Samuel Parker in 1835, "and their children barefooted and barelegged in the snow."

The coastal Indians were also frequently described as "dirty." Indeed, the filth may have been greater at the stable salmon fishing villages than among more mobile horse tribes that moved frequently and left their litter and sewage behind. The stench was particularly overwhelming at The Dalles, where the huge conglomeration of Indians, racks of drying salmon, horses, and dust created a community as odoriferous as it was colorful. Artist Paul Kane complained of the coastal Indians: "Their habits are extremely filthy, their persons abounding with vermin, and one of their chief amusements consists of picking these disgusting insects from each other's heads and eating them. On my asking an Indian one day why he eats them, he replied that they bit him and he could get his revenge by biting them in return."

Still, one must wonder about reports of poor sanitation. The river Indians were reported as frequent and skilled swimmers who may have gotten wet more frequently than the fur trapper newcomers. And Chinook habits did not seem to discourage sexual liaisons, with venereal disease a problem on the lower Columbia for both Lewis and Clark's company and the later Astorians.

Alexander Ross comments with comic approval on the cedar bark string skirts worn by Chinook women, a bit similar to the grass skirts of the Polynesians: "It does not screen nature from the prying eye; yet it is remarkably convenient on many occasions. In a calm the sails lie close to the mast, metaphorically speaking, but when the wind blows the bare poles are seen." Lewis and Clark made much the same observation.

The Salish language of the coastal tribes consisted of clicks and guttural sounds that twisted European tongues. In short order, whites adopted the Chinook jargon, trade language of a few hundred more easily pronounceable words. The jargon was soon influenced by, and influenced, English. The slang term "hootch" for homemade liquor comes from Chinook jargon, for example, and "pehlten" came to mean "drunk" after Indian observation of alcoholic Archibald "Judge" Pelton of Fort George.

These were the people who so fascinated Gairdner, with Comcomly their most famous representative. Native to a village situated on Baker Bay behind Cape Disappointment, the chief brilliantly used his close ties to the newcomers to achieve huge influence, a position that declined only when the Bay headquarters moved from Astoria to Fort Vancouver. He received a medal from Lewis and Clark, became a skilled bar pilot for incoming ships, allied himself through marriage of his daughters to the fur traders who established Fort Astoria across the river, and managed to serve as middleman for much of the fur trade. A hint of Comcomly's political instinct is suggested by two contrasting incidents when the British took over Fort Astoria and renamed it Fort George in 1814. The Clatsop chief Coboway had been given a paper by Lewis and Clark dated March 18, 1806, and Coboway preserved this carefully, regarding it as a totem of powerful magic. But when he innocently and proudly showed the paper to North West Company trader Alexander Henry, the Scot rudely threw it into the fire and gave the bewildered chief a British replacement. Comcomly, in contrast, was well aware of the international struggles among the white men. He first offered to fight for the Americans against the King George Men. When it became apparent the Astorians were going to sell out rather than defend their fort, he immediately switched sides. The chief got a full British dress uniform and sword from the warship *Racoon* when it arrived to take Astoria, and the next day had himself paddled by canoe across the river in full dress, a British ensign flying off the stern. An assessment typical of the sometimes narrow European view comes from Ross: "We had some time ago found out that the sordid hope for gain alone attached this old and crafty chief to the whites." As if anything but a sordid hope for gain attached the traders to the Indians.

As the fur traders traveled up the Columbia the dense forests gave way to treeless plains, and Indian culture changed with the climate and landscape. The tribes included the Yakima, Cayuse, Walla Walla, Umatilla, Wanapum, Spokane, Nez Perce, Snake, Bannock, Shoshone, Kootenay, Flathead, Pend d'Oreille, and Okanogan, to name just some. Their culture had been revolutionized by the horse, and in summer some ranged as far as the Great Plains to hunt bison. Salmon, however, was still a staple used for food throughout much of the basin, from The Dalles to central Idaho. One early immigrant train was startled near Idaho's Salmon Falls by an aged Snake Indian wearing nothing but a top hat and vest who cheerfully traded two salmon for a button and ambled away, giving the overlanders their first taste of the famous fish. Immigrant Samuel Francis called the salmon he sampled at Fort Boise in 1852 "the best fish I ever ate."

Handsome and hardy, these horse Indians had a freedom and self-confidence that still appeals to the imagination. Lieutenant Lawrence Kip left this description from the treaty council at Walla Walla in 1855: "About 2,500 of the Nez Perce have arrived. We saw them coming on horseback in one long line. They were almost entirely naked, gaudily painted and decorated in their wild trappings. Their plumes fluttered about them, while below, skins and trinkets and all kinds of fantastic embellishments flaunted in the sunshine. Trained from early childhood almost to live on horseback, they sat upon their fine animals as if they were centaurs. . . . Beads and fringes of gaudy colors were hanging from their bridles, while the plumes of eagle feathers interwoven with the mane and tail fluttered as the breeze swept over them, and completed their wild and fantastic appearance."

They were swift at adapting to what they considered the best parts of white culture, trading for guns, metal kettles, and wool blankets. The Plateau tribe of Chief Moses (who got his name while a missionary school student taught by Henry Spalding and for whom Moses Lake is named) acquired chickens, potatoes, and cattle at Fort Vancouver as early as 1825.

From the beginning this relationship was uneasy, however. The white newcomers were aggressive and restless, insisting upon free passage across tribal lands and building forts where they pleased. This caused particular problems in the Columbia River Gorge, where the inhabitants were accustomed to controlling traffic up and down the river. The Indians retaliated by refusing to trade, throwing stones, and trying to steal the gifts the whites would not leave. Until disease destroyed native power, it was considered unwise by fur traders to venture through the gorge in parties of less than sixty armed men. Natives at the Cascades, where Bonneville Dam is now, confidently faced off a war expedition of eighty-five North West Company trappers in 1814, sending the *voyageurs* back to Astoria in meek retreat.

We read constant complaints about Indian theft, but Native Americans saw the issue differently. The whites had too much and hoarded it. Taking some of their goods was both a way to redistribute wealth and to exact proper tribute to the power of the local inhabitants. Ross recalls a time when Indians at The Dalles got a peek at the trade goods in the ninety-pound trade bundles. The chiefs "could not comprehend why people who had so much as we were not more liberal" with gifts and tribute, he wrote. The need for mobility and communal cooperation made accumulation of large amounts of individual wealth among Indians impractical. Missionary Henry Spalding noted with puzzlement, "The chiefs have no power of levying taxes, and they are so much in the habit of contributing their own property for individuals or public good that they are not generally wealthy." Many explorers and trappers also commented on the Indian love of gambling. Modern anthropologist Eugene Hunn has theorized it was popular in part as a means to redistribute wealth: why not let luck rule how goods were distributed?

White arrogance precipitated some early conflict. Frequently told in the Pacific Northwest is the heroic story of Marie Dorion, the Indian bride of Pierre who bore a child during the arduous Wilson Price Hunt march of the Astorians. Marie later accompanied her husband back to the Snake River country to trap, and when he and eight companions were massacred she led her two surviving children through the winter desert in a hard, heroic trek until finally rescued by friendly Walla Wallas. Not always mentioned is what probably precipitated the native attack: while camped at the mouth of the Palouse River, Astorian John Clarke had detected an Indian attempting to steal a goblet. Though Clarke demanded and got the goblet back, the trapper promptly hanged the accused thief in front of the shocked and horrified tribe, which would never have executed a person for such an offense and had never seen a death as cruel as hanging.

Two years later Alexander Ross went to the Yakima Valley to trade for horses and found a huge encampment of three thousand men, uncounted women and children, and nine thousand horses that stretched for six miles along the Yakima River. His party was teased and tormented by the gathered warriors while trying to trade until Ross finally averted a fight by offering his own knife to a chief as a gift, the moment of inspired generosity instantly turning an enemy into a friend. In encounter after encounter, the natives seemed to expect, and respect, a charity that whites had a hard time coming to grips with.

Some natives were no doubt mystified by the extent of the newcomers' power, at one point presenting a party of trappers with two dead children and a request they be brought back to life. When artist Paul Kane drew a portrait of a Cowlitz woman and then later returned, village children ran from him and hid. He learned the woman had since died, and the natives feared he had somehow robbed her of her life force by capturing her in a drawing. An Umatilla village was initially terrified of Lewis and Clark, fearing the Corps of Discovery had come from the sky.

The natives knew their landscape. In what to trappers appeared inhospitable sagebrush desert, Plateau tribes could find a hundred food plants and one hundred and thirty used for medicines. In his work with modern Yakima Indians who have retained traditional knowledge, Hunn found they could identify two hundred and forty different animals and two hundred and fifteen useful plants, even though their aboriginal language lumped together under one name attractive but nonessential wildflowers. Foods included not just berries and roots but Oregon grape, duck eggs, pine lichen, sunflower stems, the cambrium layer of Ponderosa pine, wild carrots, and pine and hazel nuts.

Their skill was notable. Thomas Manby, a British seaman,

said the male Indians "never move without their quivers, filled with arrows, all of which are stained with various colors, and pointed with the flint made exceedingly sharp; they seldom miss a mark at twenty yards, and will often kill a bird at forty." The Chinooks of the coast were powerful swimmers and expert canoeists. Their ability to utilize the big trees astounded observers. "In order to appreciate their patience and their industry," wrote fur trader Gabriel Franchere, "the reader needs only to know that we found not one ax among them. They use a two-inch chisel, usually made from an old file, and a hammer that is nothing more but an oblong stone. With these wretched instruments and some wedges made of hemlock knots, oiled and hardened by firing, they cut down cedars twenty-four and thirty feet in circumference, dig them out, and fashion them into canoes, or they split and transform them into beams and planks for their houses."

Plateau Indians could start a fire in moments by rubbing two pieces of wood together, catch and cook a breakfast of small river fish in minutes, pin and defang rattlesnakes, set broken bones, and heal horrendous cuts. The tribes built large, comfortable homes of cedar and reed mats, wove watertight baskets, and boiled water in them by dropping in hot rocks. They were initially free of many serious diseases known in the white world.

Their life was freer but more directly dependent on nature than ours. They moved with the sun and seasons, camping on the Columbia during salmon runs and moving at other times to take shellfish, game, birds, berries, and roots such as wapato and camas. Yet life was not easy, particularly in the dry interior. Missionary Henry Spalding said Indians of the Columbia Plateau worked harder to survive than whites did. Anthropological study has detected telltale growth lines on the leg bones of children suggesting seasonal famine.

Natives were organized less by tribe than by family, clan, village, and band. Their chiefs had no real authority beyond whatever respect they commanded, and directed things by consent. The coastal tribes included more participation by women in trading and decision-making. Lewis theorized that this is true in any culture where women could share equally with men the labor required for food; a diet heavy in fish, roots, and berries allowed Chinook women to participate in most aspects of food gathering.

The explorers and trappers noted with approval the Indians'

care for their elderly and gentler discipline with children, who were more likely to get a dunking in the Columbia than a spanking.

The Indians were baffled by the aggressive drive and push for change by the whites. When Ross decided to travel (for little reason except curiosity) from Fort Okanogan to Puget Sound across the north Cascades, it was only with difficulty that he persuaded three reluctant Indians to accompany him as guides and helpers. As the party plunged deeper into the mountains the Indian unease grew, and finally after one was injured and another terrified by a windstorm, they refused to go farther: they saw no point. Ross and his guides ended up sulking in silence around a campfire with neither understanding the motivations of the other, a standoff illustrative of a wider truth. The European newcomers were from elsewhere, and if they trapped out or overgrazed or cut or mined or farmed an area to exhaustion, their experience told them they could move on. Geography was fluid, a map of opportunity, something to be exploited.

To the Indians, geography was more fixed. Most tribes had inhabited the same area for as long as memory and oral tradition reached. They knew their home territory down to individual rocks and trees but had no abstract tools such as map and compass to help venture beyond. There was no place they could move to and duplicate their sense of belonging.

One can get a sense of this when viewing the Indian petroglyphs along the banks of the Columbia. Here the Indians commemorated hunts, raids, and successful spirit quests or shamanistic powers, but the strongest message in the rock art is the rock itself. It is fixed to a place, not portable. The artist could not take it down from the wall and pack it to another house. This was home. There was no other.

Nature was an unpredictable spirit to be placated, not an enemy to be conquered. Flood control became one of the primary rationales for damming the Columbia River, but Native Americans looked at the issue entirely differently. Here is a description of annual flooding told by Martin Louie, Sr., an elder of the Colville tribe that was displaced by Grand Coulee Dam: "The north changes the world. In the winter the snow comes, covers the land. When it breaks in the spring, the mountains and hills will gather all the deteriorated stuff and bring it down to the Columbia, the main channel, and take it away. What goes out in the ocean will never return. And we have a brand new world in spring. The high water takes everything out, washes everything down. That's why we pray to the water, every morning and night." This is not an attitude found in Army Corps of Engineers literature.

Native Americans readily tried farming and ranching, creating some of the first small irrigation works in the Columbia Basin, but only as a supplement to their traditional life. Later some became successful farmers and ranchers, but there was never cultural agreement on this new industry. In the 1870s a prophet named Smohalla began to instruct the Indians of the mid-Columbia River. "My young men shall never work," Smohalla said. "Men who work cannot dream, and wisdom comes to us in dreams." But wasn't it work to dig camas root, work like the white farmers do? "This work lasts only a few weeks," Smohalla said. "It is natural work that does not do them any harm. But the work of the white man hardens soul and body. Nor is it right to tear up and mutilate the earth as white men do. . . . You ask me to plow the ground. Shall I take a knife and tear my mother's bosom? Then when I die, she will not take me to her bosom to rest. You ask me to dig for stone. Shall I dig under her skin for her bones? Then when I die I cannot enter her body to be born again. You ask me to cut grass and make hay and sell it and be rich like the white man, but how dare I cut off my mother's hair? . . . We simply take the gifts that are freely offered. We no more harm the earth than would an infant's fingers harm its mothers breast. But the white man tears up large tracts of land, runs deep ditches, cuts down forest, and changes the whole face of the earth. . . . every honest man knows in his heart that this is wrong."

"*We take the gifts that are freely offered.*" No phrase better sums up the gulf between the two cultures, the way gift-giving mirrored the Native American approach to life and non-Indian economics undermined it. The system Europeans saw as progressive some natives viewed as ultimately corrupting. Yet even among the Indians there was no unanimity on these difficult questions. At one point Smohalla debated a tribal colleague named Homli who was an apostle of modernization, Smohalla urging a return to the banks of the Columbia and his rival a try at adapting to the reservation. Two-thirds of the assembled listeners followed the modernist, not Smohalla.

• • •

The Columbia's natives told animal stories about heroes such as Coyote and Raven that exhibited human intelligence. Coyote in particular recurred along the river, mischievous and shrewd, imperiled and then triumphant, not just by magical power but by wit. An Indian Odysseus rather than an Achilles, he is more truly human than either. Historian David Chance explains: "At times Coyote seems like the slinking or playful animal that we occasionally see in the woods, looking at us over his shoulder with intent eyes. But in many tales he is very much a man—the ambiguity is important and intended—for he has the power to change his identity at will. . . . One must not suppose that Coyote is portrayed as a highly moral character. He is usually much more interesting than that. Like the average person, he is a mixture of inconsistencies; his actions are often evil or foolish, his sense of humor quite risqué. He is sometimes very greedy, frequently careless, and his notion of his own worth is usually inflated. But these are all foibles that can be safely laughed at in a coyote."

"Coyote . . . teaches by example," anthropologist Hunn writes, "and he exemplifies all the good and bad qualities of the human animal. Coyotes instruct while inspiring obedience to an ethic of mutual respect and concern. They inspire modesty, honesty, generosity, forbearance, forethought and courage. They etch in the children's memories a living map of their surroundings, a land peopled with creatures and forces of nature that are fully animate and virtually human; in fact, they once were fully human. Here, art clearly serves survival, strengthening the ecological, social and spiritual balance on which the hunter-gatherer life depends."

Another animal that united these tribes was the fish. The spring, summer, and fall salmon runs would arrive in succession, and the river also offered suckers, squawfish, mollusks, waterfowl, and steelhead. The various tribes called the Columbia Nch'I-Wana or Chiawana, Tacoutche-Tesse or Enbotquatqua: Big River. It was the resource that took care of them. The Indians believed the salmon ascended the stream to benefit mankind, died, and returned to life to renew the cycle.

No one can be certain how many fish swam up the Columbia River in presettlement times or how many the Indians caught, but both numbers are believed to be enormous. Lewis and Clark estimated the Indians of the gorge area alone prepared thirty thousand dried pounds of salmon annually. By the 1940 calculation of

J. A. Craig and R. L. Hacker, if fifty thousand Indians each ate a pound of salmon a day, which seemed reasonable judging from the diet subsequently recorded by visiting anthropologists, the annual aboriginal catch was 18 million pounds, a number that would likely translate to one to two million salmon per year out of a run estimated at 10 to 16 million fish. A 1986 estimate by the Northwest Power Planning Council was 42 million pounds. Anthropologist Keith Muckleston of Oregon State University in Corvallis calculates the Indians caught 4.6 million to 6.5 million individual fish. By comparison, the catch in the river recently has averaged five to eight million pounds, or fewer than one million fish—it fell as low as 85,500 fish in 1983, and was virtually shut down in 1994.

For many river Indians salmon provided at least 40 percent of their total calories. It was roasted, boiled, smoked, or dried into a flaky powder that could remain edible for several years. Big game such as deer and elk probably made up no more than 10 percent of the diet. Fish were so critical that during the Pacific Northwest Indian Wars the tribes were suspected of stalling negotiations in the spring of 1857 to give time for the salmon to return in order to supply the coming campaign. A good salmon run dictated how much time natives would have for other pursuits such as fur trapping. West of the Rockies, the Bay Company saying was "No salmon, no furs."

The fish weighed anywhere from six to a hundred pounds and were not easy to catch. Entering the river to spawn, they fed little and were reluctant to take bait, defeating the best efforts of baffled Hudson's Bay Company tackle fishermen. Downriver, Indians employed fiber nets that could reach the length of a football field. Upriver, the fish would congregate at the foot of falls and rapids to gather strength for leaps as high as ten feet, and at these falls Indians congregated to catch them. At powerful Celilo Falls just upstream from The Dalles, fishermen would stand on rickety platforms jutting out over the water and use dip nets or spears on long poles. At Kettle Falls, missionary Pierre DeSmet recorded, "It was a common occurrence . . . to take three thousand salmon in a day."

A First Fish Ceremony was held to celebrate the spring return. On April 19, 1806, at Celilo, Clark recorded: "There was great joy with the natives last night in consequence of the arrival of the Salmon; one of those fish was caught, this was the harbinger of good news to them. They informed us that those fish would arrive in great quantities in the course of about 5 days. this fish was dressed and being divided into small pieces was given to each child in the village. this custom is founded on a superstitious opinion that it will hasten the arrival of the Salmon."

On the coast the first salmon was caught, carefully brushed with moss, slit lengthwise, its heart burned and eyes swallowed, and its mouth was filled with clean sand. Astorians were initially confused after their arrival at the Chinook unwillingness to supply spring salmon the first four weeks of the run unless the whites promised they would only be slit lengthwise, not crosswise, roasted instead of boiled, and entirely consumed the same day they were caught. Anything less, it was believed, imperiled the return of the fish in the future. Explorer David Thompson was equally surprised by the willingness of the tribes to let large numbers of salmon go by to spawn, even when their members were hungry.

In 1855, newly appointed Washington territorial governor Isaac Stevens set out to make his mark in history by resolving the "Indian issue." Stevens had already scouted a potential path for a transcontinental railroad to Puget Sound, gold had been discovered near Fort Colville, and settlers who had been largely confined to Oregon's Willamette Valley and the Sound were anxious to expand into the interior in search of minerals and farmland.

Stevens wanted the Indians immediately confined to reservations so that land boundaries could be made clear. To do so he had to virtually invent for the Northwest tribes the concept of nations, of chiefs, and of property, and explain it in the Chinook jargon of three hundred words. At just the Walla Walla Treaty Council, one of several Stevens hurriedly held, as many natives showed up—an estimated five thousand—as the Territory's entire white population. Native "signers" touched the hand that touched the pen that made an X next to their name. In a series of ten treaty councils from Washington's coast to western Montana, Native Americans surrendered 64 million acres.

"My people, what have you done?" Nez Perce chief Looking Glass exclaimed when he arrived at the end of the Walla Walla Council after a three-year absence on a buffalo hunt. "While I was gone you sold my country."

The one thing tribal negotiators insisted on was their right to the fish, to use the annual gift of the river. The land they could reluctantly give up; salmon were the foundation of their economy.

It wasn't long before the Columbia's first inhabitants realized the import of what Stevens had forced upon them. He promised them two years to move to their new reservations but opened their lands to settlement twelve days after the last treaty was signed. Miners swarmed eastward, were killed, and war began. On his trip back from western Montana to Puget Sound the governor was briefly besieged by howling Walla Walla braves.

And Comcomly's head? It indeed made it to England for display, where it resided for one hundred and seventeen years in the Royal Naval Hospital Museum and survived a bomb attack during Hitler's blitz. In 1952, Burnby Bell of the Clatsop County Historical Society requested the skull's return to Astoria. Loaned in 1956 to the Smithsonian, it came home a final time in 1972, at the insistence of Chinook descendants. It is buried near Comcomly's native village site at Illwaco.

7

In Heathen Lands to Dwell

Arrival of the Nez Perce Indians at the Walla Walla Treaty
Council, May 1855. *(Washington State Historical Society)*

The Cascade Mountains receive their name from a rapid that no
longer exists, the six-mile-long Cascades of the Columbia now
drowned by the pool behind Bonneville Dam. At dawn on the
morning of March 26, 1856, however, the Columbia still made the
last, full-throated roar of its long fall from Canada through this
narrow corridor, foaming over ledges and threading past rocky islands. Here, Yakima war chief Kamiakin recognized, was the
river's most strategic choke point.

Kamiakin had come to war in slow, desperate frustration as
he watched wagon trains trundle to the Columbia Basin. The
Yakima tribal strategist had initially experimented with the economy of the newcomers in the 1840s, trading horses at Fort Vancouver to start a cattle herd east of the Cascades. His antipathy to

the whites grew with their numbers, however, and Kamiakin was ultimately called the Sullen Chief by pioneers. By 1855 he was so furious at Governor Isaac Stevens's arrogant insistence that his tribe be confined to a reservation that at the Walla Walla Treaty Council he bit his lips until they bled. When prospectors began stampeding across Yakima land less than two weeks after the treaties were signed, resentment exploded. Six miners and an Indian agent were killed, Kamiakin routed a company of army regulars in October, and the tribes subsequently made seemingly coordinated attacks across Washington Territory. The chief sent Yakima and Klickitat warriors to control the Cascades the following spring. The most famous pitched battle on the banks of the Columbia River was about to begin.

The spot was well chosen. To a traveler ascending the Columbia, the river pierced the mountains like a gate through a wall. Travelers encountered sheer basalt cliffs at Cape Horn on the north shore and the gray knob of Crown Point on the south. Dark, fir-shrouded mountains confined the river in the miles beyond. The gorge here was the path of the fur traders, the route of the salmon, the corridor of storms, and a funnel for the wind. Until disease depleted their numbers, this breach had been firmly controlled by river Indians. Now the shrunken Cascade tribe uneasily shared the portage area with shops, a small-gauge portage railway, a warehouse, a sawmill, a saloon, and a blockhouse called Fort Rains, this last named for Major Gabriel Rains, not the dreary weather. If the tribes could seize the settlement they could block troops, supplies, and reinforcements at Fort Vancouver from reaching the simmering war on the plateau.

Indian timing was excellent. Most army troops posted at The Dalles were leaving for a spring campaign on the plateau, with only nine soldiers left at Fort Rains. And while war had started the previous year, the settlers at the Cascades were about to be taken by surprise. Their cluster of buildings seemed far removed from the heart of the uprising in eastern Washington. Even the sight of natives dressed in warrior regalia at nearby villages had not caused alarm. Workers departed as usual March 26 to construct two bridges for the new railway.

Then the woods erupted with gun smoke.

A shower of bullets killed one man and wounded several. Survivors ran to Bradford's store. More than forty people crowded inside in fear and confusion, four women joining the men in the fight. Survivors were saved by the fortuitous presence of nine government muskets being shipped upriver to the army: the guns were hastily unpacked, loaded, and fired, halting the native surge. Nearby buildings began to burn. A Walla Walla settler who peeked outside was shot through the brain, dying instantly. Another Indian took aim at a Mrs. Wilkins when she burst from the trees, running desperately for the store. Before he could shoot, a man named Bush fired and killed him.

The noise was cacophonous: the whooping cries of the Indians, screams of the wounded and the terrified, the roar of muskets, shouts from confused people on both sides trying to organize an attack and a defense. A steep hillside overlooked the store and the Indians were able to hurl rocks against the building, shaking the wooden structure with dull, vibrating booms. Firebrands and hot irons hit the roof. Desperately short of water, the defenders poked an opening in the shingles and extinguished the blazes with pork brine. One wounded man, shot through the wrist, was trapped in a hollow on the riverbank. His wife and children anxiously watched and waited as he tried, and failed, to reach the store in the crossfire. He would lie there for two days before rescue, dying soon afterward.

At Fort Rains, surprised soldiers and settlers suffered three killed and eight wounded by the time the survivors gathered in the blockhouse. Again they stood off the natives. Across on the Oregon shore the steamboats *Wasco* and *Mary* came under fire as they built up steam to escape to The Dalles. A black man named Dick Turpin grabbed a gun, jumped from the *Wasco* to a flatboat, and was shot, falling into the river and drowning. Pilot Hardin Chenowith ran up to the pilothouse and lay on the floor to steer by responding to directions shouted from the lower deck, bullets splintering the boards just over his head. As the boats pulled away some settlers rowed out in skiffs to clamber aboard, while others remained pinned down.

The natives set fire to houses, a sawmill, and lumberyards. As night fell they lit Bradford's new warehouse, turning the scene too bright to risk trips to the river for water. The besieged settlers initially survived on two dozen bottles of ale and a few bottles of whiskey, but when these gave out a friendly Spokane Indian trapped with the whites volunteered to take a pail to the river for water. He stripped naked, sprinted to the river when the warehouse fire quieted, and returned with a full bucket. He eventually filled four barrels.

Stalemate ensued. The settlers were too weak and frightened to rout the attacking natives, while the natives had no weapons to pry out a fortified foe. The battle was reduced to sniping. Rescue for the besieged came on the third day when the *Wasco* and the *Mary* returned from The Dalles with a load of blue-coated soldiers and a barge carrying horses. Help also arrived from Fort Vancouver. The U.S. Army had established a permanent post at the Bay Company site in 1849 after the international boundary had been established, and a settler escaping in a boat had alerted the new post. A young lieutenant named Phil Sheridan led a party of dragoons upriver. As they drew near, a bullet grazed the future Civil War general's nose, killing a soldier next to him. Sheridan hoped to trap the Indians between his force and the contingent under the command of Lieutenant Colonel Edward Steptoe that had arrived from The Dalles, but an ill-timed bugle call by Steptoe's men alerted the Indians and allowed the Yakimas and Klickitats to melt into the mountains.

The soldiers could only round up frightened Cascade Indians left behind. Eventually nine were hanged, though later evidence suggested relatively few of these Indians had participated in the attack. Residents at the Cascades lost sixteen dead and twelve wounded. A last fierce attempt by the Columbia River's original inhabitants to assert control had failed, a result ordained by the events of the previous two decades.

Indian resistance in the Pacific Northwest was an act of desperation, coming too late to have any hope of success. Along the Columbia the farmer and miner had followed the trapper, and change piled upon change. The odds for Native Americans worsened after the battle at the Cascades. By the time the Nez Perce made their epic fighting retreat toward Canada, in 1877, steamboats thronged the river, Columbia River wheat was being shipped to Liverpool on an imposing fleet of tall ships, Portland's waterfront was lined with brick and cast-iron buildings, and the telephone had been invented. Yet it was not superior technology that first doomed the river people. The agent of change was not guns or steam engines, but microbes and Scripture. The result was catastrophic.

Disease killed far more in the American West than bullets or arrows. The Oregon and California Trail pioneers, for example, died in numbers on their trek variously estimated at between one in seventeen and one in twenty-five. Only a small fraction was due to combat with Indians. Historian John Unruh, Jr., calculated that between 1840 and 1860 some three hundred and sixty-two immigrants were killed by Indians and the immigrants in turn killed four hundred and twenty-six natives: about 4 percent of the twelve thousand immigrants Unruh calculates died traveling west. Nine out of ten whites who succumbed died from disease, particularly cholera.

The toll was far worse among the natives. The reason that Oregon's Willamette Valley has Anglo place names such as Portland, Salem, and Eugene while Washington State has Indian names such as Spokane, Yakima, Tacoma, Wenatchee, and Seattle is that disease came first and most completely to Oregon's lower Columbia and Willamette tribes who traded so avidly with the sea captains and fur trappers. By the time significant numbers of pioneers settled in the Willamette Valley, few Native Americans remained. Smallpox struck in 1775, 1801, 1836, 1853, and 1862. An 1830 malaria epidemic killed not only Chief Comcomly, but an estimated 75 percent of the natives in the vicinity of Fort Vancouver. University of Washington anthropologist Robert Boyd has estimated that by 1841, smallpox, measles, influenza, dysentery, whooping cough, typhus, and typhoid fever had reduced lower Columbia tribes an estimated 92 percent from their numbers at the time of Lewis and Clark, or from fourteen thousand to twelve hundred. Native Americans were increasingly powerless, evident in the disposition of their lands. In 1851 the survivors on the lower river ceded the lowest sixty miles of the Columbia and land for tens of miles on either side for $91,300.

The same pattern was occurring east of the Cascades and north on Puget Sound. Measles, contracted either during a raiding party to California or from Oregon Trail immigrants, killed a third to half of the Cayuse and substantial numbers of Walla Walla and Nez Perce in 1847. The powerful Yakima declined from an estimated seven thousand at the time of white contact to two thousand by the time Isaac Stevens insisted on the treaties that led to the 1856 attack on the Cascades. During the 1855–58 war across the Northwest, tribes probably mustered at most two thousand warriors to combat a Pacific Northwest white population already at least ten times that size. "Half of all North American Indians died of European diseases before Europeans ever saw them," Idaho state archaeologist Tom Green has noted.

The lower Columbia tribes called the 1830–32 measles epidemic the Cold Sick. Surviving natives did not dare touch the bodies to prepare them for burial. Indians burned some of their own villages in a futile attempt to contain the contamination. In desperation they resorted to their sweat lodges and cold plunges into the Columbia, a traditional remedy that only accelerated the toll. "The living sufficed not to bury the dead," a trader recorded, "but fled in terror to the seacoast, abandoning the dead and dying to the birds and beasts of prey. Every village presented a scene harrowing to the feelings; the canoes were there drawn up upon the beach, the nets extended on the willow-boughs to dry, the very dogs appeared as ever, watchful, but there was not the cheerful sound of the human voice."

Artist Paul Kane saw a dozen riverside villages wiped out by dysentery. "They died of this disease in such numbers that their bodies lay unburied on the river's banks, and many were to be met with floating down the stream," he wrote.

Some whites attributed the devastation to the will of God. "Has the fiat, then, gone forth," wrote Britisher John McLean of Fort Vancouver, "that the aboriginal inhabitants of America shall make way for another race of men?" Few whites recorded any guilt or sorrow over this apocalyptic annihilation, or wondered whether the culture that was succumbing had anything to teach the one supplanting it.

It was in the midst of this catastrophe that most settlers first saw, and judged, Indians. The social decay resulting from these levels of mortality had to be enormous. In 1842 eight of ten Clatsop children born were reportedly left to die or were killed by parents unable to care for them. One account by pioneer Joseph Gervais, who lived with the Indians, reported seeing babies in the devastated villages sucking with futility on the breasts of dead mothers.

Aboriginal culture showed other strains. Women had been purchased for sex, alcohol had become a trade item, and new teachings and ideas were challenging ancient beliefs and moral-ity. Missionaries undermined Native American self-confidence and economy by insisting on a conversion to agriculture. "No savage people, to my knowledge, has ever been Christianized on the wing," asserted missionary Henry Spalding, who founded the Nez Perce mission at Lapwai, Idaho. If migratory hunters and gatherers were to be saved from damnation, many missionaries reasoned, they had to be held to a lifestyle that kept them in one place long enough to be indoctrinated.

No story better illustrates the tragic collision of cultures than that of Marcus and Narcissa Whitman, two idealistic Presbyterian missionaries from upstate New York who set out to save "the heathen" and, faced with skepticism and indifference to their teachings, turned instead to the promotion of white immigration to the Columbia country. In their eleven years of missionary work in the Walla Walla Valley, the Whitmans failed to fully convert a single Native American to their stern and demanding creed. They did, however, see the Cayuse they had come to save devastated by white disease. Mission resident Nathan Kimball described in 1847 "dead Indians hanging across the [mission] fence, the same as you would hang a sack of wheat, waiting for coffins." In response, the Cayuse finally exploded into violence, turning the Whitmans into martyrs that only accelerated white political control of the river country.

The Whitman story began in 1831 with the Nez Perce and Flathead delegation that journeyed to St. Louis to seek the white man's "Book of Heaven" and whatever spiritual power it could bring. A garbled version of this visit, interpreted by Protestant churches in the East as a plea for missionaries, was printed a year later in the *Christian Advocate and Journal*, a publication of the Methodist Episcopal Church in New York.

First to respond in 1834 was missionary Jason Lee. For protection in making their way west, Lee and four associates joined the commercial expedition of Nathaniel Wyeth. This Cambridge merchant had first marched overland to the Columbia two years before to challenge the Hudson's Bay Company for the Pacific Northwest fur trade and the river's rich runs of salmon: his first group of twenty-four employees imposingly armed and identically dressed in coarse woolen jackets, pantaloons, striped cotton shirts, and cowhide boots. This military display did not prevent thirteen from deserting during the hard overland trek, however, and by the time Wyeth reached Fort Vancouver most of his supplies were gone.

Undiscouraged, Wyeth returned East for reinforcements and subsequently built Fort Hall in eastern Idaho and Fort William on Sauvie Island, just downriver from Fort Vancouver. The fur trade was in decline, however. Wyeth's fur company partnerships fell apart, his Hawaiian laborers deserted or died of disease, a supply ship arrived too late to capitalize on salmon runs, and fourteen employees were killed by Indians. Wyeth's New England nets and fishing techniques worked poorly. Undercut by the Hudson's Bay Company, he left the Northwest after four years. However, his journeys back and forth helped establish the path of the Oregon Trail, and his 1834 trek brought Lee to the Willamette Valley.

The missionary's choice of the valley was puzzling since it was hundreds of miles from the Nez Perce and Flatheads who were reportedly anxious for Christian teaching. The Flathead were embroiled in combat with the Blackfeet, however, and Lee reasoned that the agricultural potential of the Willamette site could make it a headquarters for a network of missions elsewhere in the Northwest. Indeed, Lee's organization did add additional missions in western Oregon and western Washington between 1836 and 1838.

The missions did Native Americans little good, however. Indians west of the Cascades were dying in such large numbers, and so resisted conversion, that the posts were far more significant as an aid to white pioneers than as a civilizing influence on tribes. Lee instead became an enthusiastic proponent of white settlement and American political recognition of Oregon, returning to the East in 1839 and then sailing back to the Columbia with fifty-one new settlers in what was dubbed the Great Reinforcement. After consuming more than $100,000 and converting almost no one, Lee was recalled in 1843 for having spent too much on "secular activities" (encouraging American pioneering) and failing to account properly for his expenditures.

While Lee concentrated his activities on the lower Columbia, other missionaries began reaching the interior. In 1835, Samuel Parker of the Congregational Church recruited a young doctor named Marcus Whitman to help him scout potential mission sites. The pair got an escort across the Plains by joining the annual fur traders' caravan to the Rockies. Whitman removed a three-inch iron arrowhead from the back of famed mountain man Jim Bridger there, a feat that impressed both the trappers and watching Nez Perce and Flathead Indians. The natives indicated they were indeed anxious for aid, so Whitman returned East to recruit volunteers. Parker scouted ahead, reached Fort Vancouver, and then returned to the United States by sea after leaving some letters of advice.

The thirty-two-year-old Whitman persuaded a minister named Henry Spalding and his wife, Eliza, to change the site of their intended mission from Missouri to Oregon. Then he married Narcissa Prentiss, an idealistic, pretty, but somewhat naïve twenty-seven-year-old schoolteacher with romantic ideas about missionary work and a fine singing voice. At a time when no white woman had yet crossed the continent, the momentous decision of the couple to go to the Columbia awed their neighbors. When the Whitmans were wed on February 18, 1836, the ceremony ended with the hymn, "Yes, My Native Land! I Love Thee!" As the song built the congregation began to falter, overcome with the knowledge that in the morning the couple would set out for distant Oregon. When the last stanza was reached, only Narcissa's voice could be heard above the sobs in the church. She sang:

> In the deserts let me labor,
> On the mountains let me tell,
> How He died—the blessed Savior
> To redeem a world from hell!
> Let me hasten, let me hasten,
> Far in heathen lands to dwell.

No wagon had yet made the journey, and some doubted the missionaries' wheeled vehicle could even cross the Rockies. The missionary group planned to join the annual trek of traders from St. Louis to the fur rendezvous at Green River, Wyoming, and proceed from there to the Nez Perce country, where the present-day states of Washington, Oregon, and Idaho join.

The missionaries' route would be followed by tens of thousands of immigrants in the next two decades. The path of Lewis and Clark up the Missouri River had already been abandoned for a more direct and level passage up the Platte River to South Pass across the Rockies, a rise so flat and gentle that many travelers did not recognize when they had crossed the Continental Divide. What became known as the Oregon Trail then traversed the barren Snake River plain and crossed the Blue Mountains to reach the Columbia River.

Finding South Pass had been one positive result of the ill-fated Astorians. Robert Stuart and six companions had discovered the pass as they returned east in 1812. Just two weeks after the Stuart party arrived in St. Louis, a newspaper noted, "It appears that a journey across the continent of North America might be performed with a wagon, there being no obstruction in the whole route that any person would dare to call a mountain in addition to it being very much the most direct and short one to go from this place to the mouth of the Columbia River." This proved too optimistic. The first wagons did not cross all the way to the Columbia until 1841, five years after the Whitmans and Spaldings.

For such an ambitious trek, a more unpromising combination of missionaries can scarcely be imagined. Spalding had courted Narcissa, been rejected when he proposed marriage, and later married the plainer, deeply religious Eliza Hart. Henry Spalding was of illegitimate birth, shy, quick-tempered, and lacking in the social graces the somewhat snobbish Narcissa put high value in—and he had also made it clear he judged Narcissa as lacking the commitment for serious religious work. Marcus Whitman was energetic and ambitious but unable to win consensus from other missionaries. Narcissa was brave and well-meaning but missed her family, disliked solitude, and had no training or experience in adapting to other cultures. These two mismatched and ill-prepared couples were joined by a carpenter, William H. Gray, whose contentious personality made him almost universally disliked. His later written complaints to the missionary board in the East forced Marcus Whitman to make a dangerous and unprecedented midwinter return across the Plains to reverse a decision to close the missions.

These and later missionaries never developed a happy unity. The same strong-minded idealism that fired people with Christian zeal made it difficult for them to cooperate. They quarreled almost constantly about strategies and goals, resulting in separate stations being set up hundreds of miles apart. The Asa Bowen Smiths eventually quit their mission at Kamiah to start over in Hawaii, and Gray gave up his intended mission at the mouth of the Yakima River to homestead in the Willamette Valley. At Tshimakain, Cushing Eells admitted in 1846, "We have been here about seven years & I don't know that we have reason to think one soul has been converted to God." One early Columbia Basin missionary, Asa Munger, went insane and died after nailing himself like Christ to his fireplace, expecting to rise again on the third day.

Such bizarre tragedy was unimagined as the party optimistically set out. A miscalculation by Spalding resulted in their having to hurry to catch up to the fur trade caravan, but once this was done the traveling was easier. During a rest break at Fort Laramie, Narcissa became pregnant. The missionaries' wagon made it across South Pass, establishing that overland pioneer transit to the West Coast was theoretically possible—though the two women prayed that the trouble-plagued vehicle would be abandoned long before the doggedly determined men finally conceded they had to. The wagon finally broke down for the final time along the Snake River in southern Idaho. Whitman and Spalding converted it to a two-wheeled cart they took as far as Fort Boise, then abandoned the cart and continued by horse to the Columbia at Fort Walla Walla and then by canoe to Fort Vancouver, arriving on September 12, 1836. Except for a scattering of fur posts and Lee's mission, the Northwest was still mostly empty of white settlement. Seventeen or eighteen non-Indian families, about ninety people, lived in Oregon's Willamette Valley. There were virtually no settlers north of Fort Vancouver or east of the Cascade Mountains.

Change was under way, however. The same year the missionaries arrived saw operation of the first steamboat on the Columbia, *The Beaver*. While Factor John McLoughlin was unimpressed with the craft's performance and soon dispatched it to Puget Sound (it consumed forty cords of wood a day, could not ascend the Cascades, and thus could not reach any other Bay post on the Columbia) its shipment from London was a symbolic indication of the Columbia's significance as the primary communication and trade corridor between the Northwest coast and the interior.

Narcissa was taken with the opulence of Fort Vancouver, calling it the "New York of the Pacific." Fields and pastures occupied forest clearings for fifteen miles along the Columbia and five miles inland. Outside the central log stockade, *voyageurs,* Hawaiian Kanakas, Iroquois trappers, and native Indians lived in a bustling community of more than seven hundred people. Inside, the Scottish directors of the Bay operation lived and dined in segregated, baronial splendor. To discuss accounts and strategy, they met each midday in the handsome white house of chief factor John McLoughlin for meals on fine blue china that were changed with every course. Narcissa was able to buy linen sheets, white blankets, and cookware at the fort for her new home.

The man who led this enterprise was a six-foot four-inch physician named John McLoughlin whose wild shock of white hair resulted in his being dubbed the "white-headed eagle" by the natives. Stern and kind, ambitious and intimidating, he reigned like a wilderness duke.

McLoughlin was tough: he crossed the continent to his new job in a record eighty-four days and his Bay Company superior, Sir George Simpson, described him as "such a figure as I should not like to meet on a dark night in one of the bye lanes in the neighborhood of London." When a stuffy pastor criticized his common-law marriage to a Chippewa woman, McLoughlin soundly thrashed him. The chief factor was no frontier roughneck, however. Educated and visionary, in his two decades at the new post he started a library and school, and provided river transport, food, tools, seed, and credit to American settlers entering the Oregon country. The Bay Company also supported visits by British naturalists. Scottish botanist David Douglas, for whom the Douglas fir is named, was sent to the Columbia in 1825 by the Royal Horticultural Society of London. He crisscrossed the Northwest for two years, traveling seven thousand miles at a pace of up to fifty miles a day. The natives called him the "Grass Man" for his tireless collecting and cataloguing of plants. Ornithologist and physician John Townsend came in 1834 and was called the "Bird Chief" for his collection. Fort Vancouver had an exhibit of stuffed animals and Indian artifacts that naturalists had collected.

The Columbia's bar permitting, annual supply by sea with goods from England permitted certain luxuries. And each spring, a company "express" of new recruits and mail would cross Canada and boat down the river from Canoe Camp, collecting the winter's production of furs from lesser forts along the way. The *voyageurs* would stop just before their arrival at Fort Vancouver to don their most brilliant sashes and feathered caps, then sweep up to the shore below the stockade with a chorus of song that was answered by a salute of cannon fire. After celebration and meetings the furs would be loaded on the supply ship for its return to England and the procession of bateaux and canoes would reverse upriver with trade goods for the winter season. By early fall the last boat would be back at Canoe Camp and men leaving the Columbia District would form a fall express eastward across the Rockies, carrying return mail.

This imperial network initially kept rival Americans out. Simpson ordered virtual fur extermination south and east of the Columbia to discourage competitors. A party of thirty-five or forty Bay men was sent annually to the high, cold desert of the Snake River plain to trap out all furs, a mission that came to be dreaded for its risk of Indian attack, storms, hunger, and rough travel. "I got home from the Snake, thank God, and when that Cuntry will see me again, the beaver will have gould skin," wrote one Bay man. The final Snake River expedition of the Bay Company's Peter Skene Ogden in 1829–30 was marred when nine men were drowned and five hundred beaver skins were lost at The Dalles. When Joseph Paul subsequently died of beaver disease, Ogden lamented, "There remains now only one man living of all the Snake men of 1819, and rather extraordinarily all have been killed, with the exception of two who died a natural death."

It was into this corner of British Empire that the American missionaries proposed to settle, with McLoughlin's blessing and help. Spalding chose a mission site in Nez Perce territory on Idaho's Clearwater River. The Whitmans ignored McLoughlin's advice and chose a place amid the Cayuse tribe in the Walla Walla Valley at Wai-i-lat-pu, or "The Place of the Rye Grass."

The couple's reasoning is understandable. Wai-i-lat-pu was a spot both pleasant and strategic, next to the Walla Walla River where the grass was stirrup-high. Just ten miles from the fur post of Fort Walla Walla, it was on the most direct route between the Great Plains and the Columbia. It was twenty miles from good timber, however, and agriculture had to be initiated from scratch. Arriving in November when food was scarce, the couple had to kill and eat ten horses that winter to survive. Nor was it in the territory of tribes that had requested missionaries. While the Cayuse spoke Nez Perce, they were of mixed opinion about these newcomers. Skilled at horse breeding, they owned so many—some families controlled fifteen hundred ponies—that the term "cayuse" came to be a term used throughout the West for any Indian pony. These proud people were not at all certain they needed salvation.

The hardworking missionaries soon managed to construct buildings that eventually reached the comfort of what had been left behind in New York State, but tragedy clouded their early effort. Narcissa gave birth to her only child, Alice Clarissa, on her twenty-ninth birthday, March 14, 1837. At the age of two the child drowned in the Walla Walla River, an accident of intense sorrow and self-blame from which Narcissa may never have fully recovered. She sat with her dead child for three days, only agreeing to her burial after the body began to decompose.

In compensation the Whitmans took in orphans. The year after Alice Clarissa's death, mountain man Joe Meek persuaded the Whitmans to care for his child Helen Mar, whose Nez Perce mother had deserted Meek. Then Jim Bridger sent his mixed-blood daughter Mary Ann to live with the Whitmans. The missionaries also took in seven children from immigrants Henry and Naomi Sager, who died on the Oregon Trail. By 1844 the Whitmans had direct responsibility for eleven children and taught several more. No school had been started for the Cayuse.

For the Columbia's native inhabitants, the eleven years following the Whitmans' 1836 arrival brought tumultuous change. Disease continued to deplete their numbers. Just as ominously, non-Indian numbers began to grow. By 1840 there were about one hundred and fifty Americans in the Willamette Valley. That year thirteen Americans traversed the Oregon Trail. In 1841 twenty-four arrived, and in 1842 the number was one hundred and twenty-five. As a precaution, the Bay Company ordered establishment of its post at Victoria on Vancouver Island in case the lower Columbia wound up in American hands. It was a wise move. In 1843, Whitman returned from his confrontation with the mission board and led the first big wagon train of a thousand people: the Great Migration. By 1846 the American population of the Oregon country had swollen to six thousand. With the influx of American pioneers the United States pressed its claim to the entire area, including present-day British Columbia. The presidential campaign slogan "Fifty-four-forty or fight" referred to that geographic parallel. Britain was unwilling to accept that claim, but also realized the difficulty of holding the boundary at Fort Vancouver. In 1846, the United States faced war with Mexico and Britain war in India, and neither wanted a clash over the distant, undeveloped Northwest. The two countries compromised by extending the Forty-ninth Parallel boundary, already in use across the plains, to the Pacific.

American occupation of the river region seemed far from inevitable when the Hudson's Bay Company ruled its fur empire. Many thought pioneering across such a huge distance was at least impractical, at worst fatal. The same year Whitman was helping guide that first great wagon train, Britain's *Edinburgh Review* predicted that "Oregon will never be colonized overland from the eastern United States." Horace Greeley's *New York Daily Tribune* agreed, warning that "we do not believe nine-tenths [of the immigrants] will ever reach the Columbia alive." In reality, 350,000 Americans traveled West between 1840 and 1869, the majority to California but a substantial share to the Northwest.

Just why they did so remains something of an historical mystery. There was still plenty of unclaimed farmland in the Midwest and the two-thousand-mile journey was expensive and hazardous. Certainly the pioneers were not necessarily skilled frontiersmen or even knowledgeable farmers or craftsmen: many set out hopelessly overloaded with only a vague sense of what they needed to bring or where the trail led. The route was soon dotted with furniture, trunks, stoves, sacks of food—and graves. And yet they came, year after year after year.

Some were motivated by patriotism, the claims of Manifest Destiny. Others wanted first pick of land. To a few, the epic distance itself was attractive: they could flee past failures, social restrictions, the slavery issue, failed romances, or boredom. Certainly the move to greener pastures was perhaps the defining idea of American history, an assumption that persists today. Americans still move to escape the boredom of the small town and the aggravations of the big city, to get away from irksome neighbors or to find new friends, to discover a place unspoiled where they hope their own new home will not contribute to spoiling. And having come so far, the pioneers immediately set about trying to change the Columbia River country into something resembling the place they had come from. At Fort Vancouver, the

Bay Company's formal dinners tried to duplicate European culinary ritual. At the Whitman Mission, the missionaries used irrigation ditches to try to duplicate the farm landscape left behind in upper New York.

The Americans wanted to extinguish the wilderness. In 1858, Lieutenant John Mullan, who would help site a new road across the basin, recorded: "Night after night I have lain out in the unbeaten forests, or the pathless prairie, with no bed but a few pine leaves, with no pillow but my saddle. In my imagination [I] heard the whistle of an engine, the whir of the machinery, the paddle of steamboat wheels as they plowed the waters. In my enthusiasm I saw the country thickly populated, thousands pouring over the borders to make homes in this far distant land."

The most hazardous part of the Oregon Trail was in the Columbia Basin. The establishment of military posts on the Great Plains, the lack of mountains, and the plentiful grass and water in spring made the first half of the trip relatively easy. Once across South Pass the dangers multiplied. About 90 percent of the pioneers killed in battles with Native Americans were killed west of the Continental Divide. The Snake River plain was hot, dry, dusty, and monotonous. Oregon's Blue Mountains were steep and the Columbia River was dangerous. Rafting its gorge came at a time when families and their stock were exhausted. "O! the dangers of that river!" Narcissa wrote in 1838. "Scarcely a year passes without the loss of several lives. We have been told that the [Hudson's Bay] Company has lost upwards of three hundred men in the Columbia."

For all practical purposes the Oregon Trail ended at The Dalles, a hundred miles short of the promised Willamette Valley. The immigrants had the difficult choice of trying to either run the river or take a rugged ninety-mile toll-road detour across the Cascades on the shoulder of Mount Hood. Many ventured onto the Columbia, some with disastrous results. In 1843 the Applegate family built rafts and lost three drowned and another crippled for life.

A particularly heartbreaking account is that of Elizabeth Geer, whose family made the trek in 1847. Setting out for Oregon on April 21, they arrived at The Dalles on October 27 without serious mishap. By then the mountains were too snowy to cross, so on October 30 the Geers and the Adam Polk family began constructing a raft to descend the Columbia. Tired, broke, and hungry, the two families traded a shirt to Indians for half a peck of potatoes.

Lashing together eighteen logs, the pioneers took the wheels off their wagons, put the vehicles on their rude vessel, and shoved off on November 2. The logs weren't buoyant enough to carry the weight, and the cold river water ran three inches high over the top of the raft. Rain was incessant and gorge winds kicked up steep waves. By November 5, Adam Polk was seriously ill. No one could get properly warm; even when they tied to the bank at night, their fire could not defeat the savagery of the wind. By November 8 the settlers had one day's food left. Polk died the next day.

Geer's husband left to find food and came back November 10 after buying fifty pounds of meat. Once more the party pushed off into the broad river, but the wind forced them to shore. It took Geer's husband and her son an hour and a half to secure the raft to the bank, water now knee-deep over the logs.

With no alternative, they pressed on. On November 14 the party finally reached the crude portage road around the Cascades of the Columbia. They unloaded their wagons, reattached the wheels, and set out. Here are excerpts from Geer's diary:

> *Nov. 15.* Rainy day.
>
> *Nov. 16.* Rain all day.
>
> *Nov. 17.* Rainy weather.
>
> *Nov. 18.* My husband is sick. It rains and snows. We start this morning around the falls with our wagon. We have five miles to go. I carry my babe and lead, mud and water almost to my knees. It is the worst road that a team could possibly travel. I went ahead with my children and I was afraid to look behind me for fear of seeing the wagons turn over into the mud and water with everything in them. My children gave out with cold and fatigue, and could not travel, and the boys had to unhitch the oxen, and bring them, and carry the children on to camp. I was so cold and numb that I could not tell by the feeling that I had any feet at all. We started this morning at sunrise and did not get to camp until after dark, and there was not one dry thread on one of us—

not even my babe. I had carried my babe and I was so
fatigued that I could scarcely speak or step. When I got
here I found my husband lying in Welch's wagon, very
sick. . . .

Nov. 20. Rain all day. It is almost an impossibility to
cook and quite [impossible] to keep warm or dry. I froze
or chilled my feet so that I cannot wear a shoe, so I have
to go around in the cold weather barefooted.

Nov. 21. Rain all day. The whole care of everything
falls upon my shoulders. I cannot write any more at present.

Nov. 27. Embarked once more on the Columbia on a
flat boat. Rain all day, though the waves threatened
hard to sink us. Passed Fort Vancouver in the night.
Landed a mile below. My husband has never left his
bed since he was taken sick.

Nov. 28. Still moving on the water.

Nov. 29. Landing at Portland on the Willamette,
twelve miles above the mouth, at 11 o'clock at night.

Feb. 1. Rain all day. This day my dear husband, my
last remaining friend, died.

Despite such tragedy the majority of pioneers who set out
for the Columbia River country did succeed. One reason was Fort
Vancouver's McLoughlin. He provided boats in the Columbia
River Gorge, employed the newcomers in construction, gave the
starving food, and by the spring of 1844 had advanced $31,000 in
company credit to more than four hundred needy settlers. This
was shrewd business: most of the loans were paid back, the stim-
ulation of the economy inflated prices, and supplying the newcomers proved lucrative. It also, however, invited Americans into
the region when America and Britain still contested ownership, a
consequence that drew increasing criticism from McLoughlin's
superiors.

When the boundary issue was finally settled, McLoughlin
quit. Tired of being criticized by his superiors and frustrated that
they did not press prosecution of the killers of his son after a
brawl in Sitka, he moved to Oregon City and became an American citizen. Rather than getting a warm welcome from the settlers
he had done so much to help, McLoughlin was regarded as a rich

Briton and his move a cynical land grab. Missionaries had squatted on land McLoughlin had claimed in 1829 at the Falls of the Willamette and in ensuing court action he lost much of the Oregon City holdings that should have made him rich. Visionary, kind, fair, imperious, violent, and ultimately more loyal to his employers and the new pioneers than they were to him, he died bitter and mostly alone.

Another reason for immigrant success was the missionaries. They guided wagons, dispensed advice, and experimented with agriculture, Whitman's mission becoming an important stopover for exhausted families. Some elected to winter there rather than face the Columbia or Cascades in autumn.

This work signaled a critical shift in the couple's interpretation of their role. Increasingly the missionaries saw white settlement as the hope of the Columbia River country. It would swamp native culture, forcing Indians to convert and assimilate. While the Spaldings had proved adept at learning Nez Perce and translating the Bible into terms that tribe could understand, the Whitmans never warmed to the Cayuse. Narcissa found herself repelled by the curiosity and familiarity of the Native Americans. She considered the tribe's sexual mores, gambling, horse racing, and dancing to be sin and the entire people doomed to damnation unless they had an evangelical Protestant conversion—and did not hesitate to tell the Cayuse so. In her letters she regularly referred to them as "heathen" and herself as "alone."

Marcus was often away on medical or political missions and found the task of encouraging white settlement more rewarding than trying to convert the Cayuse. In 1844, Whitman wrote his parents that he regarded the missionary effort as futile: "Although the Indians have made and are making rapid advance in religious knowledge and civilization, yet it cannot be hoped that time will be allowed to mature either the work of Christianization or civilization before the white settlers will demand the soil and seek the removal of both the Indians and the mission. What Americans desire of this kind they always effect, and it is equally useless to oppose it or desire it otherwise. Indeed, I am fully convinced that when a people refuse or neglect to fill the designs of Providence, they ought not to complain at the results; and so it is equally useless for Christians to be anxious on their account. The Indians have in no case obeyed the command to multiply and replenish the earth, and they cannot stand in the way of others doing so."

The Cayuse found little appeal in the cultural change the missionaries offered. "We must use the plough as well as the Bible," wrote missionary Elkanah Walker, "if we would do anything to benefit the Indians. They must be settled before they can be enlightened." Farming was hard and tedious, the idea of sin seemed depressing, and the religion joyless. The natives were simply mystified when Mount St. Helens erupted in 1843 and the missionaries at The Dalles broke into a joyful hymn, "How Awful Is Our God!" It made no sense to them that Marcus Whitman could not be provoked into a fight—he turned the other cheek on two occasions when struck—yet would beat Cayuse who stole from his garden. In 1842 some of the Cayuse deliberately turned their horses into the Whitmans' cornfield. When Marcus protested, he was asked, "What have you missionaries ever paid for this corn land?" The answer, or course, was nothing. The frustrated natives came close to assaulting Marcus with an ax.

Whites meanwhile both criticized the mission for making money by selling supplies and used it as a temporary resting point. In 1846 fifty immigrants wintered at the mission en route to Oregon, and as winter began in 1847, seventy did so. "Oh! I wish I had a little chamber where I could secrete myself!" Narcissa wrote of the growing pressures.

Things were little better at the Spalding mission. Native enrollment at the Lapwai School fell from two hundred and thirty-four in 1842 to zero by 1847. Spalding had imported sheep and had become obsessed with protecting them from predation by dogs and wolves and from theft by the Nez Perce. He requested enough poison to kill twenty thousand wolves. The Hudson's Bay Company's Frank Ermatinger remarked that "Mr. Spalding had got so that he did nothing but whip Indians and kill dogs." The stage was set for disaster.

By the autumn of 1847, about nine thousand non-Indians had settled in the Oregon country, two-thirds of them in the upper Willamette Valley just south of the Columbia River. That same season, measles and dysentery killed half the Cayuse tribe within two months. Marcus Whitman's attempt to halt the epidemic proved fruitless. It was Cayuse tradition that an unsuccessful medicine man could be killed by relatives of the dead patient.

Tom Hill, a mixed-blood Delaware Indian living at the mission, had already told the Cayuse the sorry fate of eastern tribes like his own. A rumor began that Whitman was spreading a poison in the air. William Gray had lent credibility to such stories by putting an emetic in potatoes to discourage Indian theft. Perhaps the Cayuse had also heard that after the Astorian ship *Tonquin* was blown up in 1811, Astorian fur partner Duncan McDougall assembled the natives at the mouth of the Columbia, held a bottle in the air, and warned it contained smallpox he would unleash should Fort Astoria be attacked. The Indians called McDougall "the Great Smallpox Chief."

When the situation finally exploded on November 29, 1847, there were seventy-four people at the Whitman mission. The Cayuse struck after lunch. As one brave distracted Marcus Whitman by starting an argument, another tomahawked him from behind. John Sager, one of the adopted orphans, reached for a pistol but was killed before he could get it. Mary Ann Bridger, another adoptee, ran, crying, "They have killed father!" Then a shot rang out, apparently a signal for Indians in the yard to begin a general assault. Narcissa went to a window and was quickly hit in the left breast. She fell screaming, then staggered up and helped organize a temporary defense of children and wounded men in an upstairs room. Finally warned by the Indians that the building would be set on fire, she came downstairs. Upon seeing her husband's mutilated body she collapsed on a sofa, weak from loss of blood. What must she have thought at that moment, if she remembered the brave hymn and idealism on her wedding day more than eleven years before?

Two men, the wounded Andrew Rodgers and the mixed-blood Joe Lewis, picked up the sofa and carried it outdoors. Then Lewis dropped his end, jumped out of the way, and the Indians began firing at Narcissa and Rodgers, killing both. As Mrs. Whitman's body rolled into the mud one Cayuse grabbed her head by the hair and struck her face with a riding whip.

The death toll eventually mounted to fourteen as adult men were hunted down. Narcissa was the only woman killed. The remaining women and children were taken into captivity, where at least one was sexually abused and two children, including adoptee Helen Mar, died of measles. A month after the massacre the survivors were ransomed by Peter Skene Ogden for sixty-two blankets, sixty-three shirts, twelve muskets, ammunition, and tobacco.

The result of the assault was the opposite of what the desperate Cayuse must have hoped. Instead of discouraging white settlement, the war encouraged it. Congress had procrastinated on pleas to organize an Oregon Territory because of the debate over whether to permit slavery in the Northwest. After the attack on the Whitmans, Helen Mar's father, Joe Meek, hurried to Washington, D.C., to demand immediate political recognition and protection. The buckskinned mountain man made the trip in a record two months and was a sensation in the capital as he graphically described the horrors of the Whitman massacre. On August 13, 1848, a bill creating the Oregon Territory was passed and Meek was appointed U.S. Marshal.

Meanwhile five hundred Oregon militia volunteers marched to the Walla Walla Valley to punish the tribe. The main body of Indians eluded pursuit for two years but, unable to collect adequate food, finally surrendered five of their members to the whites to end the "war." All five were hanged in Oregon City, the hangman being Meek.

The hanging showed that if the Native Americans had not converted to evangelical Christianity as the Whitmans had hoped, they had remembered some of its teachings. Facing the noose, Cayuse leader Tilokaikt reminded his captors, "Did not your missionaries tell us that Christ died to save his people? So die we, to save our people."

The Whitman tragedy opened thirty years of intermittent Indian-pioneer warfare in the Pacific Northwest. Natives rarely concentrated the firepower necessary to rout their foes, while whites proved inept at catching their opponents. The army did not so much outfight the tribes as outlast them. When the soldiers finally triumphed at the Battle of Spokane Plains, they shot eight hundred horses to help break tribal power. Armed with new Sharps rifles that fired minié balls with twice the range of trade muskets, the troops killed or wounded scores of Indians without the natives being able to get close enough to make their own guns effective.

The defeated tribes were confined to reservations. West of the Cascade Mountains these enclaves tended to be small sites located near traditional fishing rivers. To the east they were larger, and a number of separate tribes and bands were consolidated on each one: fourteen different groups on the Yakima Reservation, for example. On the lower Columbia River and in Oregon's Willamette Valley, no reservations were provided and no treaties ever ratified; most of the aboriginal inhabitants were already dead of disease.

On-and-off conflict continued in the deserts of the southern Columbia basin along the wagon routes. In 1877 the Nez Perce of northeastern Oregon and southeastern Washington stumbled into war as their lands were invaded and they made an epic fighting retreat across Idaho and into western Montana, hoping to escape to Canada. Their political chief Joseph—his tribe decimated with casualties, his people starving and frozen, their livestock lost or dead—finally made his famous speech in which he concluded, "From where the sun now stands I will fight no more forever." In 1878 the Bannock of southern Idaho rose a final time and were crushed.

Defeated in war, depleted by disease, the Indians seemed likely to disappear from the course of Columbia River history. Certainly they disappeared from many history books. Over the next century of constantly shifting federal policy their reservations were whittled in size, their natural resources exploited, their languages forbidden, their religion banned, and their children taken from their parents and sent to government boarding schools. Grand Coulee Dam inundated thousands of acres of prime Colville Reservation land and fishing sites, blocking salmon access to more than one thousand miles of productive river. The tribe had to move their school at their own expense, lost telephone service along the shore that was not restored until 1975, were stuck with some of the highest electricity rates in the state, and got no compensation for their lost salmon. "The promises made by the government were written in sand and then covered by water," tribal chairman Mel Tonasket once summed up. In the spring of 1994 the federal government finally offered a $53 million lump-sum settlement for damage caused by the dam, plus $15.3 million per year in annual compensation.

The Colville claim was forty-three years old when that offer was made. In the 1950s the federal government had actively sought to eliminate reservations, disband tribes, and assimilate individuals. Many natives did move off reservation, intermarry, and seemed to lose their tribal identity. But the tribes, and reservations, persisted with dogged stubbornness. The river's original inhabitants saw everything the new culture had to offer and still chose to cling to a part of their own.

By the 1960s the treaties that had been so hastily negotiated and so brutally enforced came back to haunt the conquerors. They included that seemingly harmless clause reserving fishing rights. In 1855 the language may well have seemed of negligible consequence; there were more fish in the river than anyone could use and it was obvious from experience on the lower Columbia that the Native Americans were on the road to extinction anyway. But the tribes did not disappear.

"No people," remarked Indian Affairs superintendent Thomas Harvey in 1846, "are more tenacious of what they consider their rights than the Indians." The statement proved prophetic. Nearly one hundred and fifty years later the tribal perception of rights would force a painful reexamination of what the Columbia had become.

The Whitman mission today is a pleasant spot, with a path winding along the site of old mission buildings, a trickle of water running down a reconstruction of the Northwest's first irrigation ditch, and the National Park Service trying to regrow a patch of native rye grass in a valley transformed by agriculture. There is a stone obelisk to the Whitmans on an adjacent hundred-foot grassy hill and a mass grave for victims at its base. The mission has no monument to the Cayuse, whose descendants were moved to Oregon's Umatilla Reservation.

Their ghosts whisper like nagging memory in that same rye.

8

The River That Was

Kettle Falls before it was drowned by Grand Coulee Dam's
Lake Roosevelt. *(University of Washington Library)*

In the summer of 1887 a peculiar-looking Canadian steamboat
plowed upstream toward Columbia Lake, the origin of the Columbia River. A less imposing vessel can scarcely be imagined. Of
all the steamboats that were beginning to thrash up and down the
waterway, this may have been the sorriest. There was the problem, for example, of telling the steamboat's bow from its stern,
since the good vessel *Cline* began its maritime career as a square
pile-driving barge: a confusion compounded by the boat's tendency to swing sideways to the current, giving an observer four

choices as to what might represent the steamboat's front end. The river was so shallow that the *Cline* regularly ran aground, forcing the cursing passengers to unload much of the cargo, jump down into waist-deep water, and lever the craft over an offending bar. Firewood was so green it had to be soaked in coal oil, and the boat's rude engine was built around the carcass of a Manitoba steam plow. The vessel's ungainliness was not helped by the five-thousand-pound sawmill boiler it towed. The *Cline's* only excuse for being was that the upper river's proper steamboat lay on the river bottom, its hull pierced by a snag.

No matter. William Adolph Baillie-Groham was in a hurry to start his empire before winter set in and figured the *Cline* was river-worthy enough to get him to the Columbia's headwaters. A decade of hunting and travel in the wilds of North America had given the English gentleman a certain resourcefulness. Three years before, his permit to redirect rivers had required him to put a steamboat on Kootenay Lake, a navigation improvement the British Columbia government had extracted in return for letting the Englishman have his way with the Columbia River. The gentleman entrepreneur avoided customs duties on his imported British steamboat by convincing Canadian authorities it was an agricultural implement that could pull a plow across annually flooded farmland. Baillie-Groham shipped the boat by rail to Sand Point in the Idaho panhandle and then hired a crew to move the *Midge* forty miles overland to the Kootenay River by pushing it on log rollers, narrowly escaping being crushed under his flagship in the process. Once the *Midge* was afloat he persuaded Indians to cut wood for its boilers in return for getting to blow its whistle. He then disposed of the craft as quickly as possible, its new owner dubbing the tubby little vessel the *Mud Hen.*

Now, as president and Canadian representative of the Kootenai Syndicate Ltd. and charterer of the *Cline,* Baillie-Groham exercised the prerogative of rank by claiming the towed sawmill boiler as his sleeping place. The steel cylinder was the only place that kept dry in the persistent rains, and he got the idea from an enterprising dog. It was smart to get as comfortable as possible; the one-hundred-mile journey to Columbia Lake took twenty-three days.

At least the scenery was glorious. To the east rose the Canadian Rockies and to the west the Selkirk and Purcell ranges, each climbing nearly a mile above the river valley. Dense forests shrouded the mountains and a hundred creeks chattered down from a thousand square miles of ice fields. The land was almost completely wild; a gold rush in the 1860s had played out and left mostly ghost towns in an area dubbed "the attic of North America." The electorate for one seat in parliament in Victoria consisted of just eleven men, and a crisis of democracy ensued when five were for one candidate, five for another, and the eleventh was kept so drunk by both sides that the presiding electoral officer refused to accept a ballot from such a "corpse."

Baillie-Groham's plan was simple and audacious. He was hiring two hundred Chinese laborers to dig a 6,700-foot ditch that would divert the Kootenay River into the source of the Columbia, tripling the upper Columbia's flow. Baillie-Groham did not particularly care what this would do to the Columbia: his scheme was designed to eliminate summer floods in the Kootenay Valley near present-day Creston. This would make arable some seventy-five thousand acres of rich alluvial farmland on the lower Kootenay River that his Kootenai Syndicate Ltd. of London had been promised by the Canadian government in return for promoting settlement.

"Once a ditch was cut," Baillie-Groham reasoned, "the rushing Kootenay, at that point a rapid stream some three hundred feet wide, would do the rest. By turning off such a large quantity of water it was expected that the overflow of the bottom land three hundred miles further down would be prevented." This was not the first time such a plan had been attempted. Nineteen years before, some two dozen miners had tried to divert the Kootenay into the Columbia in hopes of searching for gold on the resulting dry riverbed, a scheme that proved beyond their capabilities.

Baillie-Groham promised backers—who included a British general and a member of Parliament—more than a sevenfold profit from the canal's estimated £32,740 cost, earned by selling the farmland once the diversion was dug. Canada, anxious for a larger population of settled farmers, gave cautious approval after specifying he include a hundred-foot-long lock to control the exchange of water and navigation between the two rivers. Now, nine years after his first visit to North America on a hunting trip in Wyoming, Baillie-Groham intended to make his mark.

What a character he was. In his books, particularly *Fifteen*

Years Sport and Life in the Hunting Grounds of Western American and British Columbia, the distant relative of the Duke of Wellington comes across as curious, an astute observer, self-deprecating, roguish, visionary, sly, prudently timid, and ultimately ineffectual. He remained thoroughly European in his sensibilities, never an immigrant, never quite sticking. He was one of a class of gentlemen-adventurers who came west with the new railroads, hunting big game and exploring new mountains. Dubbed "top shelfers" by bemused Americans who snickered at their lace-up boots as "string shoes," the gentry were the target of guide offers by such dubious characters as Bearclaw Jones and Scalp Jack. The culture clash sometimes continued in the wild. Baillie-Groham related the tale of one English baronet who hauled a tin bathtub along, then demanded upon camping that his cowboy-hire fill it, declining to bathe in a nearby creek. His American employee thought about this for a while, decided he had enough of these class distinctions, and pulled out his gun. "You ain't quite the top shelfer you think you is," he informed the baronet. "You ain't even got a shower-bath for cooling your swelled head, but I'll make you a present of one, boss." The cowboy emptied his revolver into the tub and rode off.

Now Baillie-Groham was going to engineer some rivers, or so he hoped. After the ensuing fiasco he later confessed, "I feel no desire to have this work, as carried out, go down to posterity as either proposed or desired by me."

Baillie-Groham reasoned he was only intending a union of two rivers that nature had probably joined and separated several times before. His proposal, however, had already been compromised to the point of failure. He later complained that requirements swelled the canal cost twenty times: an exaggeration intended to explain to London investors why they lost so much money on a nonsensical dream.

The work actually proceeded on schedule. The sawmill was assembled in just ten days as Kootenay women watched silently from the edge of the woods. It cut more than half a million board feet of lumber for the locks, housing, store, and sheds. The soil was soft enough to let work proceed steadily, and a lock one hundred feet long and thirty feet wide was duly completed. When the Englishman's wife arrived by a newer steamboat the next summer—gamely loading wood along the way for the boilers and using a Mexican saddle for a pillow—she found her husband the

self-appointed postmaster and justice of a bustling little town he
had dubbed Groham. Less than two years after the *Cline*'s slow
voyage, on July 29, 1889, the canal was completed at a cost of
$100,000, about twice the original construction estimate.

The canal never fulfilled its intended purpose. Baillie-Groham was not allowed to keep the lock gates open long enough in
the summer snow-melt season to prevent flooding of his intended
agricultural empire. The lock was too small for most of the new
steamships to use between the two rivers, and the area too undeveloped to warrant much boat traffic anyway. Only three ever
passed. The *Gwendoline* did it twice, going from the Columbia to
the Kootenay in 1893 and from the Kootenay to the Columbia the
following year. In 1898 the larger *North Star* appeared. It was
twenty feet longer than the lock so its captain simply blew out the
gates with dynamite, letting the resulting gush of water carry him
through. The lock was never rebuilt and the canal quickly silted
to the point of uselessness.

Baillie-Groham moved to the other end of the Kootenay
River and started work to widen its outlet to the Columbia. If he
couldn't divert flood waters coming into the Kootenay, perhaps
he could hasten their exit. This work was no more successful, and
when the Englishman went to London to seek reimbursal for the
personal funds he had dumped into this scheme, the Kootenai
Syndicate Ltd. refused.

The farm project was eventually taken over by the Albert
and British Columbia Company, which decided to use dikes instead of trying to rechannel the Kootenay. Completed in 1892, the
dikes flooded out the next year. They were repaired in the 1930s,
and again destroyed by flood waters. A forest fire that same
decade destroyed the ghost town of Groham. Nature briefly fulfilled Baillie-Groham's vision in 1948, when a flooded Kootenay
burst through the old canal for a few weeks. The channel was
later plugged to keep the two rivers separate, and today is an
overgrown, half-filled ditch west of the new sawmill town of
Canal Flats. Groham Narrows, the downstream outlet, was
widened by the West Kootenay Power & Light Company when it
built its dams, and modern Libby Dam in Montana finally controlled enough Kootenay runoff to accomplish what Baillie-Groham desired. Eventually, about twenty-eight thousand acres of
the seventy-five thousand he had sought to develop were farmed,
and the Creston Valley today is indeed the beautiful mountain oa-

sis the Englishman dreamed of. Intriguing as a schemer and inept
as engineer or entrepreneur, Baillie-Groham is more than just a
footnote to history. In his simple and naïve boldness, he is representative of the growing enthusiasm to manipulate rivers. The Industrial Revolution had created new confidence in the ability of
man to improve the environment through engineering, a confidence that was about to transform the Columbia.

In 1873 the Corps dynamited its first river obstruction, John
Day Rock. In 1877, a decade before Baillie-Groham began work on
his canal, the U.S. Army Corps of Engineers started a much more
elaborate canal and lock project to bypass the Columbia's Cascades. Just one year before Baillie-Groham hired the *Cline,* work
started on the jetties at the Columbia's mouth.

So if Groham's ditch came to nothing, his intention to control nature was hardly unique. Eighty years after his abortive attempt, some Canadians seriously proposed diverting Canada's
portion of the Columbia into the Fraser River through a forty-
mile-long tunnel bored through the mountains. This would allow
Canada's share of the Columbia to power dams on the Fraser.
Only the objection of British Columbia's commercial fishing industry, which depends on the Fraser for its millions of spawning
salmon, scotched the idea, leaving the Fraser an undammed, fish-
healthy river as an instructive contrast to the Columbia.

This idea was followed by an even more fantastic proposal to
divert the waters of the Yukon and Tanana rivers south down the
Rocky Mountain Trench toward the United States, where the flow
would be split. One branch would lead east to the Great Lakes
and another south to Mexico. Called the North American Water
and Power Alliance, the $100 billion plan (in 1960s dollars) would
have created a man-made river in the West a thousand miles
longer than the Mississippi. This proposal came at the very summit of the twentieth century's engineering confidence, an enthusiasm that collapsed soon afterward with the growth of the
environmental movement, American preoccupation with Vietnam, the Arab oil shock, stagflation, and so on. Dreams are still
on the drawing boards of reversing the Arctic rivers of Canada
and Siberia to water southern deserts, or of diverting the Congo
to irrigate the Sahara. In 1928 the German engineer Hermann
Soergel even proposed a scheme called Atlantropa to dam the
Mediterranean at Gibraltar and the Dardanelles and let it shrink
by evaporation to expose new farmland. This was the develop-

mental era to which Baillie-Groham marks a beginning. The Columbia was about to change. What was it like before its submis-
sion?

Baillie-Groham's years of hunting and wilderness travel had
made him an astute observer of the natural world. He marveled at
the salmon runs already beginning to disappear. Some of the
gravel bars that grounded the *Cline* were spawning beds. The fish,
he wrote, swam all the way to Columbia Lake, where "the salmon
beds extended for three or four miles, ridge following ridge, the
depth of water at the top of each crest hardly exceeding a foot."
These were likely the beds of sockeye salmon that spawn and
spend their early lives in lakes, migrate to the sea, and then swim
prodigious distances as adults to return to their natal gravel.

In the river proper were chinook salmon spawning beds, the
birthplace of the famous "June hogs" that grew in excess of one
hundred pounds as they stored reserves of oily fat in their bodies
to sustain them on their long swim. "Because of their size, when
you packed them into cans, only one slice of salmon was necessary to fill the can," salmon packer Francis Seufert of The Dalles
recalled in his memoirs. "When the customer purchased this can
of Royal Chinook salmon and took it home and emptied it, he
found just one nice chunk of salmon the size of the can, rich in
oil, fine color, excellent texture and superb flavor. This salmon really deserved to be called Royal Chinook. It had no peer in the
canned salmon markets of the world."

Seufert was particularly proud of the quality of the salmon at
his part of the river. "The cold river water had firmed-up the
flesh," he said. "[The salmon] brought to our cannery were often
so firm that it was nearly impossible to pack them into salmon
cans. A fresh salmon slice would actually jump up one side of the
can when you pushed the slice down on the other side. How the
crews cussed when they had to hand pack such firm fish! When
you pitched them onto the cannery floor the salmon actually
sounded the same as when a man strikes his leather riding boots
with a buggy whip."

Overfished, these salmon were already in decline. The chinook catch on the Columbia peaked three years before Baillie-
Groham started his canal. When the Englishman recalled his
experiences shortly after the turn of the century, it was with nos-

talgia for a lost world of abundance. "Forty years ago the number of fish who reached these beds," he wrote of the upper Columbia in Canada, "was so great that the receding waters would leave millions of dead salmon strewn along the banks, emitting a stench that could be smelled miles off, and which never failed to attract a great number of bears. Though I have never performed the feat of walking across a stream on the backs of fish, which many an old timer will swear he has done, I have certainly seen fish so numerous near their spawning grounds that nowhere could you have thrown a stone into the water without hitting a salmon."

As early as a century ago, in 1894, the U.S. Commissioner of Fish and Fisheries warned that it "is beyond question that the number of salmon now reaching the head waters of streams in the Columbia River basin is insignificant in comparison with the number which some years ago annually visited and spawned in these waters."

Baillie-Groham admitted to misgivings about the civilization he represented. "So reckless of the future are your true builders of the Great Western Empire, as they call themselves, that no consideration whatever is given to the future outlook," he warned. "Let every salmon perish, let the species become extinct, provided the next few years' harvest fill their tin cans and their capricious pockets." It did not occur to Baillie-Groham to include himself in this condemnation.

The swirling tide of salmon seeking to spawn struck every explorer with wonder. Lewis and Clark found Columbia River water so clear at its junction with the Snake that they could peer twenty feet down into its depths in October and see salmon muscling by. The junction today is a collision of the brown Snake, heavy with eroded farm soil, and a murky green Columbia. Downriver at the Cascades, the Reverend Samuel Parker observed the region's huge trees in 1835 and noted, "The water of this river is so clear that I had an opportunity of examining their position down to their spreading roots."

Salmon initially seemed as inexhaustible as the buffalo. "The number of dead salmon on the shores and floating in the river is incredible," marveled William Clark in 1805. Artist Paul Kane encountered so many spawned out and dying salmon on a river passage that his party could not find a place free of their decomposing stench to beach their boat. "I have been obliged to travel through a whole night trying to find an encampment which would be free from their disgusting effluvia," he complained. This attitude toward dead salmon persisted for more than a century; author Earl Roberge in his 1985 book on the Columbia called them "a cruel and unnecessary waste." In fact biologists have realized in recent decades that this "effluvia" was critical to the life of the rivers; salmon in effect were nutritional packets from the sea and their spawned-out bodies fed the entire food chain along streams, from eagles to insects. When dams began blocking the salmon runs in the twentieth century, some rivers became so nutrient-starved that resident fish populations plummeted. In this sterile environment, a few upriver factories boasted that their organic pollutants actually helped river life more than they hurt.

The Columbia had a visible power and majesty difficult to imagine today: at Wenatchee, the roar of its rapids could be heard a mile from its banks. It was seasonally erratic; in spring it would rise twenty feet at Vancouver and fifty feet at The Dalles, submerging Celilo Falls from view. The river was studded with basalt islands, many disappearing each spring as the water rose.

"Through and down Fivemile Rapids [at The Dalles] the river when high or in flood was wild, with whirlpools as much as twenty feet across constantly to be seen," Seufert recalled. "I have seen huge bridge timbers used in railroad trestles come floating down the river, enter Fivemile Rapids and be sucked into one of those whirlpools. The whirlpools would stand the timber on end, and then suck it down and out of sight. Then these huge whirlpools would break and a huge boil would rise from the center of the pool and the water would boil up and above the flooding river. Sometimes the boiling river was five or more feet higher than the surrounding water. Huge back eddies would form along the shore, and would actually rush upstream. The current must have been rushing downstream at least twenty miles an hour. . . .

"There was absolutely no chance of survival if you fell in. And any number of men who worked on the boats were proud of the fact they didn't know how to swim. Their philosophy was simple: if you fell in the river you didn't have a chance, so why try to swim and struggle? . . . Drowning among Indians was common, for they were often pulled off their fishing scaffolding into the river when big salmon hit their dipnets. Those big salmon would actually sometimes pull a man into the river. . . . If one of the Indian fishermen fell into the river and was swept to his death, then immediately all of the Indian fishermen could stop fishing for the day and would not return to the river until the following day. I remember being down at Tumwater and looking up at Celilo Falls. Unknown to me an Indian had lost his life in the river and the word had swiftly spread to all the fishermen. They quit en masse, every Indian fisherman on the rocks simply walked off the fishing site together. It was a sight you could never forget."

In the United States above Bonneville Dam, the river today runs free in only two places: Hanford, left undammed because a reservoir would flood reactor sites, and above Northport, near Canada. A narrow, twisting road follows the Columbia as it was for a few miles toward Canada, a place remarkable not for spectacular scenery but simply as a spot where the current runs free. Few witness this kind of Columbia River. American parks and campgrounds dot Lake Roosevelt created by Grand Coulee Dam but none front this free-flowing river. At a point where it splits around two rocks the Columbia comes to life, the noise of the river almost startling after the muffled reservoirs. Even more so is its brawny speed, the surface breaking into boils, eddies, and whirlpools sweeping backward with sucking force. The urgency is impressive. I understood how sternwheelers that braved the six-mile run down the Cascades of the Columbia, their paddles run up to full power to maintain enough momentum for steerage, reportedly powered through in less than seven minutes, implying a speed exceeding fifty miles per hour.

Everything about the Columbia was noisier, faster, more robust then. Five places on the river were nearly impassable to boat traffic: Death Rapids in Canada, and Kettle Falls, Celilo Falls, The Dalles, and the Cascades in the United States. Dozens of others were difficult and hazardous. Even in October, the year's low-water point, Clark recorded "the horrid appearance of this agitated gut swelling, boiling and whorling in every direction."

The Little Dalles near the international boundary almost killed explorer and British Columbia surveyor David Moberly, who when describing his trip reported, "Sometimes one end of the canoe became the bow, and sometimes the other end." (The Dalles comes from the French word for pavingstone, which is what the steplike basalt formations in parts of the river reminded the *voyageurs* of.)

Celilo Falls was the most famous representative of the river's power. It was a basalt series of islands, rocks, rapids, narrows, and finally horseshoe-shaped Tumwater Falls, a cataract that could disappear from view in spring floods and measure as high as twenty-two feet at low water. Celilo was too low to be an imposing Niagara, but it carried far more water with the same kind of awesome energy. Its spray soaked the natives who stood on narrow wooden fishing platforms built over the raging water. The community was large, colorful, dirty, and redolent of decomposing fish, waste, and wood smoke, a mart throbbing with the power of the river and the excitement of trade.

The primeval Columbia simply looked different. Not only was it swift, but it was narrower and studded with towers and castles of basalt. Only a few of these outcrops escaped dynamiting or drowning by dam reservoirs. Broad bars of flood-washed boulders, gray sand beaches lined with cedar canoes, bright white water rapids where waves mounded higher than a man: all are gone.

So are the great cold snaps that periodically froze the river over, coyotes scampering across the ice to feed on trapped waterfowl. The chain of reservoirs pooled the water into heat reservoirs that moderated the climate along the river canyon, making it warmer in winter and cooler in summer. Before the dams, Wenatchee businesses would saw ice out of the Columbia, bury it in sawdust for preservation, and use it the next summer to cool apples being shipped east in boxcars.

The untamed river oscillated wildly. At peak floods the St. Lawrence River carries only twice its lowest flow. The Columbia at The Dalles flooded in 1894 at thirty-four times the volume of its lowest flow. At Revelstoke in Canada, the difference from flood crest to drought ebb was one hundred times. The Columbia had seventeen major floods in the ninety years from 1858 to 1948.

Even in ordinary years the difference was dramatic. "The river rises at The Dalles in June during the melting of the snow in the mountains 52 feet perpendicular over the [normal] water level," Lieutenant Charles Wilkes recorded. A government survey of the river above its junction with the Snake in 1881 estimated an average current of 3.5 miles per hour, a brisk walking pace, but added that the Columbia reached more than fifteen miles per hour in Spokane Rapids. As far down as Fort Vancouver the river remained unpredictable. In 1852 a young army officer named Ulysses S. Grant decided to grow potatoes for sale to hungry miners in California. The capricious Columbia washed the future President's crop away.

The river was emptier of people. It was difficult to use as a highway, was too confined by hills and canyons to offer much good farmland, and wasn't close to markets. As late as 1870, only eight hundred whites lived north of Walla Walla and east of the Cascade Mountains. As late as 1921, Madison J. Lorraine could row down the Columbia from source to mouth and encounter few large towns and no true cities until Portland and Vancouver. Instead he counted 109 rapids and waterfalls. They included Redgrave Canyon, Surprise Rapids, Kitchen Rapids, Canoe Encampment Rapids, Twenty-three Mile Rapids, Death Rapids, Eighteenmile Rapids, Twelvemile Rapids, Sixmile Rapids, Fivemile Rapids, Threemile Rapids, Kettle Falls, Grand Rapids, Spokane Rapids, Box Canyon, Hell's Gate, Long Rapids, Entiat Rapids, Foster Creek Rapids, Rock Island Rapids, Cabinet Rapids, Gualquil Rapids, Island Rapids, Priest Rapids, Coyote Rapids, Bull Run Rapids, Umatilla Rapids, Devil's Bend Rapids, Owyhee Rapids, Blalock Rapids, Four O'Clock Rapids, Rock Creek Rapids, Squally Hook Rapids, John Day Rapids, Celilo Falls, The Dalles, and the Cascades of the Columbia. All are gone.

These barriers were so feared that Lorraine was told several times he was a fool to row them alone. Historian Murray Morgan describes graphically in his 1949 book, *The Columbia*, how the river smashed his kayak in a wave below Grand Coulee, breaking struts and shearing off cleats.

Death Rapids got its name not from a drowning but from the tragedy of seven North West Company trappers in 1817. Sent from Canoe Camp to winter at Spokane House because five were too sick to cross the Rockies, they lost their supplies when trying to line their canoe through the rapids from shore. The seven had no choice but to struggle on down the thickly forested Columbia toward Spokane House. Already sick and now weak from hunger, the men began dying. After a brief debate, the living agreed to keep going by eating the dead. One by one they died, and one by one they were eaten, until only two were left, half-insane from fatigue and starvation. The last two survivors, Dubois and La Pierre, eyed each other uneasily as they struggled along the seemingly endless river. Finally Dubois jumped La Pierre in a last, desperate attempt for food. La Pierre, however, had a knife, and, striking swiftly, he slit the other's throat and feasted. Then he staggered to Spokane House and rescue.

At least that is the story he told. We have only the word of La Pierre, the last survivor, that he lived by self-defense.

Between these rapids were patches of smoother water where river travel was easier, including remote Kinbasket Lake at the Columbia's Big Bend in Canada and that nation's lovely Arrow Lakes farther south. Even these could be dangerous, however: in 1895 the propeller steamboat *Arrow* swamped in a sudden squall, her crew drowning.

The landscape has also changed. East of the Cascades, what are now rolling wheat fields were prairies of bunch grass, wild rye, Idaho fescue, and Sandberg blue grass. The irrigated farm-lands around the river were mostly sage steppe supporting ante-lope, deer, rabbits, rattlesnakes, and a host of birds. Columbia Basin native plants such as sand grass, needle grass, Indian mil-let, and bearded wheat grass were wiped out by overgrazing from sheep and cattle. Blue bunch wheat grass is so rare that surviving patches have been mapped for preservation in the eastern gorge. Naturalists discovered that New World plants which had never suffered intensive grazing could not compete with Old World weeds that hitchhiked in sacks of wheat seed. Jim Hill mustard, China lettuce, alfilaria, yarrow, pigweed, Canadian thistle, quack grass, tarweed, morning glory, and cheat grass overwhelmed the natives. Hanford farm fields abandoned fifty years ago have not returned to native range because of the persistence of foreign weeds.

The oasis islands of brilliant green produced by irrigation water were absent, of course, and the undisturbed Columbia Basin struck many as inhospitably dry and bleak. "If ever there was Indian Country, this is it," Major Gabriel Rains said of the brown range around The Dalles, meaning "Indian Country" as a descriptive insult.

Meriwether Lewis called the land around the junction of the Snake and Columbia "one continuous plain . . . great quantities of prickly pears, much worse than any I have before seen."

After the railroad came through in 1883, one traveler judged that the construction settlement of Ainsworth near the present-day Tri-Cities "boasts of a few of the best people, the largest num-ber of bad men and women, and the greatest amount of sin, dust and general disagreeableness of any place its size on the Coast." Another traveler at Wallula asked if the incessant wind always blew that way. "No, the rest of the time it blows the other way," he was told. And when a Pasco booster told a skeptical visitor that all the area needed to thrive was good people and water, the visitor replied, "Yes, and that's all that Hell needs, too."

The wildlife picture was mixed. There was less waterfowl in the interior of the Columbia Plateau than today because excess irrigation water has created marsh. There may have been more waterfowl along the Columbia, however. When the British under Lieutenant Broughton explored the first hundred miles upriver, "We startled flocks of geese which would make such a noise that if near them it was impossible to hear each other speak," recorded John Sherriff, a master's mate. The overall loss of wildlife habitat because of river development outweighs that created by new ponds and reservoirs. Federal reservoirs alone drowned a thousand square miles, much of it rich bottomland with the best wetlands, pasturage, and trees.

Many forests east of the Cascades were different. Natives burned some to encourage the rejuvenation of food plants and grasses. As a result, the pine forests had larger trees, spaced more widely apart, and in a more parklike setting than the denser, brushy second growth common today. Later loggers cut the largest Ponderosa pine in a practice known as high-grading and left the weaker trees to reseed into much denser groves. The result has been stands susceptible to insect and fire devastation, producing what the U.S. Forest Service told me are some of the "sickest forests in the United States."

West of the Cascades were trees so titanic they were difficult for the first pioneers to cut down, and forest so dense it was difficult to hack trails through. River canoes were the preferred means of travel. The river in spring would undercut and topple some of the huge fir on its banks, the trees nosing down the river like bristling submarines. At the ocean they would be cast up on the beaches into gigantic silver barriers of driftwood.

The river below Vancouver and Portland was marshier than it is now, a place of meandering side channels and boggy wetlands inundated each summer with flood. Here the young salmon flushed down from the mountain spawning grounds by the rush of snow melt would pause and feed before making the transition to the ocean. More than half of this biological cornucopia is gone now, diked, dredged, and filled.

The junction of river and sea was broader and stormier. "The mouth of the Columbia River," wrote Alexander Ross, "is remarkable for its sand bars and high surf at all seasons, but more particularly in the spring and fall, during the equinoctial gales: these sand bars frequently shift, the channel of course shifting along with them, which renders the passage at all times extremely dangerous." The Hudson's Bay Company considered the bar so treacherous that Fort Vancouver kept an extra year's trade goods and supplies on hand in case the annual replenishment ship could not get into the Columbia's mouth.

For all its capriciousness, the Columbia proved vital to early settlement. Portland has been called the city that gravity built. It did not have the mill power present at Oregon City's Willamette Falls, nor the fertile plains of Vancouver across the Columbia. But it was located a short distance up the Willamette River at a point Massachusetts sea captain John Couch declared was the farthest seagoing ships could venture. Portland was at the junction of trade coming down the heavily populated Willamette Valley and down the Columbia. Couch, Asa Lawrence Lovejoy of Groton, Massachusetts, and Francis Pettygove of Maine staked out adjacent claims in 1849 to establish what would rapidly become the river's biggest city. Pettygove won a coin toss and got to choose a name, unimaginatively selecting that of the principal city of his native Maine. Lovejoy was no better: he wanted to call it Boston. The older settlement of Fort Vancouver across the river took a different direction as an army post. The seasonal rise and fall of the Columbia and a blocking sand bar made Vancouver's shoreline a poor place for a port.

If the Columbia was not a perfect highway for commerce the surrounding mountains were worse, so river dwellers made the best of it. Their tool was a remarkable invention already plying the Mississippi and Missouri, the stern- and side-wheeled steamboat. Drawing as little as a foot of water, these vessels nosed far up the tangle of streams in the Columbia Basin to supply boom towns and cattle empires. By putting the boat's boiler up on deck and near the front so the breeze fanned the flames, these craft eliminated a deep hull. In the half century or so of steamboat supremacy on the Columbia Basin's rivers, at least fifty-four were wrecked, twenty-nine burned, and at least four blew up—but they were relatively cheap to build and so superior to land transportation before the railroads that the Oregon Steam Navigation Company demanded, and got, tonnage rates as much as ten times those levied on the Missouri.

The genius behind this extortion was Captain John C. Ainsworth, a former Mississippi boatman who came West for the California Gold Rush, hooked up with an entrepreneur building a modern steamboat on the Columbia, and arrived in Oregon to skipper the *Lot Whitcomb,* a sidewheeler named for her owner and launched on Christmas Day, 1850. A cannon blew up during the obligatory salute, killing one celebrant, but otherwise the launch celebration was an enthusiastic success. The new craft steamed from Astoria to Oregon City in ten hours and was so superior in looks and elegance to the earlier side-wheeler *Columbia* that it refused to meet the slashed rates the *Columbia* offered.

Oregonians were entranced by the one-hundred-and-sixty-foot white boat with its twin stacks, twelve-mile-per-hour speed, paneled cabins, and dining hall. Elizabeth Markham couldn't resist singing its praises in a poem sent to the newspaper *Oregon Spectator:*

> *Lot Whitcomb* is coming!
> Her banners are flying—
> She walks up the rapids with speed;
> She ploughs through the water,
> Her steps never falter,
> Oh! That's independence indeed.
> Old and young rush to meet her,
> Male and female to greet her,
> And waves lash the shore as they pass. . . .

And so on.

The *Lot Whitcomb* was not the Columbia's first steamboat. As mentioned, the *Beaver* had briefly plied the river in 1836 before transfer to Puget Sound. An Oregon City man named Truesdale built an eighty-two-foot boat powered by six horses plodding on a treadmill, and actually ran it to Portland and back once before disappearing from history. In 1849 the navy steamer *Massachu-setts* entered the Columbia to belatedly bring troops for the Cayuse War, which had already ended. But it was the *Columbia* and *Lot Whitcomb* that in 1850 truly launched the Columbia's steamboat era.

The timing was fortuitous. The Indian War of 1855–58 made the two-stage passage from Portland to The Dalles profitable, with rates hitting thirty dollars a ton. By 1860, Ainsworth had decided to monopolize Columbia River steamboat traffic by organizing the Oregon Steam Navigation Company, a conglomeration of existing boats to which he added the rights to the portage railroads and roads at the Cascades, The Dalles, Celilo, and other choke points. Shortly afterward gold was discovered in Idaho, and OSNC struck it rich. By 1862 it was charging $120 a ton for freight from Portland to the new town of Lewiston, Idaho. The *Tenino* earned $18,000 on a single trip to the Idaho gold fields. In 1862 the steamboat company built a six-mile railroad on the Washington shore around the Cascades and a fourteen-mile road on the Oregon shore from The Dalles to above Celilo Falls. Steamboats would journey to an unnavigable part of the river, unload passengers and freight for a portage around, load them onto a new boat at the second navigable stretch, and so on. At low water, cargo between Portland and Lewiston had to be handled fourteen times to get around river obstructions. Passengers took two days to get from Portland to Wallula, a drive of a few hours today.

Wheat floated down the river was handled so many times that its price in Portland, where it was loaded onto ships, was double what it brought farmers in Walla Walla. The first problem was getting wheat to the rivers: the Snake and Columbia were as much as two thousand feet below the farmed plateau. A wagon trip to the canyon bottom required constant braking on the way down and an exhausting pull for the animals back up. Reasoning he could enlist gravity rather than fight it, in 1879 a Northern Pacific railroad engineer named Sewell Truax built a four-inch-square pipe, thirty-two hundred feet long, from the crest of the Snake River canyon to the river. When the first wheat poured down the grains traveled so fast they ground into flour or burned through the pipe, but baffles and upturns were placed every hundred feet to reduce speed and friction. Soon wheat pipes fed steamboat landings around the Columbia Basin. At Orondo, north of Wenatchee, a tramway was built that operated like a ski lift, bringing sacks of wheat down and taking coal, machinery, and lumber back up.

Walla Walla had a different problem. The city's strategic spot as a military post and its location in a rich agricultural valley had made it the biggest city in Washington Territory by 1870. Its wheat farmers, however, had to haul their grain thirty miles to the Columbia, using six- and eight-horse teams that charged exorbitant rates. Dr. Dorsey Syng Baker tired of the town's idle talk of someday getting a railroad and decided simply to build one. He collected a crew of unemployed cowboys and Indians to make a grade, traveled to Pittsburgh to buy an engine and car wheels, and hired local carpenters to build cars. It is not true that the "Rawhide Railroad" ran down its tracks on strips of leather, but it *is* true that Baker used wooden rails topped by a thin strip of iron to save money. In 1875 the line began. The iron had a disconcerting habit of working loose and impaling the bottom of the cars as they went over, and even when not speared the train took three to seven hours. Still, the cost of shipping a ton of wheat to the river fell from six dollars to a dollar fifty.

Not surprisingly, farmers welcomed the arrival of better railroads with relief—yet once they had a taste of railroad pricing they decided they didn't want to give up river transport either. Exorbitant Northwest railroad rates came under the scrutiny of the Interstate Commerce Commission as early as 1887. The piracy was so bad that growers clamored for navigational improvements on the Columbia. Farm fear of being at the mercy of transportation monopolies continues to influence river policy today, creating opposition to any environmental proposal that would threaten the current competitive transportation trinity of train, truck, and barge.

While travel was complicated on this river system, it was as elegant as the times allowed. Many steamboats were outfitted with padded seats, lady's salons, smoking parlors, bars, dining rooms, staterooms, and decks for strolling and admiring the scenery.

River travel above Wallula, near the junction of the Columbia and Walla Walla rivers, advanced slowly because of rapids. Here the river pointed north and had few inhabitants. Not until 1858 did the first steamboat reach Priest Rapids, and not until 1879 did a steamboat winch itself by line through them. It was in 1888 that the steamboat *City of Ellensburg* pulled itself through Rock Island Rapids and reached the site of Wenatchee. Kettle Falls did not get steamboat traffic until 1911. Despite expensive government river improvements to get the boats that far north, they were unable to compete with railroad rates.

Occasionally steamboats were brought down through the rapids to move from one part of the river to another, always at considerable risk. The first such passage was accidental: in 1858 the underpowered *Venture* was launched at the Upper Cascades, seized by the current, and swept into the rapids before her crew could react. One man panicked, jumped, and was drowned, but the *Venture* and the rest of its crew survived, proving the passage was possible. The *Shoshone* proved unprofitable on the upper Snake after gold claims played out, so Ainsworth ordered her brought down through Hells Canyon. The resulting careening ride down bellowing rapids almost destroyed the boat: she struck rocks so many times that debris preceded her downriver, leaving residents of Lewiston to presume the boat had been lost. Yet her crew gamely ran the *Shoshone* ashore and used cabin lumber to make repairs, continuing onward and sparking a celebration at Lewiston when they finally emerged. Eventually the boat was piloted all the way down to Portland, Ainsworth himself taking her through the Cascades.

Going upriver was worse. It typically took three days for a Columbia steamboat to thrash seventy miles upstream from Bridgeport to Sanpoil. The *Colonel Wright* took several days to battle one hundred and sixty miles up the Clearwater River, then shot all the way down to Wallula, a distance of three hundred miles, in just twenty-four hours. Another steamboat spent eight days battling one hundred miles up the Snake into Hells Canyon, finally gave up, and was washed back to Lewiston in five hours.

Wrecks were common, and occasionally boilers blew. In 1857 the *Elk* blasted its Captain Jerome into a tree on the banks of the Willamette. He survived unharmed. The *Gazelle* killed twenty-eight when it erupted a year later. When the *Annie Faxon* exploded in 1893, the ship's purser was widowed on his honeymoon. His bride, who had been standing next to him, disappeared in the explosion.

These accidents were relative rarities, however, like airplane crashes today. The boats were appealing. Their scheduled regularity was a sign of order. With their churning wheels, smoking stacks, and brilliant white deck houses, they had a beauty residents mourned as they were slowly eclipsed by the railroad and automobile. The *Moyie* operated on Lake Kootenay in Canada until 1957, but in most areas the steamboat reign was over by World War I.

The unsatisfactory river conditions the steamboats battled meant that settlers could not be satisfied with the Columbia as explorers found it. True, the boats were designed for shallow, hazardous river passage, and yes, there was a sense of the explorer or pioneer in their captains. "The sensation to me," said Ainsworth, "of entering a water that had never before been divided by the prow of a steamer, was beyond description." Yet the Columbia and Snake in their natural condition were simply too difficult to travel. The federal government was beginning to provide the budget and expertise for large engineering works, and the steamboat industry's very success had created a constituency to improve the Columbia and Snake into something more navigable. It was an effort that began with a congressional appropriation to build a canal and locks around the Cascades in 1876 and ended ninety-nine years later with the opening of a "seaport" in Lewiston.

CHAPTER

9

Out Here

A steamboat plies the mid-Columbia beneath basalt bluffs.
(*University of Washington Library*)

It is late summer afternoon and the Tidewater Barge Lines tug
Challenger, pushing five thousand tons of wheat and wood chips
from Idaho to Vancouver, is sinking like a slow elevator in the
lock at Ice Harbor Dam. This is the last dam on the Snake River
before its junction with the Columbia, and the fourth of eight
locks we are passing in our long descent to the sea. When boxed
in the concrete rectangle of a lock, "the tow" of tug and barge
drops about a hundred feet each time. Ice Harbor's mechanical
step down after thirty-two reservoir miles of flat water is dramatic illustration of a modern river's engineered obedience.

The lock was built in five-foot-high concrete pours like a

layer cake. I count the strips to measure our stately fall; every two of them, perhaps, represent a tamed rapid now drowned under twenty or forty or a hundred feet of water. The Indian village that the dam buried at this site was called Sumuya.

At the bottom the lock is shadowy and cool. Its wet walls, slick with brown algae, rise to frame a confined rectangle of blue sky. The heads of spectators peer over the lip at us, forming tiny ovals. A few dam sightseers always seem on hand to watch our passage and until the water begins to drop they often pepper the crew with questions about the makeup of the cargo or how the heavily loaded barges manage to float. The questions are not stupid but the "sagebrush sailors" have heard them all a hundred times, and when asked what an empty, high-riding barge is carrying, sometimes they reply, "Sailboat fuel." Conversation is easy. While the locks are eighty-six feet wide, the barges are eighty-four. The tow slides into them like a knife into a sheath.

From a distance even large dams such as Ice Harbor can appear modest in the immense landscape of the Columbia Plateau. Going through the locks, however, makes apparent the engineering achievement a dam represents. We are so deep it feels as if we have been lowered into a huge grave. The one-hundred-and-five-foot lock at John Day Dam is the deepest in the world and by the end of this voyage we will have dropped seven hundred and thirty-two feet in all. At the upstream end of the Ice Harbor lock leaking water hisses around dark steel doors ten stories high, the spray urgent evidence of the weight of water they are holding back. The downstream gate is a brighter silver. I watch it from the front of the foremost barge, enjoying a relative quiet. The five hundred feet of assembled cargo give a temporary respite from the unceasing vibration of the tug engines, their drone a constant companion on this three-day, three-hundred-and-fifty-nine-mile trip. When the lock empties to the level of the Snake at the foot of the dam the downstream gate rises upward between two concrete towers, like the portcullis on a castle. The effect is dramatic. As the gate lip nears the surface the sun outside makes the water glow underneath like lime gelatin, and a fish is caught on a steel shelf and lifted clear of the water, skittering and flopping before bouncing back into the river. Then the steel curtain breaks clear with a backwash of current and desert wind rushes through the gap to whip spray across the barge. The gate slides home in its uppermost position like a poised guillotine. The tow crews don't like these overhead gates: in winter the spray is cold and sometimes the water freezes until accumulated ice breaks off and rattles down on the tow as it passes underneath. I walk the narrow deck of the barges back to the tug, stepping over steel cables and taking care not to slip on small drifts and rills of spilled wheat. Thirty percent of all U.S. wheat exports move down the Snake and Columbia by barge, rail, and truck. Our wheat barge is two hundred feet long and carries thirty-five hundred tons of grain.

Power is applied and the tug moves out onto the river, its metal floor vibrating. In the pilothouse there is the smell of diesel exhaust, cigarette smoke, wood chips, and river water. Wheat chaff is caught by the wind and blown back toward us in a brown flurry. We churn downriver by following a narrow channel just a few yards from the north shore. Water boils up between the barges from hulls that plow fourteen feet below the surface, almost twice as deep as comparable barges on the shallower Mississippi. The bow wave is a three-foot hump of frothy green. A squall breezes across the river a few miles downstream, forming a black horizon of rain cloud and dust with the sun above it turning the water silver. A speedboat follows us for a mile or two, playing in the tow's wake. We get a wave from a fisherman sitting on a lawn chair in the shade of his camper, his pole planted twenty feet from the river. Gulls weave across the stern, looking for stunned fish that the eighty-five-inch tug propeller may kick up. The canyon of the Snake opens up and brown, sun-blasted hills roll away to irrigated fields.

I am, in the words of the tow crew, "out here." The men and women who ride these tugs and barges spend fifteen days straight on the river: six hours on watch, six off. There is no newspaper, no television, no telephone, and no shore leave. The riverbank is often just a hundred yards away, but it might as well be a hundred miles. There is the river, and the tow, and nothing else. "It's more of a lifestyle than a job," I am told, several times.

The goal of making the Columbia and Snake rivers into a smooth water highway persisted in the national imagination almost from the time Robert Gray first sailed past Cape Disappointment. As soon as population warranted and expertise allowed, the dogged effort began. In 1876, Congress appropriated the first ninety thousand dollars to plan a lock and three-thousand-foot canal around the Cascades of the Columbia. The Army Corps of Engineers soon after launched work on a fourteen-mile canal around Celilo Falls. In 1881, Lieutenant Thomas Symons of the Army Corps of Engineers surveyed the river above Wallula and warned it would cost at least $3 million to make the middle Columbia navigable. Congress was undaunted. In 1890 it appropriated $70,000 to begin that work.

Like many other government projects before and since, these early efforts to tame the Columbia took far longer, cost much more, and worked more poorly than hoped. Bad weather, flooding, labor problems, and lack of money delayed completion of Cascade Locks for twenty years. Even after opening in 1896, the locks required modifications not completed until 1914, some thirty-eight years after the project started. The final price tag of $4.1 million was more than three times the original estimate. And by the time the project opened the heyday of the Columbia River steamboat was already over: a railroad ran down both banks. The Celilo Canal was not completed until 1915. Scarcely used, it was completely idle by 1919.

No matter. This tinkering soon gave way to real transformation. Rapids would not be bypassed or obliterated, they would be flooded. The complex ecology of the river bottom was about to be drowned.

Thinking about rivers had changed. Vessels designed to negotiate swift, rock-studded waterways carried too little cargo to compete with the new railroads. No longer would boats be designed shallow and maneuverable to overcome river obstacles: instead the river would be designed to accommodate deep-draft ships or barges, the latter driven by tugs with small, cost-efficient crews. The means would be dams to convert unruly rivers to lakes. As solely a navigational improvement this made no economic sense: it would be far cheaper to subsidize or regulate shipping costs on the already-existing railroads. Dams, however, could be justified as multiple-purpose facilities. President Theodore Roosevelt, whose name would go on the nation's first large-scale hydroelectric dam in Arizona in 1911, summarized the new thinking in 1908: "It is poor business to develop a river for navigation in such a way as to prevent its use for power, when by a little foresight it could be made to serve both purposes. Every stream should be used to the utmost." It was the promise of more electric power, not barge transportation, that was used as the prime justification for the staircase of dams and locks to Idaho.

Even with such cost-sharing it was never deemed sensible to try to make the Columbia navigable north of its junction with the Snake River. By the time the Columbia River's first dam at Rock Island was started near Wenatchee in 1929, middle-river steamboat traffic had been dead for more than a decade. Five steamboats burned in a spectacular fire at Wenatchee's docks in 1915 and the commerce never recovered. Accordingly, no provision was made for a lock allowing river navigation above Rock Island, and no commercial river traffic uses the Columbia above the Tri-Cities today. When Rock Island was updated in the 1970s and new turbines were barged upriver, they had to be portaged around Priest Rapids and Wanapum dams on giant tractor-trailers as *voyageurs* once portaged canoes.

Downriver the situation was different. By the early 1930s farmers in Minnesota could ship by rail to New York, a distance of one thousand miles, for fifty cents a ton. Eastern Washington farmers were paying $4.80 a ton to ship by rail to Portland or Seattle, a distance of less than four hundred miles. The railroads rescued farmers from a steamboat monopoly only to substitute one of their own, and there was a growing demand to break the railroad stranglehold. History recorded that when the Erie Canal was completed, freight costs from the Great Lakes to New York City dropped from one hundred dollars to five dollars a ton. Shippers wanted the same advantages in the Pacific Northwest.

Bonneville Dam near Portland, completed in 1937, drowned the Cascades of the Columbia with its reservoir, making Cascade Locks obsolete. The dam was fitted with the river's first modern lock (which later proved too small for the huge barge assemblies it spawned and was replaced in 1993). Meanwhile, Pacific Northwest farmers were convinced that Bonneville must only be the beginning. In February 1934 the Inland Empire Waterways Association was formed and a Walla Walla salesman named Herbert West was appointed to represent it. West, who was later elected Walla Walla mayor, pushed tirelessly for a chain of dams and locks from Bonneville to Lewiston. He became an indefatigable ally of the Army Corps of Engineers and when the last dam in the chain was completed in 1975, West became the second person in the nation to get the Corps' Civilian Service Medal.

Another key figure in the battle was longtime Washington senator Warren Magnuson. President Kennedy once observed during a speech in Seattle that "Maggie," the powerful chairman of the Senate Commerce Committee, was less than a spellbinding orator. However, the President went on, during a lull on the Senate floor "Maggie would reach in his pocket and mumble, 'I've got a little bill here I'd like to introduce'—and next thing you know, Grand Coulee Dam would be built!" The funny story was not strictly true; Grand Coulee Dam was planned and started before Magnuson reached Congress in 1936. But Kennedy's anecdote was descriptive of the Snake River process. The Corps was having difficulty justifying the dams economically, and Magnuson's effort in the early 1950s to get them started was repeatedly rebuffed by Congress. In 1955 he quietly persuaded a House-Senate conference committee to add an innocuous $1 million to begin construction of Ice Harbor. It was all the Corps needed; from then on they could request money to "complete" the chain. At the effusive 1975 celebration in Lewiston proclaiming the waterway's completion, only Idaho governor Cecil Andrus cast a sour note. He warned that the new waterway could mean doom for Idaho's salmon runs. "I want to point out," Andrus said, "that the cost of this system has been horrendous, both in dollars and in cost to our natural resources."

I fly into Lewiston. From the airplane the Palouse wheat country is a rolling sheet of shaved gold and the sky a hazed, milky blue. The Clearwater and Snake rivers that join at this spot cannot be seen as we bank into the airport; instead there is a gash across the Columbia Plateau marking their deep, winding canyons. At their junction is the most inland port on the U.S. West Coast.

The first tug I will ride is the red and white *Outlaw:* it sports a picture of the cartoon character Yosemite Sam painted on its side by crewman Greg Majeski. At one hundred and four feet in length, the vessel is longer than the *Columbia Rediviva* Robert Gray sailed around the world. The *Outlaw* (Tidewater tugs have names worthy of dreadnoughts, such as *Challenger, Rebel,* and *Defiance*) arrived at Lewiston at 2:30 A.M. and picked up a barge loaded with thirty-six of the ubiquitous metal containers shifted so routinely these days from ship to barge to truck to rail to airplane. Inside are 2 million pounds of pickles. After waiting twelve hours for a chip barge to be filled at the Port of Wilma a few miles downstream, the tug points toward the sea and chugs past the junction of the Clearwater and Snake, myself as sole passenger.

A visitor would have to be informed he is at the meeting of two mighty rivers: the junction today consists of the arms of a reservoir created by Lower Granite Dam. Lewiston crouches below the new lake behind a levee, the dike landscaped into a park and jogging path by the Corps of Engineers as part of the public relations campaign encountered everywhere to demonstrate the recreational superiority of tamed reservoirs over a free-flowing river.

The Port of Wilma is a flat, arid landfill opposite Clarkston, Washington, backed by fawn-colored grass hills where basalt outcroppings run along the bluffs like ribs on starving cattle. The reservoir bank is littered with industrial scrap: rusting tanks, abandoned cable spools, bald tires, abandoned winches, and broken sheets of fiberglass roofing. There are aluminum and concrete grain silos, a web of power lines, and mobile homes used as company offices. A large flock of geese lives on spilled grain. A sawmill chews scraggly second-growth pine into chips that dribble down a green chute into waiting chip barges. These are nothing more than floating metal boxes the size of a basketball court. The chips are ground into paper pulp by the mills that dot the river.

The tug pilothouse sits on a tower forty feet above the river, giving a panoramic view. The *Challenger*'s house has carpeting, wood paneling, and brass and silver controls to control two propellers and four rudders, a combination that allows a tow to move almost sideways. With its three thousand horsepower this tug probably boasts more energy than the entire nineteenth-century Columbia River steamboat fleet put together, and the heat of its engine exhaust makes a rippling mirage of the American flag off the stern. Bill Kellum, a friendly, white-haired navigator who has worked on the river for thirty years, begins to juggle and assemble the tow. He orders the deckhands to temporarily tie off some barges and churns ahead to pick up others, trying to achieve the right sequence for balance and wind control. For greater maneuverability the balky vessels are pushed, not pulled, but remain awkward in high winds and waves: the side of a chip barge is like a sail two thousand feet square. Kellum is particularly cautious because the container barge has been overloaded toward its front and the bow tips toward the river. "If I push too fast I could bury it," he explained. "Ninety percent of the people coming into the wheelhouse try to get things done too fast. That's when you get accidents. You have to slow down."

Departing Wilma, we pass under the "Someday" bridge, so named because its pillars were placed years before Lower Granite Dam was completed in anticipation that someday they would help span a new reservoir. The Columbia-Snake waterway is very much a planned place and our route is smooth, broad, and deep. Yet much of the river country remains little changed from when Lewis and Clark descended its canyons. There are no towns on the Snake River between Lewiston-Clarkston and its junction with the Columbia River—the canyon is too steep and narrow for houses or highways. The farms are on the plateau two thousand feet above us, and the voluptuously rounded canyon hills remain treeless and austere: a brilliant green for a few weeks each May and then brown the rest of the year. A subtle sign of human modification is the faint pattern of "terracettes," beaten into the hillsides. They look like contour lines, or a thousand hiking trails stacked on top of each other. They have been created over the past century by grazing cattle and sheep that follow the terracettes to feed.

There are four crewmen on this leg of the trip. Two swap six-hour shifts to steer the boat and two trade off to couple and uncouple the huge barges with steel cables and winches: we frequently drop off and pick up barges in a bewildering shuffle in response to customer demands and shipping schedules downriver. When not rearranging the tow the deckhands may chip and paint for an hour or two, cook, wash dishes, or clean. Dick Ashdown is sixty-one years old and still doing this paced but sometimes hard and dangerous work in a climate that can frequently exceed one hundred degrees in summer and reach subzero temperatures in winter. Ashdown once had two fingers pinched off by a cable. When he returned to work a month later he found the blood-stained glove he had been wearing still lying on deck, so he put his hand in it. The severed tips of his fingers were still in the glove.

Captain Keith Wiest came onto the river twenty-three years ago after being introduced to Tidewater Barge Lines by his Boy Scout troop master, while crewman Majeski is a thirty-three-year-old powerfully built deckhand in a muscle shirt and black boots, sour about a pending divorce that is an occupational hazard for these crewmen gone two weeks at a time. These men have little sympathy for second thoughts about the wisdom of damming the river.

"When this river ran free and clear, it didn't do jack shit for anybody," Majeski says.

"If they wanted to save the salmon, what did they put the dams in for?" asks Kellum.

"It just seems to me it's too late to go back," says Wiest.

As evening approaches the hills are burnished with a last burst of sun and the clouds become pink and incandescent. Then there is darkness. The rim of the hills forms a channel for a brilliant band of stars, a river of light glittering overhead to balance the soft, syrupy black one under the hull. The dams are an occasional brilliantly lit concrete oasis. At each one the lock tender uses a fishing pole to snag a canister held up by Majeski that contains the tow's cargo information. The numbers are reeled in to become part of the statistics used in Congress to justify these dams.

I sleep for a while—the tugs are roomy and comfortable enough that I have my own cabin—and am awakened at 3:00 A.M. for a transfer to the *Challenger*. The *Outlaw*, halfway down the Snake, is handing off to a new tug and taking other barges back to Lewiston. The stars have disappeared and a windy chop has come up. We are at Lyons Ferry, bridged now by a highway and a railway bridge two hundred and eighty feet above the river. My new home is much like the old. As on the *Outlaw*, half the crew of four is asleep.

There is no pause to rest in the night. The $3 million tugs are too expensive to leave idle and the engines never shut off. Neither does the pace seem hurried. On our trip downriver the tugs chug at seven or eight knots. With lock passage and barge transfers we average about five miles per hour, lending a nineteenth-century stateliness to our journey. Still, modern symbolism creeps in. One of the new wheat barges we pick up has been purchased from Columbia Marine Lines. Instead of cutting away the huge round sign on its side that proclaimed "CML," it has been painted over by Tidewater into a huge, yellow happy-face button that grins at the shoreline.

As the *Challenger* leaves Ice Harbor Dam and approaches the junction with the Columbia, the crew talks about past accidents.

The water churning out from the powerhouse turbines or roaring down a spillway can seize an unwary tow. Pilot Al Sheridan, dressed in a Hawaiian shirt and Marlboro cap, remembers one that broke his tow in half, the twist of the current snapping the thick steel cables. Another time a barge came loose with Majeski aboard, spinning slowly around in the whirlpools below the face of the dam before he was rescued. A railroad drawbridge came down on a tug being piloted by Doug Burrows, crushing the top half of the wheelhouse as he desperately tried to throttle by underneath. Burrows dropped to the carpet as the bridge beams shattered the windows, buckled the door, and sheared off the roof. A similar accident occurred on the Columbia to the reconstructed brig *Lady Washington*, snapping off her masts. The history of the Columbia is in part the drive to replace people with machines of ever-greater efficiency, and the railroads are no exception. Some of their drawbridges are unmanned, relying on remote sensors to alert them to passing boat traffic.

The tow enters the Columbia, a marriage of brown and green. There is no visible current; McNary Pool had turned the meeting of these two rivers into a lake. The parks and bridges and buildings of the Tri-Cities make it difficult to imagine what it must have looked like when Lewis and Clark paddled down here to an Indian camp, the land dusty and treeless. In the late nineteenth century there was a sign planted on the desert near this junction, reading "Watch Pasco Grow." For years that is all there was. That sign.

We pass through the flood-eroded bluffs at Wallula Gap and make most of the long, boring run down McNary and John Day pools at night. The river here is broad, spotted with a few islands, and framed with monotonous barren bluffs that hide the farms behind them. With morning the land begins to rise as the river carves its way through the eastern foothills of the Cascades. We glide over Celilo Falls, nothing reminiscent of the thunder the Columbia made here. The Dalles is still narrow, but the river is no longer "whorling and boiling" as it was for Lewis and Clark. The first trees appear. Marine clouds mound on the west side of Mount Hood.

At Hood River the gorge winds stiffen to create a white-capped chop. Wind surfers rise and blossom on the water. They fall in the swells, clamber back aboard, lift their sail like the opening of a butterfly's chrysalis, and race away, crossing the broad river in a couple of minutes. The Columbia has become a mecca for this sport. The predictable upriver wind and slow downriver current keep the craft on a steady track for a day of play back and forth across the river.

Most sports look silly when viewed with detachment and this is no exception; there is an exuberant mindlessness about the crisscrossing that is amusing because the surfers pursue it with almost religious zeal. One afternoon I watched them skip across the swells like colored stones, breathless and drugged from the sun and the water, their hard bodies braced like a strut of their craft. Most seemed terribly serious and unsmiling, though one scooped up the decaying body of a spawned-out chinook salmon in midriver and skidded ashore, gleefully scattering his friends with its decay. Here and there a bored wife or girlfriend sat reading a book and waited for her mate to exhaust himself.

Yet to dismiss the sport as vacuous is unfair. These people make a connection with the Columbia that commercial interests miss, drawing sustenance from the water that has nothing to do with kilowatts generated or food produced. When resting they sat hypnotized by the Columbia's grandeur, the wind their breath of life, the gorge their temple. Sheridan compared their flit to "mosquitoes," but the wind-surfing industry is as dependent on the reservoirs as Tidewater Barge Lines: neither could sail the untamed Columbia.

We arrive at Bonneville at night, under a half moon. Floodlights throw the surrounding fir trees into sharp relief. Two Indian fishing platforms built of drift lumber jut out over what was once the famous Cascades. The new lock under construction isn't completed during this transit so the tow must be divided and taken through the old one in two stages, a laborious process that consumes most of the night. Below the dam the barges are reassembled into a tow eight hundred and seventy feet long, the length of an ocean liner. We are now back on free-flowing river and a current is discernible, though modest since we are so close to sea level. Water boils out from the final powerhouse, coating the Columbia with curds of foam for several miles.

At 6:30 A.M. we set out on the last, easy stage to Vancouver, forty miles away. Aluminum motor homes are parked along Bradford Island where gunfire crackled in the battle of 1856. Fishing poles jut over the water, and some families are starting a morning fire. Mist swirls in the heavily forested hills, and the entire character of the river has changed to a soft watercolor of greenish-grays. Multnomah Falls, feeble in late summer but still the fourth highest in the nation, draws a white line down its cliff.

What I have just floated down is the closest thing that exists to the Northwest Passage that Peter Pond and Robert Rogers and Thomas Jefferson dreamed of: a man-made, stair-stepping lake laid over one of the most cantankerous navigational rivers in America. It is beautiful in its placid way, undeniably efficient, stupendously expensive, eerily quiet except for the rumble of the tug, and as deliberately boring as a freeway.

The engineering achievement is greater than the traffic the passage carries. Only rarely did we have other boats for company on our journey—but we often were overtaken by diesel trains and trucks rumbling up and down both sides of the river. The history of the Northwest has been dictated in part by the technology of transportation: the sailing ship, the canoe, the wagon, the steamboat, the railroad, the barge, and the highway. The Great River of the West became a corridor of commerce through the construction of locks, trestles, sidecuts, bridges, and embankments so thorough as to become redundant. Each new type of vehicle brought more development that required additional types: the steamboat made necessary the railroad as a balance, the railroad the barge, and the centralized regulation of all these the freedom of the automobile and flexibility of the truck. Dams are the American pyramids, and the Columbia our Valley of the Kings. As the *Challenger* approaches the docks at Vancouver where some of the cargo will be handed off to seagoing ships, I think back to one spot we passed on our seventy-two-hour journey that seems perversely symbolic of a building urge both heroic and vain: Maryhill.

It is, *Time* magazine once described, "the world's loneliest art museum." Perched on a bluff above the Columbia near a rocky river bottleneck known as Hell's Gate, Maryhill is the monumental mansion of reinforced concrete built by Sam Hill. It is a house Hill's wife refused to live in, a "Castle Nowhere" for a utopian community no one ever came to. Absurdly out of scale, place, and time, Maryhill is charming in its idiosyncratic art collection, puzzling in its remoteness, and sad as an attempt to give meaning to a peripatetic, ill-focused life.

The view from Maryhill is magnificent, and clearly is what drew Hill to this remote spot. Wrapped behind by the Klickitat Hills, the mansion looks down the river past orchards and wheat silos toward snowcapped Mount Hood. When Hill started work on a planned model community there in 1907, Maryhill was served by neither roads nor ferry. Railroad trains did rumble by, however, and it was railroad money that made Maryhill possible. Sam was the son-in-law of James J. Hill, creator of the Great Northern. He was also an apostle of concrete and a promoter of paved highways, and is buried on a bluff at Maryhill that appropriately looks down on train, freeway, and dammed pool.

The first serious proposal to build a transcontinental railroad had come in 1844, when the first big wagon trains were just beginning to traverse the Oregon Trail. Asa Whitney, a New York City merchant, proposed that Congress sell him 78 million acres of empty federal land for sixteen cents each, forming a swath sixty miles wide from Lake Michigan to the mouth of the Columbia River. His corridor would cross the Rockies at South Pass where the wagon trail did and Whitney would use sales of the land to finance his railroad. The ambitious idea was rejected by a Congress split along regional lines over where a railroad should start from or go to. However, the idea to cross the continent with rails and finance it with grants of land stuck. Between the Civil War and 1890, seventy-two thousand miles of track were laid in the West. To help pay for it, Congress gave the railroad barons more than 116 million acres of land—an area nearly twice the size of Oregon—plus $64 million in bonds. Many of the railroad land grants were traded and sold in the Pacific Northwest to form the basis of future timber empires, and the checkerboard pattern of square-mile land grants can still be seen in the clearcuts of the region's mountains.

Plenty of visionaries foresaw the railroad's potential. Western promoter George Wilkes argued that a transcontinental would provide the shortest path from Europe to Asia's commerce. Missouri senator Thomas Hart Benton prophesied that with a railroad to the West, "emigrants would flock upon it as pigeons to their roosts, tear open the bosom of the virgin soil, and spring into existence the long line of farms and houses, of towns and villages, of orchards, fields, and gardens, of churches and school-houses, of noisy shops, clattering mills and thundering forges, and all that civilization affords to enliven the wild domain from the Mississippi to the Pacific." Philosopher Herbert Spencer predicted that railroads would unite disparate cultures and put an end to tribalism and hatred: optimism that would also be voiced for the telephone, airplane, satellite communications, television, and the computer.

A Missouri businessman forecasted a more realistic observation: "It will suit the energy of the American people. They love to go ahead fast, and to go with power. They love to annihilate the magnificent distances."

It would take almost four decades for Asa Whitney's dream of a railroad to be realized on the Columbia; the line from Chicago to Portland was not completed until 1883. Building the transcontinentals cost $100 million, nearly twice as much as the entire federal budget in the first year of the Civil War. It was a project as forbidding as if business today proposed a moon colony costing $2 trillion. Accordingly, before encouraging entrepreneurs to plunge ahead, Congress ordered a survey of several competing routes. Isaac Stevens made the most northerly exploration in 1853 on his way to his new appointive job as territorial governor of Washington.

The surveys were of limited use. The most obvious route—that of the Oregon Trail—was ignored because so much was known about it. The remaining surveys returned with valuable information about the general landscape but few engineering details about the grades, tunnels, and fill that might be required. Any decision on the best path was further hampered by Secretary of War Jefferson Davis. He favored a southern route to prevent the North from monopolizing railroad commerce. The Civil War eliminated the southern routes from consideration, California had laid tracks east from Sacramento toward the Sierras, and so the central route seemed to make the most sense. In 1862, President Lincoln, a railroad enthusiast, chartered Missouri's Union Pacific and California's Central Pacific. They met in Utah on May 10, 1869.

Lincoln chartered the Northern Pacific to the Columbia in 1864. It would run from Chicago to Minneapolis and then west across the Dakotas and Montana to Spokane. From there it would angle southwest to the Columbia River Gorge and Portland, then turn north to Tacoma, on Puget Sound.

More lines followed in a frenzy of development in which every hamlet dreamed of becoming the next New York and every entrepreneur thirsted for a steel-rail empire. In the Pacific Northwest, two more lines were built after the Northern Pacific. A branch of the Union Pacific followed the Oregon Trail route. And in 1893, Jim Hill completed his Great Northern from Minneapolis to the Columbia at Wenatchee and across the Cascades to Everett and Seattle.

The speed of railroad construction crews could be breathtaking. On April 28, 1869, Chinese and Irish laborers in Nevada combined to lay ten miles of track in twelve hours. The Great Northern laid six hundred and forty-three miles of track across the plains between April 2 and November 19, 1887, a rate of nearly three miles a day. And a San Francisco reporter recorded one-half mile of track laid in just twenty-eight minutes.

Tunnels were bored, canyons bridged, mountains sidecut. Much of the work was done by the Chinese; when the Northern Pacific was built across eastern Washington to the Columbia the seven thousand Chinese laborers outnumbered the whites seven to one. The railroads had turned to the Chinese in desperation for labor, and then found they were harder-working, more reliable, more fearless, and less complaining than most of their white counterparts. They didn't drink, didn't frequent the trackside whorehouses, bathed every day, and drank their water as boiled tea, avoiding the stomach sicknesses that felled white laborers. They also earned only half as much. The Chinese also became a labor mainstay in canning and mining. By 1870 there were more Chinese living north of Walla Walla than whites.

The transcontinental's impact was enormous. The six-month wagon train trip or dangerous sail around Cape Horn was reduced to less than a week. The three-hundred-dollar fare for a quick route across Panama was cut to one hundred dollars for first-class rail travel, forty dollars for immigrants. In the thirty years wagon trains had been traversing the West, three hundred and fifty thousand had made the journey. In just the first full year of transcontinental railroad operations on the single route open in 1870, one hundred and fifty thousand people rode. Half a million used the train to migrate to the Pacific Northwest in the 1880s. By the end of the decade they were arriving at a rate of nearly a thousand per week.

The Columbia was the obvious railroad route through the Cascades. Trains needed a grade of no more than one hundred and sixteen feet to the mile, a rise barely perceptible to the human eye. River valleys provided the ideal slope. Thousands of miles of riverbank were turned to railroad embankment and fill in the West. Streamside wetlands were destroyed, biologically significant shallows and pools were silted over, and stream-shading vegetation was cut back. At the time, such damage seemed hardly to dent the sprawling wilderness—but the propensity of railroads and highways to follow rivers would have severe cumulative impacts on riparian ecology.

The man who brought the first transcontinental to the Columbia River was German-born Henry Villard. A scion of a well-connected German family, he had rebelled against his father, sailed to America, and worked as a Chicago and New York newspaperman who covered the Lincoln-Douglas debates and the Civil War. His fame as a reporter resulted in German investors asking him to represent them when the Kansas-Pacific railroad went into receivership. Villard successfully stood up to the demands of financier Jay Gould, and with this success in hand he came to Oregon in 1873 to represent German bondholders of the stalled Oregon and California Railroad. This line had laid tracks up the Willamette Valley but plans to reach San Francisco had stalled in a national financial panic. The industry's distress was Villard's opportunity, and he became one of a triumvirate of ruthless but visionary transportation entrepreneurs—the other two are steamboat monopolist Captain Ainsworth and Great Northern director Jim Hill—who played key roles in the development of the Columbia Basin.

Villard had a genius for building colossal financial empires with other people's money, coupled with an inability to keep them from collapsing after overextending himself. He took over control of the O&C on behalf of the investors, purchased Ainsworth's Oregon Steam Navigation Company for $5 million, added the "Rawhide Railroad" of Dr. Dorsey Baker, and combined all this into the Oregon Railway and Navigation Company. Even though he now owned the Columbia's steamship line and the government had started construction on Cascade Locks, Villard built a railway line through the Columbia River Gorge anyway, following the Oregon shore. Meanwhile he borrowed $8 million from eastern investors, bought stock in the Northern Pacific to win a seat on the board, took over control of that railroad, and linked its line with his. In five years the German had become one of the most powerful and famous businessmen in America.

Then his empire collapsed from its precarious financing. Villard returned to Germany to recoup his reputation, bounced back to the United States to help organize the Edison General Electric Company in 1889, and by 1890 was overextended again. He was forced out by J. P. Morgan and the Vanderbilts.

This meteoric streak was played out against intense regional rivalries in the Pacific Northwest. While Villard's railroad eventually continued north from Portland through Kalama to Tacoma on Puget Sound, Washington residents interpreted his choice of the Columbia for the rail corridor as an Oregon triumph that funneled the lion's share of trade to Portland. The decision rankled. Historically Portland had been the path to the interior even though Seattle boasted the better port. Only with a railroad of its own through the Cascades could Seattle hope to compete directly for the commerce of the Inland Empire.

Puget Sound's first big break came when Villard's empire crumbled and the Northern Pacific was taken over by eastern investors led by Jay Gould. The new railroad barons decided in 1887 to split the freight of the Northwest interior between the two rival ports. Traffic south of the Snake would be routed down the Columbia to Portland, while traffic north would go to Puget Sound. The Cascades Tunnel was bored through the Cascades between Yakima and Tacoma in what was an astounding engineering feat at the time.

Seattle still longed for a direct line of its own, however, and looked to Jim Hill. This Minnesota tycoon was the most brilliant of the railroad barons: entering the game too late to get lavish federal land grants, he had to make his line pay for itself. He did so by improving track engineering to allow trains to haul more weight, promoting settlement, and wheedling political concessions from cities and towns anxious for a station. He masterfully extracted a swatch of free land from Spokane by amiably threatening to bypass the city if it did not cooperate. Hill also settled an old land claim against the federal government by getting title to Northwest timberland he subsequently sold to friend Frederick Weyerhaeuser. Hill brought farming to eastern Montana, created true cities out of places such as Wenatchee, and encouraged experimentation with irrigation, seed, refrigeration, and transport.

Once Hill's railroad crossed the Cascades, Portland's head start as the region's primary city could not overcome the Columbia's disadvantage as a harbor. By 1910, Puget Sound was shipping twice as much wheat as its Oregon rival. Industry and shipping concentrated on Puget Sound, Seattle passed Portland in population, and by the mid-twentieth century Washington had twice the population of its older neighbor.

The railroads made possible large-scale development of the Columbia River country. Between 1880 and 1890, 2.5 million acres of new farmland were opened in Washington, Oregon, and Idaho by the settlers the railroads brought. Trains allowed shipment of meat, wool, wood, and minerals to distant markets. What had been relatively modest logging near streams and bays with horses and oxen became industrial-scale harvest wherever a spur railroad could be put. By late in the nineteenth century, Northwest mills were processing a million board feet of lumber every day.

With Villard's empire evaporating and Jim Hill remaining based in Minneapolis, it was Hill's son-in-law Sam who left on the Columbia a physical monument to this era: Maryhill. Unable to achieve a happy family life or live up to the business acumen of his famous father-in-law, Hill tried to build above the river an agricultural utopia instead.

Sam Hill was intelligent, energetic, creative, charming, hapless, egotistical, restless, and probably manic-depressive. It is illustrative of Hill's personality that he started three different books in 1923 and finished none of them, that he acquired and shed companies without leaving any particular stamp of success, that he claimed to undertake a secret diplomatic mission during World War I that may have existed only in his imagination—and yet he retained the friendship of royalty and the rich. He played the part of empire builder even if he had no acumen for its accomplishment.

He is a peripheral figure in Columbia River history except that he represents the instinct of Euro-Americans to modify the environment they find themselves in. He left in the Northwest three peculiar monuments to his own eccentricity: the mansion of Maryhill, a nearby concrete replica of Britain's Stonehenge, and the white Peace Arch that stands on the U.S.-Canadian border at

Blaine, Washington. Hill also contributed money to the controversial marble monument "from his white friends" over Chief Joseph's grave at Nespelem, Washington, having met the famed warrior in 1905.

Hill was a handsome and ambitious lawyer practicing in Minneapolis when he met Mary Frances Hill, daughter of the rising railroad baron. It was coincidence that the couple shared the same last name. When they married on September 6, 1888, the thirty-one-year-old Hill made his fortune and lost his happiness. He got $200,000 in railroad stocks and bonds that he successfully parlayed into a respectable fortune in the stock market. But he could not please his wife as a husband, his children as a father, or Jim Hill as a son-in-law, and spent an estimated $2 million to $3 million on the homes and monuments he left behind in psychological compensation.

For a time Sam Hill appeared to be a rising star in his father-in-law's employ, but by 1901 he had left. Exactly what went wrong is unclear; he wrote the railroad baron, "That I have often been an embarrassment to you I am sorry for, but no one has ever lost any money through me, even those enterprises which at one time looked doubtful, being, I trust, now established." Then he left Minneapolis to start over in the Pacific Northwest. His wife would not follow him, preferring the social life of Washington, D.C. She would not divorce him either. Hill's daughter Mary became severely depressed and was eventually institutionalized. His son remained distant despite Hill's clumsy attempts to spoil him. Sam once brought home from Japan a professor named Yamushita to teach the boy judo.

In the decade after leaving James J. Hill's employ, Sam plunged into a whirlwind of activity. He took over a natural gas company in Seattle and fought a bitter competitive war with rivals that ended in consolidation in 1904. He bought a huge summer home in Massachusetts, a mansion in Seattle, and a ranch in eastern Washington that later provided much of the acreage for Pearygin State Park. He ran a struggling Portland telephone company eventually absorbed by Bell, built another mansion in that city, and bought and ran two cargo ships that went broke.

Hill was also a restless traveler. He made at least thirty-two round trips to Europe and circled the globe seven times, learning to speak German, French, and Italian fluently. He carried only a small black bag on his journeys; he had dozens of special suitcases stocked with clothes and toiletries and placed in leading hotels and clubs throughout the world. Hill had two dozen globes custom-made in Berlin that he sent to friends as gifts: knowledgeable about geography, he liked to lecture friends while pointing to these globes. Some judged him charming, others a bore. In 1916, Hill made a bizarre trip west from Seattle to Siberia and across the length of Russia, claiming to bear diplomatic messages. His mission had no discernible effect on World War I. More amusingly, he once met a newlywed couple in Seattle who could not find a hotel room and, pretending his mansion was a guest house, put them up for $2.50 a day. They were puzzled by the absence of other guests but delighted at the price for such luxury.

Hill had at least two mistresses: secretary Annie Laurie Whelan and the more flamboyant Edith Mona Bell. The latter was a character in her own right who rode bareback in Wild Bill Cody's Wild West Show, competed in rodeos, and swam the chilly, twenty-mile-broad Strait of Juan de Fuca. She later outscooped her male colleagues to become San Francisco's first female crime reporter. When Hill was dying, she posed first as a nurse and then as a janitor to sneak into his hospital room, possibly to persuade him to leave a larger inheritance to her.

Sam also had a close relationship with Loie Fuller, a possible bisexual who was famous at the turn of the century for her Folies-Bergère dances with flowing veils, an act that later inspired stripper Sally Rand. He was so close to Queen Marie of Romania that in 1926 she agreed to come to the remote bluff at Maryhill to dedicate the concrete shell of Hill's mansion as an art museum. Whether either relationship was sexual is unknown.

Hill named the seven-thousand-acre tract he bought in Klickitat County for his wife and daughter—but his wife never saw it, his daughter was committed, and the mansion was never finished in Hill's lifetime. A shortage of money and typical loss of interest led Hill to abandon the project in midcourse. It was Loie Fuller who persuaded him it could be converted into a museum. When Queen Marie made a highly publicized trip across North America and bewildered reporters by climaxing it with a visit to the treeless, windy spot above the Columbia, she found it necessary in her dedication speech to try to explain. "Sam Hill is my friend," she said. "He is not only a dreamer but he is a worker. Samuel Hill once gave me his hand and said if there were anything on earth that I needed, I had only to ask. Some may even scoff, for they do not understand. But I have understood. So when Samuel Hill asked me to come overseas to this house built in the wilderness, I came with love and understanding. Samuel Hill knows why I came, and I am not going to give any other explanation. Sometimes the things dreamers do seem incomprehensible to others, and the world wonders why dreamers do not see the world the way others do."

Hill was certainly odd. A biographer of Queen Marie described Hill as a "raving American eccentric . . . a giant, aging sheepdog of a man with a cherubic face, a shock of white hair and a penchant for building ramshackle monuments to pipe dreams." In middle age he looked a bit like Santa Claus.

If Ainsworth had represented the steamboat and Villard and Jim Hill the railroads, Sam Hill can take some credit for introducing the automobile to the Pacific Northwest. At the turn of the century the car was a rich man's toy and paved highways barely existed. Hill became a leader in the Good Roads Movement, at the time largely a campaign for the elite who could afford cars. As an example of the trendy enthusiasm, five hundred Portland businessmen journeyed by train to the Columbia Gorge in June of 1914, paying seventy-five cents each to join county laborers for five hours at constructing the Columbia River Highway.

That highway was one of the engineering wonders of the age, its half-abandoned ruins today exhibiting a grace and craftsmanship that put modern roads to shame. Hill pushed for a design that would mimic some of the mountain highways he had admired in Europe, urging the hire of Italian stonemasons who built bridges and guardrails. Constructing a paved highway through the steep gorge was a remarkable feat. Early portage trails and railways had been supplanted in 1872 by a crude wagon road for which the Oregon legislature appropriated $100,000, but the dirt track was steep, muddy, and impassable in winter. Some believed a proper road could never be built. Hill helped scout the highway's route on a rugged two-day hike and spoke for it often. Completed in 1915 and stretching three hundred and sixty-three miles from Seaside on the Oregon coast to Pendleton, east of the Cascades, the road was the Northwest's first rural paved highway. In the gorge it weaved in and out of tunnels, rolled across graceful arched bridges past waterfalls, and became the subject of numerous postcards.

With completion of this highway, today's freight triad of

boat, train, and truck was foretold. The two-lane Columbia River Highway was important for another reason, however. It was arguably the first significant environmental consciousness-raiser on the river. "Nowhere in the world is there such magnificent scenery as can be found along the Columbia River," Hill once proclaimed in a speech in Minneapolis. Something so lovely needed roads to give its beauty an audience, he believed. With steamboat excursion traffic in decline after the turn of the century, the highway made the Columbia accessible again. State parks were established on the Oregon shore where the highway ran, while none were created on the inaccessible Washington side. This started a tradition of gorge protection among Portland residents that helped keep factories out when Bonneville Dam was completed and led to the creation of a National Scenic Area in the gorge in 1987.

The crowning work of Hill's frenetic life was supposed to be Maryhill. He brought his interests in roads, natural beauty, utopian communities, and monuments together on the north bank of the Columbia. His intention was to create a model farm community patterned after the Quaker settlement of Whittier, California, one of several attempts to create idealized communities on the Columbia.

Maryhill is located on the steep Klickitat Hills at a point Hill billed as "The Land Where the Rain and Sunshine Meet." He wrote to his brother Richard, "We have found the Garden of Eden . . . the most beautiful country I have ever seen." He wanted, he explained later, to battle the growing urbanization of American life. "I believe in man on the land," he said, anticipating arguments that would be made for Columbia Basin irrigation projects. "We cannot afford to have our producers leave the land and come to the city and become parasites. We want our girls to stay on the farm and become the mothers of a virile race of men and not just go to the city and become manicurists, stenographers, and variety actresses. We want our boys to stay on the farm and not succumb to the lure of the Great White Way or become chauffeurs or clerks."

The site was undeniably beautiful, but no garden. The land was treeless and most of the acreage Hill acquired comprised steep grassy bluffs of no agricultural use. This was not where the rain met the sun either: adequate rainfall for farming stopped ten or twenty miles to the west. There was no wood for fuel, the wind was unceasing, and grasshoppers ravaged the crops. It was hot in summer and cold in winter. The Columbia's rapids below Maryhill were so bad that supplies had to be barged a mile upstream and driven along the riverbank in blowing sand. Hill brought his own gasoline-powered ferry to challenge the rapids and gave up after it hit a rock on its first try. Locals called the entire scheme "Hill's Follies," their dislike for the project reinforced when Hill pushed out existing farmers to plant Maryhill and then failed to attract newcomers. His dryland orchards failed.

Frustrated as a farmer, Hill turned to engineering. He was fascinated by the utility of concrete in an age of brick and stone, and hoped to make Maryhill a highway proving ground. Beginning in 1911, Sam built ten miles of serpentine paved road up the steep bluffs in a demonstration project that cost him over $100,000. The "Maryhill loops" climbed eight hundred and fifty feet in 3.6 miles to join a dirt road to nearby Goldendale. These experiments were the first paved highways in Washington: a road to nowhere behind his Castle Nowhere.

The enthusiast used concrete to re-create the Neolithic monument Stonehenge, the "stones" made of reinforced concrete cast in molds to present a rough-hewn appearance. They were set and stacked to form a completed circle, a duplication of how the original must have appeared in Druidic times before present-day disrepair. Unlike the Salisbury Plain Stonehenge, however, the American replica is overpowered by the towering hills of its landscape, which destroyed its usefulness as an astronomical calendar. The hills loom so high that the sun cannot clear them in time to allow light and shadow to line up correctly between carefully aligned pillars. It was a typical Sam Hill oversight, as was the anthropological confusion that led Hill to build it as a memorial to Klickitat County's dead in World War I. He wrongly believed that the original Stonehenge had been a place of human sacrifice. The monument today affords sweeping views of the river and provides a popular gathering place for would-be Druids, witches, bikers, and amateur astronomers during eclipses or the turn of seasons.

The passion for concrete carried over into the mansion. Work began on the Flemish-style home in 1914. The most unusual feature was that Hill used no wood; the walls and floors were made of reinforced concrete and steel lath. The main house was sixty by ninety-three feet, a d long ramps on either end extended the structure to four hundred feet. This allowed another Hill enthusiasm, the automobile, to be driven directly up to heavy copper doors ten feet high. The home was wired for electricity twenty years before power would reach the site and had five miles of copper piping for water and heat.

As World War I dragged on, work on Maryhill slowed and then stopped. Hill realized his farming community was never going to materialize. It was clear his family could not be persuaded to move there either. Moreover he was short of money, caused by the financial foundering of his Home Telephone Company in Portland. By the time of the museum's initial dedication in 1926, Maryhill had become so derelict that a caretaker had to burn down a decaying eyesore of a barn before Queen Marie arrived. "The people attending the dedication ceremony must have felt, in varying degrees, incredulous, amused and embarrassed that this lonely hulk was to be taken seriously as a future museum," Hill biographer John Tuhy noted.

Hill's life drizzled to a quiet end and he died in 1931. The museum was finally completed by 1940 with money from his estate. Construction of highways along both shores of the Columbia allowed forty-nine thousand people to visit Maryhill the first year it opened. It has had a steady stream of visitors ever since. Today's edifice is striking in its very remoteness, and houses a collection as eccentric as its builder: Rodin sculptures, odd pieces of furniture, a collection of chess sets, items from Romanian royalty.

As unlikely as Maryhill is, its extravagance recalls railroad wealth and its concrete solidity foretold the river's dams. Placed with more enthusiasm than careful thought, Castle Nowhere is an artifact that represents the culture that developed the river, just as the petroglyphs recall the natives that came before.

The Inland Empire

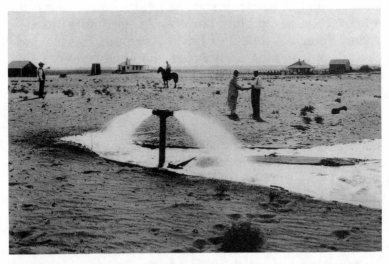

An early irrigation attempt on the Columbia Plateau at Moses Lake before construction of Columbia River dams. This is on land under development by the Moses Lake Land and Irrigation Company. *(University of Washington Library)*

The sagebrush bluff called Crow Butte pokes like a fat thumb into the homeliest stretch of the Columbia River: the low, dry bluffs that run sixty miles east to west from McNary to John Day dams. The river here, treeless and lightly inhabited, gets five to eight inches of precipitation a year. "That puts us just slightly ahead of the Mojave Desert," said Bud Mercer. The severity of the landscape can be gauged from the name of the rocky hill that looms over the western edge of Mercer Farms: Golgotha Butte. So bleak is the area that the desert on the Oregon shore is partly occupied by an army ammunition and nerve-gas depot, a bombing range, a hazardous-waste landfill, and the basin's sole coal-fired power plant. A new regional landfill on a bluff in Washington collects garbage from as far away as California. Yet between these installations are the irrigated crop circles of rich farmland that grow enough calories to feed Seattle. Despite this stinginess of nature, Mercer has become a potato, corn, beet, carrot, and grape grower.

Crow Butte wraps part way around a shallow lagoon created by John Day Dam. On the lagoon bank is a squat concrete pump house with several pipes that disappear into a hillside of sage and dry grass. There is no other evidence of what the structure is for: no farm or field or house or sign. When I followed a gravel road up and over the desert bluff, however, I came into a broad valley as jarringly green as a field of plastic Astroturf. This is where the pipes come out, and the result is four thousand acres of food. The land is watered by spindle-legged "center-pivot" irrigation systems that straddle the crops like giant robotic insects, swinging endlessly around hundred-acre circular fields on fat rubber tires. The Mercer pumps siphon up to a hundred cubic feet of Columbia River water every second, equal to the flow of a respectable creek. The water is free except for the cost of pumping and has allowed the conversion of the Mercer family's onetime thirty-two-thousand-acre cattle ranch into a smaller, more manageable vegetable farm. It has cost the family $7 million in irrigation equipment, buildings, and machinery to get to this point, and their land has turned into a minicommunity of fourteen houses, offices, barns, a food-processing factory, thirty full-time employees, and at least seventy seasonal workers. A huge American flag flaps in the hot summer breeze in front of Mercer's modest office.

"It just depends on water," explained Linda Mercer, Bud's sister-in-law, who works at the Columbia Crest vineyards that tap the Columbia a few miles upriver. "If you don't have water, the land isn't worth anything."

As told by the federal Bureau of Reclamation and the irrigation lobby, the history of the Columbia Basin is pretty simple: dry land plus harnessed water has resulted in new wealth and cheap food. Agriculture is the greatest American success story. Nowhere does this success seem more striking than in the Horse Heaven Hills around Mercer Farms. Treeless fields, shimmering in the sun and a crystal mist of sprayed water, stretch for miles before dissolving into a hazed horizon.

Reality is a bit more complicated. Settlers came late to the self-proclaimed "Inland Empire" of the Columbia Plateau. They were brought by the railroads, which promised to export economically whatever the newcomers could grow. The pioneers had two prophets to choose from.

The first was Major John Wesley Powell, the explorer who lost an arm at Shiloh and used wooden dories to lead the first expedition down the fearsome rapids of the Colorado River into the Grand Canyon. Powell traveled widely in the Great Basin and Colorado Plateau and concluded in an 1876 report that the West simply did not have sufficient water to support a large population. If all the region's rivers were tapped, he warned, they would irrigate only 1 to 3 percent of the land. He urged that allowable homestead size, set at one hundred and sixty acres in the moist East, be modified in the West. Settlers should either be granted smaller forty-acre parcels in irrigable valleys that a family could realistically ditch with the hand tools available, or be granted up to 2,560 acres for dryland farming and ranching. Powell suggested that rangeland be held in common, that unused water rights revert to the government, and that political boundaries should follow the natural boundaries of river basins, not arbitrary lines across a map. The major was right, but most of his ideas were ignored.

The other prophet was Ferdinand Vandiveer Hayden. This self-trained geologist was a bombastic, self-promoting employee of the U.S. Geological Survey who—with more optimism than scientific evidence—declared that "rain follows the plow." His theories seemed to get anecdotal support from brief wet cycles in the late nineteenth century. Hayden believed that as the prairies and deserts of the West were cultivated the ground would absorb more rainwater, rather than having it run wastefully away in rivers. As the soil stored more water more of it would evaporate to increase atmospheric humidity, creating still more precipitation, thicker vegetation, moister soil, and so on, in an ever-wetter upward spiral. Nature would smile upon human development and forests would march West in the wake of the pioneers. Hayden was wrong but he promoted his error tirelessly, and people anxious for land of their own wanted to believe. When nature did not conform to these predictions, the settlers who had been betrayed by fanciful science decided to deliver through engineering what the sky would not.

Rain did not follow the plow. Wheat farming in eastern Montana promoted by Jim Hill's Northern Pacific Railroad produced the nation's first dust bowl in the 1890s. Periodic cycles of dry weather after 1910 in Washington forced farm abandonment along the mid-Columbia River. The answer to this crisis, however, was not less development but more. It fueled the campaign for irrigation that eventually led to Grand Coulee and other Columbia and Snake River dams. The cattle and sheep industries in the Columbia Basin had already slumped because of overgrazing and disappearing range. Farmers made new mistakes, plowing with hope in places where a moment's look at sage and sand should have warned them that adequate moisture did not exist. Rather than concede Hayden was wrong and Powell right, the farmers turned to irrigation. Grady Auvil, a successful apple grower on the banks of the Columbia north of Wenatchee, pumps three to four feet of water each year on his trees, an artificial supplementation equal to annual rainfall in Seattle. "I vowed early in life that I wouldn't grow anything I couldn't water myself," the vigorous eighty-seven-year-old explained. "I hear wheat growers crying, 'When's it going to rain, when's it going to rain?' It rains when I want it to, here."

Once engineering of the West got started, it fed on itself. Successful irrigation created communities that pressed for still more successful irrigation in order to grow. Reclamation bureaucracies sprang up to serve this demand and developed a built-in bias toward engineering watersheds. The government granted millions of acres to railroads to help them finance their lines, the railroads founded towns to create business and land sales for their trains, the towns demanded irrigation water to create a farm base, and the resulting food provided a transport need to justify the investment in the railroads in the first place.

The need to water crops provided a rationale for dams that could also generate power, and the need for electricity provided a rationale for dams that could also water crops. The new energy drew new industries such as aluminum smelting to the thinly populated Pacific Northwest, creating the manufacturing base for larger cities that needed still more food. Much of the development occurred along riverbanks, and the new residents needed ever-larger and ever-more-remote dams to protect them from flooding. It all seemed so self-evident, a civilization with its own powerfully circular logic.

As a result, western water development pyramided into ever-more complex empire, requiring ever-greater government intervention to keep the system functioning. The system of canals and pumps and water rights grew not because of some national food policy that favored Idaho potatoes over Astoria salmon, but because of local boosterism, individual attempts at exploiting opportunity, and serendipitous leaps in technology.

This chaotic evolution devoured many who tried to benefit from it. Irrigation proved costly and required the skills of the engineer, the accountant, the mechanic, and the marketer as well as the farmer. Of thirty-five growers who plunged into irrigation with Mercer by the late 1970s, just three are left. The ten-thousand-acre farm next door required a $10 million line of credit to get started. Six different owners in succession lost money trying to carry such debt and turn a profit. Mercer Farms itself began not because the family wanted to leave the cattle business and grow vegetables, but because, back in 1964, their feedlot at Prosser was forty long, dusty miles away.

At that time the family ranched fifty square miles it had acquired during the Depression and it took one hundred and twenty acres in this rain-starved country to support a single cow. Bud Mercer grew up a cowboy, riding sage desert next to a river with two and a half times the flow of the Nile.

Cattle are fattened for the slaughterhouse in a feedlot but the nearest one in Prosser was inconvenient to the remote ranch. The Mercers wanted to build their own on their land, but needed hay to feed the penned cattle. Hay needs water, and in Idaho farmers were beginning to lift water directly out of new Snake and Boise river reservoirs with powerful electric pumps run by the plentiful, cheap electricity from the Northwest's new dams. "That got us excited about being able to do the same thing," Mercer said. John Day Dam was being constructed downriver on the Columbia, and in 1968 the resulting pool backed up past the Mercer ranch. The reservoir level would be kept within a narrow range a pump house could tap.

The Mercers got a permit from the state of Washington to take water out of the Columbia. There was no charge for the water, no review of pumping's impact on fish, and no debate about whether the state could or should allow siphoning of the river's flow. Western states had vigorously asserted their authority over water rights for as long as they had existed—even on rivers such as the Columbia, which touched more than one state and crossed an international boundary. Appropriation of rivers had been key to western development.

The Mercers planted their first crop in 1969. Besides cattle feed, they signed a contract with the Utah and Idaho Sugar Company to grow five hundred acres of sugar beets.

At first, everything went wrong. Circle irrigation equipment was new, imperfect, and broke down constantly: if Bud set ten circles going in the morning, seven would be out of action by afternoon. The underground pipe pulling water from the Columbia was defective, exploded, and had to be dug out and replaced. Vegetables required expensive fertilizers and pesticides, the family learning what worked and what didn't through costly trial and error. Yet they managed to turn a profit the third year. By that time it was becoming apparent that the cost of watering land for pasturage didn't produce the profit of watering it for vegetables: it can take nearly four thousand gallons of water to put one pound of beef on American tables. They began to phase out the cows. The one hundred and twenty acres that would support one range cow could grow a staggering five million pounds of potatoes or carrots if given Columbia River water, fertilizer, and pesticides. Slowly Bud tripled his farmed acreage, bought out his brothers, expanded into vegetable packing, and sold the surplus range. Hundreds of farmers up and down the Columbia and Snake were doing much the same thing. The big investment that was required attracted big companies: John Hancock Insurance, U.S. Tobacco for wine grapes, Boeing as a way to lease land it no longer needed for testing its bombers. Along McNary and John Day pools today, 320,000 acres are watered by about 1.5 percent of the Columbia's flow. None of this acreage is part of a federal reclamation project, as is the land due south of Grand Coulee: it is financed privately, pumping either directly from the river or from wells in the aquifer fed by the river. But without the pools and electricity provided by the dams, it would not be possible.

The sophisticated agricultural fiefdom of a Bud Mercer is the result of a lengthy, complex, and experimental development of the Columbia Basin that had no master plan until the Army Corps of Engineers produced its grand blueprint for damming the main river in 1932. It grew in fits and starts in restless pursuit of opportunities through pork-barrel politics and without much public debate, environmental impact statements, or coherent national farm policy.

Columbia River agriculture that followed Astoria's first weedy garden plots can be dated to 1826, when the Hudson's Bay

Company ordered farming on its posts to lessen reliance on provisions from Europe. Farming had been a disappointment at Fort Astoria but it thrived on the prairie benchland of Fort Vancouver a hundred miles inland. By 1830 the supply of food from England could be stopped, and by 1835 the fort was provisioning homeward-bound ships.

In 1826, Lieutenant Emilius Simpson visited Fort Vancouver and presented a packet of apple seeds he had carried in his pocket from London. The result astounded later visitors. "The greatest curiosity," John Townsend observed in 1832, "is the apples, which grow on small trees, the branches of which would be broken without the support of props. So profuse is the quantity of fruit that the limbs are covered with it, and it is actually packed together precisely in the same manner that onions are attached to ropes when they are exposed for sale in our markets."

Once the Pacific Northwest began to become self-sufficient in food—not difficult, given the small population at the time—export markets had to be developed to allow future agricultural growth. The first such market was Hawaii, where flour, fish, and lumber were exchanged for coffee, sugar, rice, molasses, and salt. Provisions were also sold to the Russian posts in Alaska. Cattle were driven north to the Willamette Valley from California to start herds, and by the winter of 1843–44 the Whitman missionaries could finally substitute beef for the horsemeat they had been eating since their arrival in the Walla Walla Valley. In the decade of 1835–45, grain production in the Willamette Valley swelled seventeen times.

The "Inland Empire," however (a name eventually coined by Spokane newspapers for the Columbia Basin east of the Cascades), did not look very imperial in the middle of the nineteenth century. Most pioneers pushed through the arid region to the wet Willamette Valley or the lumber towns around Puget Sound. The Columbia's rapids hampered transportation and the interior was remote from any markets. While the valleys watered by such rivers as the Yakima, the Walla Walla, the Umatilla, the Wenatchee, and the Okanogan showed promise, they were separated by steep mountains, bleak expanses of sage and sand, and thirty-seven hundred square miles of scablands carved by the Spokane floods. Walla Walla prospered by supplying miners, but in 1855, when Wasco County took in all of eastern Oregon, it had just thirty-five residents.

Those who finally did try to stick east of the mountains experimented with almost comic doggedness. They tried tobacco, ginseng, grapes, sorghum, and cotton. They imported llamas and camels. One Danish immigrant had heard Washington had a lot of trees and showed up in the middle of the state's desert expecting to log. More scientifically, Moxee Farm near Yakima was founded in the 1880s by Gardiner Hubbard, the founder of the National Geographic Society, and his son-in-law Alexander Graham Bell. They ran a number of experiments to see what would grow in the region and, until their tobacco was destroyed by frost, briefly manufactured cigars called Fleur de Yakima.

Those who pioneered endured a wide, treeless, dusty country that could be crushingly lonely. Initial refinements could be rare: one shack was papered in rattlesnake skins. Most families started in tents, sheds, sod houses, or roofed pits, and graduated to a rude, unpainted board shack of wood skidded down from the mountains during winter snowfalls. Most of these cabins had less than four hundred square feet and were furnished with no more than a stove, bed, and table. The green lumber typically shrank after construction, opening cracks. The homes were cold in winter and hot in summer and so drafty the dust couldn't be kept out. A few settlers went insane in the stark landscape and for a scrap of visual relief, some women decorated their cabin windows by stringing empty eggs gathered from the nests of the long-tailed magpies that glided over the sage. As late as 1925 only 7 percent of the area's farms had electricity and only 10 percent had running water.

The McGregor family represented a rare success without irrigation, creating a profitable sheep and wheat ranch at the dry junction of the Palouse and Snake rivers. The emptiness of the landscape remained hard to bear, however, particularly for the women. "I know that there is something in that country that doesn't like us!" Elgin McGregor wrote. "It will purr and relax in the sun of spring and Indian summer so long as you leave it alone, but it will turn malicious and malignant if you try to make it serve you, and in the long run it will probably destroy us all. Maude [McGregor] was horribly depressed by it and [my husband] John and I were both aware of it. He said it wanted to be given back to the Indians, and I'm sure he often wished it could."

Development of this region came in overlapping stages, each tending to reinforce the others. In rough order came missionaries, miners, cattle, wheat, sheep, and, by the turn of the century, irrigated agriculture. Wheat, sheep, and irrigation all flourished only after the completion of the railroads.

What first drew the newcomers east of the Cascades were gold strikes, in Colville in 1854 and in British Columbia's Kootenay region and in Idaho in the 1860s. Miners needed to eat and the Cascades and Coast ranges formed a snowy, thickly forested barrier that prevented easy supply from the coast. Cattle that brought forty dollars a head in the Yakima Valley could fetch up to a hundred dollars if driven to the mines. The Okanogan Valley to the north was a natural corridor leading into Canada and before the legendary cattle drives from Texas started, the drives of the Columbia Basin were born. An estimated 22,000 head pushed up the Okanogan Trail to the mines in ten years, and in the 1870s 72,000 head of Columbia Basin cattle were driven to Wyoming to stock ranches there. By 1879, Yakima County had an average of seventy-one cows for every family. Cattle kings such as Ben Snipes ran up to 125,000 head in the Horse Heaven Hills between The Dalles and Yakima.

The Columbia remained so difficult to navigate that it was Walla Walla at the junction of trails, not Wallula on the river, that swiftly became the dominant city in Washington Territory. "To you in Walla Walla," a representative of the Canadian mines wrote, "we must look for flour, bacon, fruit &c., but we can return you gold dust worth $18 an ounce." Supplies moved by sea to Portland, up the Columbia to Walla Walla, and then by trail to the distant claims. The community was for a generation the largest in Washington Territory, not surpassed in population by Seattle until the 1880s.

British Columbia boomtowns were no less flamboyant than their American counterparts, many rushing from frantic development to ghost towns in a few years. Typical was Sandon, the slowly restored ruins of which can be visited today. It sprang up in 1893 in a heavily forested mountain valley along the shores of a creek and within four years had twenty-four hotels, twenty-three saloons, one hundred and fifteen prostitutes, and five thousand other residents. In 1900 it burned down, the start of a long decline confirmed when the mines played out. A testament to its early glory is the hydroelectric generating plant that still hums up the hill from town. It is the oldest such working plant in British Columbia.

Not only was the beef in the British Columbia mines American, so, too, for a long time, were the miners and capital. Western Canada did not have the work force, decent roads, or railroads to reach its mineral wealth because of its rugged topography. As a result, the Yankees invaded up the north-south valleys. So complete was the initial American domination that during 1888 and 1889, all the stamps sold in Nelson, B.C., were American. The best mines discovered in Rossland, B.C., were all quickly sold to Spokane investors: the fabulous LeRoi sold to Americans for $30,000 and subsequently produced up to $84,000 in ore each day. The huge smelter at Trail, B.C., was created by F. Augustus Heinz, a New York engineer who had impressed the mineral-savvy residents of Butte, Montana, by wringing new profits out of the supposedly exhausted Rarus mine. American rail lines built north by Daniel Corbin provided ore transport. Resenting this de facto colonization, Canada enlisted the aid of the Canadian Pacific to buy Heinz out and extend its own lines south toward the border, reasserting control.

The reign of the cowboy was brief. There were no controls on overgrazing and the grass deteriorated rapidly. There were also no barns or winter feed to keep the cattle alive in severe weather. The herds lost up to 80 percent of their number in the winter of 1880–81 and again in 1889–90. At the same time, railroads brought a flood of settlers who began to claim and fence the range. The depression of 1893 was the final blow that wiped Snipes and many other cattlemen out. His last fifteen hundred cows were auctioned shortly before he left to try his luck in the Yukon gold rush. Cattle would bounce back only after irrigation began producing feed to replace the range that had been lost.

Wheat came next. After the initial growing experiments of missionary Henry Spalding, officials began touting the potential of the land. In 1873, L. P. Beach, surveyor general of Washington Territory, set off a flood of settlement by proclaiming the fertility of the rich Palouse region. Farmers learned the treeless soils could yield astonishing quantities of wheat when cultivated: so astonishing that the crop could compete with California despite the difficulty of shipping down the Columbia; so astonishing that the Senate would order a study of "the rainless regions of Washington and Oregon" to try to figure out the soil's secret. Washington senator John H. Mitchell sent a sack of Columbia Plateau soil to the Smithsonian for analysis in the 1870s. It reported back that the dirt resembled the volcanic, seemingly inexhaustible soil of Sicily that had been cultivated for thousands of years. The conclusion was touted for years to encourage settlement. Newspapers proclaimed the interior Northwest as "the best poor man's country in the world."

In 1868 the Northwest broke San Francisco's monopoly on wheat trade to England and by 1895 the Columbia River "wheat fleet" peaked at one hundred and fifty-four ships. Initially, the majority of the wheat came from the Willamette Valley, aided in 1873 by a lock that opened at Willamette Falls and allowed barge shipment to Portland. A trickle of Inland Empire wheat was transported on the Columbia by flat-bottomed barges driven upriver by wind and down by current. That trickle became a flood when the first railroad was completed up the Columbia in 1883. From 1890 to 1910 Washington was adding 100,000 acres of new wheat land a year, and its production soared from nine million bushels to 37 million. By 1905 wheat was the region's biggest crop and the Columbia region had passed California as the biggest wheat-producing area west of the Continental Divide. Californians used irrigation to switch to higher-value vegetable and fruit crops.

The resulting golden landscape of Washington's Palouse Hills inspired novelist Zane Grey to call it a "lonely, hard, heroic country," and it is a place today of stunning, austere beauty. Rural roads ride up and around the swell of plump hills like the track of a boat on an ocean, and during the riotous green of a wheat country spring, when the new stalks glow and ripple under a scrubbed sky, one has the sensation of rolling from peak to trough in some gigantic ocean storm.

Cattle faced competition from more than just wheat land homesteaders. A new animal entered the plateau that could thrive on overgrazed scrubland. Sheep were cheap to buy, would seemingly eat almost anything (including poisonous weeds—they were dumb as wood), they multiplied quickly, and they were inexpensive to keep: a single sheep man and his dogs could handle up to three thousand animals. Their chief product, wool, would store indefinitely and was easy to transport. Pendleton, Oregon, had been platted in 1869 and its woolen mills soon thrived on the huge herds and produced the famed Pendleton shirt; the existing woolen mill at Washougal on the Columbia just west of the Columbia River Gorge is a legacy of this era. By 1900 there were eight times as many sheep as cattle on the Columbia Plateau: 1.1 million. Cowboys put up some feeble resistance, burning a few sheep-herding structures and shooting animals in central Oregon, but they soon surrendered to changing economics.

Typical of the transition were Peter and Archie McGregor, who in 1882 demonstrated the new efficiency of cross-continental rail and boat transport when they took just sixteen days to travel from Toronto to Dayton, Washington, via San Francisco and Portland. Unable to afford a horse, Archie subsequently traveled on foot to look for well-watered land to farm—once covering sixty miles without food—and actually staked a one-hundred-and-sixty-acre claim at Steamboat Rock. He soon abandoned any serious thought of crop-growing in the desert in favor of ranching, however. Like other settlers disappointed that the best farmland was already taken, he began herding sheep for another rancher. Slowly acquiring stock of their own, the McGregors went from a thousand to twenty-two thousand sheep in just ten years.

It was a lonely life in a stark landscape. "I felt the first days as long as weeks at home," William McGregor wrote to his sister in 1892, "but it is healthy out here." Food consisted mostly of dried fruit and mutton, with occasional cans of Carnation evaporated milk, tomatoes, or corn—hacked open with a butcher knife—to relieve the monotony. Bread dough was mixed by opening a fifty-pound flour sack and mixing a paste on top, then frying it in a pan. Faithful dogs were legendary. One herder and his dog shepherded a mountain flock over hills and through canyons for a full week to avoid an advancing forest fire. Another missing dog returned still herding a lone wayward sheep he had been guarding for a week. In the empty country men and dogs could become bonded. One McGregor herder committed suicide when his dog failed to return to camp.

If cows were pushed aside by sheep, sheep in turn gave way to human settlers. Open range shrank in Washington's Whitman County from 1.3 million acres in 1897 to just 380,000 acres twenty years later. The county's population rose 60 percent. Between 1890 and 1910, Yakima County numbers increased nearly ten times, to 41,709. Most of the desert around Moses Lake was occupied by optimistic farmers by 1905. Cities grew at dizzying speed. Between 1900 and 1910, Portland and Tacoma doubled in population, and Seattle, Vancouver, Spokane, and Boise tripled. Sheep range was further restricted by the creation of national Forest Reserves at the close of the century, which would later become National Forests that restricted grazing. The final big roundup of wild horses at Ephrata occurred in 1906, signaling an end to its Wild West era. Even the McGregors were diversifying from sheep to wheat. By 1925 they had seven thousand acres of grain, using fifty-four wagons and three hundred and thirty-four horses and mules to harvest it.

By the close of the nineteenth century, three developments were transforming the Columbia Basin into the Inland Empire. They were promotion, mechanization, and irrigation.

Promotion was used to draw settlers, market apples, sell the merits of dams, and take Washington's wine industry from nonexistence in 1960 to the nation's second biggest in the 1980s. The Columbia is a river and basin that was consciously created as the product of people's dreams, schemes, and determination to overcome the limits of nature. Each new settler, community, or industry tied its well-being to further immigration and development, creating an almost religious fervor for environmental transformation that remains the dominant political attitude to this day.

The trend accelerated with the coming of the railroads. The Northern Pacific needed western development to generate business, and in 1883 it printed 2.5 million pamphlets to promote it. The railroad took out ads in one hundred and sixty-seven U.S. and twenty-five Canadian newspapers, sent an exhibit car to ten states, and blanketed Europe with eight hundred and thirty-one agents in the British Isles and one hundred and twenty-four on the Continent. In Washington State alone, the railroad sold 389,000 acres of its grant land in 1896, a million by 1889, and two million in 1901. It helped that the period from 1893 to 1897 was unusually wet, producing numerous reports about the promise of agriculture in the desert. Promoter Louis Frey distributed slips of paper proclaiming "Keep Your Eyes on Pasco," sold $120,000 worth of land in the dust-blown town, and poured the money into more advertising. Spokane banker Orris Dorman boarded immigrant trains to distribute pamphlets on land for sale. Booklets advertising Yakima were passed out at Chicago's Columbian Exhibition in 1893. Railroad baron Henry Villard helped the Oregon Immigration Commission to print five different pamphlets in

German and one each in Swedish, Norwegian, and Danish, all urging immigration.

Jim Hill was an equally tireless promoter of agriculture along the path of his Great Northern, depositing immigrants with wheat seed in eastern Montana and convincing Julius Beebe of Boston to invest in apple orchards in Wenatchee. Beebe's apples filled enough boxcars to form a line more than four miles long.

Apples are Washington's most famous crop. Appropriately, the world's earliest known apple-leaf fossil, dating back 50 million years, has been found in the Okanogan Highlands. The idea of growing modern apples in treeless desert took a leap of imagination, however. Wenatchee appeared the unlikeliest of spots for an apple capital. The Cascade foothills roll down to the west bank where the city lies, providing relatively little flat land for farming. The Columbia Plateau on the east bank is a desert, rising more than a thousand feet above the river. The area looks too steep, too dry, and too brown to grow anything.

The swift fall of the Wenatchee River, however, gave the gravity slope needed to irrigate benchland. And apples, farmers discovered, thrived in the long, hot summer days produced by the northern latitude. Sensing opportunity, Hill had a town site laid out next to his railroad and provided money to buy earlier primitive irrigation ditches and enlarge them. The railroad's Wenatchee Development Company got a $15,000 loan from Hill in 1896 to form the Wenatchee Power Company.

None of this was altruistic: the railroad development firm sold $100,000 of new lots in Wenatchee in just five days. The town went from four hundred and fifty-one residents in 1900 to four thousand by the time the irrigation canals began delivering water in 1904. The builder of Wenatchee's canal system, W. T. Clark, solicited Seattle's Rainier Club to back an extension of the canal system across the Columbia. Wealthy members financed an automobile bridge in 1908—the river's first—that supported a pipe to bring Wenatchee River water to the east bank. Six thousand new residents followed the water in just a few months.

Washington growers stole the nation's apple market with astute promotion. On the advice of eastern buyers they abandoned helter-skelter growing of scores of apple varieties and concentrated on a few that could be advertised, stocked, and marketed as fruit staples. Red Delicious, Winesap, Jonathan, and Rome Beauty were the big four, supplemented in more recent years by such varieties as Australia's Granny Smith or Japan's Fuji. The farmers also went for appearance. Red Delicious is arguably not the best-tasting apple; it is almost too sweet and loses its crispness. Growers convinced America that Red Delicious is what an apple should look like, however, and today its shape and color is the one schoolchildren everywhere draw: a victory, some will admit, of looks over substance. The industry organized into cooperatives and stressed quality over volume, culling marred fruit and using it for juice or applesauce instead. And whereas eastern growers had traditionally shipped apples in bulk barrels, Washington growers invented the apple box. Foothills were logged for pine to build 22 million to 26 million of the containers each year. The boxes were covered with brilliantly colored paper bearing memorable brand names and sometimes the fruit was individually wrapped. A Wenatchee competition picked "Skookum" (a Chinook Indian trade jargon word meaning "good") as a major brand name. Its logo of a beaming Native American became a well-known symbol early in the twentieth century. There were Skookum Indian dolls and a Skookum Indian singer on the radio.

The farmers did not stop with marketing. Growers experimented with warehouse cold storage to allow a long selling season, with chemical sprays to keep apples flawless, with thinning techniques to keep them big, and with refrigeration to allow their fresh delivery. The first refrigerator railroad freight cars appeared in 1902, with insulated sides and compartments at either end to hold ice. In hot weather the train had to reice six to eight times between Wenatchee and Chicago.

By the end of World War I, Washington had risen from 1.5 percent to 15 percent of the nation's apple production, overtaking New York. (At present, Washington gets three times the apple sales receipts of any other state.)

No one better represents the triumph of this industry than Grady Auvil, a sharp-witted overseer of one of the largest and oldest apple farms on the Columbia. When interviewed in 1993, he had lived on the river for all but two of his eighty-seven years. The two hundred acres of trees he has on the hills north of Orondo are watered by wells that suck from the aquifer replenished by the pool behind Rocky Reach Dam, and he has six hundred additional acres downriver. Auvil's family came to the Columbia in 1908 and he has watched everything from steamboats to ski boats churn past his farm in the period since. "We've gone from the mule to the moon in my lifetime," he remarked, "and it's pretty remarkable."

The completion of Rocky Reach Dam raised the Columbia at the farm sixty feet and forced Auvil to move six houses and lose sixty acres, but he has few regrets about the physical changes he has seen. "That dam has created more recreation than the river ever did," he said. The area along the reservoir below his farm has been turned into a park.

The production Auvil squeezes from eight hundred acres is astounding. He employs more than eighty people full-time, has four hundred seasonal workers, and every year grows 800,000 boxes of apples and cherries: tens of millions of apples from his farm alone. The soil is not exceptionally good, he explained, but the climate is, and a single apple tree can produce twenty bushels of apples. All of the Columbia River's irrigated apple acreage combined would cover an area about ten miles wide and twenty-five miles long, or about the size of the metropolitan sprawl of a single large American city. This is sufficient to produce 10 to 12 billion apples annually, or two for every person on earth.

When the Auvil family planted their first orchard in 1928, trees were spaced about one hundred to the acre. Now farmers plant as many as fifteen hundred to the acre and train them onto taut wires like grape vines. It costs $10,000 to $20,000 an acre to set up such an apple orchard, but the close spacing can produce a first crop in as little as three years. By the time an orchard is five years old, the right apple variety and a good market can recoup the original investment in just two years more. An average yield is a thousand boxes of apples per acre, and a top-producing stand might give two thousand or even three. Auvil, who averages two thousand to three thousand, still isn't satisfied. Scientists have measured the solar energy falling on a field and have determined that five thousand boxes can be produced.

Auvil's farm illustrates a couple of trends common to the agriculture of the Columbia River. One is its racial makeup. As recently as 1980, 90 percent of Auvil's summer help was white but now is almost entirely Hispanic. In the Yakima Valley, the number of Hispanics rose from thirty-seven in 1930 to forty-five thousand in 1990. Six lower valley towns—Grandview, Granger, Mabton, Sunnyside, Toppenish, and Wapato—have Hispanic majorities. This new mix is a return to the Columbia's early pioneering history when the region was a rainbow of Scots, French, Native Americans, Hawaiian Kanakas, free blacks, Asians, and Mexicans. The mining boomtown of Three Forks, British Columbia, which burned in 1894, was described as "a cosmopolitan Babylonian town" by the *Slocan Prospector*, boasting "Canadians, Americans, English, Irish, Scotch, French, Italians, Caucasians, Negroes and Japanese." More crudely, the *San Francisco Bulletin* in 1862 described The Dalles, at the time a wild Gold Rush supply center so unruly that at one point it was briefly ruled by a mob, as composed of "Saxon, Celt, Teuton, Gaul, Greaser, Celestial and Indian." Asians provided much of the labor force. Author Linda Tamura has calculated that Japanese in Washington and Oregon soared from 385 in 1890 to 16,347 by 1910, drawn by salaries often less than half that of whites but twice their earning potential in Japan. America was portrayed in Japan as a paradise. "I pictured that even the flies would be different," one woman told Tamura. Instead, several thousand died from the work, accidents, and violence of the Northwest frontier.

Racism increased in the decades after the Civil War. The Chinese were literally loaded on boxcars and railroaded out of Tacoma in the 1880s. Chinese were also forced out of the smaller Washington community of Tekoa in 1881. When a newcomer from China wandered into town a few days later and innocently asked about work, he was promptly hanged. A white man who showed up at a Walla Walla concert with a black wife was tarred and feathered by a mob of fifty hooded men. Attitudes were ugly and blatant. Apparently ignorant that its first store was built and operated by the Chinese, the *Chelan Falls Leader* editorialized on August 13, 1891: "We have no objection to the Chinese—in China. He has the same right to life, liberty and the pursuit of happiness as other human beings have, but his tastes and mode of life are so dissimilar and distasteful to white people—he comes so near being human swine—he is so full of leprosy and opium, he is so altogether undesirable that we have no use for him. . . . There will never be any room in Okanogan County and especially Chelan Falls for Chinese. The Chinese must go. Paste that in your hat." In large part they went, if not killed first: Chinese miners were massacred by both natives and white gold thieves on the Snake, Palouse, and Okanogan rivers. In one attack by white outlaws on the Snake's Douglas Bar, thirty were slaughtered.

• • •

The other change Auvil represents is intense modernization. His family began with twenty-five acres and now has eight hundred, started with horses and turned to mechanization in relief. The same trend occurred everywhere along the river. The size of the average wheat farm east of the Cascades doubled, to three hundred and twenty acres, as the combine revolutionized its harvest. The first such machine arrived from California in 1888, requiring five men and thirty-two horses to operate. It "combined" the previously separated tasks of reaping and threshing the wheat. Three years later the Holt Company of Stockton, California, invented a "sidehill" combine with a leveling device that could operate (with difficulty) on the steep, rolling hills of the Palouse and Walla Walla regions. The combines were a nightmare to operate—the huge horse teams could easily become entangled and the driver kept a bucket of rocks on his seat to throw at lagging or straying animals—but American agriculture had taken its first giant strides toward replacing people with machines. In 1880 half of all American workers were employed on a farm. By 1990 it would be less than 2 percent.

The invention of first the clumsy steam plow and then the gasoline engine freed farmers from the horse, allowing millions of acres that had been devoted to animal pasture to be converted to human food. So many animals were surplused that French army officers came to the Columbia during World War I to buy up animals for transport. A twenty-horsepower tractor could harrow three times as fast as a horse team and plow seven times as fast. At the same time fertilizers appeared. They doubled wheat production by 1910 with no addition of acreage. All this meant that farming was no longer the unskilled occupation of the hardy pioneer. It required land, water, and money.

In the fields around John Day Pool, farming has entered the space age. Fred Ziari is a former agriculture professor turned Hermiston consultant who has tied crop production to satellite technology. Bud Mercer is linked to Ziari's office by computer modem and gets daily updates on weather forecasts, past water use, and suggestions of how much water should be applied the next day. Infrared satellite and aerial photographs of the irrigation circles are used by Ziari to analyze how crops are growing and to suggest adjustments in water application, fertilizers, or pesticides. Remote sensors in fields sense humidity, soil moisture, and temperatures, and use traps to make insect counts. This information is relayed to the central computers. Ziari also uses infrared sensors to inspect irrigation pump wiring, detecting a breakdown that could have cost $20,000.

"I was born in Iran, came to the United States when I was seventeen, and have traveled a great deal," Ziari said. "To me, the Columbia River system is a marvel of human ingenuity. This is a complete marvel. There is a reason we can get food so cheaply. *This* is the reason for it."

Auvil, Mercer, and Ziari all center their enterprises on water, and as railroads poured hundreds of thousands of people into the Columbia Basin, water was what many of them lacked. Farms collapsed on the margins of adequate rainfall. Spokane grew by 67,554 people from 1900 to 1910 and then halted the next decade. Walla Walla lost 20 percent of its population in the same period. Predictions that dry Whitman County would reach half a million in population proved laughable, and speculative schemes collapsed. Chicago residents had been sold lots in a "Cascade City" that was nothing more than central Washington sagebrush. Four lots in a never-to-be boomtown of Kendrick were purchased by Archie McGregor for $1,591 in 1890 and sold twenty-six years later for $52.

While dry areas withered, communities such as Yakima boomed. Its story is illustrative of what was happening around the Inland Empire. Once more the railroads played a key role. When the Northern Pacific pushed its new railroad line up the Yakima Valley toward the Cascades and Tacoma and bypassed Yakima by a few miles, the community dutifully put its buildings on log rollers and moved them to where the railroad went. And when the Cascades Tunnel was completed in 1889, settlers filed on 257,000 acres in the Yakima Valley. They had the dirt and they had the railroad. All they needed was water.

The man who would bring it to them was a forty-four-year-old, fast-talking traveling salesman named Walter N. Granger. Energetic enough to have made a sales income of $15,000 a year at a time when a good income was a tenth of that, Granger later moved west for his health and as a hobby built small irrigation systems in Montana. With this experience to recommend him, Granger was summoned to St. Paul by Northern Pacific manager Thomas F. Oakes and offered an option on ninety thousand acres of railroad land in the Yakima Valley at $1.25 an acre if he would help build an irrigation system. The pair formed the Northern Pacific, Yakima and Kittitas Irrigation Company, appropriated a thousand cubic feet per second of the Yakima River's flow, and broke a bottle of champagne over the outlet gate to the first diversion canal on March 26, 1892. Granger mapped out two new towns, Sunnyside and Zillah, the latter named for Oakes's daughter. The Northwest water rush was on.

By 1905, Granger's system had been bought out by a group of Seattle investors headed by Roland H. Denny, son of one of the city's founders. It boasted seven hundred miles of canals and laterals serving thirty-six thousand acres. Other counties east of the Cascades scrambled to follow and by 1920 all nineteen eastern Washington counties had some kind of private irrigation system. By 1928, before Grand Coulee Dam and its irrigation project had even been approved, there were 3.6 million acres of irrigated land in the Columbia Basin above Bonneville Dam, stretching from eastern Idaho to Hood River, Oregon.

Irrigation did not prove to be simple. Sprinklers did not exist yet and ditches were dug perpendicular to a field's furrows. The trick was to get enough water to produce a "head" and overcome the friction of liquid against the dirt, but not so much that soil and seed began to wash away. Waste was common because getting water to flood the far end of a field required enough to surge past that point. None of this was mechanized, and farmers had to learn by trial and error how to siphon water from their lateral: some sucked on the tubes as if they were siphoning gasoline rather than hand-pumping them. Irrigation canals became clogged with weeds and debris, leaked, and occasionally slumped. Nor was there provision to keep fish out of the canals being diverted from rivers. Salmon would be swept down a canal and left, flopping and dying.

Water supply was undependable, rivers running low in late summer just when irrigation reached its peak. Private irrigation companies recognized a need for water storage reservoirs in the mountains but lacked the financing or expertise to build them. Inevitably, they began to turn to the federal government for help. A region that would later pride itself on conservatism and independence became in part the creation of Uncle Sam.

Irrigation was not new to the West. Southwestern Native Americans had irrigated parts of Arizona and New Mexico for centuries. It was the Mormons in Utah, however, who first undertook irrigation on a large scale. They broke ground on their first canals in 1847 and by 1865 had irrigated 1.5 million acres, fed by a thousand-mile network of main canals.

Irrigation subsequently spread to Colorado, California, Idaho, and finally Washington and Oregon. Accordingly, scores of companies around the Columbia plunged into irrigation as a land development scheme: some successful, some not, and some little more than frauds. Clarkston started as an irrigation development by Boston engineers called Vineland, but plans to bring water to the central Columbia Plateau failed. The McGregors tried to tap artesian wells, with no sustained success. Tacoma and eastern businessmen pooled $500,000 to divert the Palouse River but the project was never finished. Columbia River Orchard Company promoters were found guilty of offering $4 million in fraudulent bonds on a one-hundred-and-fifty-two-acre tract. Arcadia Orchards Company north of Spokane tried to promote gravel benchland as prime farm sites and went bankrupt.

This troubled history resulted in growing intervention by an initially reluctant federal government. The Desert Land Act of 1877 was the first attempt by Congress to promote irrigation, granting six hundred and forty acres to an individual willing to irrigate it for three years. The law failed because few individuals could afford the expense of developing such a large tract of land with the primitive tools available. In 1894, Congress went a step further and passed the Carey Act to encourage state-private partnerships in financing irrigation projects. The law accomplished little in Washington and Oregon but was a success in Idaho, where 60 percent of all the land ever watered under the law is located. The largest private irrigation works in the nation began tapping the Snake River and gave birth to the community of Twin Falls.

Elsewhere it was apparent that more government intervention was needed. Few asked if western irrigation should succeed, even though it was so expensive it could not pay its own way as private enterprise. Government aid was seen as vital in order for the West to develop and overcome the economic and political domination of the East.

There was no question that water supply was inadequate: seven thousand claimants contested in court for Yakima River water alone. Engineers for Granger's Washington Irrigation Company simply blew up a diversion dam of the rival Union Gap Irrigation Company at Cle Elum Lake. Armed guards patrolled canals. Only large federal storage reservoirs, investors argued, could avert water wars.

In 1902, Congress passed the Newlands Act creating the Bureau of Reclamation, essentially decreeing that irrigation had become so important to the development of the West that it required federal aid and management. The immediate effect in the Columbia Basin was the construction of several large reservoirs on tributaries of the Columbia and Snake to provide sufficient water, plus a federal takeover of struggling private irrigation companies. In 1915 the bureau built the three-hundred-and-forty-nine-foot Arrowrock Dam above Boise, the world's tallest at the time. Other storage reservoirs were built on the Yakima, Umatilla, and Klamath drainages.

The first large dam built on the main-stem Snake River was the bureau's Minidoka, completed in 1909. Minidoka was also the bureau's first attempt in the Northwest to expand irrigation beyond existing private systems into new territory. It was successful in drawing settlers, but farm prices were so depressed in the 1920s that 40 percent ended up as tenants of their better-financed neighbors. The huge investment irrigation required began to favor consolidation of land in fewer, larger farms owned by richer settlers, a trend kept only partially in check by legal limits on how much land farmers could acquire.

The Bureau of Reclamation picked its initial projects carefully and was initially reluctant to take over in the Yakima Valley, reasoning that it appeared to be a relative success as a private enterprise. Northwest congressmen saw the bureau as an answer to ending increasingly acrimonious fights, however. Washington congressman Wesley Jones found a report stating that three-quarters of irrigable land in the Yakima Valley still awaited development and persuaded a reluctant government to step in. The Washington Irrigation Company sold its system to the bureau for $640,000, the Northern Pacific Railroad sold reservoir sites high in the Cascades, and by 1907 the government was delivering water in the Yakima Valley and moving on to the Kittitas Valley upstream. By 1909, just seven years after its creation, Reclamation was responsible for watering 125,000 acres in the West.

It was clear history was forming a pattern along the Columbia that made development of the main river inevitable. Like the Mercer farm, each small step toward utilizing the Columbia made the next seem logical. Each public and private step to promote development left in place a constituency to demand still more development, creating a climate in which balance was increasingly difficult to achieve. It was not driven by demand for food. American farmers had become so successful that commodity prices collapsed after 1920 and did not recover until World War II: the very time in which Grand Coulee Dam was planned and built primarily as an irrigation project. By this time, however, irrigation was seen not as an end but a means toward other political ends of providing jobs, of generating electricity, and of promoting development. Bureaucracies had been created that were anxious to sustain their own momentum. A river, they promised, could remake not just a farm but society, too: the new engineers could remake the world.

And to a degree they did. The Columbia Basin is green testimony to the effectiveness of this vision. The victory could never be final, however, because such development inevitably drew still more people chasing what remains a scare resource: fresh river water. The Yakima's first upstream reservoirs postponed rather than resolved water battles: by the 1980s concern over disappearing salmon runs renewed the water fight and once more new reservoirs, storing more water, were proposed as a partial solution by the region's congressmen.

The Columbia's tributary valleys proved a warm-up to the ultimate transformation. The big river itself still ran unruly and free; when the Bureau of Reclamation was created, the dream of capturing the Columbia and diverting it to the "Big Bend" country around Moses Lake appeared too expensive to be feasible. Bureau commissioner F. H. Newell took a look and said such a project "must be left for a future generation."

Now that generation was about to step on stage.

Franklin Roosevelt gives an address at a 1935 eastern Washington rally celebrating the start of construction of Grand Coulee Dam. Seated with him is Frank Banks, chief of the dam construction. *(Washington State Historical Museum)*

In late July of 1880 the newest addition to the steamship and railroad empire of Henry Villard steamed up the Columbia to Portland's docks, bringing visual proof that the world was about to be transformed. The thirty-two-hundred-ton *Columbia* had been outfitted in New York with the latest invention from Thomas Edison: one hundred and fifty of the new electric "lamps" (the term "lightbulb" had not been coined yet) and four "dynamos" (the word "generator" was also not yet in common use) to power them. The dynamos, which reminded the Edison men of a reclining woman with her legs sticking up, had been dubbed "Long-legged Mary Anns" in dubious honor of a frequent visitor to their New Jersey lab complex. To avoid offending Victorian sensibilities, however, the name had been modified for public use to Long-*waisted* Mary Anns. Each could power up to sixty of the bulbs. As the brilliantly illuminated ship circled the Horn on its way to the Columbia, it drew excited crowds at Rio de Janeiro, Valparaiso, and San Francisco. By the time the ship reached Portland half the bulbs had burned out, but even when half-lit the *Columbia* was like a flame at the Willamette docks, proclaiming the banishment of darkness. A few weeks later wires were run ashore and a light was suspended over First Street. "The powerful rays lighted up the whole neighborhood to the brightness of day," the *Oregonian* reported. "Thousands visited the light and the vessel." After being a subject of scientific curiosity for centuries, electricity had finally been harnessed to a practical purpose. Villard, flush from his successful consolidation of business on the Columbia, became the newest investor and board member of the Edison Electric Company. In the next century the Columbia River would change almost beyond recognition.

Adoption of electricity in the distant Pacific Northwest was swift in the years after the *Columbia*'s illuminated voyage. In 1882, Villard installed an Edison incandescent lighting system on his Ainsworth dock in Portland. The same year, the Tacoma Mill Company installed earlier, cruder arc lights (where the illumination is produced by current arcing between two wires) at its factory in that city. The first hydroelectric power plant in the region was installed in 1885 at Spokane Falls, powering twelve arc lights in Spokane with current that ran on bare, uninsulated wires. The same year a small dam and waterwheel were built to light a mine and mill at Hailey, Idaho. Also in 1885 the first Pacific Northwest power company to sell centrally generated electricity to different customers was built at Jackson Street in Seattle to supply the waterfront. By that time lightbulb prices had fallen to thirty cents, or one-quarter the price they were five years before—but still about two hours of a laborer's wages.

It is difficult to realize today how extraordinary this invention promised to be. Electricity promised to be more than merely a brightener of dim rooms. It was going to change the world.

The Industrial Revolution had been a mixed blessing for Americans. While production of goods soared, it had produced stifling air pollution (Pittsburgh alone counted fourteen thousand smokestacks), urban slums, and brutal working conditions. The gap between rich and poor had widened as industry and transportation networks were increasingly controlled by huge corporations, trusts, tycoons, and robber barons. Wealth in the nineteenth century was more narrowly concentrated and meant a far greater distinction in everyday experience than it does today. The rich could afford servants to conduct the backbreaking tasks of chopping wood, fueling stoves, washing clothes, processing food, hauling and heating water, tending lawns, and harnessing animals. To be rich was to enjoy a higher satisfaction of life's basics: to be cleaner, warmer, and better-fed. As late as 1932, social critic and New Deal enthusiast Stuart Chase felt it useful to compare the benefit of electrically driven running water with the labor of a hypothetical woman on his Virginia farm, fetching water from a well two hundred and seventy-one feet from the house and sixty-five feet below it. He estimated that in a year's time she would carry twenty-seven tons of water fifty-six miles uphill: "The equivalent of eight round trips up and down Pike's Peak, destroying twenty-seven ten-hour days."

Electricity promised to change all that. It would pump, it would heat, it would cook, it would clean, and it would banish the tyranny of the solar day. No longer would people feel compelled to "go to bed with the chickens and rise with the dawn." It would give to anyone the kind of physical luxury only the rich had ever experienced. It was clean, eliminating open flames, smoke, ash, and soot. It could be shipped from place to place by wire, not by barge or coal car or wagon. It would allow the dispersal of industry and people from the crowded, unhappy cities, and remove the temptation of the farmer to move to town for basic conveniences. "A family with rural electrification," author John Gunther would write, "is at one jump removed from the peasanthood."

The magic of this new energy source comes through in the recollection of Anne H. T. Donaldson, the wife of a Grand Coulee Dam engineer. Assigned housing in the contract engineer's community of Mason City built below the dam, she drove to it shortly after its construction. She was fascinated by the rows of trim new houses without chimneys, their heat supplied by three slender wires:

"We drove out through the first blinding blizzard of the winter, the last twenty miles entirely in second gear, unable to see beyond the hood of the car or steer straight on the icy road. Arriving cold and hungry, I found that they had forgotten to 'connect up' the just completed house assigned to me. The three rooms were piled to the ceiling with crated furniture from the secondhand stores in Spokane. It was icy cold and damp; there was no kitchen range, heat or water. In less than an hour all these important details had been supplied by a simple process of hooking up. The house was marvelously warm and dry, dinner was cooking on an excellent electric range—rented from the company at $2.50 a month—and I had become a convert to electricity. . . .

"We women have become electrically minded, and use freely all the wonderful appliances on the market—water heaters, refrigerators, washing machines, vacuum cleaners, coffee percolators, toasters and irons. All the more difficult problems of housekeeping are thus solved for us. We have strength left over from our daily tasks to help with the big achievements. To interest ourselves in the school, in organizing the several churches to be built shortly, to visit the sick, the recreation hall, the movies and the library. Yes, we really have time for books and study. . . . If the government will be able, by harnessing these great waterways of our country, to develop electric power to the point of practical everyday use by all the people, there will be a new era of emancipation, a veritable new deal for women."

This was the kind of optimism that made the damming of rivers seem unchallengeably sensible.

Electricity had a more subtle effect on American society. An ax, hand pump, or wood stove were things any common person could understand. Electricity was not. Edison was dubbed by the press the "Wizard of Menlo Park," implying an almost magical knowledge ordinary mortals did not share. In 1924, *Graphic Survey* magazine noted, "Electricity is such a subtle commodity, at once so beneficent and so terrifyingly destructive, that we regard it and its high priests with a kind of awe."

Increasingly, decisions on technological change would be deferred to a scientific and engineering elite that, while expert in its field, was often profoundly ignorant of the social or environmental side effects of its work. The costs of harnessing the Columbia were not so much overwhelmed by the benefits, or even willfully ignored, as simply not thought about very deeply. The engineers who would transform the river had no experience in thinking about such costs.

An example of the problem is a 1924 Fisheries Board hearing on a proposal by subsidiaries of General Electric to build a $100 million dam and manufacturing complex on the Columbia at Priest Rapids. The subject of the hearing was salmon, and the understanding of the problems posed to fish by a dam across a river was not very sophisticated. Britain had been requiring fish bypass facilities on its dams since 1870, but the practice had lagged in the United States. Even though the principle was well known, attention focused on getting adult fish upriver past the dam, not the more difficult problem of getting young salmon down.

Dam engineer M. O. Leighton said he was willing to do what he could for fish, but clearly viewed the entire matter as outside his area of expertise or responsibility. "I judge the authorities do not really know much about it because they practically all disagree, and it has been exceedingly confusing to get any base data on which to proceed," he told the commission in explaining why the dam's plan had little provision for salmon. "One eminent fish man confessed two days ago and said, 'We really don't know.' You fish people are mightily skillful in catching these fish to put into cans. Cannot you be just as skillful in getting these fish to be raised up over a dam? Why not? What's the difference? Surely we out in the Northwest, as I know it, are not going to lie down before a little problem like that. If we had been of that disposition, we would not have had the Northwest here."

Had it been built, the dam would have been ninety feet high. No fish ladder—a series of stepped pools arranged like a staircase to allow salmon to leap easily from one to the next and finally swim past the dam—had yet been built to that height and worked, Oregon fish commissioner F. P. Kendall pointed out. "We have got an investment of $35 million or $40 million in the salmon industry at the present time," Kendall told E. A. Sims, chairman of the Fisheries Commission. "Is that to be sacrificed for a new industry, a new development?"

"I take it that your idea is that no satisfactory fishway can be constructed for this dam," Sims said.

"If you guarantee a satisfactory fishway I will vote yes now," said Kendall.

"Are you willing to admit that American ingenuity and engineers are beyond the possibility of figuring out the problem of this fishway?"

"I do not say it cannot be done," Kendall replied. "I say it never has been done."

• • •

Waterfalls were quickly tapped to provide the power of falling water but the number of feasible sites was limited. What society needed was something to back up water and funnel it to fall artificially. What was needed were dams. A dam's energy capacity is determined by the volume of water pushing its turbine blades and the height the water is falling from. A cubic foot of water falling through seven-hundred-and-twenty-six-foot-high Hoover Dam is the equivalent of eight horsepower.

Dams today seem simple and commonplace. There are more than fifty thousand large ones in the United States today, "large" meaning structures at least twenty-five feet high or that back up at least 16 million gallons. Despite their ubiquity and long ancestry—the ancient Egyptians built dams—engineering of high dams remained uncertain. In Spain, the one-hundred-and-sixty-foot high Puentes Dam, built in 1790, collapsed in 1802 and drowned six hundred. In Britain, the Dale Dike collapsed in 1864 and drowned two hundred and forty-four. In the United States, the Johnstown Dam collapsed in 1889 and drowned twenty-two hundred, the worst dam disaster in history in terms of lost life. So disturbing was the failure rate of dams that in 1834, when the one-hundred-and-twenty-foot-high Ascutney Mill Dam became the first high masonry arch dam in America, companies were so afraid it would collapse that none would build mills below it and the stock of the dam company plummeted. A rifle manufacturer finally used its power in 1845, however, and the dam is still standing today.

French engineers first applied modern mathematics and engineering to dam design in the 1800s, creating the principles for the construction of the mammoth hydroelectric projects of the twentieth century. The Snake River's Minidoka Dam of 1909, eighty-six feet high and 4,475 feet long, did not initially generate power but was significant in demonstrating the feasibility of damming a large river with an earth structure. The Bureau of Reclamation followed this in 1911 with the two-hundred-and-eighty-foot-high Theodore Roosevelt Dam in Arizona, at the time the highest rock masonry dam in the world. Built to supply irrigation water, hydroelectric generators were also installed at the insistence of engineer Louis Hill. The experiment was so successful that the bureau convinced Congress to allow power generation revenues to defray the expense of irrigation projects in the future, making them more economically justifiable. At the same time, Congress asserted federal jurisdiction over water power on navigable rivers: from now on the federal government would decide who built power dams and who didn't, and would reserve the best sites for itself.

Reclamation's confidence grew. When Hoover Dam was built beginning in 1928, it used more concrete than all the fifty dams the bureau had built up to that time, and yet it was finished two years ahead of schedule in 1936. The engineers called it their "warm-up for Grand Coulee," which, while no longer the world's biggest dam (Brazil's Itaipu and Venezuela's Guri generate the most power; Canada's Syncrude Tailings is the earth dam with the biggest mass), remains today the largest concrete structure in the world.

The damming of the Columbia came slowly, however. A small generator was placed at Priest Rapids in 1907, but there was neither the engineering experience to block that large a river nor the need for the vast quantities of energy it could produce. Pacific Northwest utilities had plenty of smaller rivers to harness first, and the region was still sparsely developed and had little industry. Just as important, the electric revolution had become embroiled in politics.

Small power plants and electric utilities proliferated throughout the United States after Edison's inventions. In 1895, Seattle alone had thirty different private electric power companies to serve a population of only fifty thousand. Consolidation was inevitable. Conservationist Gifford Pinchot called for a publicly run "Giant Power" network to sort out the confused and overlapping utility systems. "It will be not the hand that rocks the cradle but the hand that turns the electric switch that will rule the land," Pinchot said.

Private industry moved first. By 1900 those thirty companies in Seattle had consolidated into the Seattle Electric Company, which in turn was absorbed in 1912 by a nationwide holding company called Stone & Webster. This evolved into Puget Sound Power & Light, the company that would build the first dam on the Columbia River at Rock Island. By 1912 ten giant holding company groups led by such capitalist giants as John D. Rockefeller, Jr., and Samuel Insull controlled 60 percent of the electric business in America, and by 1930 the control of the big ten had reached 75 percent.

The early chaos had created a parallel push for consolidated public ownership. Four cities started public power agencies the same year Edison opened the first central power steam plant in New York. By 1924 there were 3,084 public power systems. In the Pacific Northwest, Vancouver started municipal-owned service in 1889, Tacoma in 1893, and Seattle in 1902. In 1904, Seattle built the nation's first city-owned hydroelectric project on the nearby Cedar River. Almost immediately these public power systems were thrown into competition with their private counterparts. Seattle City Light's rates were so low that its private competitors were forced to cut their rates roughly in half, and the utility boasted that the result was more electric stoves in Seattle than any city in the nation. The two competitors pushed lines down the same streets, fighting for customers house by house. This struggle between public and private power would be a constant undercurrent to the debates about damming the Columbia River.

The public power lobby charged that private utilities were managing out of shortsighted greed and that government control of electricity was imperative to protect American freedoms. "Nothing has been imagined that even remotely approaches [the Power Trust] in the thoroughgoing, intimate, unceasing control it exercises over the daily life of every human being within its web of wires," warned a 1925 report to the Pennsylvania legislature.

Private companies responded that Pinchot's idea for a public power network was socialistic, and in 1919, Interior Secretary Franklin Knight Lane recommended a "Superpower" system run by private power companies instead. Private power, its capitalists argued, would in the long run prove more efficient than a public bureaucracy, and they flip-flopped Pinchot's argument to contend public control of electricity would give government too much leverage over private lives. "The key issue in America today," Henry Swift Ives told the National Electric Light Association in 1925, "is whether the American people desire to preserve the institution of individual rights in property or substitute therefor community ownership supervised by a socialist oligarchy. This country cannot exist half socialist and half free any more than it could have existed half slave and half free."

The privates had had a disquieting preview of what was to come during World War I, when the federal government moved ahead with a dam on the Tennessee River at Muscle Shoals in Alabama to provide power for munitions. This public entry into the power business was bitterly opposed by private industry. They saw their business being undercut by a government with unlimited access to tax revenues and cheap bonds. Private power paid taxes, its spokesmen argued, while public power did not.

As a profit-making business, however, the privates were reluctant to extend lines into rural areas where customers were few. When they did so they sought to charge higher rates for the added expense of serving isolated houses or farms. They were also conservative about the risk of overbuilding their generating capacity, fearing the electricity would not be used or that surpluses would drive down rates. While public power advocates promised tirelessly that cheap power from dams on the Columbia would attract new industry, private utilities saw a Northwest still woefully undeveloped despite years of inexpensive electricity in cities such as Seattle and Tacoma. While it was private Puget Power that started the first dam on the Columbia at Rock Island in 1930, the dam was initially only thirty-four feet high and remains the smallest on the river. The larger holding companies based in the East did not follow through to develop bigger sites such as the one proposed at Priest Rapids.

As a result of this hesitation, by the 1930s the federal government was asserting control over dam construction on the river. J. D. Ross was the outspoken chief of Seattle City Light before he became the first director of the Bonneville Power Administration that would market federal power from the Columbia. He said private utilities made a fatal error in not moving swiftly in the 1920s to develop the river. They didn't, Ross charged, because they wanted "to corner the supply and hold up the price."

The battle over the best way to tap the Columbia River at Grand Coulee to irrigate central Washington's dry interior became part of this battle between private and public. So did the question of building Bonneville Dam upstream from Portland, which would dump huge new sources of cheap power on the market. Public power proponents saw damming the Columbia as offering, in the words of campaigning presidential candidate Franklin Delano Roosevelt, a "yardstick" of cheap electric rates against which other rates could be measured. "The cheaper the power, the more of it is used," Roosevelt would forecast later at Grand Coulee Dam. "We are going to see electricity and power made so cheap that they will become a standard article of use, not merely for agriculture and manufacturing, but for every home within reach of an electric transmission line."

Watering central Washington's Columbia Plateau had been a dream at least since 1892, when developer Lachlin MacLean first proposed that a giant trench be dug across the Big Bend of the river and the Columbia diverted into it. Alternately, he proposed that a dam a thousand feet high spill the river across the plateau. Certainly the geography of a river wrapping around the basalt plateau made some kind of diversion obvious, but the depth of its canyon made MacLean's diversion ideas seem impractical. In 1915 the Bureau of Reclamation made its first survey of the Columbia's development potential, but no plan emerged from that study.

Then, in July 1918, an Ephrata attorney named William "Billy" Clapp hit upon the idea of using the Columbia's ancient riverbed at Grand Coulee to funnel the water southward. The river had already done its own digging, Clapp realized. Use the coulee and no giant trench was needed, nor such a colossal dam. If the fundamental problem was getting Columbia River from one elevation to another, nature had already done much of the work.

A few days later the flamboyant publisher of the Wenatchee *World*, Rufus Woods, motored into Ephrata on one of his regular trips for news. Woods had first seen his infant apple town while traveling with his identical twin, Ralph, on their way to the Klondike Gold Rush, drifting back after the pair lost most of their money in Alaska. He plunged into local journalism and politics and was offered the failing *World* in 1907, when its circulation was only four hundred and sixty-five. By the end of his third year at the paper's helm, Woods's enthusiastic promotions of himself, his paper, and central Washington had pushed the newspaper's daily sales past twenty-five hundred.

Energetic, bombastic, visionary, contradictory, and extroverted enough to travel as a clown in a circus in 1936, Woods made no pretense of being an objective journalist. He reveled in using his paper to promote economic development for the region he had chosen. He trumpeted the virtues of local apples, talked tirelessly of development schemes, advocated a lottery that allowed whites to acquire a large share of the Colville Indian Reservation, and made himself regionally famous by touring the far-flung rural communities with a newfangled touring car, finding stories and snapping pictures. He milked the car for publicity by proclaiming it a "Traveling Office." Woods also had a deliberate policy of naming neighboring towns as frequently as possible in his publication and holding down the mention of "Wenatchee" so that families throughout the area would think of the *World* as their paper.

Driving the hot, dusty streets of Ephrata, Woods dropped by the office of W. Gale Matthews at the Grant County Title and Abstract Company. Matthews urged him to go talk to Billy Clapp about a new irrigation idea. The subsequent story, published July 18, 1918, is probably the single most famous newspaper article in Pacific Northwest history. "Formulate Brand New Idea for Irrigation Grant, Adams, Franklin Counties, Covering Million Acres or More," it was headlined. It is generally credited for launching the long public debate about Grand Coulee Dam.

The story was not, however, on page one, as frequently recounted. It was on page seven, had no illustration, and shared space with several advertisements. Modest in length, it occupied less than one-quarter of the page, being squeezed by a picture from the war in Europe and homey stories about picnics, illnesses, visiting relatives, and sock-knittings in the communities of Mansfield, Squillchuck, and Rock Island. If Woods had the foresight to know he was launching construction of the biggest concrete structure on earth, he did not betray it with the story's play. He threw out the idea with neither quotes or qualifications, beginning, "The last, the newest, the most ambitious idea in the way of reclamation and the development of water power ever formulated is now in process of development."

The story's timing was excellent. With other irrigation projects established and the world war drawing to a close, there was new interest in flexing American muscle in development schemes. The story was remarkable in neatly summing up the idea, linking irrigation to hydroelectricity by explaining how power would help pump the water up into the coulee, and identifying the key problem. "The whole idea is not an intricate one," Woods wrote. "The one outstanding feature of the project is its immensity." From then on Woods was a tireless supporter of the dam over bitter opposition from Spokane, skeptical critics, and readers who wearied of countless stories on the virtues of Grand Coulee. Years afterward he never hesitated to remind subscribers that the *World* had promoted the idea first.

"Baron Munchausen, thou art a piker," one reader scoffed when the story first appeared. But when Roosevelt finally approved $65 million to begin construction, fifteen years after that first story, Woods walked out and read a telegram announcing the decision to a stunned newsroom. "I always knew it would happen," he said with uncharacteristic quiet. Then he went back into his office.

Grand Coulee has since been enshrined in American mythology as such an outstanding success that the era's critics who called it a "white elephant" or "as useless as the pyramids" have subsequently looked foolish. Yet their concerns were reasonable. They worried that there was no need for the irrigated food, and the nation still has farm surpluses today. They objected that the cost of irrigation would prove too expensive to justify; while accountants could argue the cost has been paid back by government power sales, it has never been paid back by farmers. They said there would be no market for the power. World War II proved that wrong, but the prediction was logical. When Rock Island Dam was competed in 1932, it alone had twice the capacity of the power the Northwest was then using—and yet the federal government was planning to start Bonneville and Grand Coulee dams as well. Just the first powerhouse at Bonneville was initially designed with enough power to meet the need of three Portlands at that time. The Pacific Northwest had had cheap power rates from smaller dams for a generation, skeptics pointed out, and yet there had been no stampede of industry to the region.

The debate over Grand Coulee was not long in getting started once Woods's 1918 story appeared. Elbert F. Blaine had been Roland Denny's attorney when the latter invested in Yakima Valley irrigation and had since become one of reclamation's strongest proponents, an aide to Washington governor Ernest Lister. He became intrigued with an alternate plan to tap the rivers and lakes of the wet Idaho panhandle with a one-hundred-and-thirty-mile-long canal that would bring water to central Washington by gravity. Several months after Woods's first article, or two weeks before Christmas of 1918, Blaine and Lister ordered the state's hydraulic engineer and geologist to drive a snowy route from Albeni Falls in Idaho to central Washington, taking barometric readings along the way. The trip proved the route was indeed downhill and required no pumping, as a dam at Grand Coulee would.

In his 1919 message to the legislature, Lister endorsed a "Big Bend" irrigation project and $100,000 was appropriated to start studies on the competing schemes. (James Ford, secretary-treasurer of the Spokane Chamber of Commerce, later argued successfully that to avoid confusion—there are several Big Bends in North America—enthusiasts should substitute the name Columbia Basin Project.) By 1930 two dozen different studies were done, coming down on all sides of the issue.

The most famous was the 1922 examination by Panama Canal builder George Goethals, whose six-day visit to the region was more of a triumphal tour by a national hero than a transit-and-core-sample engineering survey. Local communities did their best to honor the celebrity; Ephrata entertained the famous officer by putting on a rabbit drive. Goethals declared Grand Coulee "a perfect dam site" but favored the canal as less complicated. (Once his fee was pocketed, Goethals told Congress the next year he was against big government irrigation projects at all.) Other studies sent a mixture of messages. A 1922 state report favored the dam. The Federal Power Commission concluded in 1922 that it needed more information; the Columbia Basin Irrigation Commission said in 1924 that the costs of the two plans were equal; and a federal reclamation consultant in 1927 said irrigation was worthwhile but declined to back either plan. A number of regional and national newspapers were opposed to a dam as too expensive and, in the words of the *Washington Post*, "a misuse of federal authority." Two key federal agencies, however—the Bureau of Reclamation and the Army Corps of Engineers—were growing increasingly confident of their ability to harness huge rivers and of the combined benefits of flood control, power, and irrigation. Once it became apparent that Hoover Dam was going to harness the Colorado successfully, the larger Columbia became the next logical goal. "So far as public opinion is concerned, the Columbia Basin project stands before Congress in an entirely different position than before," Reclamation commissioner Elwood Mead would tell the Spokane Irrigation League in 1931. "People are no longer afraid to undertake great enterprises such as this one."

The political maneuvering between the "pumpers" (the dam proponents who wanted to use Grand Coulee's electricity to pump river water up and over into the coulee) and the "ditchers" (the Spokane canal enthusiasts) went on for fifteen years and was intense, polarized, and sometimes comic. The 1931 picnic in the Coulee to counter the canal rally in Lind was not the only example of mobilizing public demonstrations. When the Spokane group announced a ten-day tour of the area by congressmen that included just one hour at the dam site, lobbyist James O'Sullivan raised five dollars to buy two hundred and fifty two-cent stamps and invited prominent people from all over the state to the sixty-minute stop. Woods urged general public attendance with his *World,* schools obligingly dismissed classes, and Wenatchee shopkeepers organized a thousand-car caravan to the river. When the congressional train parked at Coulee City, thousands of people were on hand to greet them and accompany them down the coulee to the proposed dam location. "Now all in the world we want, gentlemen, is a slab of concrete right across here!" Woods boomed into the loudspeakers.

The dam's merits were duly recited, the hour expired, and the Spokane hosts began whispering it was time to leave. Woods and O'Sullivan had planted allies in the crowd, however, and as the congressional delegation began to shift and stand, a chant went up: "We want Smith of Idaho!" Unable to resist the chance to make a speech, Addison Smith stepped to the microphones. When he finished, to encouraging applause, it was, "We want Allgood of Alabama!" The distinguished gentleman from Alabama could do no less than comply. And so on. Accordingly, three hours were spent at the dam instead of one. Just as important, the congressional delegation noted that the next day's rally in Pasco by canal enthusiasts mustered only fifteen hundred.

There was quieter lobbying as well. O'Sullivan got Reclamation commissioner Arthur Powell Davis aside in the early 1920s and urged him to look at the idea for Grand Coulee Dam. Clarence Dill, who had attributed his 1922 election to the U.S. Senate in part to his openness to a dam as well as a gravity canal, eventually became a persistent supporter. One of the greatest coups was pulled off by Senator Wesley Jones, the same Jones who as a congressman had persuaded Reclamation to take over irrigation of the Yakima Valley. When Congress appropriated money to study dams on the Missouri River in 1929, Jones got Dill to go with him to President Hoover and get the President's backing for a $600,000 study of the Columbia by the Army Corps of Engineers. Canal proponents might have successfully blocked this study had they known about it in time, but Jones quietly slipped it into a routine rivers-and-harbors bill. This study, headed by Seattle district engineer Major John S. Butler, was the most decisive in Columbia River history. It became known as the 308 Report for the number assigned it by the House of Representatives. Completed in 1932, it recommended a series of ten dams on the river, including upstream flood-control projects in Canada. It declared Grand Coulee Dam more feasible than a canal, and estimated the cost of the dam for irrigation at eighty-five dollars an acre if power was sold to subsidize farming, versus four hundred dollars for the canal from Idaho. The 308 Report signaled victory for the "pumpers." Over the next thirty years this blueprint would be followed closely.

The environmental debate over the fate of the Columbia River was over before it began. There was no environmental review of the Corps' plan, and to a Pacific Northwest locked in Depression, there was never any serious question that river development was the way to go. "I don't remember writing anything about people objecting to the dam in the 1930s," recalled Hu Blonk, the reporter who covered day-to-day progress at the site. Roosevelt was elected President the same year the 308 Report appeared and was looking for job-creating public works projects the next spring. He was less interested in irrigation than employment, but the dams appeared ideal to accomplish both. Just two years later the President was already mentioning the possibility of sending barges upstream through the dams to wheat country, a plan that wouldn't be realized for four more decades. "This is a dream, my friends, but not an idle dream," Roosevelt prophesied.

Since either the canal or the dam would get water to the Columbia Basin, the bitter rivalry between Spokane and the smaller towns to the west on this issue might seem puzzling. Why would farmers or merchants care which method was used? In fact, the fight was a battle in the wider national war between private and public power. The reservoir created by a huge dam at Grand Coulee would drown a proposed dam site at Kettle Falls that privately owned Washington Water Power had filed for. Suspiciously, the filing had come just ten days after the Bureau of

Reclamation authorized core drilling to test potential dam foundations at the Grand Coulee site. More important, a federal dam would create a surplus of cheap public power to undercut private rates. This in fact happened when the federal dams on the Columbia began operating and public utility districts formed; private rates fell in competitive response.

Regional jealousies also came into play. The smaller towns west of dominating Spokane were frustrated that the "power trust" had been slow to extend electricity to rural customers. They were wary of Spokane's control over the placement and timing of any irrigation. Rural residents also wanted a "postage stamp" electrical rate system, similar to that used by the government for the mail, in which power cost the same regardless of how remote the customer.

The Pacific Northwest's infusion of newcomers that had been brought by the railroad between 1890 and 1910 had made the region one of the most liberal, experimental, and pro-union in the nation. The International Workers of the World, or "Wobblies," had organized workers suffering deplorable conditions in the logging camps and mines. While ultimately unsuccessful as an organization, the IWW did prompt an improvement in working conditions and focused public dissatisfaction with private industry. Seattle had experienced a general strike in 1919; Portland journalist John Reed extolled the Russian Revolution in his book, *Ten Days That Shook the World*; and eastern senators blasted the nation's fourth corner as "the Soviet of Washington." This all helped set the stage for a campaign that in the years after World War I would give the region the highest ratio of public power ownership in the country.

The push started when freshman Washington legislator Homer Bone took out a six-thousand-dollar mortgage on his own home and launched an initiative campaign in Washington to allow the creation of a statewide public electric utility. He based the idea on the Ontario Hydroelectric Commission, a provincial organization formed in 1906 to electrify that part of Canada because there was insufficient private money to do so. The "Bone Bill," as it was called, was the private utility industry's worst nightmare. They easily blocked Bone's idea in the 1923 legislature. When he took his measure to a public vote the following year, private power spent at least $175,000 to defeat him. (That is the minimum identified by the Federal Trade Commission; some newspaper accounts estimated the complete cost at closer to a million dollars.) The state was blanketed with mailings, pamphlets, and surveys condemning public power. Later federal hearings revealed that the private power industry ransacked their opponents' offices, staged bogus rallies, and destroyed opposing petitions. Bone's own campaign was so inept that it failed to include a statement of its arguments in the Voter's Pamphlet published by the state government before the election and distributed free to all residents. "I was held up to ridicule and scorn in every corner of the state and emerged a ruined man," Bone recounted.

The tide soon turned, however. Increasingly impatient that most Northwest rural homes remained without electricity, the state Grange voted in 1927 to support a more moderate proposal. This would allow the formation of "public utility districts" on a local instead of statewide level. Meanwhile, the reputation of private power was declining. An influential study showed that the privates paid less in taxes than they overcharged in rates. While utility holding companies had performed a valuable service by reorganizing the nation's helter-skelter private power system into efficient grids, they also discouraged competition, pushed up rates, watered stock, and overextended themselves in their drive for consolidation and control. In 1927 the U.S. Senate refused to seat Frank L. Smith of Illinois and William S. Vare of Pennsylvania because of the scandal surrounding their massive contributions from utility trusts. The trusts' partial collapse after the 1929 stock market crash destroyed private power's reputation as the best qualified to look after the public's interest in electricity.

The debacle had ruined Samuel Insull, a onetime secretary to Edison who had become one of the most powerful utility figures in the country. A "little Insull" collapse in Oregon by the Portland Electric Power Company cost thousands of small investors their savings, further souring the public's impression of private power. During his 1932 campaign for President, Roosevelt told a Portland audience that the holding companies were "financial monstrosities" that had cost ordinary investors their savings.

The weather also seemed to conspire against private power. In 1929, drought began in the Pacific Northwest and the private hydroelectric facilities had so little water they could not meet demand, increasing doubts that these companies could be relied on to provide a vital service.

In 1930, Bone and the Grange submitted the new public

power proposal under a revamped initiative procedure in Washington and Oregon. With the Depression deepening, it won in both states. Public utility districts that formed in response needed a source of electricity, creating potential customers for federal dams on the Columbia. That same year Julius Meier, a public power advocate, won the governorship of Oregon, and in 1932 Clarence Martin, another backer of public power and development of the Columbia, won election as governor of Washington. Back in New York, Franklin Roosevelt was reelected governor in 1930 after creating a public power agency for his state.

It was into this atmosphere, in the fall of 1932, that Roosevelt brought his presidential campaign to the Columbia River. He stopped first in Seattle, drawing the biggest crowds in city history to that point, and pledged his support to the controversial Bone.

Then Roosevelt went on to Portland and made clear the battle lines. Electricity was a right, not a luxury, Roosevelt said, and public power could be the "birch rod in the cupboard" to hold private rates down. "Judge me by the enemies I have made," he thundered. "Judge me by the selfish purposes of those utility leaders who have talked of radicalism while they were selling watered stock to the people and using our schools to deceive the coming generation. My friends, my policy is as radical as the Constitution of the United States. I promise you this: Never shall the federal government part with its sovereignty or with its control of its power resources, while I am President of the United States. . . . the next hydroelectric development to be undertaken by the Federal Government must be on the Columbia River!"

Roosevelt did not, however, specifically promise either Grand Coulee or Bonneville dams. He masterfully kept the region in suspense for months after his election. Senator Clarence Dill had met with Roosevelt in Albany as early as January 3, 1931, to solicit a promise to build Grand Coulee if elected. After the election he gave the President-elect a summary of the proposal. Then came its estimated price tag: $450 million. Suddenly Roosevelt seemed to back off. "I hadn't any idea that this project was so big," he said. "I'll have to go to bed with this."

When Dill came to the White House after the inauguration to again press for the dam, Roosevelt was charming but cagey. Dill was about to get a lesson in political bargaining and Roosevelt's skill at pork-barrel politics. The President was being pressed for public works all over the United States, including the Tennessee Valley Authority, and he was determined to make his generosity to the Columbia River clear.

"It's too big," he at first told Dill. "It's so big we can't build it now. It will produce so much power, we can't sell it all." Dill countered that the power could come on line gradually. Roosevelt then objected that there was too much land proposed for irrigation, that it would add to existing surpluses that had destroyed farm prices nationwide. "Why, the farmers would run me out of the White House. Think of the cost of this project, 450 million dollars. Why, that's more than the Panama Canal cost!"

Dill's temper began to rise. He reminded Roosevelt of his promise in Albany to build Grand Coulee. He also reminded Roosevelt how he had helped swing the Maine delegation to his nomination. "It's no bigger," Dill said heatedly, "than it was when I telephoned you that Senator Barkley had traded his favorite-son delegates to be instructed for you in exchange for the agreement to make him temporary chairman of the Chicago convention, and you said, 'You've done it again. Congratulations!' and then you added, 'If we win, I'll build your dam!' " Western support had been critical to Roosevelt's nomination at the Democratic convention, and he had subsequently carried every western state.

Dill was about to go on, but as later recounted by historian Wesley Arden Dick, Roosevelt held up his hand. "Wait a moment, Senator, sit down." The President took up a cigarette, inserted it in his famous holder, lit it, and slowly blew the smoke upwards. Then he looked at Dill. "Let's build a low dam," Roosevelt said.

A low dam? This would defeat the entire scheme of hoisting river water up into the Grand Coulee. When Dill asked him what he meant, the President suggested building a Grand Coulee dam just one hundred and fifty feet high instead of the five hundred and fifty proposed. This would produce some cheap power and quick jobs, and then when the depression was over it could be heightened to provide irrigation. Forty million dollars, the President suggested, should be adequate.

Dill countered with $100 million. Roosevelt said $60 million was as high as he could go. Dill said that wasn't enough to span the Columbia River. Roosevelt replied, "Listen, Clarence, modern engineers will do anything if you tell them what you want. Go see Dr. Elwood Mead [the head of the Bureau of Reclamation]. Tell him I want plans drawn for a low dam at Grand Coulee for $60 million." It would, he promised, get the dam going. It was a "foot in the door."

Dill went away partly mollified, but Roosevelt was not done toying with the Northwest. Dill learned a few months later that Grand Coulee had again been put on the shelf pending completion of studies of a market for the dam's power. Harness the Columbia River! Who would use all that energy? The region was nothing but an economic colony of salmon canneries and wood mills. Dill got another meeting with Roosevelt to protest the delay and the President, playing the good cop, called in Interior Secretary Harold Ickes to play the bad.

Ickes began to explain that it was unclear who would buy the dam's electricity, sinking Dill's hopes. Roosevelt abruptly interrupted that a low dam would produce only 250,000 kilowatts, only an eighth of what had been originally proposed. Surely that power could be utilized, he told his interior secretary.

"Now I want this money allocated at your next meeting," he said to Ickes.

"All right, Mr. President, if that's what you say," Ickes replied.

"That's what I say," Roosevelt answered.

Oregon representatives were going through the same suspense. They wanted Public Works Administration funding for a dam at either Umatilla Rapids or the Cascades of the Columbia. Roosevelt expressed support for $25 million for a dam at the Cascades, to be named Bonneville, but only if a suitable foundation could be found. The Washington shore at the point was little more than the broad rockslide from Table Mountain that had created the Cascade rapids in the first place. Finally the Corps of Army Engineers reported that they had found a feasible site. Roosevelt assured Oregon senator Charles McNary and Congressman Charles Martin the money would be forthcoming and the good news was announced in Oregon. Congress then adjourned, in late spring of 1933.

What followed, however, was ominous silence. Martin returned to Washington, D.C., in September to learn what was going on. He discovered that Roosevelt had reportedly cooled to Bonneville because of the engineering difficulties of the site. The President's secretary brushed the congressman off without an appointment. In a panic, Martin called McNary, who was ill, and insisted he hurry back to the capital. The pair went to the White House and announced they wouldn't leave until granted an audience. Roosevelt agreed to see them, greeted them with charm, and mentioned that $250,000 had been granted for further study. The Oregonians regarded more study as only an excuse to shelve "their" dam and had dubbed the quarter million dollars the "Ickes kiss-off."

Martin countered that the Corps had finished its own study in July, pulled the favorable report from his pocket, and began to read from it. "When I had finished," Martin recounted, "to my surprise he asked no questions but, looking first at the Senator and then at me, raised his arms and said, 'I can go for thirty-six million dollars.' "

Clearly Roosevelt had made up his mind before the pair had walked into his office. Martin grasped his hand and said, "By this act you will harness the Columbia and give us an unlimited supply of the cheapest power in the country; you will rebuild the Northwest."

"That is exactly what I wish to do," Roosevelt replied, beaming.

By this maneuvering Roosevelt had made political heroes of both himself and the Northwest representatives whose votes he needed for the New Deal. The low-dam proposal for Grand Coulee was upgraded by 1935 to the plan for full height. Since the foundation had been built to accommodate a high dam, this two-step process did not delay construction.

At their peak the two projects employed about ten thousand and brought on line a surplus of power just when it was most needed, at the start of World War II. When the dams were approved, however, all the details of where the power was to go, what it would cost, or when irrigation would begin were yet to be worked out. Yet the Pacific Northwest Regional Planning Commission, created by the federal government in 1935, recognized what controlling the Columbia would mean. It noted that 13 percent of the nation's land area had only 3 percent of the population, and that the Northwest's economy was chiefly a seasonal extractor of raw materials. Electricity would change all this, and the Columbia River dams would be "in all probability more far-reaching than any public work or group of public works heretofore planned or constructed by the nation."

12

The Biggest Thing on Earth

Abandoned farm before irrigation came to the Columbia Plateau. (*Washington State Historical Society*)

Block 40 of the Columbia Basin Project is a rectangle of farmland about forty straight-line miles south of Grand Coulee Dam. On color-coded Bureau of Reclamation maps it looks like a green finger pointing toward the Main Canal. While the dam was completed by the beginning of World War II, the dream of irrigating the desert had to be postponed until after that conflict. It was 1951 when Block 40 became the first large section of the Columbia Basin Project to get water. The liquid poured down the concrete rivers and gushed into laterals through gates controlled by hand-turned wheels, branching like a circulatory system until the flow arrived finally at the high point of each eighty-acre farm unit. The farms were oddly shaped, irregularly drawn by government surveyors to follow contour lines so that gravity could carry the delivered water to all parts of the fields. Back then the feeder ditches ended in an austere plateau of sand and basalt and abandoned pioneer farms, the kind of place most people would call a wasteland.

Irrigation utterly changed it. The landscape today is still flat and broad and largely treeless, except for rows of poplars and elms given free by the Soil Conservation Service to retard wind erosion. In summer, however, it becomes a song of chlorophyll and shimmering sprayed water, improbably green in a place where heat energy ripples the air above arrow-straight gravel roads.

Block 40 is so open that it provides views as far as Mount Rainier a hundred miles to the west, and the starched sky so big that farmers can sometimes see approaching storms hours away. When Mount St. Helens erupted in 1980 the ash drifted in ominous dark clouds toward the Columbia Plateau like the end of the world before finally sifting down as gray, gritty snow. Ted Osborne worried that the light-colored ash would reflect too much light and heat away from his fields and so he plowed the ash under, reseeded, and got thirty-two bags of beans per acre that year, his best crop ever.

A fringe of low basalt cliffs marks the northern extent of Osborne's three-hundred-and-fifty-six-acre farm, the sage steppe beyond a reminder of what the land used to look like. Other basalt outcroppings near their house betray the difficult rockiness of their land. Tired machinery sits on lichen-encrusted lava, and a long mound of stones picked off the fields runs next to the gravel road. The cairn is a wry monument to human ambition, the result of a campaign to sift the soil deeply enough to allow the cultivation of potatoes. The rocks eventually won, however: Osborne could never dig away enough of them and so grows wheat and beans instead. The exposure and scale of this landscape struck me as a bit intimidating: the farms have tended to swell in size over time (the Osbornes started with just eighty acres), and the houses of the nearest neighbors look like white dots on a green horizon. The people here are closer to each other in spirit, however, than in the city where I live. They all shared the challenge of pioneering. "I wouldn't have stuck it out if we didn't have such fine neighbors," I was told by Barbara Osborne, Ted's wife.

She is eleven years younger than her husband, has struggled with him on this land for four decades, and instead of being ground down she exhibits a grace that comes from having accomplished a difficult task with skill and perseverance. When I met the Osbornes they were about to celebrate their fortieth anniversary on this farm. The lilac near the back door, grown from a cutting because the couple was too poor to afford shrubbery when they moved here, was about to bloom, as it had every such celebratory Memorial Day weekend. Their pleasant but modest house is still built around the bones of a surplus tarpaper construction shack the couple purchased as their dwelling in 1953. When trucks moved it onto the plowed land, the site was so empty that the house stuck up like an ark on a brown flood. There was no plumbing until the pair mortgaged their Ford for a thousand dollars to do the first remodeling. There was no telephone service either.

Now elms and willows shade a brilliantly green lawn around the Osborne house, providing a sense of enclosure from the emptiness beyond. Block 40 can get blazingly hot in summer, frigid in winter, and windy all the time, but Barbara has learned to appreciate its flat beauty, so different from the enclosing folds of rolling wheat country where she grew up. She led me out through a barbed-wire fence to the irrigation ditch their children used to float on in inner tubes, the water a silver thread that wound back and back toward the Columbia. A hawk shrieked from a nearby tree at our intrusion, and a wheeled irrigation line hissed water on new beans. Where the ground was too stony to plow, wildflowers bloomed in cracks in the basalt. "It was exciting," she said of reclaiming the desert. "But it was a hard life. What made it bearable was that everyone was in the same boat."

Ted Osborne was seventy-three years old when I met him and was still dragging and setting metal irrigation pipe each morning of the growing season. He is a shy, ruddy-faced, big-nosed, genial, and honest man, and if you had asked the people who planned Grand Coulee Dam what sort of farmer they had in mind for its benefits, they would have pointed to someone very much like him. He has spent a lifetime turning this sandy, rock-strewn stretch of plateau into a productive farm.

His family homesteaded the property in 1907 and subsequently prayed for rain for more than two decades. "It sure didn't produce much without water," Ted said. By the Depression they had lost the farm to taxes and moved to Ephrata, where Ted's father took a job delivering mail and Ted found himself growing up around the men who dreamed up what they later called "The Biggest Thing on Earth." His family rented their house from Gale Matthews and his father played pinochle with Billy Clapp. Ted mowed Billy's lawn, pleased that the generous lawyer always gave him a quarter instead of the dime he'd expect elsewhere. As a teenager Ted later went to work to build Grand Coulee Dam, realized with growing excitement that the family's old homestead was in line for the first liquid benefit, and ultimately used the wages he was earning to help buy the farm back.

A pioneer settlement nearby was named Gloyd and so the Block 40 wives called themselves the Gloydettes. They met the first Friday of every month to push for schools, organize a 4-H Club, and trade homemaking skills. The first appearance of a bookmobile was cause for excitement. The rare entertainment was a trip once or twice a month to the drive-in movies at Soap Lake. Barbara took comfort in a large kitchen cabinet with a marble shelf for rolling dough that was called a Kitchen Queen. "The marvelous thing about this is that it was mouseproof," she said. "That, and a Kirby vacuum cleaner, helped keep me sane."

It was a ditch rider who first taught Barbara about canning and gardening. If some parts of the Columbia Basin Project are technologically complex, others are reassuringly simple. A farmer who wants a certain amount of water the next day typically fills out a requisition slip, slips it in a glass mason jar, and screws the jar onto a lid nailed on a post along the irrigation canals. The person who picks up these messages and phones them in to the water master is the ditch rider, and there are nearly a hundred of them in the Columbia Basin Project. They drive a route like a mailman and serve as a link among the scattered families.

Actually delivering water down a ditch can be complex. A certain head and gradient is needed to push the liquid where it is needed. Start a wave down a canal and its energy will travel at about six miles per hour, or four times faster than the water particle itself. That energy time determines the water delivery time. Yet a water master also has to take into account leakage and evaporation and the fate of waste water as it continues downhill. There are thousands of gates in the ditches to control the flow, a computerized alarm system to warn when one goes haywire, and seven small hydroelectric plants along the canals to recapture some of the energy of the diverted water. The employees in the Reclamation headquarters basement in Ephrata still wear cowboy boots, but a lot of their work now is done on computers.

This irrigated complexity has become controversial in itself, as we shall see at the end of this chapter.

• • •

The dream of Grand Coulee Dam was a part of the area's consciousness for as long as Ted can remember. He vividly recalls the 1934 visit of President Roosevelt, who observed the bustling pit along the Columbia where the dam was going to be and then motored down the Grand Coulee to see where the irrigation water would go. Ted took a prize watermelon he had raised to Soap Lake and was thrilled when FDR himself selected it from a display that extended for ninety feet along the road. He still remembers the President's ringing voice booming out in a speech to the crowd, asking the question Roosevelt already knew the answer to: "Do you people want the low dam, or the high dam?"

"The high dam!" they roared.

"Then you shall have it," Roosevelt replied, flashing his famous jubilant smile.

"I've always remembered that," Osborne said quietly. The high dam assured water would get to his family's farm. So popular was the New Deal that later, when the dam was rising, it was almost impossible to find an admitted Republican to serve on the election board in the construction towns around the site.

Ted went to work as a laborer on Grand Coulee in 1937, when he turned eighteen. "I was scared to death half the time on that project." Hillsides erupted in a roar of dynamite, concrete buckets swayed by overhead, water dripped and hissed through small leaks in the cofferdams that temporarily held back the river, and thumping pumps threw the leakage right back. A one-ton rock in this environment was called a "pebble," and a boulder had to reach three tons to earn the name of "rock." There were shrill whistles and growling machines and rattling conveyer belts more than a mile long. The belts rumbled by about as fast as a man could run, taking excavated dirt out and bringing gravel for concrete in. One day, setting a record that has never been broken, the men at Grand Coulee poured 20,696 cubic yards of concrete, enough to pave the equivalent of forty football fields to a depth four inches thick.

Osborne graduated to drilling and grouting the bedrock at Grand Coulee's base. A dam is only as good as the foundation it sits on, so the engineers dug down through the glacial till of the Columbia's river bottom to bare granite, drilled holes in the rock, and pumped a pressurized liquid slurry of cement called grout to fill any fissures that water might creep around. The failure to achieve a watertight foundation at Teton Dam in Idaho is suspected as the flaw that led to the collapse of the three-hundred-foot-high earth structure in 1976, killing seven and destroying or damaging four thousand homes.

The grouting done, the rock was thoroughly cleaned before the first level of concrete was poured. It was not just shoveled clean, or even swept clean, but scrubbed clean with "brushes, sponges, wire brooms, water and air hoses," in the words of Hu Blonk, the on-site correspondent for the Wenatchee and Spokane papers. "So clean must the granite bedrock be before concrete can be poured on it," he wrote, "that it is possible, although perhaps not appropriate, to eat one's meal off of the rock without danger of foreign atoms sneaking in."

There were seven thousand workers. When men weren't being killed or injured—and seventy-seven died building Grand Coulee Dam—they were passing out from heat exhaustion and being dragged into the shade. They consumed fifteen thousand salt pills a day in summer and lined up so tight in the beer halls when their shifts ended that they could scarcely turn around. They managed to quaff enough, however, that the initial lone law-enforcement officer, Francis McGinn, made more than a hundred arrests for urinating in the street. They drank, they fought, they gambled, and one of the supervisors gained the envied reputation of being able to cuss for three straight minutes without repeating himself. Some workers amused themselves with black widow spider fights, and one foreman put a foot-high fence around his new house to keep the rattlesnakes out of his yard.

Construction boss Harvey Slocum was so fond of the whorehouses up on B Street that when the girls complained of the heat he had sprinklers strung across the tar roofs to cool the buildings with water. That charity didn't get Slocum into trouble but his drinking did. When he was fired, Hu Blonk diplomatically wrote it was for "ill-health." A day or two later, when the reporter walked into the Continental Cafe, he heard Slocum angrily call his name. Blonk walked over to where the fired boss was sitting at the counter.

"What's the matter, Harvey?" Blonk asked.

"You put in that goddamn paper of yours that I was canned because of 'ill health,' " Slocum protested. "Now you know damn well I got canned because I was drunk!"

There were gamblers and pimps and bootleggers and drug dealers and pool sharks and petty crooks. The madams had names like Big Edna and Big Grace and ran bawdy houses with titles like the Spar, Gracie's, the Red Rooster, and the Seattle Rooms. It cost two dollars a trick but just ten cents to shuffle around the floor with the taxi dancers: girls from poor families who roomed together and restricted their labor solely to dancing. Intermission had to be called periodically in the dance halls in order to shovel out tracked-in mud in winter and sweep out blown-in dust in summer.

One New York newspaper called Grand Coulee "the cesspool of the New Deal." Senator Clarence Dill was accused in newspaper accounts of having profited by buying up lots around Grand Coulee in anticipation of the dam he had championed, and decided not to seek reelection. Journalist Richard Neuberger, however, a future U.S. senator for Oregon, described the area as simply colorful in a 1937 article for *Harper's* magazine. "The real estate agent wears a checkered vest and derby hat. Taxi-dancers in gaudy dresses line the walls of twenty beer parlors. Fist fights break up two or three drinking bouts. A dozen brothels with fantastic names cater to several thousand womanless males, and the ladies from the sporting houses swear vehemently as dirt seeps through their sandals and spatters their toe nails when they walk along the boardwalk to the beauty parlors that flank the main street."

The dam site was divided by community and rank. Government engineers were at the top of the pecking order in the U.S.-built community of Coulee Dam. Private contractor supervisors were across the river in another town called Mason City. Ordinary laborers were scattered in towns called Grand Coulee, Grand Coulee Heights, Grand Coulee Dam City, Delano, Electric City, and Osborne.

The New Deal government village of identical homes was a deliberate contrast to the beer halls up the hill. Frank Banks, the supervisor in charge of constructing the dam, was a personable but rigid teetotaler who, assistant Philip Nalder recalled, used to check the garbage of his engineers for liquor bottles. "It was like living at an army post," recalled Nalder's wife, Mibs. "The children assumed the rank of their parents."

The Northern Pacific had to build thirty miles of new spur

line to service the remote location and initially there was no decent road to the site. When both Almira and Wilbur put up signs proclaiming themselves as the "Gateway to Grand Coulee," saboteurs from the rival town sneaked out and sawed the proclamations down. The mud was so bad in winter that one enterprising farm boy brought his tractor to the intersection of the county road and B Street, waited inside the office of the Grand Coulee *News*, and pulled out bogged freight trucks for five dollars. Blonk was informed that local resident Bob Mummy had found a good-looking hat lying unattended in the mire. When Mummy stooped to pick the hat up he was surprised to see a man's face underneath, peering up at him. "Think nothing of it," the man said. "There's a wagon load of hay and two horses under me."

Housing was initially almost nonexistent. Blonk started in a shack with no plumbing and the bucket he used for water would freeze over on winter nights. An impoverished family named Reed couldn't afford any place to stay when they came and so they dug a cave in a hillside, installed a drum stove inside, hung a blanket at the door, and camped there with their new baby.

It was all they needed to get started. The New Deal and the dam were promising them a job, and with it the promise of a new life.

Grand Coulee would be the biggest dam on the Columbia, but not the first. Almost six months before the big one was started, four thousand workers completed the river's most human-sized and homeliest dam, plugging a rugged stretch of river south of Wenatchee called Rock Island Rapids. Grand Coulee draws hundreds of thousands of tourists a year, but Rock Island does not even have a visitors' center. With a "head" between the reservoir brim and the Columbia at its foot of just forty feet, Rock Island is the river's lowest as well as oldest dam. Even its new powerhouse is humbly roofed with corrugated metal like a Quonset hut so the top can be lifted off like a lunch bucket to allow cranes access to the generators inside. Rock Island seems almost quaint compared to the severe behemoth that is Grand Coulee: its first generators have hardwood instead of steel rails and their General Electric insignia glow in proud, polished brass.

Rock Island was built by Boston-based Stone & Webster, the electric holding company that controlled Puget Sound Power and

Light. By the end of the 1920s it was clear that Puget needed more power and that the Columbia River was the most obvious untapped source. Engineering had advanced to the point where a low dam across the river seemed both affordable and feasible, so Stone & Webster applied for the Rock Island site in 1928. It received a license thirteen days before the Crash of 1929 and, despite the depression, work began in January 1930. Only four of ten planned generators were initially installed because of the depression's impact on power demand.

Rock Island was a logical site for the Columbia's first dam. The fall of its rapids provided the necessary depth for a reservoir while the island split the Columbia in two. This made it relatively easy to divert the river's flow onto first one side of the island and then the other, allowing the foundation of each half of the dam to be built in turn on a dry riverbed. The location had other advantages. It was adjacent to the Northern Pacific railroad, making it easy to deliver construction supplies. There were existing transmission lines nearby. The low height of the dam and resulting small reservoir meant that little valuable farmland would have to be flooded and thus paid for. The river had deposited gravel and sand nearby that could be used for concrete. Throughout the West, rivers have conspired in their own obstruction by producing the raw materials needed to make dams.

Rock Island's length was more than a thousand feet shorter than Grand Coulee and its initial head was less than a tenth that of the bigger dam. (It was later raised six additional feet.) The techniques used at Rock Island became standard for many of the dams that followed, however. When dams are built in high, narrow rock canyons—such as the Columbia's Revelstoke in British Columbia, completed in 1984—rivers are frequently diverted through tunnels bored in one cliff. Most of the Columbia River sites were too broad and the river volume too great for this technique, so cofferdams were used instead. A horseshoe-shaped enclosure was built out to a mid-point of the river and its interior pumped dry. The loose rock and sand at the bottom of the horseshoe were excavated to bedrock, cracks and potholes were filled with grout, and the dam foundation rose from there.

Once the foundation piers had risen above normal river level, the cofferdam would be disassembled and moved to the other half of the river, allowing the water to pour between the half-finished abutments on the first side. When the full set of piers was completed across the river, each opening between them could be shut off by smaller, prefabricated metal cofferdams, and the complex system of penstocks, outlet tubes, and spillway gates would be completed as the dam rose. Grand Coulee, for example, is pierced by sixty outlet tubes that allowed the river to pour through as it was completed.

The cofferdams were impressive achievements in themselves. The temporary dams were built of sixty-foot-square "cribs" made from twelve-inch-thick timbers that stood, in Grand Coulee's case, up to one hundred and ten feet high. The bottoms of these enormous wooden baskets were cut to rest snugly on the river bedrock. Two dozen or more of the apartment-house-sized structures were then jockeyed into place with cables and tugs, filled with rock to pin them to the bottom, and fastened together. Then the cribs were planked over on top and overlapping steel sheets were driven around their outer sides, facing the river. The resulting work areas were huge; the cofferdams at Grand Coulee enclosed an area of sixty acres.

When work started at Rock Island no one had ever seen the bottom of the Columbia River before. The excavators were astounded by the yawning chasms, jagged pinnacles, and wide potholes the turbulent current had carved, helping explain why several steamboats had met their end at this point. These irregularities had to be filled like cavities in a tooth. While Rock Island's present head is only forty feet, its total height is up to one hundred and sixty-two feet because of its deep foundation. The roots of Grand Coulee go even deeper: that dam's lowest concrete is two hundred feet below the surface of the Columbia River that flows out from its base.

Diverting the river was only one difficulty facing the dam engineers. The most basic requirement of all, siting the dam, proved difficult at Bonneville. The location was logical enough. It was at the head of tidal influence on the Columbia, and thus was at the lowest point at which a dam could be built on the river. Upstream the river fell thirty-seven feet in seven miles, promising good water energy. Drowning the Cascades of the Columbia and installing a lock at the dam would eliminate more than a century of navigation frustration. Moreover, Bonneville's generators would be near Portland.

The loose rock of the Cascades was a problem, however.

When winter flooding halted work on Bonneville the first Christmas, in 1933, engineers were still not satisfied with their site. The flood hiatus allowed additional test drilling to be done and engineers concluded they had to move Bonneville two thousand feet downstream. Even then, building a major dam on a sloping avalanche site was a feat of chutzpah. Edgar Kaiser, the superintendent of excavation, commented on Bonneville's dubious location: "We weren't really mature enough then to see that it couldn't be done, and maybe that's why it *was* done."

With a site finally decided on, the government went to work even though plans for the structure were far from completed. The purpose was to employ people, blueprints be damned. One electrical engineer complained that workers were building the Bonneville powerhouse before planners knew what kind of generators would be installed, "the only objective apparently being the dumping of yards of concrete and the placing of tons of steel. Structural design in the office was but a jump ahead of actual construction in the field."

The dam at Grand Coulee was having its own site problems. Some 21 million cubic yards of gravel, sand, and clay that lay over its bedrock had to be removed, the equivalent of about 80 million wheelbarrow loads. Once the hillsides were cut into they tended to slide, one hillside of 1.5 million cubic yards slumping ninety feet downhill and swallowing two tractors and a steam shovel. A number of steps were taken to deal with such slides, from putting up temporary rock abutments to draining away groundwater.

Most intractable was a slurry of almost liquid mud that poured out of a crevice in the bedrock on the east side of the dam, flooding the foundation work area. Engineers first tried stemming the goo with timbers and then installed a rock crib, but the mud continued to surge over the top. Finally they hit upon the idea of freezing the mud flood until the concrete dam was in place. Pipes were inserted, ammonia brine was piped in that could freeze up to seventy tons of earth a day, and an "ice dam" forty feet high, twenty feet thick, and one hundred and five feet long was created. Blonk recalls that when supervisors told him they were building an ice dam, he thought they were pulling his leg and ignored the story—reading about it two days later in a rival newspaper.

•   •   •

When first completed, Rock Island was thirty-eight hundred feet long and cost $15 million. Bonneville began as a 1,450-foot spillway dam on one side of Bradford Island and a 1,027-foot first powerhouse and a navigation lock on the other, and cost $88.4 million. It took four years to complete, and the resulting head between reservoir brim and river averaged sixty-seven feet. In the 1980s a second powerhouse nine hundred and eighty-six feet long was completed across an artificially dug channel, so that Bonneville now spans two islands and three arms of the Columbia.

Grand Coulee dwarfs both of these. Its crest rose three hundred and fifty feet above the Columbia and its foundation reached another two hundred feet below. Its length is almost a mile, or 5,223 feet, longer than the flight deck of five aircraft carriers laid end to end. The original structure cost $300 million and adding the third powerhouse in the 1970s added another $700 million. Its nearly 12 million cubic yards of concrete represents twelve times as much as was used in Bonneville Dam. Upstream, ten towns and twelve hundred buildings had to be razed or moved to make room for a reservoir that would cover one hundred and twenty-five square miles of land. Thirty million board feet of timber were cut. A sheep herder named Cul White was hired by the Bureau of Reclamation to find Indian graves, and the Spokane Mortuary Company was enlisted to move them uphill above the reach of the water. Engineers also discovered that spring meltwater would be backed up by the new reservoir at the border because of a choke point of two islands at the Little Dalles, possibly flooding the Canadian community of Trail. After building a scale model of the problem, the Reclamation Bureau discovered that the offending rocks could simply be dynamited, allowing high water to move smoothly into Lake Roosevelt instead of mounding at the boundary.

All three dams are gravity dams, meaning they get their strength from the weight of their structure on top of bedrock, not from bracing against canyon walls. Grand Coulee at its base is nearly five hundred feet wide, angling back to a thirty-foot road on the top. While the drop from its railing seems steep, the dam is so fat it is difficult to throw a baseball from the crest and hit the river downstream. Like all dams, Grand Coulee is not completely solid—it has more than eight miles of tunnels and galleries in its interior—but it is astonishingly sturdy. It took 6 million pounds of conventional explosives to blow two hundred and sixty feet off the end of the dam to add the third powerhouse. Yet even when the main dam was no longer anchored to one of the canyon walls it didn't quiver from the weight of Lake Roosevelt. *Smithsonian* magazine once asked engineers how long the dam might last if abandoned by civilization. They guessed it would persist at least until a new Ice Age glacier or Spokane-sized flood bulldozed it off the riverbed.

Grand Coulee was poured in a series of interconnecting concrete blocks five feet thick and up to fifty feet square. Cooling pipes were laid between each five-foot layer and river water was pumped through them to speed the curing of the concrete, which otherwise could have taken two hundred years to fully set up. The joints between the blocks were sealed with grout.

With seventy-seven men dying to build the dam, the idea that some are entombed in the dam's concrete is a standard part of Grand Coulee legend. One Army Corps employee told me she had been informed bodies lie in all the Columbia dams, like some kind of blood sacrifice to the gods of hydroelectric power. Alas, while there is a grisly romance to such tales, they are not true. The concrete was not poured five feet thick at once but instead was delivered in hanging buckets that held about four cubic yards at a time, enough to fill a form a few inches thick. Cranes let the buckets down to a point only a foot or two above the last pour. To be buried a worker would have to crawl under a bucket, lie down, and not be missed or noticed by his coworkers as they spread the slurry out. It simply didn't happen. Reclamation spokesman Craig Sprankle said that as a joke, however, workers would sometimes nail a boot to the wooden concrete form, or a rubber glove in which sausages had been stuffed to resemble fingers. When the form was pulled off after the concrete was set, the foreman would find a supposed pitiful remnant of one of his employees, a discovery that would set the crew to howling with laughter.

Grand Coulee was never, of course, "The Biggest Thing on Earth" as Neuberger titled his 1937 article about the dam. The Great Wall of China is far bigger. The earth-filled Fort Peck Dam built the same time on the Missouri was more than twice as long and a dozen times as massive. The dam was, however, the biggest concrete structure ever built. At maximum power it can generate enough electricity to service six cities the size of Seattle.

When Rock Island Dam was completed in 1933, skeptics questioned the Depression-era market for its power. By the time

Grand Coulee Dam began generating eight months before the attack on Pearl Harbor, in March 1941, generators could not be installed fast enough. The defense buildup had begun. Bonneville had started generating in March 1938. By 1943, 96 percent of Columbia River electricity was being used for war manufacturing.

Most of this power went to the manufacture of aluminum. Airplanes are made out of that metal, and Seattle's Boeing alone produced ten thousand bombers during the war. Before cheap electricity, aluminum was so precious and costly a commodity that a one-hundred-ounce pyramid of it was used to cap the Washington Monument. Before 1939 there were no aluminum plants west of the Mississippi. In December of that year, however, Alcoa announced it would build one at Vancouver to use electricity from Bonneville Dam. Five more aluminum smelters followed in quick succession, scattered around the Northwest. By 1942 they were consuming three-quarters of the energy produced by the new dams, and by the end of the war the region was producing 42 percent of America's aluminum, a ratio that has persisted into the 1990s.

The aluminum smelters became the Columbia's most reliable energy customers. Unlike homes and most businesses they require electricity as tirelessly as the river flows, twenty-four hours a day. The factories would buy the product of the generators at night, when no one else wanted it. Moreover, their contracts provided that in times of shortage they could be cut off from power, eliminating the need for river managers to create surplus generating capacity. In return for granting such flexibility, the aluminum industry was awarded bargain rates. Moreover, its presence both justified and spurred rapid dam building. The plants today are not huge employers—they directly employ about seven to eleven thousand workers in the Pacific Northwest—and yet they gobble a third of the river's energy. With the world facing a surplus of aluminum capacity as Russia dumped the metal onto the world market in the early 1990s, prices slumped, and Northwest power rates climbed. Some critics argue that the region's aluminum industry should be allowed to die a natural economic death by the year 2000. This could allow the electricity to be sold at higher rates to other industrial customers that would likely employ more people. Alternately it could allow more water to be spilled over dams to help endangered salmon. The issue is complex, however.

There is no guarantee substitute customers will be found or that salmon will be helped.

Aluminum was not the Columbia's only war product. Its electricity powered shipyards in Portland and Vancouver that turned out seven hundred and fifty ships, or 27 percent of all those built in the conflict. Another fifty-five thousand kilowatts disappeared to a "mystery load" in a remote corner of the Washington desert called Hanford. Only when the atomic bomb exploded over Nagasaki did utility officials learn its purpose.

By the end of World War II the two dams produced nearly as much power as all the hydro- and steam-generating plants that had been built by the region's utilities in the previous half century—and all of it was being used. War had justified damming the Columbia River, and war transformed the Pacific Northwest. Between 1940 and 1948 the population of Washington and Oregon increased 44 percent as people swarmed into the region to work in war industries and coastal military bases. Before the first acre of Columbia Basin desert was watered from Grand Coulee's reservoir, the white elephant debate was already over. "The White Elephant Comes into Its Own," the *Saturday Evening Post* headlined in 1943.

Bonneville Power Administration publicist Stephen B. Kahn later wrote a poem to drive home the dam's role in the war. Here is its last verse:

> *On this democratic altar we have worked and scores have died.*
> *So the power of the river may turn the battle tide*
> *As our armies fight in battle, so we back them with the might*
> *Of the nation's greatest river, working day and night.*

By the time the first generators began to turn, several of the long-running disputes over management of Columbia River energy had been resolved. The arguing had been strenuous. Final hearings on creation of the Bonneville Power Administration alone, held in 1937, filled five hundred pages with testimony. What was to become of their power once it left the generators? Who would transmit it? How much would it cost? Would it benefit the region or nation generally, or the communities closest to the dams? Would it supply public systems or private, would it power industry or homes?

The first and one of the most persistent ideas was to create a Northwest copy of the famed Tennessee Valley Authority. The TVA built twenty-one dams in the Tennessee Valley in the 1930s and early 1940s, more than doubling energy consumption in that region, attracting new industry, and environmentally restoring an area of ravaged land the size of England. As such it was a model of government social engineering, and in 1935, Senator James Pope of Idaho introduced a bill to copy its success in the Columbia Valley.

Pope's legislation was the first of five unsuccessful attempts to pass such a measure. The bills never overcame conservative opposition. Republicans saw the idea as socialistic. Businesses objected that the TVA was specifically directed to "avoid sale [of electricity] to private companies or individuals doing business for profit." Existing agencies such as Reclamation and the Corps of Engineers feared their own control of the dams would be stolen by a new superagency on the Columbia. Opponents also pointed out that TVA was charged with tasks arguably already handled by other agencies or businesses in the Pacific Northwest, such as promotion of agriculture, soil conservation, and the manufacture of fertilizer.

Liberals, however, were unwilling to simply make the new power available at the dams to any takers, hoping the free market would accomplish what it so far had not: making electricity affordable to rural as well as urban customers. The compromise that replaced a Columbia Valley Authority was a new kind of federal agency that would oversee the marketing of the power, called the Bonneville Power Administration. BPA would neither build dams nor get involved in land planning like TVA, but its decisions on transmitting and selling electricity would be pivotal.

Bonneville traces its origins to a Pacific Northwest Regional Planning Board created by Roosevelt in 1933 to study issues of economic recovery. Chaired by Portland newspaper editor Marshall Dana, its most influential member was Professor Charles McKinley of Portland's Reed College. The board recommended that the federal government market the new power, rather than leave it to private industry to distribute. It rejected the idea of splitting the region into territories, each served by its own dam. It also rejected the idea of setting up a Columbia Valley Authority. Instead, it suggested, the Army Corps could be left in day-to-day charge of running Bonneville Dam, and the Bureau of Reclamation in charge of running Grand Coulee. BPA would take over when the electricity left the powerhouse. The compromise has worked as a mechanism to harness the Columbia's energy but has been too awkward to allow effective environmental planning.

Senator Homer Bone introduced a bill in 1936 to create the proposed agency, taking a cue from TVA by suggesting that the bulk of the cheap new power be reserved for public power at postage-stamp rates. G. W. Thiessen of the Oregon State Grange testified in 1937: "We are not so much interested in large industrial centers as we are in building up rural communities with local industries. These large industrial centers are simply places where vice, immorality and Communism thrive."

The Washington delegation sided with Bone, but Oregon was split. Portland was served by private power but Oregon politicians outside Portland favored public power. Oregon's legislature sided with rural interests: 70 percent of the state's farmers still had no electricity. They had supported the big federal dams, despite the threat of competing irrigation, to get it. Accordingly, Oregon senator Charles McNary came in on the side of Bone's vision of BPA. By the time Roosevelt summoned the region's congressional delegation to the White House in February 1937, it was to hash out the details. In August of that year, the President signed the Bonneville bill into law.

The agency was named for a second-rate explorer named Benjamin Louis E. de Bonneville, of dubious significance to BPA's region. Bonneville took two years' leave from the army from 1832 to 1834 to attempt to break into the fur trade and, he claimed, scout Mexican and British strength in the West. The effort was largely a failure. The fort he built at South Pass was called Fort Nonsense by his critics, his fur enterprise collapsed, and his absence led to his temporary dismissal from the army. A romanticized account of his adventures by Washington Irving made Bonneville's travels famous, however, and as proof that promotion sometimes counts for more than accomplishment, his name was applied to the regional power authority.

Having disappointed private power and industry by creating the new agency, Roosevelt subsequently dismayed them by picking the combative, visionary head of Seattle City Light, J. D. Ross, to head it.

Puget Power had been battling Ross for thirty-five years, and losing. He was an apostle of public power, low rural rates, and government control. His utility enemies had become so desperate that at one point they hired private detectives to tail Ross in hopes of turning up something to force him out of office. They were disappointed, and Ross's brief tenure at Bonneville left a permanent mark on the Pacific Northwest.

He came to rambunctious, ambitious, and untidy Seattle after an unsuccessful sojourn to seek gold in the Klondike Gold Rush. Casting about for something to do, in 1902 Ross submitted to the city a plan to build Seattle's first hydroelectric plant on the Cedar River. That demonstration of initiative and knowledge was enough to get him appointed electrical engineer of the new public utility called Seattle City Light. By 1911, Ross had risen to superintendent, and in subsequent years he secured dam development licenses on the Skagit River to give Seattle a cheap source of power, plunged into the long and bruising propaganda war between public and private power, and eventually forced competitor Puget Power out of much of the city. He was an indefatigable promoter of dams, electricity, and the social benefits of electric consumption. As early as 1928 he called for a 300,000-volt transmission line from Seattle to Los Angeles, anticipating the day when lucrative power sales to California would help justify the complete damming of the Columbia and the Snake. To whip up public enthusiasm for hydroelectric development he turned the Skagit dams into a visitor attraction, building a tourist railway and planting gardens. When Seattle mayor Frank Edwards tried to curb Ross's power in 1931 by firing him, it was Edwards who was recalled instead. The popular Ross was reinstated.

In a 1940 profile in *Harper's* magazine, it was recounted that "the corporation executives who, one after another, were sent to Seattle to manage the competing utility were baffled by Ross. Despite numerous attempts to cripple or oust him, the community refused to let him down. He became a sort of monument. His big bulk, huge head, hands like hams, slow, placid look, elephant tread, rumbled blue serge with shiny knees and elbows, and tender interest in birds and begonias—all inspired confidence. Ross knew how his neighbors felt and over a long period of years guided City Light with due regard for those feelings. In the end, public power was entrenched in the city."

Ross was appointed to head the Bonneville Power Administration on October 9, 1937, twelve days after Bonneville Dam was formally dedicated. He wasted no time in setting the direction of the new agency. Rates were pegged low and service rapidly expanded with an eye to making electricity a universal benefit. Ross launched the construction of the huge transmission lines that transported the Columbia's power across the region, nixing the idea that Columbia power would remain solely with nearby communities such as Portland. He confirmed postage-stamp rates and cemented in place the "preference clause" that promised a share of power for public utilities.

The rates he approved were astounding. When the first electricity systems were created in the 1880s, power costs in the Pacific Northwest were equivalent to several dollars per kilowatt hour. Bonneville's wholesale rate, in contrast, was set at one-fifth of one *cent* per kilowatt hour, more than 50 percent cheaper than that offered by TVA and a bargain that didn't change until 1965. Nothing spoke more powerfully of what big dams on the Columbia could do. Ross said that should mean residents could get basic lighting for a dollar a month, and all the appliances plus home heating for $7.50. Response was immediate. By 1940, private utility rates in the Pacific Northwest had been reduced by $13 million a year because of the cheap new Columbia power. A number of public utilities were able to cut their rates in half. Residential electric use soared.

Unfortunately, the success of cheap hydroelectricity in the Pacific Northwest also laid the seeds for future disaster. Nowhere in the world was wired energy so inexpensive and ubiquitous. Electric heat became commonplace in homes and businesses, while energy conservation was ignored. For thirty-five years electric consumption marched upward on charts and graphs in an unbroken slope, a trend that Northwest energy planners interpreted disastrously—shortly before the Arab oil embargo of 1974—as continuing indefinitely. With the river already dammed, Northwest utilities launched a program to build five nuclear power plants at once, not foreseeing that the higher cost of thermal power would force conservation measures and level consumption. The crash construction undertaken by a new consortium called the Washington Public Power Supply System, or WPPSS, foundered on runaway costs, questions of safety, and miserable mismanagement. The acronym was soon pronounced Whoops and became a synonym for fiasco. The price of the nuclear plants ballooned from $5 billion to $11 billion, the market for the power evaporated, and only one of the five plants was ever completed. The result was the largest bond default in U.S. history, injuring thousands of small investors.

In response, Congress passed the Northwest Power Act and created the Northwest Power Planning Council in 1980, a move that was an abrupt lurch from unbridled development to energy conservation. The addition of new generating facilities slackened, utilities helped finance insulation and other conservation measures, and by the beginning of the 1990s the BPA was aggressively pursuing wind power, energy from small gas turbines, the recycling of waste heat in factories to make power, and geothermal energy. Charged with bringing new order to Columbia River management, the council has generally drawn praise for its efforts at promoting energy conservation but has had a more difficult time gaining consensus on saving salmon.

The Pacific Northwest still has today a higher percentage of public-owned utilities than any region in the nation, as well as the nation's lowest electric rates, both directly attributable to the damming of the Columbia River and the politics of J. D. Ross. On March 14, 1939, after just a year and a half at the head of the BPA, Ross died following abdominal surgery.

His successor was Dr. Paul Raver, former chairman of the Illinois Commerce Commission. Raver did not have Ross's crusading instincts for public power, but he continued his policies and pushed for completion of the Columbia River development plan that had been mapped out by the Army Corps of Engineers in 1932. In 1945, fearful that the Depression would return with the end of war, Congress authorized construction of a dam at Umatilla Rapids to be named for the late Senator Charles McNary. Construction began in 1947. Over the next twenty-three years the remaining seven American dams on the main-stem Columbia were built, three of them completed in 1961 alone.

If the dream of damming the river had originated in schemes of how to use its water to irrigate farms, the war experience had shifted official thinking. Grand Coulee would be the only dam built for reclamation; all the others were built primarily for energy production. Five of the main river's dams were built and are operated by the Army Corps, five by pubic utility districts along the mid-Columbia in eastern Washington, and three by B.C. Hydro in Canada.

This shift in emphasis toward energy production shadowed the irrigation development scheme that had led to Grand Coulee Dam. It took thirty-five years from the time Billy Clapp first outlined his dam scheme to Rufus Woods until the first farm water reached Ted Osborne's farm. By that time the utopian ideal of using large-scale engineering to promote small-scale farming was obsolete.

There are two statistics that sum up the outcome of the Grand Coulee dream that had first brought federal dam construction to the Columbia. One is that the Columbia Basin Project irrigates an area nearly the size of Rhode Island: about 640,000 acres if one adds the pumping of well water from an aquifer incidentally fed by Project runoff, their pumps powered by Project electricity.

The other statistic is that half the land originally intended for irrigation—another Rhode Island—has never been watered, and may never be.

Support for completion of the Columbia Basin Project has evaporated like sprinkler mist on a hot Grant County day. Grand Coulee Dam worked, but people like the Osbornes were the last of the American farm pioneers. The basin farms operate with a generous taxpayer subsidy, and with today's economics federal reclamation promises no land for the landless. Few Americans could afford to buy and operate an irrigated farm today. "You either have to marry it or inherit it," Ted said.

None of this subtracts from the marvel of the irrigation project. Just one of the pumps sucking water out from the reservoir behind Grand Coulee Dam could fill five hundred bathtubs each second. The pump facility has twelve of them. "Our canals are as big as a river," noted Bill Gray, the Reclamation Bureau's chief of water and lands operations, noting that two of its major canals are longer than the Potomac. The water grows apples, mint, alfalfa, beets, beans, carrots, potatoes, grapes, cherries, and a score of other crops with technological efficiency. The Hudson's Bay

Company was pleased when it could harvest twenty bushels of wheat per acre at Fort Vancouver. Columbia Basin growers sometimes get six times as much. Irrigation as a whole consumes about 6 percent of the Columbia.

The water made Moses Lake the biggest city in central Washington and created entire new towns: Basin City, Royal City, and George. (The latter traces its name to the first President, of course, but for the benefit of future scholars I feel obliged to record that my friend and colleague at the *Seattle Times*, investigative reporter Eric Nalder, insists that George was named for his dog. I checked this tale with Eric's father, Philip, who had become the director of the Basin Project in Ephrata in 1951. Indeed, Philip recalled, George was a sheepdog, mistreated by its former blue-collar owner, and had become Eric's pet. George's unfortunate habit of menacing anyone not wearing a business suit frequently kept him on the Nalder family mind, however, and when a group of investors from Yakima outlined the plans for their new community to Philip, he said, "Why don't you call the town George," failing to mention it was the dog, not the Father of Our Country, that first brought the name to mind.)

Completion of the canals increased the number of irrigated farms in Grant County alone some six times, to 1,216, and initial enthusiasm was infectious. "You *had* to be excited about it, all the time," said Nalder. "We had a hell of a lot of pride about it." One must drive across the project to get some sense of its scale. It is largely flat, huge, and both beautiful and boring in its trim utility. The new towns, which lack any real core, seem frozen in the 1950s, when they were built. The rule-straight roads cut across fields that in late spring can be almost blinding sheets of green alfalfa and yellow saffron, red-winged blackbirds flitting through the golden stalks of the latter like winking jewels.

As remarkable as this transformation of desert is, the contribution of Grand Coulee and the Columbia Basin Project needs to be put in perspective. It represents less than 8 percent of the irrigated land in the Columbia Basin, and just over 2 percent of all farmland in the basin. If the Columbia Basin Project disappeared overnight, the overall impact on regional agriculture would be significant but far from catastrophic.

Moreover, its impressive engineering has required still more engineering to keep it working. The canals bring so much water into the desert soil that an equally lengthy system of drains has had to be installed to prevent the land from being waterlogged and drowning the roots of the crops. The two systems combined, if laid end to end, would reach more than six thousand miles.

Construction of the project had stalled at the halfway point by the 1970s as farmer enthusiasm waned. The eastern half of the intended project proved wet enough to grow dryland wheat, and therefore 90 percent of the land still planned for irrigation is already farmed. Many of those farmers observed with distaste the heavy investment in machinery and irrigation systems that their neighbors put up with in return for higher yields. Moreover, by 1989 the estimated cost of artificially watering the second half of the project was $2.6 billion, or nearly three times what Grand Coulee Dam and its canals had originally cost. Faced with such a price, even Reclamation has retreated to proposing an alternative that would water less than a fifth of the proposed acreage for $313.5 million.

The simple yeoman farmer who was to be served by the project has proved a myth. Original Reclamation law restricted a husband and wife on federal irrigation projects to ownership of three hundred and twenty acres but put no limit on how much acreage was leased. Some corporations, particularly in California's Central Valley, used that loophole to accumulate huge farms with taxpayer-subsidized water. Abuses have been less blatant in the Columbia Basin Project, but even there a few farms have swollen to the four-thousand-acre range. Instead of the original New Deal dream of land for the landless, the modern project has put fewer, more sophisticated farmers on bigger farms. The Osbornes have had to quadruple their original acreage to survive and they are typical. Grand Coulee may water an area nearly the size of Rhode Island, but it supports just over two thousand families, individuals, or corporations that actually work the land—a far cry from the 100,000 farm families originally projected.

In the 1980s, Congress reformed the Reclamation Act in an attempt to recognize modern economic realities. The new rule allows a couple to own and lease up to nine hundred and sixty acres at subsidized rates, while allowing farmers to lease more if they pay the *real* cost. The difference is substantial. The subsidized cost of supposed repayment for the dams and irrigation works ranges from two to five dollars per acre per year. (Besides the subsidized cost of the irrigation works themselves, farmers also pay an average of about twenty-four dollars per acre per year for maintenance and operation of the system.) The *true* cost of paying back the dams and canals can range from sixty to more than two hundred dollars an acre per year, depending on the federal project involved.

Despite this price difference, several dozen farmers on the Columbia Basin Project elect to farm more than nine hundred and sixty acres because water is still "the cheapest thing they've got," explained Quincy Irrigation district manager Keith Franklin. Fertilizer can run two hundred dollars an acre, treatment of the worst pests and diseases can hit three hundred dollars, and a piece of modern machinery routinely costs in the six figures. A hundred dollars or so per acre for water can seem affordable if it allows the costs of a mechanical harvester to be spread over a larger acreage.

Some economists accordingly question federal irrigation. Farmers pay nothing for the water they take, only for the cost of dams and canals and pumps to get it to them. Water withdrawn from the Columbia, however, is not really free—it is water that cannot push dam turbines or nurture salmon. In 1976, Norm Whittlesey, an economist at Washington State University, calculated that electric rate payers were losing fifty dollars for every acre-foot diverted from the Columbia. An acre-foot is a measure equal to an acre of water a foot deep, and project growers have used as much as 2.8 million acre-feet a year. When the economist looked at the economics of completing the other half of the project, the numbers got even worse: $4,500 per acre. Farmers would repay $153 of this, power sales from Grand Coulee would cover another $192, Washington State taxpayers would contribute $1,000 in cost-sharing of the project, and the rest would come from the federal treasury. This for land that is not barren desert, but is already being farmed for wheat today.

As a target for sympathy and aid, agriculture had become a victim of its own success. Food was too cheap to interest policymakers in extending canals. By the time government reclamation projects stalled in the 1970s, there were 45.4 million irrigated acres in seventeen western states, a tenth of the world's total. About a fifth of that acreage had been watered by federal projects. The biggest crop, representing 37 percent of the total, was cattle feed such as alfalfa.

Not surprisingly, environmental critics questioned the sacrifice of natural rivers for animal feed and social critics argued that river development made farmers prisoners of mechanized agriculture, cumbersome bureaucracy, and a Treasury debt that can never realistically be repaid. More surprisingly, these critics remain in the minority. They are challenging a system of belief nurtured for half a century, a conscious public relations campaign designed to control public thinking about the West's major rivers.

The House of Lies

Apple princesses representing the forty-eight states pour jugs
of water into Grand Coulee's main canal at its opening in 1951.
(Bureau of Reclamation)

Just one payment had been made on Woody Guthrie's brand-new brown Pontiac and already it was a wreck. Its upholstery was torn and stained, its fenders were dented, and a window had been broken out by the folk singer after he locked his keys inside the car. When the vehicle pulled up to the headquarters of the Bonneville Power Administration in April 1941, unwashed and unannounced, its interior was a heap of clothes, blankets, food wrappers, a guitar, Woody's wife, Mary, and three travel-weary, blond-headed children. A BPA film director named Gunther Von Fritsch had visited Guthrie in Los Angeles in early April, explaining that the agency might be looking for a folk singer to put its mission to music in a new documentary. Woody was twenty-eight, broke, and out of work, and when he heard nothing more he decided to drive to Portland and force the issue by seeking an audition. On the trip up from Los Angeles, the singer hocked the family radio to get money to feed his children.

Greeting Guthrie was Stephen Kahn, the man who had hit upon the idea of hiring him. Kahn had produced a 1939 film called *Hydro,* extolling the virtues of the new dams on the Columbia. "Ordinary people hadn't been able to afford electricity," he recalled. "The big fight was over who was going to get the benefits of those dams." Now BPA was turning the electric industry upside down: giving preference to public utilities, slashing rates, and promoting electric heat. Between 1930 and 1940 the number of public utilities in the Northwest had gone from almost zero to seventy-eight. There was a missionary fervor to the public power mission, a heady unity among believers who suddenly found themselves in power with the New Deal. When J. D. Ross was appointed as head of Bonneville, Kahn periodically drove him from BPA's Portland headquarters to Seattle so the new administrator could check on his beloved City Light. At the midway point the two would argue over where to stop for lunch, Ross preferring Centralia because it had adopted public power, while Kahn preferred neighboring Chehalis because Centralia had been the site of a lynching of a unionizing Wobblie two decades before. Two compatible idealists were clashing on the politically correct place to dine. Bonneville as created was a revolutionary agency, a little man's agency, an agency in a propaganda war with private power to convince the public of the merits of big, taxpayer-financed dams. Woody Guthrie, the eloquent Okie, could give Bonneville the common touch it was looking for. "He had the gift of gab," Kahn said. "He could talk tears out of a stone. He was genuine, though. There was nothing phony about the guy."

Kahn wanted to update *Hydro* with folk music and had been told of Guthrie by a curator of folk music at the Library of Congress named Alan Lomax. The choice was bold. Woody had not yet achieved the national fame that songs such as "This Land Is Your Land" and "So Long, It's Been Good to Know Ya" would later bring. Nor is it likely he would be hired by the entrenched and cautions Bonneville Power Administration of today. Guthrie was not, as some later suspected, a Communist, but he was a union-supporting, left-leaning crooner for the working man who had written a ballad in praise of Pretty Boy Floyd because the gangster had reputedly used some of his loot to help hard-pressed farmers pay off their mortgages. "Some will rob you with a gun, some with a fountain pen," Woody sang. He had no fondness for the business establishment. During his travels for Bonneville he met a local official who was on the telephone with the Inland Empire Chamber of Commerce. The delighted official asked Guthrie to "play some background music" for the chamber into the telephone. "I wouldn't play no *foreground* music for any chamber of *commerce*," Guthrie replied, "let alone the background."

So this was the entertainer who had shown up on Bonneville's doorstep: sleeping in the car with the family, bearded, unwashed, and charming. Kahn considered the situation, realized the singer's hire could add momentum to his own campaign to make a new film, and proposed that BPA hire Woody for thirty days, a temporary stint that would avoid cumbersome civil service employment procedures. Then he took the singer to audition before BPA administrator Raver, a neatly combed former utilities professor who wore gold-rimmed glasses and three-piece suits. Raver listened to Guthrie for an hour and then hired him for the month for $266.66, a notch above what skilled labor was making on Grand Coulee Dam. During the next thirty days the folk singer was driven up and down the Columbia River and wrote twenty-six songs, including such classics as "Roll On, Columbia," "Grand Coulee Dam," and "Pastures of Plenty." Guthrie, who liked to tell stories on himself, later claimed he wrote twenty-six songs in twenty-six days for two hundred and sixty-six dollars, which was close enough to the truth. The month was the most productive period of his life.

None of the songs had original music, all borrowing tunes from folk favorites. "Roll On, Columbia" used the tune from "Goodnight, Irene"; "Way Up in That Northwest" was sung to "On Top of Old Smokey"; and "Grand Coulee Dam" was based on the "Wabash Cannonball." The agency gave Guthrie a typewriter and desk—he was a speed typist—and a stack of books on the Columbia, which he apparently browsed through, because several verses of "Roll On, Columbia" refer to the Indian attack at the Cascades. They also put him in a car with public relations employee Elmer Buehler and sent the two on a tour through the Columbia Basin to observe the spirit of the Northwest. The pair visited a hop field, a Grange meeting, wheat fields, the desert intended for irrigation, and—at Guthrie's insistence—the

"Hooverville" of tarpaper shacks under a bridge near the Portland Sears store. The singer charmed almost everyone he met, though his heavy perspiration and failure to change his shirt took many people aback. "He had this terrific body odor," Buehler recalled. "When the windows were rolled up I could hardly take it. The girls in the office used to signal me to take him out for coffee or something to get him out of the building." On the road, Guthrie would sit in the backseat strumming his guitar and writing down snatches of song. "People would drive by and see we were an official car and see him in the back and wonder what the hell was going on," Buehler said.

Guthrie was a keen observer and a folk poet who in his brief stay managed to write what have become the most popular anthems of Pacific Northwest history. "He talked the common man's language," Buehler said. The folk singer also institutionalized a view of the Columbia River that remains the dominant perception to this day. The words to "Grand Coulee Dam" summarize the sentiment Guthrie was hired to put to song. A sampling:

> She winds down the granite canyon and she bends across the
>   lea
> Like a dancing, prancing stallion down her seaway to the sea,
> Cast your eyes upon the biggest thing yet built by human
>   hands
> On the King Columbia River, it's the big Grand Coulee dam.
>
> In the misty crystal glitter of the wild and windward spray
> Men have fought the pounding waters and met a watery grave.
> Well she tore their boats to splinters and she gave men dreams
>   to dream.
> Of the day the Coulee Dam would cross that wild and wasted
>   stream.
>
> Uncle Sam took up the challenge in the year of thirty-three
> For the farmer and the worker and all of you and me.
> He said, roll along Columbia, you can ramble to the sea
> But river while you're rambling, you can do some work for me.

Two generations later, some thinkers would regard western

dams as the most visible symbols of development run amok: their wires the buzzing, sizzling nerves of a society that in becoming technologically complex had also become regimented, stuffy, and a prisoner to its own dreams—a world that had not given people the leisure to make democracy work, as Roosevelt had hoped, but a place of quarreling special interests in which the demands for capital and specialist expertise had squeezed out the participation of ordinary citizens, leaving them frustrated and powerless. Guthrie predicted none of this. He saw the dams providing jobs. He saw the generators delivering power to farm wives enslaved by kerosene light, wood stoves, pit toilets, wash tubs, and pump handles. He saw a government using the Columbia River to try to correct the excesses of the Industrial Revolution, to truly redistribute wealth and curb fossil fuel pollution, to harness a "wild and wasted stream." He saw Grand Coulee Dam as government at its best, a prophecy of what socialism could accomplish when it triumphed. He sang these thoughts:

"All this here water just a going to waste."

"That's a good river. Needs a couple more dozen big power dams scattered up and down it . . . keeping folks busy."

"You just watch this river and pretty soon, everybody's a-gonna be changing their tune. The Big Grand Coulee and the Bonneville Dam, run a thousand factories for Uncle Sam. Everything from fertilizer to bombing planes . . . making everything from sewing machines to fertilizer . . . atomic bedrooms . . . plastic! Everything's gonna be plastic!

In "Pastures of Plenty," he prophesied:

Look down in the canyon and there you will see,
The Grand Coulee showers her blessings on me;
The lights for the city for factory, and mill,
Green Pastures of Plenty from dry barren hills. . . .

Few subjects touched him so powerfully. Here on the Columbia was not just the despair of the common man, broken by the Depression, but his salvation: giant engineering works. He scribbled madly during his tours throughout the day, refined and polished the words at night. Mary, tired of being ignored, left him with the kids in the evening and went out to see Portland. Woody paid no attention.

Guthrie recorded a dozen of the songs on acetate disk in the BPA basement but the looming war meant the movie would be postponed. The thirty days was an eventful time in his life. The Pontiac was repossessed and his marriage, already rocky, broke up. He had to hitchhike out of Portland to New York. But in 1942 he professionally recorded a half dozen of the songs, and in 1945 requested from Bonneville the lyrics of twenty-four of them. In 1948, Kahn incorporated some of the tunes into a new BPA movie, *The Columbia,* which was widely shown around the region.

By the end of the decade, however, Kahn quit Bonneville, having drawn fire from private utilities that did not like his prose-lytizing for big federal dams. It was evident that New Deal zeal was burning out. Buehler was transferred out of public affairs to a janitor's job at the Vancouver substation. In 1952, Eisenhower became President and appointed as secretary of the interior Douglas McKay, a former governor of Oregon who was an ally of private power. Interior at that time oversaw Bonneville (Energy does today) and McKay ordered the movies *Hydro* and *The Columbia* destroyed. The Guthrie songs were to be forgotten, and the models and dioramas Bonneville had used in public meetings to tout the merits of the big public dams were dismantled. Enough socialism. The new administration wanted hydroelectric development left to private companies.

This shift in political climate produced a ferocious fight during the 1950s over the fate of the Snake River's Hells Canyon. A high federal dam that would have drowned the canyon proper was discarded—for political more than environmental reasons—in favor of three smaller dams built farther upriver by privately owned Idaho Power. The shift also resulted in the five mid-Columbia dams being constructed by the public utility districts (PUDs) of Grant, Chelan, and Douglas counties instead of the Army Corps of Engineers. The PUDs were a compromise. Eisenhower opposed federal involvement, but private power could not by itself muster the low-cost financing or the electricity markets to build such huge dams. The public utilities became intermediaries, able as public agencies to obtain cheaper bonds and then

sell the power to both public and private customers. This cooperation signaled an uneasy truce to the half-century-long ideological
struggle between public and private power.

Initially, however, the Ross-Kahn era was simply put to the
flames. By chance Buehler was tending the furnace at Vancouver
when copies of the films arrived to be destroyed and so he kept
copies of each, hiding them in his basement. Kahn had also kept
copies. By the time Bonneville's fiftieth anniversary arrived in
1987, however, Woody Guthrie had been excised from its official
memory and had to be rediscovered. Audiovisual specialist Bill
Murlin launched a two-year search that turned up the old films,
bureaucratic records on Guthrie's employment, and the acetate
recordings crudely made in the agency basement. A new album
was compiled and released. By that time, "Roll On, Columbia" no
longer seemed weighted with political content and had become
the unofficial anthem of the Pacific Northwest. A sample verse:

> *And on up the river at Grand Coulee Dam*
> *The mightiest thing ever built by a man*
> *To run the great factories for Old Uncle Sam,*
> *It's roll on, Columbia, roll on.*
> *Roll on, Columbia, roll on.*
> *Roll on, Columbia, roll on.*
> *Your power is turning our darkness to dawn,*
> *So roll on, Columbia, roll on.*

When Guthrie wrote this song, the Columbia did indeed
"roll on" and "ramble" between the two big federal dams he extolled. The entire point of his contract, however, was to cement
public support for the grand federal plan to stop the Columbia
from rolling or rambling at all, to complete the 1932 Army Corps
vision of a series of ten dams, each of which would back the river
up to the toe of the next dam upstream. Woody's talent had been
harnessed to promote not only public power and cheap electricity, but the complete development of the Columbia on every available river mile. There is unintended irony in the singer's last
verse of "Pastures of Plenty":

> *It's always we've rambled, that river and I.*
> *It's here on her banks I'll work till I die.*

My land I'll defend with my life, if need be,
'Cause my pastures of plenty must always be free.

Whatever the development of the Columbia was, it was not free.

The hiring of the folk singer was only one step in an ambitious, expensive, and continuing campaign to persuade the public of the benefits of damming the Columbia River. Seventeen government photographers were hired to document the construction of Grand Coulee and Bonneville dams. Some of their pictures, such as Wayne Fuller's picture of sheep being driven across the crest of Grand Coulee Dam, have become a standard part of the American image of the Depression era.

Grand Coulee had been born and built in controversy, and the Columbia's dam builders were acutely aware that if their program was to continue, it could only be with public support. By the 1940s one in every four federal dollars spent on water projects was being spent in Washington State alone. An eastern engineer, complaining at the rate federal dollars were flowing into the Pacific Northwest for hydroelectric and irrigation development, is reputed to have remarked: "The Columbia is certainly a wonderful river. It waters four states and drains forty-eight!" The Bureau of Reclamation responded to such sentiments by setting out to make projects such as Grand Coulee a national achievement, not a regional one. In 1952, Washington senator Warren Magnuson persuaded the U.S. Postal Service to issue a commemorative stamp showing Grand Coulee Dam in order to fix an image of the dam as an American monument.

The visitor who approaches the dam today passes by a parking lot with a view of Lake Roosevelt and standards listing the names of all fifty states, a display with no apparent purpose except to reassure the out-of-state tourist that this is *your* dam, too. And when the pumps were started on May 7, 1951, and the first water flowed into Banks Lake, Reclamation had on hand jugs of water solicited from the governor of every state. The letter requesting the water had argued that every state was about to benefit from the distant irrigation project: not from the food produced, but from the market the new farmers would provide for *other* states' manufactured products. Development of the Columbia meant more customers for America! Almost every governor responded with water, the governor of Arizona sending only half a jug because he complained that greedy Californians had stolen the rest from the Colorado River. As Columbia River water surged out of the fourteen-foot-diameter pipes into the concrete canal, forty-eight pretty women recruited from the Washington State Apple Blossom Festival, each dressed in a full-length formal white dress, poured a jug from each state to feed the flow.

Just two weeks afterwards came perhaps the most famous and peculiar public relations stunt on the Columbia, the "Farm in a Day." Its initial success illustrated the energetic ingenuity the expanding federal government was capable of displaying, creating a can-do sensibility that would not erode until the Vietnam War. Its quieter failure illustrated just how difficult it was to remold society with grand engineering alone.

The Columbia Basin Project was supposed to redistribute wealth. Failed plateau homesteaders, Dust Bowl refugees, and World War II veterans would be given the opportunity to carve a new life for themselves in the desert, thanks to government water. Reclamation official William Warne said that perhaps the irrigation project was "not utopian, but as near the ideal American farming community as can be." By this time Grand Coulee Dam reporter Hu Blonk had gone to work for Reclamation to promote the project and Reclamation had decided to garner publicity by turning a piece of desert into a planted farm in a single day. Blonk had the inspired idea of awarding the farm to the "nation's most worthy veteran," to be selected by the Veterans of Foreign Wars. "This allowed us to have press releases issued by every VFW post in the United States," Blonk later recounted in his autobiography. From twenty thousand entries, a thirty-year-old veteran named Donald Dunn was selected.

Dunn had been a tank driver in European combat, returned to his native Kansas to farm, and was wiped out by a flood five years later. He moved to live with relatives in Yakima and became a farm implement salesman. Enlisting the aid of a Yakima newspaper editor, he wrote an essay about his plight. He told me that his hard luck in Kansas and decision to relocate to Washington were probably the factors that made him the winner. Six days before his third child was born, Dunn watched a farm, house, furniture, and equipment materialize on eighty acres of sagebrush in just twenty-four hours.

The event started at midnight with fireworks bursting over the selected land. Eighteen earth-moving machines and one hundred and fifty tractors went to work clearing, grading, plowing, and seeding. Five hundred volunteers swarmed onto the property to erect a comfortable, modern, three-bedroom house on a concrete pad. An open-ended Quonset hut was installed to shelter a donated tractor, furniture was carried into the house, and the couple was even presented with a dog, a cat, and the first three-cent Grand Coulee postage stamp. More than one hundred photographers snapped pictures and a crowd of fifty thousand watched as Reclamation Commissioner Michael Strauss handed over a gold-plated shovel for Dunn to turn water into a farm ditch. The event was publicized worldwide, and Dunn soon received so much mail that the general of nearby Larson Air Force Base loaned his secretary to help the new celebrity process it.

At first it seemed a fairy tale come true. Dunn slept in his new house that night, and while the lumber creaked as it settled, he said the quality of the overnight structure was impressively good. This was American prowess on display: a country that could win the world's greatest war and build its biggest concrete dam could also create a home and farm out of wasteland in the space of a day. The house still stands near Moses Lake, odd looking because of its experimental inverted "butterfly roof" in which the gutter runs down the center. The farm still operates.

Utopia could not really be built in a day, however. Dunn was soon overwhelmed. "We got more publicity than the President of the United States," he recalled. "Being a farm boy, I didn't know how to cope with it. I made a lot of mistakes." He immediately rented eighty more acres and planted grass to start a dairy, but found there were no facilities yet to process, store, or transport the milk. There were no processing plants yet for the crops that had been planted: Dunn found it would cost him more to harvest the seeded potatoes than he could get for them. The farm had also become a tourist attraction, and Dunn found himself spending more time coping with curious visitors and making speeches than farming. Within two and a half years the veteran was $63,000 in debt. "Seattle First National Bank didn't want to foreclose on the owner of the Farm-in-a-Day," Dunn recalled, but it was clear he was in over his head. The farm was quietly sold for $65,000, but the sale was publicized as $75,000. Dunn was given $10,000—"I don't know where they came up with it," he said—and he left to take a grain elevator job in Colorado, where he eventually retired.

The farm subsequently has had three other owners, and ultimately succeeded only after being combined with other holdings to make a four-hundred-and-fifty-five-acre spread. The small family farmer could no longer persist on the government's eighty-acre allocations. Government irrigation was not a guarantee of individual success, even when the recipient started out with a free farm.

With the damming of the Columbia a long-established fact and the public more jaded about promotion, river publicity is less flamboyant today. The harnessing of the river is as solid a part of the Pacific Northwest's self-image as the dams themselves, a feat so fundamentally important to the subsequent economy of the region as to almost be beyond debate. The battle would seem to be over. However, the Bureau of Reclamation, Army Corps of Engineers, Bonneville Power Administration, public utility districts, and other agencies still pump out a steady stream of brightly colored literature proclaiming the benefits of harnessing the Columbia and listing its benefits in terms of dollars, megawatts, tonnages shipped, food grown, and acres watered. The game is as old as the agencies themselves; even the name of the bureau implies that the desert is not being developed or altered but rather "reclaimed," as if it were a natural Eden and only needs a dam or two to return to its paradise state.

The government literature is dotted with pictures of people fishing, swimming, and boating the reservoirs. Most of the reservoirs have green, shaded parks, watered by the Columbia and paid for by electric revenues: these help hammer home the impression of beneficial development. Most of the dams have self-congratulatory visitor centers. Tourists are provided balconies to overlook the huge powerhouses, display rooms touting the benefits of hydroelectric development, and fish-ladder viewing rooms to watch salmon swim by. At Grand Coulee a stirring film that ends with Guthrie's "Roll On, Columbia," retells the story of an arid plateau with irrigation riding to the rescue. The movie's imagery is always of moving water, not stilled pools.

Rocky Reach Dam north of Wenatchee boasts the best, most objective museum of any hydroelectric facility on the river, an ambitious display on the region's history and the development of electricity. Yet even there the visitor's experience is carefully calculated. The entrance to the dam is positioned a quarter mile before the visitor parking lot, leading tourists on a winding road through acres of manicured lawn, lush flower gardens, and cool shade trees, all watered by the arcing spray of sprinklers. This oasis is a deliberate contrast to the dry brown hills that enclose the river. A mural in the visitor center shows the white fall of water down the dam spillway transformed into stampeding wild horses: an unstated reference to a famous Rufus Woods headline in the Wenatchee *World* extolling Grand Coulee as promising the power of "two million wild horses!" Downstairs are the windows that give a peek at salmon muscling up the fish ladder. Signs nearby explain the steps the utility is taking to mitigate damage to the salmon runs, but offer no information on what that damage is, or how the facility that visitors are walking through helped cause it. Upstairs in the theater are a series of historical paintings celebrating Columbia River history. One caption celebrates Indian petroglyphs, failing to mention that almost all the petroglyph picture sites have been drowned by dams. The final painting of a dam with its spillway open and a waterfall cascading down is captioned: "From the days of the first settlements to the present time, man has sought to harness and utilize the waters of the Columbia. How successful he has been is shown by the familiar sight of waterfalls at power producing dams along its entire course." The falls may be magnificent, but to a utility engineer they are a sign of failure, not success: whenever possible they are shut off. Water that pours over the top of a dam is water that is not generating electricity, and is kept to a minimum despite the complaints of fish agencies that desire it to flush young salmon down to the sea. Almost every dam publicity photo shows the spillway roaring with a beautiful white cascade, and every dam engineer is taught that such a sight is evidence of wasted energy and poor management.

Rocky Reach is actually superior to most of the sketchy displays at other dams, and certainly not as one-sided as the exhibits and tours at Grand Coulee. It illustrates, however, a systematic slanting of the story that makes it difficult for the average citizen to think seriously about the Columbia or any river. Most of what is stated at the dams is true, but the displays deliberately ignore other truths. We have not just harnessed the Columbia, we have turned it into a body of water utterly different from its natural state, and in doing so have deliberately thrown the entire Northwest ecosystem out of whack. None of this got much debate when it was happening—Guthrie's enthusiasm was typical—and there is little allusion to the costs of it now.

To visit a single dam, as a typical visitor might do, is to encounter a display that seems one-sided in the acceptable way that American advertising is one-sided. But to visit dam after dam after dam as I did—to see a monotonous repetition of an edited history that crosses into myth—finally began to nettle, and then irritate, and I realized the perception of the Columbia that the public draws from its powerhouses is as deliberately engineered as the dams themselves. I found myself mentally referring to each one as a Temple of Half-Truth. And as I sifted through the literature, and viewed the movies, and studied the videotapes, and tried to absorb half a century of justification for what was done to the river, I became impatient not with the argument for development but with the lack of acknowledgment that there could ever have been another side, that there was ever any question of balance, any need for honest regret, or any appreciation for the wild country that has passed. The utilities' failure to recognize this, in effect to respect what was destroyed—even if one decides the destruction was, on balance, warranted—seemed dishonest finally, a deliberate evasion of truth. So I finally thought of them as a House of Lies: a government fairy tale. Beyond the display case was reality, the Columbia as Robo-River. To Chelan PUD's credit, it began planning in 1993 an overhaul of its visitor center to discuss fish and wildlife, the environmental impact of dams, and a fuller explanation of hydropower. What is needed for those visiting elsewhere, it seems, is a lesson in how to tour a dam.

The water is different. Understand that first. It is older, dirtier, tireder than it used to be by the time it reaches the sea. There are fourteen big dams on the Columbia itself but more than five hundred major dams in the Columbia Basin, and their cumulative effect is to retard the flow of water back to the ocean. The big reservoirs keep it warmer in winter and, from their depths that feed the powerhouses, sometimes colder in summer. The water's oxygen content, sediment load, concentration of pollution, nutrient content, and biological life all change. The reservoirs segregate the water into temperature layers, the most frigid at the bottom often becoming so oxygen-depleted that fish cannot breathe there. Yet when the river is high and water is spilled over a dam, the force of its fall can drive nitrogen from the atmosphere into the water, supersaturating the river and giving fish gas-bubble disease, or the bends.

The bottom is different, too. Dams steal the energy that once transported sediment down the Columbia, turning the riverbed into a vast mud flat that concentrates many pollutants. Not only are the ancient spawning beds buried by deep, dim waters, but they are also clogged with silt. The reservoir behind Lower Granite Dam on the Snake River collects 2 million cubic yards of dirt a year—enough in six years to equal the volume of concrete in Grand Coulee Dam. Deltas form just under the surface at the reservoir's upper end because the river has trouble flushing itself. In changing from a free-flowing river to a series of oscillating pools, the Columbia's aquatic environment has changed as dramatically for the creatures that live in it as if a forest was changed to a prairie. This point was driven home when I took a canoe out on Lake Roosevelt once and paddled into a slough. When the water roiled with big fish I peered curiously over the side for salmon, forgetting for a moment that salmon were blocked forever from this part of the Columbia by Grand Coulee Dam. The fish were not salmon but carp. The water was not moving, it was still. The bottom was not gravel, it was mud. Roll on, Columbia, roll on.

The environmental changes on the Columbia are best understood by understanding the hydroelectric system that made them. Start with the most obvious feature, the dam. What can it tell you?

The most telling detail is its height. There are two basic kinds of dams on the Columbia River and its tributaries, storage dams and "run-of-the-river" dams. Of the fourteen dams on the Columbia itself, all but three are run-of-the-river. All the dams back up water, of course, but eleven are designed only to take advantage of the river's natural drop, not to store so much flow that they change the Columbia's seasonal cycle. The dams that run the show, however, are the tall ones: Grand Coulee in the United States, and Keenleyside and Mica in Canada. (There are additional storage dams on tributaries, such as Duncan in Canada and Libby in Montana.) Their reservoirs are so vast that they are in effect giant batteries: they store water as potential energy until it is needed. Grand Coulee impounds sixty times as much water as Bonneville Dam.

Another obvious clue to a dam's function and significance is its size. Big dams usually justify themselves by being big power producers. A structure's energy potential is a product of the river flow and dam height, and Grand Coulee is far enough down the Columbia to get a good flow and high enough to develop a respectable head, the gravity power of falling water that produces electricity. As a result, the dam is the river's dominant power producer: it can generate nearly three times as much electricity as the next biggest dam on the river. When Grand Coulee releases water, it sends an energy wave downstream that affects the ten American dams below it. This is not a wave one can see, but it can raise or lower river levels as much as six or eight feet over a twenty-four-hour period as the river oscillates to the daily cycle of power demand. The dam closest to Grand Coulee is tied most closely to its pulses, and so Chief Joseph boasts twenty-four generators and is the second-largest power producer on the river.

These water releases are timed to the clock. Daily electricity use is cyclic, increasing in the morning when people wake up, shower, and cook breakfast; remaining high during the day; peaking in the evening as dinner is cooked; and then steadily declining over the night. The trick for Columbia River operators is to time the pulses of the water releases downriver so they will reach varying dams at about the right period to match this demand. It takes weeks or months for a molecule of water pushed through the turbines at Mica Dam to reach the sea, but only a day or day and a half for the energy wave from a surge of water at Mica to roll through all thirteen other dams.

A third thing to remember about dams is that much of their structure is hidden by water. From the surface of the Columbia at its downstream base, the foundations of Grand Coulee extend the equivalent of an additional twenty stories downward. Half of its mass is hidden from view. Mica Dam is even more deceptive. It is only half as long as Grand Coulee, but it is two hundred and fifty feet taller and its earth construction makes it thirty-one hundred feet broad from front to rear at its base, so broad that the total volume of material in Mica is nearly four times that of Grand Coulee's concrete. Dams are even bigger than they look.

Dams also have a misleading appearance of solidity. Strong they may be, but it is an engineered strength, calculated and shaved to save money. Most Columbia River dams built after Grand Coulee do not span the river with solid concrete but have an earthen section next to the concrete to save money, and none of the run-of-the-river dams are monolithic in the way Grand Coulee is. For the most part they comprise fairly solid piers separated by spillway gate sections and powerhouse penstock inlets. Dams are also tunneled horizontally and vertically by galleries and elevator shafts to allow inspection of their interior, and are pierced by gated outlets. Grand Coulee has eight miles of horizontal passageways through its mass that lead to sixty outlet tubes, allowing passage of the river through the dam if the reservoir needs to be drawn below the spillway. In March 1952 a dam employee pushed a wrong button in an interior gallery, opened an outlet gate, and started the river pouring into the dam interior, a mistake that began flooding one powerhouse and threatened to shut down electricity over much of the Northwest. Employees waded the cold, flooded galleries and got the flow shut off three hours later, but it was a reminder of the tremendous forces pent up behind the seemingly slumbering dams.

Which leads us to another point about dams: their eerie emptiness. They are the most robotic of modern creations. The generators hum and vibrate as if in private meditation, the polished terrazzo powerhouse floors are as empty as they are spotless, the dials on long gray boxes of generating instruments seemed to wind around without the appreciation of human eyes. There is almost a cult of cleanliness: the supervisor at Rock Island Dam used to write the day's date on a paper match, hide it atop a pipe or in some obscure nook, and wait to see how long it took cleaning crews to find it and return it to him.

Finally, dams are misleading in their apparent economy. A Pacific Northwest politician need only remind his constituents that their power bills have historically been half that of the rest of America to reassure them that the damming of the Columbia was the proper choice. And yes, while dams are expensive when first built, they are cheap over the long run because of their mechanical simplicity and free fuel. Hydroelectric generators, moreover, are more efficient in squeezing electricity out of the energy of falling water than thermal plants are in harnessing the energy of coal, oil, or uranium.

The bargain rates of the Columbia River dams have been subsidized by the nation as a whole, however. To date, the federal government has invested about $8.6 billion in dams and locks and power lines in the Columbia Basin. A generous repayment schedule has resulted in the Bonneville Power Administration paying less than half this sum back in principal and interest combined over the past half century. Only a tenth of the principal, or $864 million, has been paid off. Fending away the annual attempts by the White House and Congress to recoup more of its investment has become a rite of passage for Northwest lawmakers, a test they so far have passed year after year. Both sides are weary of the struggle, however, and at this writing Bonneville was seeking congressional permission to become a public corporation to refinance its debt, clearing its books with Uncle Sam in order to receive more freedom of action. The point remains, however, that as sheer investment neither the dams nor irrigation works have paid for themselves.

Dams remain undeniably impressive, some of the grandest structures our civilization has produced. Yet they are only links in a much bigger system, a broad power network that spreads across half the continent and is controlled by computers in major cities. A dam is a valve on a far more complex piece of plumbing, and only by unifying operation of the Columbia River did engineers finally tame it.

The biggest recorded flood on the Columbia River occurred in the spring of 1894, when 700,000 cubic feet of water per second roared down the Columbia's canyon at the future site of Grand Coulee Dam and nearly 1.3 million cubic feet bellowed at The Dalles downriver. The gravel benches deposited by the high water can still be seen at the historic site of the Battle of the Cascades, just below Bonneville Dam.

The lack of riverside population prevented damage from being severe, however, and there were no dams yet to influence the flood in any event. Far more disturbing and destructive was the Columbia River flood that began shortly after the fourth dam, Mc-Nary, had started construction: about the first of May 1948. Residents were dismayed that even with three dams already on the river, none had the storage capability to control a deluge of this magnitude.

The winter snowpack in the basin had been 20 to 42 percent greater than ever recorded, depending on the measurement site, and the spring thaw had come late. When the warm Chinook winds finally arrived they came with heavy rain. The snow dissolved like butter on a hot skillet. In centuries past some of the snow would have been shaded by uncut forests, absorbed by ungrazed range, and temporarily stored in undiked wetlands and flood plains. Human development, however, sped the water back to rivers. The Kootenay began climbing an inch an hour. Grand Forks, British Columbia, flooded. Missoula, Montana, went awash from the Clark Fork. The dike broke at Bonners Ferry, Idaho, and the town filled with water. More than 160,000 acres in the upper Columbia Basin were inundated. All this fed the Columbia.

The raging river hit seventeen miles per hour just north of the international boundary. New bridge piers at nearby Northport, poured just weeks before, were undercut and swept away. At Grand Coulee the generators spun out record volumes of power and still the spillway gates were wide open, producing an artificial falls twice the height of Niagara that filled the canyon below with spray like smoke from a forest fire. Through its basalt canyons the Columbia gushed, fed by swollen tributaries such as the Okanogan, the Methow, the Wenatchee, the Yakima, the Snake, the Umatilla, the Deschutes, the Klickitat, the White Salmon, and the Wind. By the time the Columbia raced past Vancouver its flow was a million cubic feet per second, four times greater than normal. The river was so deep that it rose twenty feet against the downstream base of Bonneville Dam.

Here was Guthrie's "wild and wasted stream."

Rock Island Dam couldn't handle the flow with its spillway gates and disappeared under the river. Celilo Falls similarly vanished, its cliffs and islands submerged. Water crept up over roads and into fields. Near Pasco, a thousand families fled from a trailer park that went under. Government officials checking the extent of the damage were carried by their boat into a nearby farmer's drowned orchard. "Get your rowboat out of my orchard!" the owner shouted to the visitors as they floated by. "Get your orchard out of our river!" the men answered back.

Down through its grand gorge the Columbia poured, and out toward the plains of Portland and Vancouver. Four million people had migrated to the West Coast to work in war industries during World War II and a wartime city of housing called Vanport had been built on the flood plain between the bustling Kaiser shipyards in Vancouver and Portland, located on the Oregon shore where Jantzen Beach and Delta Park are today. It was home to 18,700 people until the dike gave way and the Columbia took it out.

Portland docks on the Willamette were flooded. The Union Stock Yards went under several feet of water. Only sandbags saved Portland's Union Station. Up and down the river, flooded fields swept away dairy cattle, plowed crops, topsoil, trees, barns, houses. Railroad traffic along the river halted. Transmission towers were endangered. Traffic into Portland's airport, protected by a levee, stopped. In all the flood killed forty-one people in the United States and Canada and caused more than $100 million in damage.

What is illustrative about this story is not just the flood's damage. In 1972 and 1974 a runoff of even greater magnitude occurred in the mountains of the Columbia Basin. This time, however, no dams were inundated, no cities swept away, no bridges destroyed. By 1972, Canada's Keenleyside had been finished and Mica followed suit in 1974, both constructed under a cooperative treaty with the United States. They provided the upstream reservoir capacity to store excess water. The flood was contained. Before the river was completely dammed it fluctuated between flood and low water at The Dalles in a ratio as high as thirty-four to one. Upriver storage cut that capriciousness to five to one, at worst. The Columbia was no longer just dammed; it was a regulated system that flowed when the computers told it to. It is as a system that the new Columbia must be understood.

Each day thousands of people roll out of bed, drive to dam power-houses, reservoir control centers, and hulking institutional administration buildings, and go to work operating the Columbia River. Linked by computer and telephone line, they juggle sometimes competing demands for power generation, flood control, fish flows, irrigation, and barge navigation. With a clack of computer keys they send waves of water energy pulsing down the basin, the reservoirs bobbing up and down in response like bathtubs.

The "dispatcher" headquarters of the Bonneville Power Administration are located in the concrete basement of its reservoir operations center in Vancouver, Washington. Built at Ross Substation ten miles from downtown Portland in order to boost its chance of surviving a nuclear attack, the high-ceilinged room is a bit reminiscent of the war room in the film *Dr. Strangelove*, though much more brightly lit. Clusters of computer terminals and telephones occupy desks on the tile floor. At either end of the room, two movie-screen-sized diagrams of the region's power grid are displayed, made of removable tiles so that modifications or damage can be displayed. On a third wall is a painted map of the rivers and dams of the Pacific Northwest. The room is secured with locked doors and guarded. The half-dozen dispatchers have the responsibility of ensuring that lights will burn and motors purr at a constant rate across the Columbia Basin, and their safety must be assured.

Greg Delwiche, chief of Bonneville's reservoir operations section, calls these dispatchers the "firefighters" of the Columbia River system, and the analogy is apt. Like firemen, they often do little but monitor a system that hums along by itself—but if something goes wrong, such as a storm or powerhouse fire or transmission line break, they are pressed into action and are expected to shuffle loads with the cool aplomb of emergency workers. "When a nuclear plant goes down in California," Delwiche explained, "we feel it here." So integrated is the power grid that the 1994 Los Angeles earthquake briefly knocked out power to my neighborhood in Seattle.

Electricity, once generated, cannot be stored. If Columbia River dam turbines spin out too much power, it cannot be tucked away until needed. The U.S. electrical system runs on a cycle of sixty hertz and excess power races this cycle past sixty, speeding electric motors and clocks. Too little power and a slower cycle causes the dimming of lights and slowing of motors called a brownout. Computers compare the generation of the Columbia River with power demand four times a second. When a consumer flicks a light switch—or rather when millions of consumers flick switches on and off—the result is sensed by the system immediately. A governor on the spinning generator opens or closes the wicket gates that control water flow past the generator blades. With millions of consumer decisions and thousands of spinning generators on hundreds of dams and other power projects, this adjustment smooths out across the system to a comforting regularity.

Bonneville's control center is tied to similar rooms at other utilities and a constant juggling act goes on to keep the system in balance, selling excess when it is present or buying surplus when needed. Some generators run at varied speed to match energy to demand. A digital dial tells operators how close to sixty hertz they are operating, and typically it is very close indeed. A comparison is made with Naval Observatory clocks four times a day and adjustments made to ensure that electric clock speeds match real time.

All this is far more sophisticated than early attempts at controlling power generation. At the eastern Washington town of Waitsburg the night operator of the first power station burned a carbon-filament lamp over his cot. When it began to glow brighter he knew lights elsewhere in town were going out for the evening and he could reduce the water flow to the turbine. When the lamp dimmed in the morning it was an indication that lights were coming back on elsewhere, so he would open the generator's wicket gates to get more water power.

So complex is the problem of reconciling human demands with river flow that there are actually four levels of control, of which the dispatchers represent the second-to-second fine-tuning. Next up the tier is the scheduling branch, a two-person operation that occupies a windowless, glass-walled, ten-by-twenty office on a floor above the dispatchers. The schedulers coordinate power demand over hours and days. When I visited, Bob Denny and Robin Swartzbaeker sat at two computer terminals that displayed seemingly incomprehensible columns of numbers. With a punch of keys this pair could determine river surges and ebbs across the Pacific Northwest. A transformer had blown in California and a transmission line was down; Robin took a call from a utility in San Diego to confer on how power was being shuttled around the break. "We avoid spill at all costs," she said, having been trained to regard unproductive water lost over the top of the dam as a waiter would regard spilled soup. "You can usually do something, be creative." Back up one reservoir for an hour, for example, so the flow of another can be fully utilized.

One step above the schedulers is a water management branch, which studies weather patterns, snowpack, river flow, and anticipated power demand. It forecasts how the river flow should be controlled in the weeks and months ahead. And above this is the contract management branch, which negotiates the sale of blocks of power and determines the river's fate for years into the future.

These four divisions are just the tip of the management iceberg. They work only for Bonneville, which is just the power transmission and marketing agency. The Army Corps of Engineers has responsibility for nine dams on the Columbia and lower Snake River, and its Reservoir Control Center is located across the Columbia in Portland at the elegant old Customs House, built in 1900. This structure is the architectural opposite of the modernistic concrete of the BPA operations center: with its ornate courtyard, winding staircases, and high, woodwork ceilings, it has been used as a backdrop for several Hollywood movies. If the office style is different, the goals are not. The Corps confers with BPA on how electricity demands will mesh with the strict rules it must follow on maintaining reservoir levels for navigation and flood control.

The complexity grows on the central Columbia, where Washington's Grant, Chelan, and Douglas counties control five more dams through their public utility districts. The needs and desires of Bonneville and the Corps are fed into a computer in Ephrata and coordinated with the plans of these PUDs. Then there is Grand Coulee, run by the Bureau of Reclamation; the Canadian dams run by B.C. Hydro; the upper Snake River dams run by Idaho Power; and finally the host of tributary dams, including the Corps' large Libby in Montana and Dworshak in Idaho, and Reclamation's Hungry Horse on the Flathead River in Montana. Each spill, turbine start-up, wicket gate opening, and power generation affects all the others. Sixty years of experience has given these agencies plenty of practice in manipulating the Columbia Basin, but the coordination remains impressive. It is governed by international treaty and formal coordination agreements that run into thousands of pages.

This elaborate structure is necessary, explained Russ George, chief of the Corps' Reservoir Control Center, because "the Columbia is not, in its natural state, a good power-producing river." In a typical year, 60 percent of the river's flow occurs in May, June, and July, the time of year when heating and lighting demand is at its lowest. Three-quarters of the river's flow occurs in the six warmest months. This produces the Columbia's most fundamental environmental problem. All of the river-related species, particularly salmon, have evolved to the river's natural cycle. Young salmon depend on the spring and summer freshet to flush them to the sea, and adults time their runs to swim summer-high water back to distant spawning grounds in the mountains. Human energy demand is exactly the opposite. We want the river turning generators in the winter, when no fish are going up or down. Energy exchanges with the Southwest—in which the north supplies summer air-conditioning and the South supplies winter heat—have modified this imbalance a bit, but in the main people and fish are at odds on when the Columbia should flow.

The lack of flooding in 1972 and 1974 demonstrated how the river's timing has been tamed. The ability to do so depends on the control of remote reservoirs such as Mica Dam's Kinbasket, an uninhabited lake with almost no roads on its shore that oscillates up to one hundred and fifty feet each year. This flattens out the Columbia's cycle of flow, releasing water in winter and storing it during the spring and summer snow melt. Lake Roosevelt behind Grand Coulee can range as much as eighty-two feet, Libby in Montana one hundred and seventy-two feet, and Hungry Horse in Montana two hundred and twenty-four feet. These dams, plus Canada's Keenleyside and Duncan and America's Dworshak and Albeni Falls, store two-thirds of the 55 million acre-feet of water that can be stored in the basin for electricity and flood control, a huge volume more than five times the total used for irrigation.

A series of formal agreements coordinates all the rivers and dams in the system, the most remarkable being the 1964 Columbia River Treaty with Canada. It was the first in the world between two nations which recognized that what happens upstream on a river affects events downstream—and that financial compensation for the benefits or costs is thus justified. The agreement was controversial when negotiated, and to a degree remains so three decades later. From the U.S. perspective the agreement allowed Canada to build three large dams with mostly American money and enjoy the benefits of their power and flood control. From the viewpoint of Canadian critics, Canada was bamboozled into giving the American Northwest thirty years of extra water at bargain-basement 1964 prices. Renegotiation of the treaties in the 1990s is expected to improve the compensation Canada gets for its stored water.

The idea to coordinate Columbia River planning across the border was first proposed in 1944. By then it was apparent that much of the Columbia's summer flow was pouring uselessly over the spillways of Grand Coulee and Bonneville dams when there was no market for the electricity. If Canadian snowmelt could be stored until winter, when energy demand was high, a second powerhouse could be added at Bonneville, a third at Grand Coulee, and additional generators could be installed at future dams.

Americans were initially preoccupied with building additional Columbia River dams of their own, but finally, in 1959, the two nations asked the International Joint Commission to explore the issue. A treaty was prepared and signed by President Eisenhower and Canadian prime minister John Diefenbaker on January 17, 1961. The U.S. Senate ratified it just two months later, but that speed only reinforced suspicion in Canada that their nation was being had by the Yankees. The benefits to America in added generation and flood control were obvious, but the gain to Canada was not. British Columbia was already building a dam on the Peace River that would supply its power needs. The proposed treaty would give the province half of the additional power the new storage generated on American dams, shipping it back across the border—but British Columbia couldn't use it. Accordingly, Canada would agree to the deal only if the Americans promised in advance to buy British Columbia's share of the added electricity.

The Pacific Northwest couldn't use the added power yet either, but it occurred to the Americans that if the Northwest could not use the extra power, the Southwest could. Congress passed a bill to allow Columbia River power to be sold outside the region, and public and private power companies in the Southwest quickly formed a consortium to buy the electricity. This consortium paid Canada $254 million up front for thirty years of the added power, plus $69.3 million for the benefits of flood control. This gave Canada the money needed to build the storage dams, adding generators for its own use. No longer were hydropower agencies at the mercy of seasonal flows. Now they could turn the Columbia on and off like a faucet.

Deciding when to turn the faucet remains complex, however. Hydro managers are in effect guessing how much water is going to pour into their storage pool in the future, which in turn is dependent on storms, snowpack, temperature, and so forth. A host of agencies have a hand in this prediction. The National Weather Service's Northwest River Forecast Center is down the hall from the Corps' Reservoir Control Center, feeding out daily predictions on river volumes and levels throughout the region. Adding their predictions are the Columbia River Forecasting Service, the U.S. Geological Survey, the U.S. Soil Conservation Service, the Columbia River Water Management Group, and the Northwest Power Pool.

A century of river records has given these agencies a good idea of the upper and lower limits of power generation. While Columbia Basin dams at peak operation could generate up to 30,000 megawatts, experience with drought has taught river managers that they can only guarantee 12,600 megawatts at the Columbia's lowest flow. This lower figure is called "firm" energy. It is the power that is promised to ordinary homes and businesses, and because it is guaranteed it is more expensive than the "interruptible" power used by the Northwest's aluminum industry. Usually, however, there is enough energy for all uses. On average, the Columbia system generates about sixteen thousand megawatts.

Even when they are confident of future river levels, the Columbia's electricity managers can't turn the faucet on and off as freely as they would like. If power were the only goal the Columbia River reservoirs would fluctuate more wildly than they do. Selling power in the winter rather than summer can triple its market value. Other considerations enter in, however.

The pool behind Bonneville Dam, for example, is supposed to fluctuate no more than five feet up or down, and Bonneville itself is used as a "reregulating" dam to smooth out the river flow downriver past Portland and Vancouver. Grand Coulee's Lake Roosevelt usually falls no more than fifteen feet from June to September to maintain the reservoir as a one-hundred-and-fifty-mile-long recreational resource. Operators are limited to raising and lowering the reservoir by no more than a foot and a half a day to avoid quick changes in reservoir weight and pressure that can collapse its banks. There can be seasonal constraints as well. In the spring of 1986, engineers declined to use Idaho's Lake Pend Oreille for storage of potential flood waters because it would push up ice on the lake's rim, possibly damaging docks and bulkheads.

Competing demands for the river are constant. The most common battle is between the needs of power and fish, but agencies also try to manage reservoir levels and current to satisfy barge operators, wind surfers, pleasure boaters, hydroplane racers, and even an annual cross-Columbia swim. The Corps' Russ George recalled one pleasure boater who beached his boat during a sudden windstorm and woke up the next morning to find it high and dry. The boater telephoned Portland and asked for a foot of water in John Day Reservoir, the longest in the lower river.

The request couldn't be satisfied: it was a weekend, power demands were low, and the flow of the Columbia had been slowed accordingly—but engineers did actually look at the numbers to see if the boater could be accommodated. Eventually friends came and dragged the boat back down to the water, but the fact that the sportsman even thought to ask for a different lake level demonstrates how thoroughly the Columbia is controlled. No need to pray anymore. Just dial the Corps of Engineers.

CHAPTER

14

The Salmon Gauntlet

Indian fishermen at Celilo Falls before it was drowned by the reservoir behind The Dalles Dam. A fish wheel is in the background. *(University of Washington Library)*

Few animals elicit the human response that salmon do. These fish reduce life to its simplest, most heroic terms. They are born, washed to the sea, grow, struggle back to their birthplace, reproduce, and die. Their carcasses fuel the river ecosystem and thus provide the energy their progeny will consume. While the Columbia has been harnessed to produce electrical energy, it has been robbed of another kind of energy: swimming packets of solar energy represented by salmon grazing on the sun-fueled food chain of the sea. Bears, eagles, seals, ravens, and sea lions depend on their annual migration. "Salmon hit all the buttons," observed Tom Quinn, a University of Washington fisheries professor. "These journeys stagger the imagination. They make love, and they die."

Salmon are part of the fish genus that includes trout and the seagoing trout called steelhead. They are a pretty fish—silvery, trim, and muscular—and are impressively big: routinely two or three feet long and three to thirty pounds, sometimes bigger. They can jump falls ten feet high, use the earth's magnetic field to navigate, find their home stream across thousands of miles, and sniff out cooler water to control their own cold-blooded metabolism. Their range is astounding; Columbia River chinook feed in the Gulf of Alaska, and a steelhead tagged at Adak Island in the Aleutians was later caught after migrating to the Salmon River in Idaho. One Canadian sockeye run swam seven hundred miles upriver in just twenty-four days, or nearly thirty miles a day.

Salmon are also accessible. They swim up fish ladders and spawn in shallow streams where people can see them. They have a distinctive, rich taste, and most years are the most valuable commercial fish species caught in the United States, valued at up to a billion dollars in the North Pacific alone. They are a superb sports fish, putting up a terrific fight when hooked. They symbolize the link between man and nature.

"Salmon and steelhead test the health of aquatic ecosystems in the same way the miner's canary tests air quality," Lewis and Clark College law professor Michael Blum has written. "As a result, anadromous fish [the term means fish that migrate to the sea and return, such as salmon and steelhead] may be considered the Northwest's most important natural resource, just as they were 135 years ago when the Stevens Indian treaties guaranteed the tribes a share of the harvest."

There are five species of Pacific salmon that spawn in North America: chinook (or king), coho (or silver), sockeye, pink, and chum (or dog). The last three are the most numerous, the first two the most prized. In addition there are two trout, the steelhead and sea-run cutthroat, which have adopted the anadromous ways of the salmon. Coho and pink may stay at sea only one year, chinook as long as seven. Chum, coho, and pink tend to spawn in streams close to the ocean, while chinook and steelhead swim farther upstream and sockeye spawn in lakes.

Migrating to the sea is an evolutionary gamble that has paid off. The sea provides food to allow prodigious growth, giving the fish that survive a physical advantage in seizing spawning territory and battling for a mate. Anadromous fish pushed aside the

less adventurous fish that stayed home and, when pioneers arrived, dominated coastal rivers from Sacramento to the Arctic.

The Columbia and its tributaries could never have accumulated the nutrients to support the tens of millions of pounds of
salmon that once annually returned. Only by feeding in the ocean
could such immense numbers be sustained. And while the danger of long migrations was high, the two thousand to five thousand eggs each female laid in gravel nests produced enough
young to make the species incredibly resilient in the face of periodic flood, drought, or other environmental catastrophe.

As Pacific salmon colonize new streams they rapidly evolve
a new genetic calendar and body type. Chinook that swim to a
system's uppermost tributaries arrive in spring when water is
highest, while those spawning farther downstream make the trip
in summer or fall. Their genes trigger their migratory timing to
match the flood cycle of their birthplace. Those swimming hundreds of miles upstream evolve the body fat to do so. Different
stocks exhibit different sizes depending on the depth of water,
height of falls, and other characteristics of the route they must
surmount. They home in on their natal stream because they have
evolved to survive there.

This has made the protection of Columbia River salmon runs
far more difficult than fish biologists originally hoped. Artificial
propagation efforts on the Columbia date back to an abortive 1887
salmon hatchery on the Clackamas River in Oregon that was soon
abandoned, and the subsequent century of experience has been
plagued with mistakes. The initial idea was to capture male and
female, squeeze both to extract eggs and sperm, fertilize, and cast
the eggs back into streams. There was little understanding of the
importance of the protective nests the mother dug in the gravel
with her tail, of salmon adaptation to a particular stream, or of
the effects of stream degradation. Few fish survived.

The development of the Oregon food pellet and disease-con-
trolling drugs in the 1960s allowed fish to be hatched in concrete
tanks on land. They were grown to about the size of a finger
(hence the term "fingerlings") before being introduced into
streams, giving them a higher chance of survival. Biologists found
they could get new generations of salmon to evolve to meet
changed conditions in a remarkably short time: University of
Washington professor Lauren Donaldson used hatchery fish to

shift the timing of a Lake Washington run from August to October to better meet the class schedule of the students he had studying them. If dams took a toll of fish moving down and up, then hatcheries simply churned out more fish to compensate.

Then scientists realized there was more to salmon survival than numbers. We were losing the DNA information in their genes.

The salmon hatchery at Big Beef Creek is approached from an unmarked dirt road that tunnels through a grove of leafy alder, winding to where the coppery stream meets an arm of Puget Sound. It is a modest place. Several weather-worn sheds and buildings roost in untended brambles. The weir and fish trap built to catch returning salmon are of rough, plain wood. The hatchery was built as a university education facility but its use has slowed as research financing has tightened. Dozens of other fish hatcheries are busier and more modern than Big Beef Creek, but it has two advantages that have resulted in its being enlisted for the genetic rescue of an endangered Columbia Basin species: it is remote enough to be reasonably secret, and it has copious amounts of pure artesian well water uncontaminated by chemicals, dirt, or disease.

A bright new metal warehouse the size of two tennis courts gleams among the tired structures, boasting sliding barn doors that can be locked securely. Inside are eight round fiberglass fish tanks as big as large Jacuzzis. Here, five hundred miles from their native lake, a generation of endangered salmon is confined for life. I peer inside the tanks and dark, four-inch-long sockeye skitter away from my shadow. These are the offspring of a fish I have dubbed Eve. In 1991 she was the only female sockeye to swim nine hundred and seventy miles from the sea and climb sixty-three hundred feet in elevation to central Idaho's Redfish Lake, a crystalline jewel tucked under the jagged crest of the Sawtooth Mountains. Eve had come home to spawn. It was a courageous effort but the mathematics of salmon mortality were against her: the odds were remote that the young of a single mother could make their way to the sea past the gauntlet of dams, escape ocean fishermen, and then return once more to their natal lake. Rather than risk extinction, biologists collected Eve's eggs, fertilized them with the sperm of three males that returned the same year, divided them between a hatchery in Idaho and tanks at the National Marine Fisheries Service (NMFS) headquarters in Seattle, and began raising them artificially. Biologists knew that if left in the wild, Eve's twenty-one hundred eggs might produce at best just one or two surviving, spawning adults. If raised in captivity, in contrast, as many as 60 percent might survive to adulthood, producing up to 600,000 eggs for the next generation. That would result in enough young to risk reintroduction into the wild. Fish biologists have never tried to rebuild a run from a single mother before, or tried to put the offspring of a captive generation back into nature. It is a gamble born of desperation. NMFS, which distrusted the chlorinated water in the center of the Northwest's biggest city, subsequently moved its share of the progeny to Big Beef Creek. The Idaho tanks were fenced with barbed wire.

This fuss was the direct result of a 1990 decision by southern Idaho's Shoshone-Bannock tribe—the tribe of Sacajawea—to successfully petition that Snake River sockeye such as Eve be put on the nation's endangered species list. It was a momentous decision. Scores of salmon runs in the Columbia River Basin had already gone extinct with little notice or alarm. Other tribes and fishing groups were hesitant to invoke the powerful Endangered Species Act, which could lead to unknown restrictions on their own commercial catch. The Shoshone-Bannock, however, were hundreds of miles from salmon in harvestable numbers and had nothing to lose.

The cost of nursemaiding Eve's genetic remnant is a million dollars a year. "Never has so much effort and concern gone into nine hundred fish," noted Marine Fisheries biologist Ed Schiewe of the Seattle survivors.

Eve, who would have died after spawning anyway, was stuffed by the Idaho Department of Fish and Game and mounted in the state capital building in Boise. Then scientists anxiously waited to see if any more sockeye would return to give her some help. Because the salmon have a four-year life cycle, Eve represented the reproductive hope of just a quarter of the population: other Snake River sockeye might still be at sea. The following year it appeared Eve might indeed be the last female: only a single sockeye made it back to the high mountain lake and biologists promptly dubbed him Lonesome Larry. While his epic swim did not win him a female partner, Larry's sperm was taken to help fertilize future generations artificially. Then, in the fall of 1993, two females and six males returned. Three thousand eggs were collected and then fertilized with sperm from the six males plus Larry, creating fourteen batches with different parents and relieving concern about catastrophic in-breeding. These fish were also raised in tanks, but some were scheduled to be reintroduced to Redfish Lake as one-year-olds and allowed to swim to the ocean on their own. The remainder are scheduled at this writing to reach adulthood in captivity.

This kind of fish production, called "captive broodstock," is unusual. It is expensive and difficult to keep salmon in an artificial environment their entire lives. Most Columbia River salmon today, however, start their lives in a human-built hatchery. Fishery agencies annually artificially raise and release more than 170 million juvenile salmon into Columbia Basin streams from one hundred and twenty-eight fish hatcheries. The Army Corps of Engineers barges or trucks up to 20 million of them around dams.

Agencies know almost 99 percent of these hatchery fish never survive to return to the Columbia River as harvestable adults. The odds for wild salmon are just as grim. Even if born on the most pristine and undeveloped of rivers, most won't make it. As a result, some officials view this last-minute attempted rescue of Snake River sockeye as quixotic. Biologists are trying to rescue a nearly extinct stock from just a trio of mothers, a stock that somehow must adapt to the same dam-by-dam river journey I made on the Tidewater barge. Returning upstream to spawn, they must pass the dams by thrashing their way up a total of more than seven hundred fish ladder steps, gaining about a foot with each jump. In other words, they must climb these artificial rapids to a height comparable to the tallest skyscrapers in Seattle or Portland.

Skeptics make other points. Sockeye salmon as a *species* are in no danger of extinction. There are tens of millions that spawn annually in Canada and Alaska, and tens of thousands that swim to the Wenatchee and Okanogan river systems in the Columbia Basin. That may be a drastic drop from sockeye runs in the Columbia that once numbered three million, but it is not extinction. "Salmon is the only endangered species you can buy off the shelf in a can," said Robert Meyers, senior vice-president of Puget Sound Power and Light, at an engineering conference.

An even greater irony is that until 1990 humans were doing their best to block and poison sockeye salmon from returning to

Idaho, making this rescue effort a textbook example of the moral quandaries posed by the Endangered Species Act.

Redfish Lake is not a pristine wildlife preserve. It is a large, cold recreational playground with a lodge, several campgrounds, and a bridge over the outlet stream so that tourists can observe any salmon that happen to struggle by. Fishermen troll for resident trout, water skiers cut wakes of cream, children wade in the chilly shallows, and their parents bask in the high, brassy sun. Yet Redfish is the only remaining refuge in central Idaho, the last of several lakes in the Stanley Basin where sockeye used to spawn and spend the first year of life. Humans are now trying to save a species they exterminated so efficiently that some fish biologists believe the original genes are already extinct, meaning a million dollars a year is being spent to resuscitate a stock that can trace its ancestry back only a few decades.

"Undoubtedly it is *not* the same fish as was there originally," argued Bill Herschberger, a fish geneticist at the University of Washington. Many biologists are less certain than Herschberger, but some utility executives believe the entire effort is absurd, like guarding a 1930s copy of the *Mona Lisa* because the original has been destroyed.

In 1910 the Sunbeam Mining Company slapped a concrete dam across the main fork of the Snake River twenty miles below Redfish Lake and installed generators to power its nearby mine. By 1912 the company had added a wooden fish ladder for salmon but it was so poorly designed that it failed to attract any fish. In 1920 a concrete ladder was built that allowed passage of at least some salmon, and a diversion tunnel that had been built to drain the streambed when the dam was constructed may also have allowed some salmon to go up and down. Yet did they? After the mining company abandoned the site, local residents who were tired of the fish blockage took some sticks of dynamite and blew out one end of the small dam in 1934.

The result is utter mystery. Was the Redfish Lake sockeye run blocked and extinguished, or did a few struggle through the diversion tunnel and later fish ladder? Were the sockeye who later spawned in the lake remnants of this gene pool? Or were they descendants of landlocked salmon called kokanee, strays from other Columbia River runs, or artificially introduced by humans? Salmon eggs from other regions have periodically been planted in central Idaho's lakes, with uncertain results. Biologists have tried to piece together the basin's natural history like detectives investigating a decades-old murder. The memories of area residents are vague. Scientists have come away with persuasive arguments on both counts: that Eve represents an ancient stock, or that she is merely a descendant of salmon that recolonized Redfish Lake after 1934.

Nearby lakes are absent of any sockeye at all. For several decades it was the policy of Idaho's Department of Fish and Game to poison the sockeye lakes to make room for trout. Kamloops trout had grown as large as fifty pounds on Lake Pend Oreille in northern Idaho, and Idaho fish agents wanted to duplicate that success in the central part of the state. The high mountain lakes were so poor in nutrients, however, that biologists believed resident squawfish and suckers consumed food desperately needed by the intended trout. Meanwhile the salmon that struggled back had little value as sports fish, their bodies having deteriorated in anticipation of spawning. Accordingly, the state decided to poison the lakes of native fish. Toxaphene was dumped into neighboring Stanley Lake in 1959, Pettit Lake in 1961, and Yellowbelly Lake in 1962. Then barriers were placed across the outlet creeks to prevent squawfish, suckers, or salmon from recolonizing. An irrigation diversion dam was built across the creek leading to Alturus Lake, blocking salmon from entering it as well. Only the largest lake, Redfish, remained unaffected. In 1960 it still produced 4,400 spawning fish.

Given this history, the belated interest in Snake River sockeye can be hard to understand. In fact the rescue seems absurd except that Eve contains something special: the only salmon genes that drive sockeye to swim that far, that high, that far south. What biologists are trying to save is not the last of the salmon, but the last of a stock of salmon that swims to an unusual place. Snake River sockeye (the name given to this run that swims the Columbia, Snake, and finally Salmon rivers in return) have been genetically endowed with the proper size, muscles, and fat reserves to make the journey.

A century ago their numbers were in the thousands, and Redfish Lake got its name from the color of spawning salmon in its gravel. By 1991 the names of the Salmon River and Redfish Lake seemed a bitter joke. Of eight tributary and lake systems where Columbia River salmon used to spawn in central Idaho, five have been completely shut off by dams. The surface area of spawning lakes available to the fish has declined 96 percent. Development and damming have already wiped out sixty-seven different salmon stocks in the Columbia Basin, and an estimated seventy-six additional stocks are threatened. The inclusion of just four of them on the endangered species list has thrown the river system into an uproar.

Until 1990 the disappearance of individual salmon stocks on tributary rivers was not considered much of an issue. Ever since the first dams had been built on the Columbia River the strategy has been to mitigate the havoc they caused by producing replacement salmon artificially. Politically, the salmon did not have to be from the same place; the hatcheries could be concentrated on the lower river to placate the powerful commercial fisheries based at the Columbia's mouth. Until the Endangered Species Act gave them leverage, the interest of tribes such as the Shoshone-Bannock in having runs reach distant streams in Idaho could be safely ignored.

Still, there *was* a white recreational and Indian commercial fishery in the interior, so as the dams marched upriver, so did the hatcheries: Congress appropriated $177 million to build hatcheries to mitigate the expected salmon losses caused by the new Snake River dams. These fish factories began to be built all over the basin, including the relatively remote rivers of central Idaho. As a result, humans dumped far more young salmon into Columbia Basin streams than had ever hatched naturally. Between 1960 and 1987 their number increased 150 percent and their combined weight shot up seven times. Even as wild runs declined 95 to 98 percent from historic levels, hatchery-raised fish kept overall salmon numbers in the Columbia at about 2.5 million: a decline of 75 to 85 percent from aboriginal times, true, but still healthy enough to sustain a limping commercial fishery. The number of returning salmon that annually swam over Bonneville Dam actually was twice the number in 1985 than when the dam was completed in 1938. Until recently, most biologists believed fish hatcheries were the only practical way to sustain salmon numbers. "In my mind, the use of hatcheries is going to continue to be a necessity to have the river produce at all," said Herschberger. "There's been too much degradation of habitat for wild runs, particularly in the main Columbia."

The very success of hatchery fish endangered the remaining wild runs, however. The hatchery fish competed for food, spread disease, bred with their wild cousins, and weakened the genetic characteristics that had enabled the wild fish to survive in particular streams. Most seriously they allowed continued heavy fishing, meaning scarce wild fish were being scooped up in the same net with plentiful artificially hatched fish. The engineered river had resulted in an engineered biology, a numbers game that allowed stocks such as Redfish Lake sockeye to slip toward extinction. "When the river system all got put together, it didn't work as advertised," summed up Ed Chaney, an iconoclastic fish consultant who has made a specialty of dogging the power planners with uncomfortable facts. "The engineers screwed up."

Until the Endangered Species Act listings changed the rules of the game, engineers did their best to ignore Chaney—not easy to do given his six-foot-six frame and gift for pithy criticism. The Boise-area consultant views the Columbia River system as the region's biggest con game, in which the costs of saving salmon are wildly exaggerated and the costs of losing them ignored. Taxpayers built dams whose benefits went to private aluminum companies and corporate farmers, Chaney charges, meaning we "communized the costs and privatized the profits. The Columbia is pretty typical of the pork barrel gone wild. They dammed it all except for fifty miles."

He regards the Bonneville Power Administration as inconsistent when it counts water released for salmon as a cost, since it applies no such charge to water diverted for irrigation, spilled through navigation locks, or shifted for flood control. Certainly these rates are as significant or more so than those to save salmon. Jim Ruff, a hydrologist for the Northwest Power Planning Council, has estimated that irrigators throughout the Columbia and Snake basins remove a total of 14 million acre-feet of water each year above Bonneville Dam, amounting to $350 million a year in lost revenue for power producers: an expenditure not equaled by salmon protection until the crisis year of 1994, when ocean fish production had collapsed.

Chaney believes salmon will only succeed when at least part of the river system, particularly the lower Snake River, reverts toward its natural condition. Two decades of artificial fixes such as loading salmon on barges and moving them past the dams have only resulted in Endangered Species Act filings. "We can't admit we don't have a technological fix to get us out of this technological mess," he said.

The Shoshone-Bannock petition to list Snake River sockeye as endangered was followed within months by one for Snake River chinook salmon, filed by a coalition of environmental groups led by Oregon Trout. That move came as no surprise once Native Americans had opened the possibility. The listing of the northern spotted owl as a threatened "indicator species" of old growth forests was already bringing the logging of ancient trees to a halt in the Pacific Northwest. Environmentalists and tribes saw salmon as an even more potent ecological indicator. Heavy logging, overgrazing, heedless road building, unwise development, and chemical-intensive farming all hurt salmon. The fish were not just a species that hunted over tens of thousands of acres, like a spotted owl. They ranged thousands of miles from the Gulf of Alaska to central Idaho, and were affected by everything that happened over that vast territory.

For a hundred years fish managers had concentrated on artificial hatcheries to sustain numbers of salmon. Overnight, the issue had changed. A utility system goal of doubling Columbia River salmon runs was not good enough even had it succeeded. (It didn't.) What was important were individual stocks because they conserved genetic information, forced environmental protection of the entire habitat, and required reconsideration of the promise that society could have its cheap hydroelectricity and its salmon, too. "What happened was, the goal posts got shifted," complained Randy Hardy, the administrator of BPA.

Part of this shift was forced by growing doubt about the hatchery program. One study of thirty hatchery runs that were robust for decades showed mysterious, troubling declines. "In the long run," said National Marine Fisheries Service biologist Robin Wapples, "it is really important to conserve the genetic resources in the wild stocks because they've been shaped by thousands of years of evolution to survive." It was genetics that produced the hundred-pound "June hogs" in Columbia River chinook runs, fish large and fat enough to make the twelve-hundred-mile swim to the Columbia's headwaters. It was genetics that powered salmon to Redfish Lake.

Yet was this realistic? The Columbia Basin was dotted with more than five hundred dams. Were biologists now to rescue battered genetic survivors? In fact there was no unanimity. The fish experts gathered in the windowless conference room at NMFS headquarters in Seattle and wrangled heatedly about whether Snake River sockeye could, or should, be saved. The nation's taxpayers had just spent half a century and $8 billion deliberately harnessing the Columbia River and altering its ecology. Now Indians and environmentalists wanted Humpty Dumpty put back together? Who said Eve was really an Eve, different in any meaningful way from other salmon?

Put in charge of answering such questions was biologist Wapples. He found himself studying the strontium content of the bone otaliths, or ear structures, in captured Redfish salmon to determine if their parents had migrated to the ocean, where more strontium exists. He ground up the cells from tissue samples, put them on a gel made of potato starch, applied electricity, and studied how different proteins moved in the electric field. If samples from two different fish show the same migration pattern on the gel, they have the same genetics. If not, then Eve and her mates are unique. Indeed, they seemed to be different. Lose this fish and the DNA code was gone, too.

Still, extinction is normal. Why not give up? "For us, that's simply not an option," Wapples said. Redfish sockeye are reproductively isolated by six hundred miles of river from their nearest cousins, and the Endangered Species Act says that isolation is enough to warrant protection. That is why grizzly bears and bald eagles are protected in the contiguous United States even though both are plentiful in Canada and Alaska. "It's not okay, under the law, to call a species extinct," Wapples said.

The grim future for Columbia River salmon had been determined as early as 1807, when a twelve-thousand-franc prize for a new food preparation method for the armies of Napoleon Bonaparte resulted in the invention of canning by Nicolas Appert, a confectionery shop owner in Paris. By 1819, Ezra Daggett of New York City had successfully canned fish. Attempts to develop a fish industry on the Columbia date to 1829, when Captain John Dennis of the brig *Owyhee* bought fifty barrels of salmon from the Indians in exchange for tobacco, sailed them around Cape Horn to Boston, and sold them for ten cents a pound. Nathaniel Wyeth's attempt to establish a commercial fishery five years later failed, however, and the resource remained largely untapped by non-Indians until 1866 when three entrepreneurs from Maine—George and William Hume and Andrew Hapgood—started a salmon cannery on the Columbia. The first season they canned 288,000 pounds of chinook. The rush was on.

Within twenty years there were fifty-five canneries on the Columbia, packing more than a hundred times that first year's harvest. Early canning crews were dominated by the Chinese, each of whom could clean a salmon in forty-five seconds and turn out a ton of canned salmon per hour. The pace quickened even more with the invention of the "Iron Chink" canning machine for smaller salmon, which could do the work of ten laborers. Just as the river's water would be free to utility companies and irrigation districts, the salmon were free to the new industry. There was no custom of restraint.

Astoria, which had slumbered in wet neglect since the Hudson's Bay headquarters had moved to Fort Vancouver in 1824, suddenly revived. It was the fishing community farthest downriver and thus the first to intercept the salmon as they came in from the sea. Because of the city's steep hills much of the new Astoria was built on pilings over the river estuary. It was a boisterous place that boasted a "swill town," a red-light district, and colonies of transplanted and mostly single Finns, Norwegians, Danes, and Chinese. Sunday church services were canceled and the ministers went fishing when the runs were at their peak. As early as 1889 there were twenty-six hundred rowboats and sailboats fishing between Portland and the river's mouth.

Regulation was inconsistent and enforcement was worse. Washington Territory banned traps or nets that blocked tributary streams as early as 1871, but it took Oregon two decades to follow suit. Oregon specified net sizes and trap spacing in 1878, but it took Washington two decades to adopt similar regulations. The coordination between the two states was so bad that it drew comment from Theodore Roosevelt in a special message to Congress on December 8, 1908. "During these twenty-five years the fishermen of each state have naturally tried to take all they could get," Roosevelt observed, "and the two legislatures have never been able to agree on joint action of any kind adequate in degree for the protection of the fishers." By the time truly effective enforcement began in the 1930s, salmon had been in decline for decades.

Wanapum tribal elders later recalled that the huge salmon runs had disappeared from Priest Rapids by 1905, more than thirty years before Bonneville Dam was completed.

The new industry initially caught only chinook. The catch of that species peaked at 43 million pounds in 1883 and then plunged from overfishing. Between 1883 and 1890, industry production fell from 630,000 cases of forty-eight one-pound cans of Chinook to 385,000.

Fish wheels appeared on the Columbia in 1879, with construction of the first one at the Cascades below the present site of Bonneville Dam. Within twenty years, seventy-six of the crude harvesters had been constructed. These large wooden water wheels were built over rocky channels where migrating salmon tended to swim. As the current turned the wheel, a wooden bucket or lip on the downstream side of the paddle would scoop up salmon, lift them clear of the river, and dump them into a deep wooden box. The fish wheels have been estimated to have taken only about 5 percent of the Columbia salmon harvest, but their looming presence and the inexorable turn of their wheel seemed like an irritating reminder of the insatiable and shortsighted greed that ruled the fishing industry. The wheels were finally banned in Oregon in 1926 and Washington in 1934, but they were only symptomatic of a widespread mania for resource depletion. It was first come, first served in a pattern ecologist Garrett Hardin would later call the Tragedy of the Commons.

As the chinook numbers fell the fishermen moved on to other species such as coho and sockeye. In 1911 the catch of other salmon species allowed a new peak of 46 million pounds of canned Columbia salmon. The salmon swam by in such numbers that owners of seine nets up to six hundred feet long lacked the strength to haul the bulging nets to the river beaches and harnessed horses to pull in the wriggling harvest. In 1921 one seine caught sixty thousand pounds of fish in a single haul.

Such bonanzas did not last. As technology improved, the catch became disastrously efficient. The gasoline engine allowed trolling on the open ocean and by 1920 there were over a thousand powered boats operating out of the Columbia's mouth. By the time Bonneville Dam was completed in 1938, the annual catch of salmon had slumped to only 20 million pounds. Americans had annihilated more than half the Columbia's salmon before the dams were built.

The dams, however, decimated what was left. Grand Coulee was built without any fish passage facilities for a number of reasons. The Reclamation Act of 1902, unlike the Federal Power Act of 1920, made no mention of fish passage—and Grand Coulee was a Reclamation dam. Besides, the resource that far upriver seemed insignificant to everyone but the Native Americans upstream. Runs represented a catch of about thirty thousand adult fish worth, at that time, about $300,000. Biologists doubted salmon could surmount a fish ladder three hundred and fifty feet high, or that young salmon could migrate downstream through a one-hundred-and-fifty-mile reservoir and past the dam. Accordingly, Grand Coulee's fish were captured, their eggs taken, and the runs were transplanted to downstream tributaries, with a mixed record of success.

Bonneville was different. It was the first dam migrating adult salmon would encounter. Bonneville was also an Army Corps dam and, as such, came under the Power Act calling for fish passage. It was only one-sixth Grand Coulee's height, making a fish ladder practical, and the runs were economically important.

While there were no detailed plans for fish ladders when the dam was approved, there were also no detailed plans for the dam: even its site was still being shifted. The 1932 Corps 308 Report that had called for ten dams on the Columbia, however, had included preliminary plans and cost estimates for adult fish passage at each dam. Accordingly, the Corps completed a plan for fish ladders and an elevator lift by September 1, 1934, about a year after Bonneville's construction got under way. The Oregon Fish Commission immediately objected that the Corps' blueprint was inadequate, starting the bureaucratic warfare between dam managers and fish managers that continues today. Oregon wanted a design that would increase the cost from $2.8 million to $3.6 million, and finally got Senator McNary's help to achieve a compromise $3.2 million. As the dam was built the designs continued to evolve, however, and the final cost was $7 million. There were three fish ladders and two elevatorlike lifts to get salmon upstream, and three smaller bypasses to allow young fish to go downstream. Most young salmon, however, were expected to pass safely through the dam turbines or over the spillway. In 1941, Thomas Roins, the assistant chief of engineers for the Corps, told Congress that dam turbines were "absolutely incapable of hurting the fish. If you could put a mule through there, and keep him from drowning, he would go through without being hurt. Before we put the wheels in, we carried on experiments with fish, and proved conclusively that the pressure of the turbines will not injure fish."

This statement proved to be misleading and naïve. The turbines would decimate any run that passed through. Still, the overall feeling at the time was uncertainty. In 1938 the U.S. Bureau of Fisheries warned, "There is no way of determining in advance whether or not the fish-protective works will be successful and what, if any, adverse effects the dam will have upon the fish supply." About half a million salmon and steelhead passed Bonneville the first year, a number that eventually grew to an average of about a million. Salmon, it seemed, could pass a single dam; the problem would come when they had to pass several, each exacting its toll. As seasons became better regulated and hatchery programs expanded, salmon runs into the early 1950s actually seemed to be recovering. Then the burst of dam building overtook conservation. By 1983 the catch bottomed out at 1.3 million pounds, about 3 percent of the historic peak.

Some had prophesied this. In 1947, when just three dams had been built on the Columbia River, writer Paul Needham predicted in the *Oregon Business Review* what would follow. "If present plans of the dam builders go through," he wrote, "the rich anadromous fishery resources of the Columbia Basin are doomed. A total of sixty-nine dam sites are now under study in this basin alone. Among these is McNary dam. If this is built, it will be the beginning of the end of the steelhead and salmon runs in the upper Columbia River. Another main-river dam is proposed at The Dalles near Celilo Falls. But the finishing touch will be the four-dam plan now being recommended by the Army Engineer Corps for construction on the Snake River to provide slackwater navigation to Lewiston, Idaho. All western fishery biologists with whom I have talked agree that this plan, if followed, will spell the doom of salmon and steelhead migrations up the Snake River as well as up its best tributary, the Salmon River of Idaho. . . ."

The Washington State Department of Fisheries was so upset by plans to dam the Snake River that it suggested three hundred and eighty-seven other dam sites that would produce power with far less biological cost. The agency was ignored. People knew what they were doing to the salmon three decades before the dams were completed, and did it anyway. When the four lower Snake River dams were built, the average death rate of juvenile salmon runs coming down the Snake River jumped from 5 percent to 70 percent.

An example of the seeming indifference of hydroelectric engineers came in 1968 when John Day Dam was being completed. Vice-President Hubert Humphrey was the scheduled guest for the dedication but the fish passage facilities and generators were not yet complete. The Army Corps of Engineers closed the dam anyway to fill the reservoir, and then spilled water over the top of the dam for a spectacular show. The lack of fish ladders and nitrogen saturation of the water from the spill killed at least twenty thousand adult chinook salmon, but the ceremony came off as scheduled.

The combination of overfishing, overbuilding, and recognition of Indian treaty fishing rights meant that the non-Indian fishing season in the lower river fell from as much as two hundred and seventy-four days of the year to a "museum piece fishery" of about thirty days or fewer. Many major runs of Columbia River salmon have had no fishing for three decades and have still not recovered. "People on the lower Columbia are still going to hang on," said Steve King, harvest manager for the Oregon Department of Fish and Wildlife. "Their motto is, 'Any season, anywhere, at any time, at any cost.'" Like the Native Americans, salmon represent to these fishermen not just dollars but a historic lifestyle. The fish, however, have reached the limit of their resilience.

The emphasis of the Columbia River salmon rescue has always been on engineering, not biology. Humans have built ladders, screens, diversions, hatcheries, and collection barges, and used strobe lights, incandescent lights, poppers, barriers, and funneled water to try to shoo the fish in the direction we think they should go. What we haven't done, contends James Anderson of the Fisheries Research Institute at the University of Washington, is "taken the fish's point of view." Salmon are the most valuable and studied fish species in the United States but, as water creatures, they are hard to see or track. No minisub has ever followed a migrating salmon. After spending a billion dollars on water flows, studies, turbine screens, bypass facilities, and hatcheries in the 1980s to double salmon runs—and instead seeing them decline by the end of the decade—biologists are only certain of just how complex the problem is.

To illustrate the challenge salmon face, let us follow the perilous life of Suzy chinook as she makes her migratory journey to the sea and back. "Nowhere in the world," wrote fish biologist Anthony Netboy, "have fish been asked to cope with so many man-made obstacles to survival. The wonder is that depletion of their populations, though serious, is not worse."

Suzy is a wild fish from central Idaho, and begins life in a natural spawning bed in a rushing tributary of the Columbia, the Middle Fork of the Salmon River. Her egg is tucked with thousands of others in the interstices between bits of gravel. Suzy's dying mother fanned the protective rock over the nest of eggs with her tail. Suzy has not yet hatched, but already existence can be hard. A drought or freeze or diversion of water for power or irrigation can leave salmon spawning beds dry. A flood can break the bed open. And even as a fertilized egg, Suzy requires oxygen. If the watery spaces between the gravel are plugged by dirt carried into the river by erosion, she will smother.

Thus only about half of natural salmon eggs on average survive to become alevins, tiny protosalmon that hatch and live briefly in the gravel. As the alevins emerge from their nest, predators, disease, starvation, and weakness sweep away more. If five hundred mother salmon lay two million eggs, just 250,000 on average will survive to become young salmon fry an inch or so long. Of these fry, more than 90 percent die or are eaten as they hunt for lake plankton or insect larvae to prepare for the long trip to the sea. Accordingly, as few as one percent of the eggs that were laid, or twenty thousand salmon fingerlings, will start for the ocean. This high natural mortality is what artificial hatcheries try, with considerable success, to circumvent.

Suzy's survival of these grim odds represents just one part of her luck. She is fortunate that her ancestors used a part of the Columbia Basin river system that has not been plugged by dams. The Northwest Power Planning Council estimated in 1993 that 54 percent of the 350,000 stream miles in the Columbia Basin are inaccessible to salmon because of the concrete barriers.

After a few months of growth it is time for Suzy to be

pushed downriver to the sea. Her trip from Idaho to the Pacific has traditionally taken twenty to thirty days in the spring freshet, the speed and murk of the runoff hurrying her past predators such as squawfish. Humans are holding water behind dams, however, and the amount of water coming down the Snake River has declined 20 to 30 percent because of irrigation diversions. As a result, the time a young chinook requires to make the trip has stretched to two or three months. This represents a grave problem. Suzy's body is timed to change, in a process called smoltification, so that when she reaches salt water she can survive in that medium. If delayed too long the smolt process can halt and reverse. Scientists are still seeking to clarify how many salmon deaths this delay can cause.

In 1984 fish agencies asked that more water be released to maintain minimal river flows in the Columbia and Snake to help hurry young salmon to the sea. An umbrella group called the Columbia Basin Fish and Wildlife Authority urged that it take no more than fifteen days for salmon to pass the gauntlet of dams. However, the agency that received this request, the Northwest Power Planning Council, was persuaded by utilities that guaranteeing timing or a flow made power planning difficult. The council inserted a subtle but crucial change, deciding instead that the dams should provide a "water budget": a block of water to be released at fish agency request. The advantage of this for the utilities is that they knew in advance how much power generation they would lose for salmon and could plan accordingly, rather than making last-minute changes to meet a targeted flow. The disadvantage for fish agencies is that the water budget was inflexible, providing more flow than is needed in wet years and not enough in dry years. Nor have biologists agreed on how much flow is enough.

Even with added water, the passage of Suzy and her cousins is slow enough to make them easier prey for predators. The squawfish is an ugly, giant minnow that can reach two feet in length and gobble a hundred young migrating salmon a day. Its numbers have exploded in the slack water of the reservoirs as salmon and trout hatcheries pour out a ready food source. Young salmon tend to mill in confusion at the upper and lower sides of each dam, making them easy pickings. To try to bring the system back into ecological balance, sports fishermen have been offered a bounty of three dollars per squawfish, otherwise regarded as worthless trash fish. In 1991 an estimated 210,000 were caught, with unknown benefit to salmon runs.

Suzy has more to worry about than squawfish. She and her wild cousins are finding the river crowded with their hatchery brethren that compete for food. They also infect the wild fish with bacterial kidney disease, an affliction that will weaken salmon just as they make the difficult physiological transition from fresh to salt water. Dumb, weak, and sick, hatchery salmon—from Suzy's point of view—are nerdish competitors lessening her own chances of survival.

As if these problems were not enough, some of Suzy's companions stray into irrigation intakes and find themselves in a concrete ditch. There are more than nine hundred irrigation intake structures in Washington, Oregon, and Idaho, and only in recent years has there been a systematic campaign to get them screened. There is no maintenance program to keep them that way. An estimated 422,000 salmon fingerlings died in irrigation canals in the Lemhi River near Salmon, Idaho, while installation of screens on Oregon's John Day River saved an estimated 500,000 fish from a similar fatal detour.

Our heroine is carried by the current down the Salmon to the Snake. At Lewiston the river begins to slow. And slow. And slow. Suzy has reached her first dam reservoir. So powerful are the spring river currents she evolved in that up to this point she has been swimming backwards, in effect simply guiding her body between the rocks. Now she is in a slack lake and has to turn around and burn precious energy to migrate. The reservoir also seems a strange place, not at all what instinct told her to expect. The bottom is mud instead of rock. Mats of river weeds grow in the shallows. Predators abound.

Near the first dam the current begins to quicken again. Suzy is pulled downward, fifty, sixty, eighty feet: deeper than she has ever gone, deeper than the wild river ever got. The light dims, then disappears. The chinook is in a huge penstock that leads to a turbine blade spinning about one revolution every second. This is not fast enough to simply chop fish up like a blender, but some are killed by being struck by the blades and others stunned by cavitation pressure in the whirling darkness. Almost before she can react Suzy is spun through the blades and spat out the bottom of the powerhouse, dizzy and disoriented, surfacing again in blinding light and a swirl of bubbles. Once more predators are waiting. The casualty rate from this perilous passage is hotly disputed, but by the estimate of the Northwest Power Planning Council, up to 15 percent of Suzy's companions died in that dam and reservoir, and will die in each of the dams to follow. Recent studies by utility biologists at Rocky Reach Dam and the Snake dams suggest that this figure is too high, with a major study under way by 1994 to track fish with electronic, rice-sized "tags" inserted in their bodies.

At some dams, Suzy's experience differs. Water is being spilled over the top to allow salmon to avoid the spinning turbines, and our chinook is spilled with it. She plunges a hundred feet in a thundering cataract so powerful that waves bounce twenty feet high off the dam's concrete spill basin, filling the air with spray. She drops and is bounced away downstream, her survival once more demonstrating the physical tenacity of young salmon. Unfortunately, the dam's waterfall can drive so much nitrogen from the atmosphere into the water that it threatens to give Suzy the same nitrogen narcosis or gas bubble disease, better known as the bends, that scuba divers can suffer. The problem was first recognized in the 1960s; in 1969 an estimated 20 percent of the chinook juveniles in the Snake River system died of the malady. There is a balancing point at which the advantages of directing salmon over the spillway and away from turbines are canceled by the danger of nitrogen supersaturation. Biologists are not certain what that point is.

Suzy swims on, sometimes passing through turbines, sometimes over the spillway, finally clearing the last dam at Bonneville. In a poor water year, the total mortality of young salmon descending through eight dams can reach as high as 97 percent.

Our heroine's difficulties are far from over, however. By the time she is in the lower Columbia she is desperately hungry but available feed has declined. Diking and dredging have eliminated wetlands that are the grocery store of the wild, rich in nutrients and thick with hiding places. In the lowest forty-six miles of the river, only 23 percent of tidal swamps and 35 percent of marsh swamps remain. Accordingly, Suzy makes it to the ocean but far later, more poorly nourished, and more battered than if she had traveled the natural Columbia.

At sea she migrates as far as southern Alaska, feeding and growing. Her luck holds. She does not encounter El Niño ocean conditions that can halt the upwelling of nutrients from the deep and depress the sea's food chain. She beats the odds by swimming past the nets of Canadian and American fishermen on her journey back down the coast. Three-quarters of all the Columbia River chinook that are caught commercially are caught at sea, not in the river, and for threatened runs this catch remains far too high. An average 74 percent of adult Snake River fall chinook were harvested in the six years prior to their making the endangered species list, despite warnings from biologists that the catch had to be limited to 55 percent to give the run a chance to rebuild.

After an absence of three years, Suzy reenters the Columbia. At the mouth she narrowly escapes a bite by a sea lion. Federal protection means marine mammal populations are exploding, a recovery that puts them at odds with endangered salmon. In 1990, 19 percent of returning chinook salmon were recorded with mammal bites, a majority of them expected to die before spawning.

On entry to freshwater Suzy stops eating. Her body is about 15 percent fat at this point, and by the time she completes her long swim back to home waters she will have consumed nine-tenths of that store. She ignores the temptation of sports fishing lures at Buoy 10 and swims purposefully upstream until she encounters Bonneville Dam. Here she pauses.

Migrating salmon are attracted to strong current. The strongest currents at dams come from powerhouse outlets or the spillway, but fish can't swim past turbines or leap a tall dam. Instead they must search for the entrance to a fish ladder, a ten- or fifteen-foot-wide slot in a structure that is typically half a mile to a mile long. Engineers have made this easier by feeding extra current into fish-ladder entrances, by having two or three ladders on each dam, and by having multiple entrances to each ladder. Still, confusion can be fatal: if salmon spend too much time finding the varied entrances in their gauntlet of dams, they will consume their fat reserves and starve to death before entering their native stream to spawn.

Suzy finds a ladder and is surprised to find it crowded with a new kind of fish. These are shad, a native of the eastern United States. At the request of the California Fish Commission, anxious to experiment with new stocks, ten thousand of these fish were brought to the Sacramento River in 1871 by a Rochester, New York, fish enthusiast named Seth Green. He carried the anadromous fish west in milk cans via the new transcontinental railroad.

Once introduced the shad thrived, and some strayed north to the Columbia. The first mature shad was caught in the river in 1880, and their numbers have been climbing ever since. In 1990, 3.7 million were counted at The Dalles Dam, eclipsing the number of salmon. Until recently, however, they were largely ignored by both fishermen and biologists, and the effect of this explosive increase on the ecology of native salmon is unknown.

On her way upriver Suzy also encounters a slalom course of Native American gill nets. Once more she is surrounded by her hatchery-bred brethren, and their adult numbers are so large that a river fishery is allowed. While the harvest is not thorough enough to threaten the hatchery runs, still more of Suzy's wild cousins are snared by the nets. Life is getting very lonely.

She finds the Snake River and encounters a new kind of barrier: warm water. Suzy's metabolism is controlled by the temperature of her environment. When the water warms, her cold-blooded system speeds up, once more consuming desperately needed fat reserves. She prefers a river temperature of forty-nine to fifty-eight degrees, and water above seventy degrees is an oven that can kill her. Since construction of the four lower Snake River dams, temperatures have averaged three degrees above normal. In periods of low rainfall and slow current they can climb toward the lethal range. Salmon have no choice but to back down into cooler water and wait, once more throwing off their biological timing. The dams have changed the schedule of water flow and pushed the peak of warm water back from July and August to September, just when salmon have evolved to begin ascending the stream.

A release of water from Dworshak Dam temporarily cools the Snake, and Suzy wearily climbs over the four lower river dams. She turns into the Salmon River and then into its Middle Fork. Her tiny brain is alive with powerful memories of river smells and contours. Finally she reaches a side creek, prepares a nest, does a slow mating dance with a promising male, and has a final ecstatic release of eggs before an exhausted death. She has triumphed. But as her life flickers out, her body drifting with the current before beaching, she has an instinctual sense of alarm. Suzy is the exception. The spawning channel is distressingly empty of other salmon. The odds are against her stock prevailing for many more generations.

· · ·

Mary Friedberg is a biological babysitter for half a million fish on a quick trip down the Columbia, but she seems an unlikely employee, even a temporary one, of the Army Corps of Engineers. The thirty-eight-year-old former Peace Corps volunteer lives in a yurt on timbered acreage east of Mount Hood with neither telephone nor electricity, one of the rare Northwesterners not wired to the dams.

We are riding on a red-painted Corps fish barge down the Snake River toward the Columbia, giving salmon and steelhead collected at Little Goose Dam a taxi ride past six more concrete plugs. The idea is to spare the Suzy chinooks of this world some of the downstream trauma just described. Without the barge ride it would take the half million salmon and steelhead in the tanks up to thirty days to travel that far; with the barge it takes less than three. It is a straightforward engineering solution to an engineering problem, and no custodian seems less likely than Friedberg, who shares her New Age opinions only cautiously with the tug crew. "I think what we need is magic," she tells me.

Friedberg opens a grate to take the temperature of the barge tank, matter-of-factly scooping out a handful of salmon that have died. On one trip she counted three thousand dead, but that mortality is still far less than would have occurred in a journey through the dams. "It's kind of phenomenal that you can take half a million fish down the river every three to four days," she remarks. I look down at the churning salmon and steelhead in the rumbling barge, the vessel vibrating to the rattle of the pumps that circulate fresh river water through its hold, our passengers packed in this technological tremble to a rate of about six per gallon. Indeed.

No exercise better illustrates the conflicting visions for the future of the Columbia River than this barge trip. It is the centerpiece and pride of the Corps' salmon mitigation program. The agency argues, correctly, that more salmon survive the barge trip than if left to make their own way through the dams. Environmentalists counter, correctly, that twenty-five years of barging and a tripling of the release of hatchery fish into the Snake have not halted the slide of several wild runs toward extinction. They believe engineers are trying to combat the effect of unnatural dams with even more unnatural barge and truck rides that leave salmon sick, stressed, vulnerable to predators when dumped (the Corps tries to spill them at night under a new moon to give the fish a chance of hiding in the darkness), and utterly disoriented. When they return as adults, barged salmon must find their way back up a river they have never swam down. If barging salmon works, environmentalists demand, why are some of the runs being barged on the endangered species list?

Upon these rocks the two groups have built their respective churches. "It's a holy war," said Ed Chaney.

Washington and Oregon officials tend to like fish barging. It is cheap. It interrupts neither electrical generation, irrigation diversion, or barge transportation of other goods in their states—and Washington alone consumes 60 percent of the hydroelectric power generated in the Columbia-Snake system. If Idaho wants a faster current in the Snake and Columbia reservoirs to push young fish migrating from its streams, Idaho is welcome to send it from its own irrigation and power reservoirs, the other two states advise.

Idaho governor Cecil Andrus, in contrast, has become the most powerful proponent of an environmentalist proposal to quicken river current by lowering the dam reservoirs forty to eighty feet during salmon migration. This "drawdown" would return the waterway close to its free-flowing state, theoretically speeding fish passage time. The Corps points out that changing the water levels would require rebuilding both fish ladders and barge locks, a project that could cost as much as $4.7 billion. But a reservoir drawdown would also relieve pressure on Idaho to find more water to send downstream. In 1991 a consulting firm called Hydrosphere concluded that Idaho farmers could conserve as much as 2 million acre-feet of water to aid fish flows, but farmers are reluctant to tackle the expense of doing so.

Biological uncertainties dog both barging and drawdowns. Scientists know that about 3.5 percent of the young salmon of the Columbia River Basin survive to return as adults. Exactly where the other 96.5 percent perish is extremely hard to determine.

Nor are biologists unanimous that speeding the reservoir current will do that much good. Typical of the skeptics of the supposed magic benefits of water flow is fish biologist Anderson. "The power interests have already given up water and unfortunately it hasn't done much," he points out. Recent studies have found almost no correlation between water flow and fish survival.

Yet barging is a dubious alternative. Just getting into a salmon transport barge is a dizzying, disorienting roller-coaster ride for a young salmon. At Lower Granite Dam they are subjected to water pressure two and a half times greater than normal as they are funneled down pipes to the waiting boats. Little Goose Dam has corrected the pressure problem, but even there the experience is traumatic. As the fish are drawn by the reservoir current toward the dam turbines, a screen looms ahead. Instinctively flinching, the salmon are directed to swim into a dark slot leading back upward through the center of the dam. The current lifts them like an elevator up to a horizontal six-inch pipe where they shoot with almost fire-hose force into a concrete millrace running the length of the dam. The fish are swept down to a three-foot-wide metal flume that runs a third of a mile from the face of the dam to a waiting barge. To maintain the proper 3.8 percent slope, the chute curves around in a complete loop, reminiscent of a water-slide ride in an amusement park. The salmon skid out the bottom of this onto the top of a grate where they can be inspected or counted, and then fall through the grate into a steel tank. Here an electric motor starts to whir and a screen begins squeezing the salmon toward one end of the tank, where a door opens to beckon them into another dark pipe. Through this they finally fall vertically into a covered barge.

"At what point," asked environmental writer John Daniel, "does human intervention turn a wild species into a captive artifact?"

As traumatic as this trip may be, the death rate during the barge ride is only 2 to 7 percent, a fraction of dam mortality. So enthused are some Corps and National Marine Fisheries Service biologists about barging that some have proposed building yet another dam. This would be called a "fish capture facility" and be located at Lewiston, at the head of Columbia-Snake navigation. A concrete barrier would funnel migrating salmon from the Clearwater and Snake rivers into barges just before they entered the first reservoir above Lower Granite Dam, giving them a lift across all the slack water pools.

This is not the only engineering solution being proposed. The most elaborate and least likely is to build an artificial river next to the real one: a sixteen-foot-wide concrete canal, complete with fake rapids, resting pools, and an overhead screen to ward off preying birds. This would carry fish downstream along the river's railroad grades, leaving the real river to the business of providing power, watering crops, and floating barges. The cost would be at least $5 billion, however, and no fish biologist is willing to guarantee that such a substitute would really work. Less ambitious are plans already under way to improve the bypass channels young salmon use to get past dams. Yet these are just as controversial: at Bonneville Dam's second powerhouse, an elaborate new bypass system wound up killing more salmon than the turbines did because it turned into a feeding chute for downstream predators.

A more promising solution has materialized by accident: the most successful Columbia River dam at fish passage is Wells, about forty-five miles north of Wenatchee. Difficult geology forced engineers to construct there the world's first "hydrocombine" dam in which spillway and generators are located at the same point, instead of having the powerhouse off to one side. This means that the river's full current pulls salmon to where the spillway bypass is, rather than having the strongest current pull salmon to the powerhouse. Nearly 90 percent of young salmon pass over Wells's spillway using only 10 percent of the Columbia's flow, allowing the rest of the water to be used for power. Remodeling dams to mimic Wells, however, would cost billions of dollars.

Hatcheries are also being reformed. A new Washington Department of Fisheries facility at Rocky Reach Dam relies on well water to eliminate contaminating bacteria, contains chillers to maintain optimum temperatures to time the hatching of eggs, and provides more water per fish and more frequent vacuuming of fish wastes. Rubber mesh has been installed in egg trays to simulate natural gravel.

Other hatcheries are experimenting with allowing their fish to spend a longer period of their juvenile life in streams, trying to combine the hatchery advantage of protecting eggs with the wild advantage of teaching young salmon to survive in a rugged environment. This program is bitterly controversial, however, because it threatens to blend wild and hatchery genes. A proposal by the Yakima Indian Nation to try it has been tied up in argument for years.

Biologists are so divided over what works and what doesn't and are so tied to the institutional philosophy of whoever has hired them that Chaney calls them "biostitutes."

"Science has become a commodity rather than a standard," said Ted Strong, the Yakima Indian who is director of the Columbia River Intertribal Fish Commission. "Too many groups can go out and buy science, and then use science to reaffirm a political decision."

Scientific uncertainty has certainly become a rallying point for river industry. Research is designed to be contentious but the squabbling only confuses policymakers. One need only find enough biologists to create confusion in order to paralyze and continue the status quo—a status quo in which the Columbia is an energy resource, not a biologic one.

Uncertainty has become useful for environmentalists as well. They have been skeptical and unsupportive of proposed additional studies that might undermine their conviction that water flow is key to salmon recovery. The complex truth has become a potential threat to the religious creed of both sides.

Ted Bottiger, a member of the Northwest Power Planning Council that oversees this rescue effort, recalls two incidents that illustrate the polarization. One was a visit to his Olympia office by a utility executive, who dumped cans of sockeye salmon on Bottiger's desk. It didn't matter that the sockeye represented were caught two thousand miles away in Alaska. The point was that the Power Council was demanding costly concessions for a species being caught and canned by the millions. The other was a visit by an environmentalist with a fistful of red candles. The candles represented sticks of dynamite, she told Bottiger, and under the dictates of environmental protection laws, the only discretion he had was to decide which dam to blow up first.

When a University of Washington fisheries professor named Donald Bevan was put in charge of the recovery team seeking ways to save Snake River sockeye and chinook runs from extinction, one thing quickly became apparent from his study of the Columbia River system.

"No one's in charge," Bevan said.

"That's right, no one's in charge," agreed BPA administrator Hardy, the one person who comes closest to actually overseeing the Columbia River mess. Hardy thinks his agency is being forced to throw money at the salmon problem with no evidence it is doing any good. "There is a lot of dogma and very little data," he said.

Columbia River salmon research is wide yet shallow. It has

been neither well-organized nor systematic. No agency has ever laid out the key questions that need to be answered to restore salmon runs effectively, and then devised and financed an orderly research program to answer them. Studies with conflicting statistics are fired back and forth like bullets in a shoot-out. Many are duplicative, most are not peer-reviewed, and almost all are too limited in scope. By 1992 the Army Corps of Engineers could count thirteen new studies under way trying to finally answer fundamental questions about salmon survival. Ideally, such answers would have been in hand before the first dam was built.

Proposals to unify fisheries management of the river date back half a century to proposals for a Columbia Valley Authority. Milo Bell, an early fish-ladder designer, also urged unity as the dams were going up. He was ignored. No agency, state, or tribe wanted to surrender authority, and so no one has it. Instead, the gauntlet that Suzy chinook must swim includes twenty-three different fishery agencies and Indian tribes, more than a dozen power agencies, and brigades of industry, farm, and environmental groups all clamoring for influence. "If you want to understand what is going on in the Columbia," advised University of Washington fisheries professor Ray Hilborn, "it's whoever wants to increase their budget."

The Northwest Power Planning Council has attempted to bring some coordination, writing a plan and getting federal dollars to help implement it. Reasoning that there was no certainty about what would work biologically, the council zeroed in on reforms in four broad areas at once: hydroelectric dams, habitat, hatcheries, and harvest. It has no enforcement power, however, and has failed to achieve any philosophic consensus among the warring interest groups. Its initial salmon strategy of doubling the size of Columbia River runs has foundered on drought and fisheries mismanagement.

Some argue that as enchanting as vibrant salmon runs might be, the quest to save them is economically unjustifiable. The Columbia and Snake provide $3 billion in power per year, water $5 billion in irrigated crops, support eleven large aluminum mills, and move 8 to 10 million tons of cargo by barge. The river's salmon industry, in contrast, produces fish that at the most optimistic estimate create revenues about a twentieth as large. (In 1982, however, economist Phillip Meyer estimated the value of the fish already lost to dams at an additional $372 million a year.)

The salmon that survive persist at a subsidized cost in bureaucracy, hatcheries, and lost power revenues that equals $50 to $200 per adult fish produced, far more than they are worth as food. An estimated $500 million has been spent on hatcheries, ladders, and other improvements on Columbia dams alone, and spilling water has arguably cost the region so much hydroelectric energy that it has eaten up the energy savings of a decade of expensive conservation projects. Common sense might suggest that the salmon's reign on the Columbia has ended, like that of the buffalo on the Great Plains.

Nonsense, said Michele Dehart, director of the Columbia's Fish Passage Center in Portland, another agency trying to help coordinate river management. It represents seven state and federal fishery agencies and thirteen Indian tribes, and its job is to demand adequate water flows in the river from the Bonneville Power Administration, the Army Corps of Engineers, the Bureau of Reclamation, and the utilities. This puts Dehart, a biologist, on an inevitable collision course with other powerful river interests, and her implacable insistence on the need of salmon for water makes her controversial. One scientist called her the "Ice Queen of the Columbia."

Of course the various sides are at war, and *of course* she is controversial, she reflected. "The mission is difficult. Anadromous fish and maximum revenue don't easily coincide." The promise when the dams were built was that hatcheries would make up the damage, that we could dam the Columbia and only gain, not lose. It was a lie, she said. "It's not true you can have everything. You have to give some things up." Rate payers already spend about 4 percent of their electric bill on fish programs—one to two dollars per person per month for a typical household—and might have to spend a percent or two or three more if biologists are heeded.

"What does society want to do here?" Dehart shrugged. "We're not going to freeze in the dark if we sustain the salmon runs, but we're not going to get back to historic levels of salmon production, either. It all boils down to money."

Dan Huppert, a marine economist, said the cost to help salmon is insignificant in a regional economy of $189 billion. "There are a lot of games being played," he said. "Every interest group has an incentive to overestimate the costs to it."

Still, perhaps salmon enthusiasts are living in the past. "We gave up the river to get a nonpolluting, renewable energy source," argued Al Giorgi, a fish consultant employed by the utilities.

It's not too late, countered Dehart. She, and Chaney, and Shiewe, and many others want to keep trying things: to draw down water, to raise Eve's offspring, to see what works. The new name for this kind of experimental action is "adaptive management." Kai Lee, a former Power Planning Council member who now teaches at Massachusetts's Williams College, has written a book suggesting the analogy of a compass and gyroscope. Science is the compass, setting the necessary biological and technological direction, he said. Politics is the gyroscope, keeping biological zeal in balance. Adaptive management is a way to get beyond dogma and opposing ideals, to experiment systematically and find something that works.

No one will ever again walk the Columbia River on the backs of migrating salmon, Dehart conceded. "We're just in a situation where they've got everything," she said of the hydroelectric engineers, "and we're trying to get some of it back."

15

The Poisoned River

Reactor and processing complex, Hanford Nuclear Reservation.
(Washington State Historical Museum)

In 1992 the Columbia was listed by the environmental group
American Rivers as the most endangered river system in the nation. The intention of the listing was to call attention to the environmental consequences of the river's ambitious damming more
than contamination of its water. Most of the Columbia's course is
through lightly inhabited areas and its huge volume dilutes any
wastes. Accordingly, judging the river's level of pollution is difficult. The Columbia is not a muddy river like the Mississippi or
Colorado, nor a bearer of concentrated industrial pollution such
as the Cuyahoga River near Cleveland, which once literally
caught fire. People swim it, fish it, and use it for drinking water,
after filtering and treatment. Its flow is so large, averaging 150 billion gallons a day, that the Columbia itself has traditionally been
of less environmental concern than its tributaries.

Yet environmentalists have counted forty-four major industrial polluters in the river's basin such as pulp mills, canneries, and smelters. There are forty-three federal Superfund sites outside the heavily contaminated Hanford nuclear reservation, places with such serious toxic pollution that they require a federally supervised cleanup. The upper Clark Fork flood plain around Butte, Montana, which is part of the basin, is the nation's largest Superfund site: a one-hundred-mile corridor of toxic mine tailings that leach into the water. The Hanford nuclear reservation contains another fourteen hundred separately identified polluted sites. Basin fish have periodically exhibited elevated levels of dioxin, mercury, furans, and radioactivity. The Columbia Basin's population has climbed two and a half times since 1933, and the basin's cities and towns use the Columbia and its tributaries to carry off their sewage, sometimes with only partial treatment and occasionally not even that. Portland has sewer pipes connected to storm sewers that, during rainstorms, flush seven billion gallons of raw sewage a year into the Willamette and Columbia.

Putting all this into perspective is not easy, particularly since this kind of pollution has been the status quo for a hundred years and only in the last generation has begun to be cleaned. Some understanding of the river quality that has been lost can be found near tributary headwaters. The Middle Fork of the Salmon River, for example, is like a sheet of molten glass, the water so brilliantly clear that the granite boulders below seem to glow with green and yellow fire. The transparency dims as the Middle Fork falls to the main stem, which is nearly opaque. The sediment and nutrient and chemical load grows when joined by the Snake, and gets heavier still after the junction with the Columbia. There is nothing new in this. Woody Guthrie's wild and wasted stream has long been used as a convenient sewer.

Cannery owner Francis Seufert recalled the prevailing attitude earlier in this century: "Garbage was always a problem around the cannery and the mess house. Seufert's Cannery [at The Dalles] sat on the edge of Fifteenmile Creek, about a quarter of a mile from where it emptied into the Columbia River. . . . All garbage from the mess house was tossed over the fence into the creek. This included all dented cans, wooden boxes, paper boxes, buckets, odds and ends of all kinds that would accumulate around a salmon cannery. If anyone asked what to do with any kind of debris, he was told to just throw it into the creek. Twice a year the creek in flood or high water from the Columbia would sweep away all the debris. . . ."

The folk belief of early pioneers was that rivers naturally cleaned themselves within seven miles of any dumping. The belief was wrong. By 1942 the National Resources Planning Board was already warning that "the pollution of waters in a number of areas of the Pacific Northwest [is] a growing menace. . . . Quite generally, the cities and industrial plants discharge raw sewage into streams."

Logging was relatively small and localized in the Columbia Basin until 1894, when the new railroads cut shipping rates to spur business. By 1909 there were three hundred lumber mills in the mountains that fringe the Columbia Plateau and logging volumes in northern Idaho shot up fourteen times. The cutting was so severe it pushed back the boundary of the Rocky Mountain foothill trees that reached into the Palouse country some ten to twelve miles. Cigar-shaped bundles of logs a thousand feet long, fifty feet wide, and thirty feet deep would be chained together on the lower river, containing up to six million board feet of timber. These would be towed into the Pacific Ocean toward mills near San Francisco.

The cut-over lands bled sediment that clogged salmon spawning beds. A third of the Forest Service's three hundred and forty thousand miles of logging road are in the Pacific Northwest, and these dirt sidecuts on steep, easily eroded hillsides dribble dirt into the region's streams. Clearcuts turned the Northwest from vegetated sponge to picked-over hillsides where snow and rain slipped off the land like water down a cookie sheet. Forests that had shaded snow and stored water were decimated. The streams they fed began to dry up in the summer.

Placer mining, in which streambeds are torn up to get at gold by washing gravel, also contributed to the decline in water quality. Idaho's Blackbird Mine dumped so many heavy metals into Panther Creek that salmon and steelhead runs had been destroyed by 1970.

The plowing of the Columbia's grass and sage plateau also released erosion, fertilizers, and pesticides. Each spring, Palouse Falls in southern Washington turns from white to brown as snowmelt washes eroded topsoil off surrounding farms. Until soil conservation practices were instituted in the 1960s to bring the loss under some control, the equivalent of a hundred-and-sixty-acre farm with topsoil eighty feet deep was being swept over the falls every year. The basin's rivers still carry an estimated load of 170,000 tons of eroded dirt annually.

Such damage accumulates. In 1990, biologists revisited three hundred miles of streams in the Columbia Basin first surveyed between 1936 and 1942. They found that half to three-quarters of the pools used by fish had disappeared because they were plugged with eroded sediment. In Idaho, 57 percent of a surveyed sixteen thousand miles of streams were affected by erosion caused by human activity, four-fifths of that mileage displaying intermediate to high levels of sediment. The erosion problem is worsened by grazing livestock that strip protective vegetation from stream banks, crumble the dirt into rivers, and defecate in the water. Fish production in ungrazed streams is 2.4 to five times greater than where cattle and sheep live, biologists have discovered.

The Columbia's tributaries are frequently in sad shape. The South Fork of the Salmon supports only a quarter of the fish it could if cleaned of logging sediment. Sixty percent of the Grande Ronde River, or three hundred and seventy-nine miles, has been judged by biologists to have degraded habitat because of farming, logging, or grazing. The Tucannon was shortened as much as 20 percent and lined with levees, destroying salmon habitat. The Wallowa is listed by the Environmental Protection Agency as "severely polluted." The John Day suffers from high temperatures and poor water quality. Release and storage of water for irrigation causes flows in the Cle Elum, Yakima, and Tieton rivers to fluctuate as much as 300 percent in a twenty-four-hour period. Yakima River temperatures at Prosser occasionally reach eighty degrees, lethal to any migrating salmon.

Tributary streams are sometimes sucked dry. The Umatilla, Yakima, and Walla Walla have all periodically run out of water because of irrigation diversions. So much irrigation water is taken from the Snake River that it nearly goes dry below Milner Dam, just east of Twin Falls.

Plowing and grazing has also eliminated 94 percent of the sage steppe desert on the Columbia Plateau that is home to a number of species moving onto the endangered list, including the desert night snake, pygmy rabbit, sharp-tailed grouse, and numerous songbirds. Undisturbed sage steppe is rarer east of the Cascade Mountains than old-growth forest west of them.

Because the river is dammed, it allows contaminants to accumulate in reservoir mud where they are absorbed into the food chain. Resident fish in both Lake Roosevelt behind Grand Coulee and below Bonneville Dam have shown toxic contamination. In Lake Roosevelt heavy metals and dioxins from Canadian industry have been found more than one hundred and fifty miles downstream near the dam itself, and by the early 1980s cadmium levels in Lake Roosevelt fish were the highest of one hundred and twelve samples taken across the nation. The fish had also absorbed lead, zinc, dioxin, furans, mercury, copper, and arsenic.

The Columbia's new stagnant shallows are weedy, the plants consuming dissolved oxygen needed by fish. Cold, dark reservoir depths have an opposite problem. The lack of sunlight halts the growth of bacteria and plankton that form the base of the food chain, starving the depths of nutrients. These changes have shifted the fish population away from salmon and toward hardier species like shad, squawfish, carp, walleye, bass, catfish, and suckers.

A remarkable survivor is the sturgeon. This armor-plated prehistoric fish has reached lengths of eleven feet and weights up to thirteen hundred pounds; it can live more than a century. Unlike anadromous salmon, sturgeon reside in the Columbia full-time. The commercial fishery of white sturgeon in the river peaked at six million pounds in 1892 and then collapsed from overfishing. When catch-size limits were finally imposed in 1950 to protect large, sexually mature fish, the sturgeon slowly began recovering. There are an estimated 800,000 to 1 million in the Columbia Basin today, but their habitat has been segmented by dams, and in some tributary waters such as the Kootenay the species is in danger of extinction. Some of the sturgeon that persist have lived in the river long enough to retain a memory of the Columbia before the dams. What must the sturgeon have thought when the current finally stilled, the river began to deepen, and they prowled upstream and down to find themselves boxed by walls of concrete, their range now limited to a reservoir pool?

The new lakes the dams have created are pretty, but they have not replaced the complex riparian zone that a meandering, seasonally flooding river creates. Ninety percent of the basin's animals depend on streamside areas for some part of their life cycle and a thousand square miles of riparian habitat has been lost. As a result, Washington's Department of Fish and Wildlife has estimated, 120,000 game birds dependent on that landscape were reduced to two thousand, thirteen thousand fur-bearing mammals were reduced to five hundred, and ninety-five thousand wintering songbirds were reduced to three thousand. "River basins were also the natural migratory corridors for many land animals," said Peter Paquet of the Northwest Power Planning Council. "With the dams in place, we've blocked those corridors." (American dam reservoirs as a whole have flooded an area of land about equal to the size of Vermont and New Hampshire.)

Besides directly altering the river, humans have accumulated growing piles of waste on the shorelands around it. The Idaho National Engineering Laboratory has injected 16 billion gallons of radioactive waste into the Snake River aquifer. An army nerve gas depot near Umatilla, Oregon, just a few miles from the river, has dotted nineteen thousand acres with nine hundred concrete "igloo" bunkers to hold ammunition and poison gas. The ammunition has been removed and the site is being closed down, but cleaning and destruction of old ammunition has produced a three-hundred-acre plume of contaminated groundwater that has been placed on the Superfund list.

The region's hazardous waste landfill for toxic chemicals is near the Columbia at Arlington, Oregon. A bombing range is at nearby Boardman. The army's Yakima Firing Center, where troop maneuvers are held, also borders the Columbia. Large cities such as Seattle and Portland have begun using dry Columbia Basin desert sites as landfills for their garbage, shipping it east by truck and train.

None of this is under the supervision of any single agency. Pollution-control duties are split between the federal Environmental Protection Agency and the ecology departments of the various states, plus their Canadian counterparts in British Columbia. Habitat protection is the responsibility of a host of agencies, including the Forest Service and Bureau of Land Management. No single entity "owns" the Columbia. The states have granted individual water rights, the federal government has asserted authority over power dam sites and navigation, and the tribes have treaty fishing rights. Nobody is in charge of maintaining the environmental health of the river, or of even measuring it. Ask government how polluted the Columbia is and the answer is, "We don't really know."

• • •

In 1850 a writer surveying the Hudson River reportedly wrote, "It would outrage man's sense of justice if that broad stream were to roll down to the ocean in mere idle majesty and beauty."

Rivers were to be used, and if that meant some pollution, so be it. The *Trail Creek News* summed up attitudes prevailing in 1900 when it commented on concerns about fumes emanating from the new smelter built on the Columbia at Trail, British Columbia. "There are those who claim that smelter smoke is injurious to health," the paper noted, "but when it first rolls forth from the lofty chimneys of the Trail Smelter, heralding the advancement of progress of the West Kootenay District and signifying the doubling of the present working forces of the mines . . . every man will take his hat off to greet the smoke which will come to them as balm to the nostrils of the progressive North American."

The resulting pall got so bad that the trees in the Trail Valley were largely dead by the 1920s. "There were no grass or trees here when I was growing up," recalled Bob Fletcher, a seventy-one-year-old retiree who gives tours of the smelter. Trail had become a cockpit of acid rain and sulfuric soil.

Trail today is a tidy Canadian town just north of the international border overshadowed by the biggest smelter in Canada: a hulking, soot-stained fortress of sheds and pipes and smokestacks that consumes more electricity than a city of 250,000 people and from which discharge pipes run down a steep bank to the Columbia like the legs of a spider. Periodically the river burps as fresh waste water from an underwater outlet causes its surface to bounce with an eruption.

The smelter still processes more than 700,000 tons of concentrated ore per year, producing 300,000 tons of zinc. By-products include 2.5 tons of gold every twenty hours. To produce such volumes the plant uses and discharges 63 million gallons of river water every day, and despite new controls some waste still goes into the rushing river. As of 1993 the smelter released about five thousand pounds of phosphate, three thousand pounds of ammonia, forty-five hundred pounds of fluoride, seven pounds of lead, two pounds of zinc, fifteen pounds of cadmium, three pounds of arsenic, and four pounds of mercury into the Columbia every day. The smelter's environmental record is also periodically marred by accidental acid spills into the river. This is actually an improvement, however: what used to be thirteen piped outfalls into the river has been reduced to five, and the daily three hundred and fifty tons of sulfur stack smoke that used to fog the air have been cut to twenty.

At the smelter's southern end a long pipe injects a slurry of water and black sand into the river, the sand being the slag from lead, zinc, and silver smelting. Each day four hundred tons of this pours into the Columbia. Cominco, the smelter owner, used to assume that the heavy metals in the slag were bound tightly to the grit and could not affect the river's biology. The assumption was false. The sand has drifted more than fifty miles south to Kettle Falls and is the source of much of the heavy metal pollution of Lake Roosevelt fish.

Cominco has announced that river dumping will stop by December of 1996, with the slag moved to a land disposal site instead. These plans, however, hinge on remodeling of the existing lead smelter. A first attempt in 1989 to convert to an oxygen smelting technology to reduce pollution didn't work well, and the company is testing an alternative. Construction is also tied to the company's quest for a Canadian tax break, and when I talked to the company's manager of environmental health, Graham Kenyon, the issue was still undecided. It is Kenyon's job to assure nearby communities that the smelter's emissions do not represent a health threat, and the lively jousting that ensues has given him a certain wry sense of humor. The smelter's four-hundred-and-eight-foot stack and its smaller chimneys were emitting a thin brown vapor the day I visited. When I asked him what it was, his first reply was "River fog." For the past three years he has kept goldfish in a tank with a floor of Cominco's slag to demonstrate its harmlessness. Goldfish, however, are carp, far less sensitive to pollutants than trout or salmon.

The smelter first attacked its smoke problem sixty years ago by converting sulfur dioxide gas to sulfuric acid in order to make fertilizer. Steady process has been made since then, yet lead, zinc, mercury, arsenic, and fluoride are emitted at the rate of about forty-four hundred pounds per day. Almost a century of heavy air pollution has so contaminated the surrounding soil that despite a vigorous reforestation campaign that has planted 2 million trees, the surrounding anemic hills are still scrubby.

The Trail Smelter is far from the only industrial polluter on the Columbia River. The Canadian pulp mill at Castlegar has released large volumes of dioxins and furans that accumulated in fish tissues. Its flyash, lime dust, and fiber formed a mat on the river bottom below the mill. Both problems have been addressed by a recent conversion of the plant to a more modern process, and measured chemical contamination levels in whitefish have begun to drop. American aluminum smelters and pulp mills dot the river at Wenatchee, the Tri-Cities, The Dalles, Troutdale, Camas, Vancouver, St. Helens, Wauna, and Longview. Chemical plants are located in Portland, St. Helens, and Kalama. Eight seafood processors discharge large amounts of waste at Astoria. Other pulp, lumber, and aluminum plants are located on such tributaries as the Willamette, Snake, Clark Fork, Kootenay, and Spokane rivers.

Concern for this degradation is, of course, a postindustrial phenomenon. There is a museum and mine tour at British Columbia's Rossland that gives some sense of the grim danger and monotony the Industrial Revolution first entailed: the dark, wet, clammy mines lit only by dim candles and oil lanterns; the cave-ins; the gas explosions; the simple slips and falls. In the Trail Smelter, recalled Fletcher, lung damage for zinc plant workers was an accepted part of the job. Until the new plant was built the old was filled with a fog of acid from the process used to leach mineral from ore, acid that pricked and burned to exact a death penalty from men wresting wealth from the earth. Few lived long after retirement. "If you stepped into the old plant," Fletcher recalled, "you'd sneeze your head off and think you'd been bitten by a thousand mosquitoes." These kinds of immediate health hazards swamped concern about subtle environmental effects.

Humans did not set out to dirty the Columbia. Rather, it seemed so big as to be immune from degradation, and competitive pressures resulted in inadequate thought about consequences.

At the nuclear complex at Hanford, a Westinghouse spokesman named George Carpenter tried to explain the chain of events that led to the radioactive fouling of billions of gallons of groundwater and the atmospheric emission of radioactivity over an area of the Columbia Basin that stretched to Spokane, one hundred and fifty miles away. "Everything seemed to make sense at the time," he said, "and so it was done."

The concrete block building that houses the abandoned core of the world's first large-scale nuclear reactor has the architectural drabness of a packing warehouse or steam plant. Clearly designed from the inside out and erected hurriedly, B Reactor looks from a distance like a haphazard cluster of children's gray building blocks with an industrial smokestack lending an exclamation point like an upright Lincoln Log. None of it gives any clue to what is within. Flat-roofed, windowless, and dreary, the building has nonetheless been declared a historic landmark. Here is where the plutonium fuel for the first atomic bomb test in New Mexico was produced, as well as the fuel for the weapon that destroyed Nagasaki. The Hiroshima bomb was fueled with uranium 235 separated from U 238 at Oak Ridge, Tennessee. When the federal government launched the Manhattan Project it did not know which fuel manufacturing method would work, so it started them simultaneously. Of course, both did.

B Reactor was deliberately built in what was considered the middle of nowhere in 1943: the sagebrush desert near the Columbia River community of Hanford, Washington. The town was named for Tacoma judge Cornelius Hanford, who had headed a consortium of investors called the Hanford Irrigation and Power Company that had platted the town in 1905. The first safety principle of the government's nuclear program was simple: make sure the facilities were remote enough that if anything went wrong, a minimum number of people would be killed. Government engineers deliberately looked for an empty "hazardous manufacturing area" of at least twelve by sixteen miles for plutonium production. The "gawd-awful" waste in the rain shadow of the Cascade Mountains fit that bill. Army lieutenant Thomas Symons visited the desert around Hanford and concluded, "It is a desolation where even the most hopeful can find nothing in its future prospects to cheer."

The design of the reactor was simple, based on the principle that if you dump enough enriched uranium into a big-enough pile, its decaying particles will collide with other atoms, start additional decay, and initiate a chain reaction. It consisted of a cube of graphite thirty-six feet square and twenty-eight feet thick, bored with two thousand and four horizontal holes several inches in diameter. Long aluminum tubes holding rods of enriched uranium were pushed into the graphite until enough were in place to start the reaction. No ignition switch was required, only water: forty-eight thousand gallons per minute to keep the temperatures of the pile manageable as plutonium slowly accumulated. Accordingly, the second big advantage of the Hanford site was the Columbia River, which flowed half a mile from B Reactor. Pipes led river water through several settling and purification tanks to the reactor, where it passed through each of the fuel rod holes and emerged at nearly the boiling point, draining away to cool briefly before being dumped back into the Columbia River. This "single pass" design—flawed because it allowed radioactive leakage to leave the reactor—would not be phased out until 1971.

Modern nuclear power plants encase their reactor with a steel and concrete containment vessel. The first eight Hanford defense reactors did not have such a safeguard to contain leaks or accidents. Nor did they bother with the complex welter of pipes and safety systems now required in commercial power plants. Had a catastrophic accident occurred there was little to prevent it from contaminating the outside environment. When B Reactor was designed, the full effects of radiation, fallout, and the difficulty of containing radioactive pollution were poorly understood.

"You have to appreciate the drama of the first time they did it," said Dennis DeFord, a historian at Westinghouse who showed me the reactor and control room. America was leaping in one step from the experimental reactor built under the stadium at the University of Chicago that generated a few thousand watts to a huge production reactor producing 250 million watts of energy. On paper it worked, but would it in practice? There were nine additional control rods of boron inserted horizontally in the graphite as the uranium was being loaded that prevented the reactor from starting up prematurely. Boron absorbs neutrons. When the control rods were pulled away the chain reaction would start. Or so scientists hoped.

As the rods were withdrawn in September 1944, the reaction indeed started as anticipated. Power climbed smoothly. The spirits of the anxious physicists rose with it. Then, a few hours later, the pile died. Enrico Fermi studied the dials in the control room. "I believe the bitch is having puppies," he muttered. He retreated to his glass-walled office. Bill McCue was a Du Pont chemical engineer who was supervising the reactor operators that day. His men watched the famous physicist talk animatedly to other project administrators behind the glass wall. When the session broke up, McCue asked what they had decided. "They were just making up a pool on when the reactor would come back to life," he was told. Indeed, after a while the reaction started again. Then died again.

Fermi worked his slide rule, talked to other administrators, conferred with colleagues in Chicago. They decided the reaction was producing a by-product isotope called xenon 135 that, like boron, was absorbing too many neutrons and shutting the reactor off. As the reactor died xenon 135 production died with it, and the isotope rapidly decayed away to the point where the chain reaction could begin again. As power built, so did the xenon isotope, leading to an endless cycle that produced the baffling rises and falls in reactor activity. If more fuel could be added, physicists calculated, the xenon 135 could be swamped by the chain reaction and overcome.

Two things were needed to make that possible. The reactor had to have room for extra fuel rods. Du Pont engineers, over the objection of the government and physicists seeking to hold down costs, had insisted on adding more slots than theory called for, providing two thousand instead of fifteen hundred. That margin proved sufficient to overwhelm the xenon 135. The other requirement was to have a flexible cooling system to handle the extra heat. "The river was key," DeFord said. It supplied the electricity to build Hanford and the coolant to keep the entire affair from melting into the earth.

Everything was designed for speed and simplicity. The control room, with its pale linoleum and green-gray metal panels, looks much less complex than a dam powerhouse control room today. The most technologically impressive wall is a panel of gauges measuring the water temperature and pressure from each coolant tube, giving scientists a clue to the heat of the reaction and thus its power. A sign above the panel calmly advises "Caution: Bumping Panel May Cause Scram," or emergency shutdown. Things were simpler then.

For more than four decades after the successful B Reactor start, Hanford supplied fuel for America's nuclear arsenal. As the nuclear stockpile accumulated to a level adequate to destroy the world many times over, however, production slowly began to wind down. By 1971 all but one defense reactor at Hanford had closed. The newer N Reactor, environmentally superior to the others because it recycled its cooling water instead of dumping it directly into the Columbia—but still, like the Soviet Union's Chernobyl, without a safety containment dome—operated until 1987. Then it was over. The five-hundred-and-sixty-square-mile reservation became a relic of the Cold War, and Carpenter compared its resulting radioactive and chemical mess to the wreckage of a "battlefield."

There are nearly fourteen hundred separate dumps sites, spill sites, tanks, and buildings to be mopped at Hanford, the remnant of a frantic weapons-building process that consumed more than 100,000 metric tons of uranium and released 467 million curies of radiation into the environment. It will take fifty years and more than a hundred billion dollars to clean up.

Accounts of the early atomic bomb program typically concentrate on the theorists working out the mechanics in New Mexico, and of course their discoveries were critical to making the weapon work. In terms of people and dollars, however, the biggest task was not assembling the bomb but producing fuel for it, since the raw material did not exist in nature. Plutonium was the most costly substance that had ever been created. Because of the electricity and water required, the two sites chosen to process uranium were located at the two dam-building showcases of the New Deal: Tennessee and its TVA, and Washington State and the Columbia River. Plutonium production was regarded as the most potentially radioactive and hazardous, so by December 1942 officials had decided to locate that process in the sparsely populated West.

Two thousand residents of the small farming communities of Hanford and White Bluffs were summarily ordered to move without being told why. Nearly seven thousand acres of farmland were taken out of production, the apple orchards chopped down. Then recruited workers began arriving in a flood until they reached fifty-one thousand at the peak. Starting with bare desert at the beginning of 1943, more than five hundred buildings were erected, one hundred and fifty-eight miles of railroad laid, three hundred and eighty-six miles of road put in, and 780,000 cubic yards of concrete poured in a year and a half. Employees endured isolation, secrecy, and bleak surroundings. Wind storms kicked up what workers dubbed "termination dust" because each sand blizzard convinced another batch of workers to "terminate" and move away. Yet just two years and six months after the site was picked, the first atomic bomb was detonated.

Most had no idea what they were working on. Rumor had it that Hanford was making high-powered airplane fuel, chemical or biological weapons, or, as a joke, fifth-term buttons for Roosevelt. When the war ended with Hiroshima and Nagasaki, the resulting attitude of the assembled workers was neatly summarized by the headline of the Richland newspaper: "Peace! Our Bomb Clinched It." The havoc was judged to have saved lives by avoiding an invasion of Japan. The War Department issued mushroom cloud pins to all Manhattan Project employees and at the end of 1945 the Associated Press ranked the bomb ahead of the German and Japanese surrenders as the year's most important story.

The resulting environmental effects were imperfectly understood and, worse, kept secret, preventing any kind of outside scrutiny that might have improved pollution control. "They [nuclear engineers] deemed themselves wise enough to determine what their fellow citizens must bear," summed up Bart Hocke of Lawrence Livermore Laboratories at a conference on "The Atomic West." Officials initially thought the health hazard from fallout was small and that to talk publicly about it would needlessly alarm people.

General Leslie Groves, the director of the bomb project, justified: "Not until later would it be recognized that chances would have to be taken that in more normal times would be considered reckless in the extreme . . . while normally haste makes waste, in this case haste was essential." While that may have been true in the case of a world war, subsequent pollution under the pressure of the Cold War is less excusable. To its credit Hanford pioneered some environmental monitoring techniques to track its pollutants. To its discredit much of this information remained secret, Hanford's engineers too often sacrificing the environment to production when the two came in conflict.

Problems began almost immediately. There were three basic production steps at Hanford, and all three released pollutants. First, raw uranium had to be encased in fuel rods. Second, the fuel rods were inserted into a reactor, where the bombardment of particles produced about a tenth of a gram of plutonium per ton of inserted uranium. After a period of days the irradiated rods would be pushed out the back of the reactor into a pool of water to cool. That led to the third stage. The rods were taken to another area when acid was used to break down the uranium and, through a complex series of chemical steps, isolate usable plutonium. Initially, resulting fumes were vented to the air in plumes that deposited harmful isotopes of iodine across much of eastern Washington and northeastern Oregon. There it was taken up in the food chain, particularly in dairy milk consumed by children. A foolish 1949 experiment called the "Green Run"—apparently designed to test radiation detection methods that could be used over Russia to gauge its plutonium production—released eight thousand curies of iodine 131 in two days. Kennewick got a thousand times the government's allowable limit of radiation, and Walla Walla got one hundred times. Scientists subsequently calculated that children northeast of Hanford had thyroid gland exposures to radioactivity several thousand times higher than normal background levels. A study to determine if disease resulted is expected to be completed in 1996.

Instead of shrinking after World War II, Hanford began expanding rapidly as the Cold War got under way. Six more plutonium production reactors were built and in the 1970s a commercial nuclear power reactor was added, another started but mothballed, and smaller research reactors constructed. Hanford also became a convenient burial ground for low-level nuclear waste from around the nation. By the mid-1980s, two-thirds of the high-level and half the low-level radioactive garbage in America was stored there.

The Columbia was directly polluted. Engineers had hit upon the idea of encasing the uranium reactor fuel with aluminum cladding, but under the heat and stress of production some of the casings broke, releasing radioactive uranium that contaminated the Columbia's cooling water. As radioactivity entered the Columbia it was concentrated in sediments, in plants and creatures that lived in such sediment, and in the fish that fed on them. As early as 1947, fish in the Columbia River were showing radioactive concentrations averaging 100,000 times the normal amount as far as twenty miles downriver. By 1955 the reactors were being pushed beyond their initial design limits because of Cold War pressures. B Reactor was pushed from its design capacity of two hundred and fifty megawatts to two thousand megawatts of power in a desperate drive to shorten the time needed to generate plutonium. This put new heat and stress on the fuel rods and led to more breaks and leakages. By 1960 the Columbia was receiving an average of 14,500 curies of radioactivity per day, or more than went into the air in the notorious Green Run.

The 1971 closure of the first eight primitive reactors halted most of this pollution, but small amounts of radioactivity continue to leak into the river from polluted groundwater. Mulberry trees at a spring near N Reactor have shown elevated levels of radioactivity in their berries, leading enterprising environmentalists to make a batch of mildly radioactive mulberry jam. It was sent to Washington's governor to emphasize the need for cleanup.

The reactors were not even the major pollution problem. Far worse was the soupy mix of chemical acids and radioactive waste produced while extracting plutonium in the fuel rods, a devil's stew that was put into steel tanks. Because these were initially considered temporary, they were built with only one shell. An estimated sixty-eight of the tanks subsequently leaked 121 million gallons of high-level liquid nuclear waste into the soil. Nor was any provision made for easily emptying the brew of radioactive sludge that remained in the older tanks, a necessary first step that baffled engineers as the cleanup got under way. By the 1990s its consistency ranged from peanut butter to concrete-hard salt cake so radioactive it could only be probed by radiation-hardened robots.

While the most concentrated and dangerous radioactive waste could be contained in tanks, the chemical processes themselves produced 440 billion gallons of additional contaminated water, a volume big enough to fill Seattle's domed stadium nine hundred times or drown Manhattan Island in a lake forty feet deep. Rather than try to build enough storage tanks to contain such a flood, it was simply poured into the desert. As a result, an estimated one hundred and twenty square miles of groundwater have been contaminated not just with radioactivity but with ninety-three thousand metric tons of chemicals carried by waste water into the ground.

Human error compounded questionable management decisions. Sand was used to temporarily trap some of the radioactive isotopes in desert soil where they could decay in place, and just two spilling basins that received waste water accumulated an astonishing four tons of uranium by-products this way. Unfortunately, the turn of a wrong valve released a torrent of acid cleaner, stripping the plutonium from the soil and carrying it down toward groundwater, producing a five-square-mile underground plume expected to reach the Columbia about the year 2185 unless halted.

Hanford still accepts "low-level" nuclear waste from other states such as contaminated machinery, clothing, tools, or medical waste. This is sealed in drums or boxes and buried in quarter-mile long trenches in the desert. The nuclear reservation is also the destination for nuclear reactors cut from retired nuclear submarines. Barged up the Columbia, they sit in open pits.

Hanford was shrouded in secrecy until 1986, when the Department of Energy released nineteen thousand pages of history and documentation that spelled out what had occurred. Suddenly the Pacific Northwest realized that it was host to the most polluted site in the Western world. In 1990 the state of Washington, the Environmental Protection Agency, and the Department of Energy entered into agreement for the most complex, costly, and ambitious cleanup program on the planet.

Unfortunately, there was considerable confusion about how to proceed. Extracting polluted groundwater is difficult, and pumping or injecting exercises that might help correct one spill can prompt another to move. Initial progress has been slow, as agencies determine which cleanup method will work best. Public interest groups forced the redesign of plants created to concentrate radioactive waste into glass that can be moved to a permanent depository. Contaminated reactors next to the river may be trucked uphill by giant tractor-trailers for encasement in concrete and final burial. While that will prevent the faint possibility of the reactor sites being flooded by a Columbia dam breakage upstream, many Hanford workers such as Dennis DeFord think such removal is unnecessary. He prefers to encase the radioactive cores in concrete where they are and then mound basalt rubble over the reactor buildings in a gigantic cone. It would create a valley of basalt pyramids along the mid-Columbia, a bizarre monument to the arms race and the folly of man.

Intriguingly, Hanford is more than just a polluted eyesore. The irony is that this poisoned reservation borders the most ecologically important stretch of the Columbia above Bonneville Dam. For fifty-one miles below Priest Rapids Dam the river flows quietly in its natural state past the abandoned reactors, undammed and largely undeveloped. Ben Franklin Dam was proposed for this stretch of the river but was never built because its

reservoir would have backed up water over the contaminated reactors.

Accordingly, what humans have made uninhabitable for
themselves has inadvertently turned into a wildlife refuge with
forty-eight rare and threatened species. The Hanford Reach is the
most productive salmon spawning area left on the Columbia.
Some 60 percent of the salmon that spawn naturally above Mc-
Nary Dam do so around the nuclear reservation. There are five
hundred deer on the reservation, white pelicans nest along the
river, and the delicate bands of mauve and pink at White Bluffs
are dotted with swallow nests, the birds thriving despite their occasional use of radioactive mud for construction. The southwest
corner of the reservation is an area of one hundred and twenty
square miles—about the same size as the underground contaminated plumes—and has been set aside as an Arid Lands Ecology
Reserve. It supports an unusual herd of three hundred elk that
live on the desert landscape. Across the river is a U.S. Fish and
Wildlife Refuge and a Washington State Wildlife Refuge, which
occupy another one hundred and thirty-four square miles. Bald
eagles congregate in summer and fall to eat the carcasses of the
spawning salmon, and coyotes prowl the bank. By the time of this
book's publication, both of these areas should have been released
from the reservation. One of the claimants for the returned land
will likely be Native Americans.

Upriver from the nuclear boundary and adjacent to Priest Rapids
Dam live a band of Native Americans who never signed a treaty,
were never granted lands, and were never given compensation
for being forced to abandon their traditional fishing sites at Hanford in 1944. These are the Wanapum, or "River People," who
numbered about twenty-four hundred in one hundred and
twenty lodges when Lewis and Clark passed by the southern
edge of their territory. The Wanapum called the whites the Up-
such, or the Greedy Ones.

When the nuclear engineers came to build the bomb, most of
the Wanapum moved upriver to Priest Rapids, where they were
allowed to settle in three abandoned houses that had been built
for the operators of the Columbia's first hydroelectric plant, the
shoreside generator constructed without a dam in 1907.
The refuge was only temporary. In 1953 dam engineers came to

the Wanapums' new village and explained that their new fishing site would be drowned by Priest Rapids Dam. The Grant County Public Utility District gave the Indians $26,000 and promised to provide housing and jobs in return for Native American agreement not to oppose construction. Wanapum Dam was already going up and the Indians bowed to the inevitable. Eventually, in 1973, the utility built the Wanapums new homes on a sagebrush bench just below the face of Priest Rapids Dam. Some of its residents work in the powerhouse or at the utility headquarters.

This enlistment of the Indians in Columbia River progress brought a mixed response of toleration and resignation by the tribe. In 1955 tribal leader Johnny Buck—or Puck-Hyah-Toot, nephew of the prophet Smohalla—spoke through an interpreter at the site dedication of the dam to be named for his tribe.

"You and I know that the white race, when they first came, looked upon the Indians as friends," the aging chief said. "We remember the first who came to the Northwest, where they met the Indians and found them friendly, and the Indians were respected. From White Bluffs to where the dam will be built, the soldiers respected those Indians and did them no harm. The dealings were attended by friendliness. We have carried on tradition and live peacefully without being bothered, or bothering, anyone.

"Going back, before the earth was born," Puck continued, "the Mighty Creator made this world. That part where we lived the Creator made. He made the earth. He spread upon the earth things for the Indian people so they could live. He gave them roots and berries. Salmon he put in their streams and he caused wild fowl and wild animals to come upon the land. These were the foods the Indian has enjoyed, the good food the Creator has given. When I think of losing these things, I think of losing my life."

The white engineers listened politely as he spoke. "I do not feel that I should get angry or say anything that a dam is to be built," Puck said. "I feel that somehow I and my people will get by as long as we have friends like are here. The Creator predicted and directed that the light shall fall upon the earth and give warming life to everything upon it. The sun will brighten and warm the body of the Indian and will preserve his body. You, and I, get this living, under that light." Then he sat down.

Puck-Hyah-Toot died the following year. Two dams were rising to inundate much of the Wanapum's traditional Columbia, and eight nuclear reactors steamed and discharged radioactive water into the rest. Smohalla had been too optimistic. The white man had wanted the desert after all. The presence of the Wanapums did not slow construction except for one brief instant.

As Puck's funeral procession passed Priest Rapids Dam on its way to a burial point four miles upriver, construction work halted for four hours as a gesture of respect, allowing the ceremony to take place with only the sound of the wind and the river. Then the hammering began again.

16

Cloudville

Wanapum Indian village at Priest Rapids, above the Hanford Nuclear Reservation. *(Washington State Historical Society)*

Cook's Landing is a four-acre peninsula of rock and fir on the Washington shore of the Columbia River, reached via a short gravel road that bumps over railroad tracks and runs down to Bonneville pool. The landing is cupped in the mountains of the Columbia Gorge and thus is sometimes wet, frequently cloudy, and always windswept. Knobby and isolated, it seems the unlikely object of a half century of legal and physical argument. There simply isn't much there: derelict automobiles rusting in the brambles, drying fishing nets, salmon smoking sheds. Up to half a dozen families have lived at Cook's at one time or another in a collection of scrap-wood shacks. The largest and most prominent of these is a dirt-floored home on the southwest shore, built with the simple gable shape of a traditional longhouse. This shelter was cobbled together from drift lumber fished out of the river, unpainted plywood, plastic tarps, carpet remnants, and bare electric bulbs. A blanket serves as a front door; inside I once found

David Sohappy's grandchildren playing Nintendo games on a television set. Winter winds whistled through cracks in the patchwork walls while David's wife, Myra, explained why she did not want to move off the river and accept government housing on an alcohol-plagued reservation. "I don't want those HUD homes," she said. "They're ugly. They're paper houses. Like living in a yellow jacket home."

Cook's Landing is the product of a complex, peculiar, and embarrassing history. When Bonneville Dam was nearing completion in 1937 its reservoir began to drown thirty-seven Columbia River fishing and home sites used by Native Americans. The government men advised the Indians living there to write their names on their houses so that the structures could be replaced after the water rose. Steps toward fulfilling that promise took far longer than building Bonneville, however. It was not until 1939 that the Army Corps of Engineers reached agreement with the Yakima, Umatilla, and Warm Spring tribes to replace the lost sites with six new ones, totaling four hundred acres. Only Cook's Landing was set aside before World War II. Not until 1946 was the first money for the rest of the replacement land appropriated by Congress. Five sites were ultimately acquired, the last not purchased until twenty-six years after the reservoir filled. Replacement housing was not built at all. The wording of the fishing site agreement was deliberately vague, and by 1953 the Corps announced that there was no requirement for it to replace any homes and that it had no intention of doing so.

The Native Americans did not take the hint and leave the river, however. They built their own rude structures. Resulting complaints by whites about unsightly hovels and uncollected garbage led to a 1957 regulatory proposal by the Bureau of Indian Affairs to ban any permanent homes, a rule that drew immediate protest from the Indians. Adding insult to injury, the government that year paid the tribes $26.8 million for the loss of Celilo Falls and other fishing sites flooded by The Dalles Dam upriver, or approximately two hundred and fifty times what it had spent on the less famous "in lieu" fishing sites behind Bonneville.

In the ensuing years the Bonneville Indians would fight for the right to live on the reservoir shore, to fish when they pleased, and for decent sanitation facilities. "My grandmother's sister lived in what is now Drano Lake, Little White Salmon River, until it got flooded out in 1938 by Bonneville Dam," David Sohappy would recall later, shortly before his death. "The Corps of Engineers promised the people that lived there the year around that they would replace the homes that were flooded out. To this day, they never did live up to their word."

From the white man's perspective the natives did not fit the engineered river. Their persistent fishing muddled attempts to manage the salmon resource for the commercial interests downstream. The Indians were poor, they were untidy, they were visible, and thus they were an uncomfortable reminder of the river and culture that had been drowned. A generation of struggle broke out to try to evict permanent squatters such as the Sohappys, a campaign broken off only in the early 1990s after public support for it had collapsed. By that time David Sohappy had been imprisoned, his health had been destroyed, and the people of the Pacific Northwest were asking themselves why the region's first inhabitants were its most impoverished group, with the highest Native American death rate in the nation. By that time politicians and federal prosecutors had turned an impoverished Indian fisherman with little formal education into a civil rights martyr, and had transformed an otherwise valueless piece of land on the wrong side of the tracks into a symbol of broken promises.

No one would have been more surprised by this turn of events than Washington territorial governor Isaac Stevens, the ambitious young army officer who had secured Native American surrender of 64 million acres of Pacific Northwest land for just $1.2 million. By 1985, Northwest tribes had sold or otherwise lost two-thirds of the reservation land that Stevens had allowed them to keep, and only one of the reservations that the government created bordered directly on the Columbia, or Nch-I'-Wana, the Big River. Stevens had achieved his bargain, however, by promising in the treaty that the Indians could continue to fish at all "usual and accustomed fishing places . . . in common with the citizens" of the Territory.

So the natives went to the river. Salmon was not just food, it was a sacrament. The river was not a "resource," it was life itself. In the century after the treaties were signed the Indians still fished the rapids and channels, still gathered at Celilo, and still moved to the cycle of the seasons and the salmon runs, marking the annual wheel of time with seasonal celebrations. Using their reservations or their new jobs in cities as a base, they carved out a lifestyle that took a middle ground between their hunter-gatherer past and the school-and-career path of the dominating culture. The Columbia remained the anchor for their self-identity, and when first Kettle Falls and then Celilo Falls were drowned, it was like the cutting of an anchor cable. When The Dalles Dam was proposed in 1947, Chief Tommy Thompson of the Celilo Indians testified against it. "I think I don't know how I would live if you would put up a dam which will flood my fishing places," he said with plaintive bewilderment. "How am I going to make my living afterward? It is the only food I am dependent on for my livelihood, and I am here to protect that."

Thompson was ignored, of course. The dam-building program never missed a beat from concern over Indian fishing rights. On April 20, 1956, fish biologist and author Anthony Netboy attended the last of the First Salmon Rites to be held at Celilo Falls. Tommy Thompson rose to bless the food, Netboy recalled, and "made a speech in his native language that was charged with emotion. Before it was over the vigorous old man was weeping."

Celilo today has been gone nearly four decades yet still reverberates in the heart of every Native American who ever fished or lived by it. "If you are an Indian person and you think, you can still see all the characteristics of that waterfall," I was told by Ted Strong, director of the Columbia River Intertribal Fish Commission. "If you listen, you can still hear its roar. If you inhale, the fragrances of mist and fish and water come back again."

As the dams choked off salmon runs and ocean fishing pressure increased, Native Americans began battling for a share of the runs that struggled up the Columbia. Their traditional fishing sites on rivers meant they were at the end of a gauntlet of fishermen extending out into the Pacific Ocean. Since the tribes fished closest to the spawning grounds, state fishery agencies imposed restrictions that frequently put on natives the burden of letting enough salmon escape. By 1960 their share of the total salmon catch had dwindled to 1 percent and the Indians became engaged in pitched, club-swinging battles with state authorities over access to the region's rivers. In 1968 fourteen members of the Yakima Indian Nation filed suit challenging Oregon's right to regulate their Columbia River fishery. The case was called *Sohappy* v. *Smith.*

• • •

David Sohappy's name is a modern spelling of the Wanapum "Souiehappie," a word roughly translated to something that is put away in a special, hidden place, or something shoved under a shelf. His band had neither signed Stevens's treaties nor fought in any Indian wars. They occupied one of the driest and bleakest regions of the Pacific Northwest, made habitable only by the huge annual fishing runs. The band was called the Sokulks by Lewis and Clark and the Ska-moy-num-acks by Ross, but in subsequent years was more commonly referred to as Wanapum, or River People.

The Wanapums were famous for their prophet Smohalla, who in the late nineteenth century combined native belief and Christianity into a new religion variously referred to as Dreamer, Seven Drums, or Washat. By this time disease and relocations to reservations had reduced the Wanapums to two hundred people, or about 8 percent of their numbers at the time of Lewis and Clark. Urging adherence to traditional ways, Smohalla counseled his followers never to leave the Columbia. He established his own headquarters at a point at the foot of Priest Rapids called P'na, or fish weir. He was a cousin of David Sohappy's great-grandfather.

When army major J. W. MacMurray was sent to investigate Smohalla as a potential troublemaker, he came away impressed. "In person Smohalla is peculiar," he reported. "Short, thickset, bald headed and almost hunch-backed, he is not prepossessing at first sight; but he has an almost Websterian head with deep brow over bright, intelligent eyes. He is a finished orator, his manner mostly of the bland, insinuating, persuasive style; and when aroused he is full of fire. The audience, to the man, seemed spellbound under his magic manner; and it never lost interest for me, though in a language comprehended by few white men and translated to me second or third hand."

Smohalla protested the idea of Indians acquiring private property for settlement, and told a Creation story that David Sohappy would have heard. The first people had wings, Smohalla said, but they tried to divide up the earth and became greedy and jealous. They fought until they had killed nearly all their number. So God was angry, and he took away their wings and commanded that the land and fisheries should be common to all who lived upon them. "God said he was the Father and the Earth was the Mother of mankind," Smohalla related, "that nature was the law; that the animals and fish and plants obeyed nature and that man only was sinful. This is the old law. After a while, when God is ready, he will drive away all the people except those who have obeyed the laws. Those who cut up lands or sign papers for lands will be defrauded of their rights and will be punished by God's anger."

This is the culture in which David Sohappy was raised, and it gave him a quiet, stubborn conviction that put him in the center of fishing rights conflicts for twenty years. Sohappy was never particularly eloquent and certainly not glib, choosing his words carefully and usually speaking quietly. He had a presence, however. He was handsome, with a broad, coppery, weathered face of strong nose and chin and mouth, his silver-black hair pulled back into braids. He was clearly intelligent, though he frequently seemed bewildered by the position modern society had put him in and frustrated by its incomprehension of his beliefs. His defiance of both state and tribal law made him a hero to some and an opportunistic fish poacher to others. At the time of his trials even Native Americans were divided over the propriety of his position.

Sohappy was born on his mother's allotted tract on the Yakima reservation but spent his early years at White Bluffs, where his grandparents fished and had a drying shed. He began fishing at age five and had only five years of formal schooling. He learned his native language and religion and was taught to gather roots, to hunt, and to fish. He initially led an adult life not notably different from many other Pacific Northwest Native Americans. He was drafted into the army in 1946 and made buck sergeant, but mustered out in less than a year because he already had a child. He lived twenty years in the Yakima Valley, halfheartedly farming his family's reservation allotment, leaving to fish whenever seasons and runs permitted. Some of the salmon were sold and others were shared in the seasonal cycle of longhouse gatherings or given to the elderly. Sohappy mixed fishing, hunting, and longhouse religious activity with odd jobs as a carpenter, electrician, plumber, heavy equipment operator, welder, and sawmill worker. When the fishing stopped at Celilo after construction of The Dalles Dam, Columbia River Indians began switching from dip nets—hoop nets pulled through the water on long poles—to long gill nets that extended from the bank into the new dam reservoirs. Sohappy's brother Aleck had moved downriver to Cook's Landing to try gillnetting. In 1965, after being laid off from a lumber mill worker job, David joined him. Myra and the children came, too.

The family never left, the Sohappys deciding they preferred to live as close as possible to traditional ways. They refused welfare, ate salmon two or three times a day, hunted, and gathered roots and berries. By the time David was imprisoned he had seven children and fourteen grandchildren. This extended family, he later estimated, averaged a legal and illegal catch of two thousand to twenty-five hundred salmon and steelhead each year, worth about $30,000. The number of salmon swimming past Cook's Landing ranged from a low of 480,000 in 1980 to a high of 1.2 million in 1986.

From the salmon came cash to support twenty people and buy boats, nets, cars, food, blankets, and clothes. They would earn sixty dollars or so from a net of fish, use it to buy gas, and drive to a Seven Drum ceremony. Sohappy advanced in his Seven Drum faith to the Feather Religion branch and became a healer, a ceremonial leader, and a counselor.

From Cook's Landing the world looked very different to David Sohappy than it did to white fishing regulators. Salmon fishing was a right Indians had retained, not a privilege granted by the conquering whites, Sohappy contended. "A privilege can be regulated and a right cannot be regulated," he said. To his mind the non-Indian ocean and river fishermen harvested to heedless, greedy excess. The whites had also built the dams without adequate compensation to the tribes, he contended. Congress had passed the Mitchell Act, which provided $200 million to build salmon hatcheries to compensate for the new dams, but thirty-six out of thirty-eight of these initial hatcheries were located below Bonneville Dam. This made sense in ensuring that the bulk of the artificially raised fish did not have to pass any dam, but it also meant that new salmon would not swim upstream where Indians could catch them.

The fisheries departments of Washington and Oregon believed iconoclastic rebels such as Sohappy had to conform to fishing regulations, however unfair, to prevent anarchy on the Columbia and extinction of the runs. Natives who ignored the rules were either outlaws or living hopelessly in the past.

In 1968, Sohappy was arrested and confined in the Skamania County jail for four nights. His plight attracted the attention of

Native American activists and in short order he found himself a legal figurehead, his name at the head of fourteen fishermen suing in federal court to challenge state regulation of Indian fishing rights in *Sohappy* v. *Smith.* The federal government, sympathetic to Indian complaints about discriminatory state fishing regulations, joined the Yakima, Umatilla, Warm Springs, and Nez Perce tribes in a similar suit challenging state authority. The two suits were combined: Sohappy and Uncle Sam on one side, state fishing regulators on the other.

Columbia River Native Americans had already scored some legal victories. A 1905 U.S. Supreme Court ruling had established their right to cross private property to reach traditional fishing sites on the river. In 1942 the Court ruled that Indians didn't need state licenses to exercise treaty fishing rights. On the rivers around Puget Sound, Washington's Indians had gained national publicity in the 1960s when they set their nets for salmon in defiance of state authority, setting off club-wielding battles with state police that resulted in repeated arrests. Now two court decisions proved revolutionary, incorporating the Sohappy claim.

The first, issued in 1969 by U.S. District Court Judge Robert Belloni of Portland, held that states could regulate treaty Indian fishing only when necessary for conservation. Native treaty rights to fish otherwise superseded state law. Belloni also said the states could not put on tribal fisheries the primary burden of allowing enough salmon escapement for spawning. Belloni did not, however, spell out what kind of fishing season this implied.

Five years later, U.S. District Court Judge George Boldt of Tacoma went much further. Few would have expected a radical decision from the conservative, bow-tied judge, a Republican appointee. But after a lengthy trial involving exhaustive testimony by anthropologists and historians, Boldt decided that a numerical value had to be put on the treaty phrase ensuring that natives could fish "in common" with other citizens. "In common" did not mean that natives simply had the same rights and regulations as whites, Boldt ruled. That would ignore the implicit promise of the Stevens treaties to preserve Indian livelihood. Native Americans were thus entitled to *half* of the harvestable salmon and steelhead heading for traditional tribal fishing grounds and stations—including the Columbia River.

The decision hit the Pacific Northwest like a bombshell. About 1 percent of the region's population had been awarded the opportunity to catch up to half its fish, a resource potentially worth hundreds of millions of dollars. Boldt was hanged in effigy by enraged white fishermen.

The Boldt and Belloni fishing decisions forced the inclusion of Native Americans in the management of the fish resource and rivers, with profound results. The tribes proved effective in adding their own biologic expertise and snaring federal grants for fish hatcheries, habitat restoration, and other improvement projects. They also brought a new environmental perspective. By forcing fish managers to guarantee larger runs to the rivers, tribal power shifted the focus on salmon from the sea to land, where the devastating changes in stream habitat were finally recognized. It forced an admission by policymakers that not only were salmon not inexhaustible, they were in long-term, alarming decline. Perhaps most importantly, the region was forced to recognize that the rapid harnessing of the region's rivers had exacted a painful ecological and economic cost difficult to reverse and impossible to ignore. If a commercial fishery for tribes far up the Columbia was to be maintained, the gauntlet of dams had to be reckoned with.

Columbia River salmon runs had been yo-yoing since the completion of Bonneville Dam, the number of salmon swimming back to the river ranging from a high of 2.4 million in 1944 to a low of just over one million in 1960. Numbers had climbed back encouragingly by 1971, only to begin falling precipitously in the 1970s. When Boldt made his ruling, about 1.4 million fish were entering the river. By 1981, when Sohappy would be caught by federal agents for selling illegally caught fish, the number was near the all-time low, or 1.1 million fish. Several things contributed to the decline. Protest fisheries directly after Boldt's ruling disrupted normal fishing season management. Just one year after the judge ruled, the last dam on the lower Snake River was completed. Drought hit in the late 1970s and river and ocean temperatures rose, both hurting the runs. And ominously, in the mind of some white fish managers, the Indian season above Bonneville had lengthened and their share of the river's harvest had reached as high as 38 percent by 1976. The agencies were reluctant to believe the natives could regulate themselves adequately.

At the root of this reluctance was Boldt's decision that Native Americans were to be allowed to catch fish in excess of their 50 percent share if the extra fish were to be eaten or used in their religious and social ceremonies. There was reportedly growing abuse of this "subsistence" loophole, however, with some of the supposed ceremonial fish being quietly sold. Could this account for the disastrous slide in the fish runs? In 1981 fears of abuse seemed to be confirmed when forty thousand adult salmon disappeared between Bonneville and McNary dams. They were counted over the Bonneville fish ladder, but not at McNary. They were not reported caught either. Where had they gone? Authorities suspected they had been poached.

Sohappy, meanwhile, found himself in a peculiar position. He did not recognize the legal authority of the federal government, the states, or the Yakima tribe. "I started looking at these law books," he later recalled to me while in prison. "I said hey, here's our fishing rights, plain. I started to think, well, if someone could get those rights back, we'd have it made."

If the people making the rules were the ones who had destroyed the Pacific Northwest's environment, it seemed to Sohappy a surrender of his values to accede to them. He had his nets in the water day and night, whether fish were running or not, as a matter or principle. He'd explain his reasoning to any fisheries agent or news reporter who stopped by. There was practicality involved. It would be impossible to sustain his traditional lifestyle if he adhered to the rapidly shrinking fishing seasons. Moreover, he proved difficult to stop. Illegal fishing was only a misdemeanor and the prosecutor in Skamania County, Robert Leick, was reluctant to prosecute the stubborn Indian: Leick sympathized with his position. Frustrated fishery agents could rarely get a court showdown to jail or fine Sohappy and so were reduced to seizing nets and boats. Sohappy estimated he lost two hundred and thirty nets over a twenty-year period, valued at $138,000. Agents in turn complained they were threatened, shot at, their cars rammed, and their boats showered with rocks.

The standoff came to a head when Senator Slade Gorton of Washington, a longtime critic of special fishing rights for Indians, pushed Congress to amend a fish and game statute called the Lacey Act. This changed illegal fishing from a misdemeanor to a felony and allowed prosecution in federal instead of county courts. Encouraged by the possibility of stiff penalties, undercover federal agents set up an elaborate fourteen-month sting operation. They constructed a fish drying shed at Celilo, hired a Sohappy nephew as an unwitting fish broker, and offered to pay top dollar for some of the river's weakest, most endangered runs. In June 1982 an affidavit was filed in federal court alleging that more than seventy people, most of them Indians, had sold sixty-one hundred fish to the federal agents. Cook's Landing was raided and Sohappy's house searched for evidence. His son Sam was handcuffed after allegedly assaulting an officer. "I don't think it's against the law for me to sell a few fish here and there," Sohappy told reporters after the raid. "We've been doing it since before the white man came. I fished all my life."

Eventually, nineteen of the seventy named were actually indicted, and thirteen convicted. Sohappy was found guilty of four felony counts, convicted of illegally selling three hundred and seventeen fish totaling forty-three hundred pounds for $9,685. Apparently angered by Sohappy's insistence that fishing rights were above other law, U.S. District Court Judge Jack Tanner handed down a stiff five-year federal prison sentence. Sohappy's appeals were rejected and in 1986 he was sent to prison. His son David Jr. got five years for selling twenty-eight fish totaling three hundred and thirteen pounds for $865. Shortly afterward, two whites who illegally sold $20,000 worth of sports-caught salmon to Seattle restaurants were charged with misdemeanors, one getting a thirty-day jail sentence and the other a one-year suspended sentence and a $1,000 fine.

Prison did what twenty years of harassment could not. It broke Sohappy's spirit and his health.

In February 1987, I and a *Seattle Times* photographer named Alan Berner—who had been taking a remarkable series of photographs of Northwest Indians—visited Sohappy at Sandstone federal prison in Minnesota. We went at the urging of his new attorney, Tom Keefe, who believed that the fundamental story of Sohappy and the Columbia River had been obscured by the court maneuverings and appeals stemming from what the press had labeled "Salmonscam." Keefe argued that his client's punishment was grossly disproportionate to his crime. We drove north from the airport in Minneapolis across a flat, frozen landscape to the trim concrete buildings at Sandstone. By this time Sohappy had been reunited in prison with his son David and his nephew Matthew McConville. I think prison officials were trying to be humane in letting them serve together, but it was odd to have the trio lined up to speak to us in orange prison coveralls, as if they were the James gang. I asked Sohappy how he had been treated by his fellow prisoners, a large number of whom were convicted drug dealers.

"They ask what I'm in for," he said. "I say fishing. 'Fishing?' they always reply. 'That's the first time I've heard of anybody in federal prison for fishing!' They can't believe it."

As we talked his voice was quiet and he seemed depressed. He didn't like prison food and missed his salmon and berries. In four months he had lost eleven pounds. A blood vessel had burst in his left eye. He was sixty-one years old, and in the next sixteen months would suffer two strokes before his final release. A third stroke in 1991 would kill him.

It was ironic that I found myself writing sympathetically about the Sohappy case. As a Northwest newspaper reporter I covered some of the early fishing battles and protests and watched attorneys argue their case when the appeal reached the U.S. Supreme Court, where Boldt's allocation of a 50 percent share of fish to the tribes was upheld. I saw the tribes as one more special interest in the perennial wrestling over the resources of the river. I had never heard of the Wanapum tribe or Smohalla or old chief Comcomly when, in 1981, the Vancouver *Columbian,* for which I worked, was tipped off that illegal fishing by both whites in the lower river and Indians above Bonneville Dam appeared to be a major contributor to the well-known decline of the fish runs. I was assigned to the story.

It was a wonderful opportunity to get out on the Columbia. I interviewed non-Indian poachers in lower-river fishing communities such as Skamokawa, rode in Fisheries Department patrol craft looking for illegal nets with night-vision scopes, and wrote about both David Sohappy and his neighbor Mary Settler, a Yakima grandmother imprisoned for ten months after pleading guilty to fifteen felony counts of selling salmon out of season. Salmon, I realized, represented to a poor fisherman an economic tide of twenty- to fifty-dollar bills. Penalties were so weak and enforcement stretched so thin that illegal fishing had become a kind of game. More than a tenth of all the criminal file space in Wahkiakum County on the lower river was taken up by the illegal fishing saga of a single family of poachers.

The theme of the resulting series was that illegal fishing,

spurred by white lawlessness in the wake of the Boldt decision and Native American abuse of the ceremonial fishery, was a major threat to dwindling Columbia River salmon. With tribal fishery regulators frustrated by their inability to crack down on poachers because of lack of manpower, authority, and political backing from the affected tribes, the stories were not sympathetic to Sohappy's position. While I quoted him about how the dams and white overfishing had decimated salmon runs, his creed that "If Indians are allowed to keep fishing, the fish will come back" did not strike me—and could not have struck readers—as very persuasive. "They flaunt the law in our face," fumed Joe Schwab, a sergeant with the Oregon State Police. I wrote then, and believe now, that unrestrained fishing meant regulatory anarchy that would doom any attempt to manage salmon survival intelligently.

What I was not told by fishery agents as I worked on the project was that the elaborate "Salmonscam" sting operation was already under way and that some of the fish being sold illegally were purchased with tax dollars. Officials were honestly alarmed by the disappearance of salmon between Bonneville and McNary dams and believed that rebels such as Sohappy were likely a major contributing cause. Unfortunately for prosecutors, the fourteen-month investigation by federal officials failed to prove that Sohappy was selling salmon illegally to anyone but their own undercover agents. The jury rejected the government's central argument that Sohappy or other Indians had led an organized poaching ring. If the Indians were criminals under modern law, they seemed disappointingly disorganized.

There were other problems with the government's case. Those arrested pointed out that they had been caught selling twenty tons of upriver Chinook salmon illegally while white ocean fishermen had been legally allowed to harvest a thousand tons of the same stock. Inadvertently, Salmonscam called attention to the lopsided fishery regulation of the Columbia River.

Most embarrassing of all was that a team of white fish experts led by National Marine Fisheries Service biologist Wes Ebel had further investigated the river and discovered that the forty thousand fish that had disappeared between Bonneville and McNary dams were not missing after all. They had not been poached. They had either milled in the reservoir pools or strayed to nearby tributary streams because the Columbia was too polluted for them to proceed upstream. Fluoride emissions from the aluminum plant at John Day Dam had blocked their normal migration.

Meanwhile my own perceptions about Native Americans and their relationship to the region's rivers and its salmon continued to evolve. My poaching stories had helped land me a job at the *Seattle Times,* and in 1985 managing editor Alex McLeod proposed that I return to the Indian fishing question from a much broader perspective. He wanted a series of stories on Washington State's Indians, an oft-ignored minority that still held title to 7 percent of the state's land and was asserting rights not only to fishing but to operating reservation fireworks, liquor, cigarette, and gambling businesses exempt from Washington law. Some tribes were reopening unresolved land claims and others that had never received federal treaty recognition were pressing for it now.

The resulting project led to a series that portrayed a minority with the highest unemployment, alcoholism, disease, and mortality rates in the region. Its most eloquent passages were the quotes of Native Americans, present and past.

"In one day the Americans became as numerous as the grass," Walla Walla chief Peopeomoxmox had remarked to Governor Stevens during the Treaty Council on his land in 1855. "This I learned [during a war party against other Indians] in California. I know this treaty is not right; you have spoken in a roundabout way. Speak straight. I have ears to hear you and here is my heart. Suppose you show me goods. Should I run up and take them? Goods and the earth are not equal. Goods are for using on the earth. I do not know where they have given lands for goods. We require time to think, quietly, slowly. You have spoken in a manner partly tending to evil. Show me charity. I should be very much ashamed if the Americans did anything wrong. . . .

"Think over what I have said."

The Klickitat River pours into the Columbia at Lyle, a small town on the Washington shore downstream from The Dalles Dam. This is the transition zone where the dry eastern hills give way to wet western forest, and this Mount Adams country is an artful mix of forest and meadow benchland, thick with wildflowers and the smell of pine. In its lower reaches the Klickitat cascades down into a shadowy, mist-filled canyon where the basalt seems to have been quarried to provide convenient steps and ledges for aboriginal fishermen. Here the Indians still fish in the Celilo way, leaning out over the foaming chutes of water and combing the current with dip nets. They reach hand over hand along long wooden handles as unwieldy as medieval pikes in order to pull the hoops through the frothy water, waiting until a bump and jerk reveals a salmon to be scooped. It is hard, wet, exhilarating work, some of the natives shrouded in mist like ghosts, the river pounding like the clamor of a factory.

Tribal members set up camp on a grassy bench beyond the lip of the canyon. They live in makeshift lean-tos of canvas and plastic and plywood and loose rock, with old mattresses and discarded sofas shoved underneath. Blankets, moldering sleeping bags, tarps, and old clothes are heaped in corners of the shelters while disintegrating running shoes, worn gloves, blackened campfire utensils, packs of cigarettes, and a salmon carcass worked by a dog typically occupy the foreground. The site is littered with food wrappers, Coca-Cola cans, and beer and liquor bottles, the air at dusk scented with pungent marijuana. These are not the Tribal Council Indians with briefcase and computer, or Bureau of Indian Affairs Indians of rule book and regulation, or even the gill net Indians with outboards and nets. These are the natives staggered by change and seeking equilibrium in the wilder country of their ancestors. They fish until they are weary, rest, and then fish some more, eating some of the catch but running most of it down to brokers on the Columbia, throwing the salmon into the beds of old pickups or the trunks and backseats of sprung-out sedans.

Alan Berner and I visited the canyon as we worked on our newspaper series, and then Berner returned by himself while I tried to slog through the complex thicket of Indian law and contradictory federal Indian policy. Finally it was time to map how the series would be presented, and so Alan printed his favorite photographs and spread them on a conference table in the *Seattle Times* newsroom. They were evocative, beautiful, sad, and ironic, capturing more in an expression or shaft of light or rude juxtaposition than I could say in a hundred news stories. To choose among them was difficult, and particularly baffling was the choice of a lead picture for the front page on Sunday. "For today's Indians," my story summed up, "positive and negative currents circle each other in a dizzying whirlpool." Who best represented

this yin and yang? Berner urged that we use a striking color portrait of a young Indian named Jim Spino, taken at Klickitat
Canyon.

I wasn't sure. I had never met Spino. He certainly played no
role in Native American politics. I called the region's natives a
"people of promise" but Spino hardly seemed most representative of that label. He had had minor brushes with the law, had
tried the Job Corps and preferred fishing. "I don't look forward to
nothin'," he had told Berner fatalistically. "Just take it like it
comes." Yet the photograph was undeniably powerful. Spino wore
a cloth headband, braids, a denim jacket. Most telling was the ambiguity of his face: proud, pained, uncertain, a scar above his upper lip, his portrait a geometry of angles in the light of the
Klickitat sun. Berner was right. The picture captured the mixed
emotions we had experienced. That weekend, Jim Spino's face
thumped down on half a million Seattle-area doorsteps.

Two days later we learned that he was dead.

He had lapsed into unconsciousness after a daylong celebration of his twenty-fourth birthday, on Saturday, December 14,
1985, just a few hours before Seattle householders picked up the
paper to study his face. The coroner concluded that the cause of
death was alcohol poisoning. Jim Spino had drunk himself to
death. He never knew his portrait had been picked to lead the series.

I didn't know what to feel. The click of a shutter had captured someone who suddenly seemed as ephemeral as a rainbow.
The same Sunday morning that his image had given him a two-
dimensional media reality, his soul was gone. All the sad statistics
I had been accumulating over twelve months had been given a
name and a face, but one I'd never met. It was ironic but also disturbing, haunting. What had he really been like?

That week, as the series ran, Berner and I drove to Spino's
funeral. The leaders of the ceremony explained over the telephone that it would be at Cloudville, a cluster of four thirty-year-
old government houses built on a sagebrush hill above The Dalles
Dam. The community was unmarked on any road map, but not
hard to find. It was just downstream the Columbia from the
drowned site of Celilo Falls. Named for the George Cloud family
that dwelled there, it stuck out plainly on the rolling desert, its
snow-crusted yards jammed with the cars of Native American

mourners. We got out of our car and looked around. The world was fuzz, the sky a lid of cloud and the land a mist-colored sheet of snow and sage. We could smell the venison and dried salmon stewing in pots in preparation for the funeral feast. We weren't sure how we would be received. The leader of the Seven Drums ceremony had given us permission to come but we did not know if the family had agreed, or even knew we were expected.

We were treated with polite and tolerant grace, it turned out, not so much welcomed as absorbed into a gathering that was more than a mourning—it was a reaffirmation of surviving life. A twenty-five-by-fifty-foot temporary longhouse with a roof of blue plastic tarps and walls of plywood had been erected on the frozen ground. Inside, the earth was covered with old carpet and colorful native rugs. A row of drummers, most of them elderly, beat out a chant punctuated by the ringing of bells, the wailing of a song dying in an eerie sigh like a breath of wind. Spino's pine casket was closed, draped with an Indian blanket. Around the coffin were mementos recalling bits of his life: a plastic deer to remember his love for hunting, a plastic sled to commemorate the way he would lead younger children in snow play at Cloudville.

A woman named Christine Lewis told us how in the old days the bodies would remain unburied for three days, just in case they reawakened from the spirit world with a message or a song. The dead were not always truly dead. Smohalla, pronounced gone, had then sat up to announce he had returned from the spirit world with new songs.

Lewis sighed. Health authorities today require embalming. Such returns no longer happen.

The funeral was not solemn. The ritual was practiced and inclusionary, with mourners walking in and out of the longhouse at will to dance, meditate, eat, and talk. They were not just grieving but finding strength in companionship. At midday, tables were erected on three sides of the longhouse, forming a U around the casket. There, a lunch was served: dumplings in salmon broth, Indian fry bread, dried salmon, berry preserves, venison stew. We ceremonially sipped water at the beginning and the end: a symbol of purity, of the centrality of water, of the river, of salmon, of life.

"He had a big heart," I was told by Spino's big brother, Wesley. "He learned hard and lived hard and gave his all to anybody.

Most everything he had, he'd just give away."

The Seven Drums chanting went on all night, dancers moving in a line in the dimly lit longhouse and singing in Yakima, nodding and stepping and then turning around in unison "to go in the right direction," it was explained. With gray daybreak it was time to go to the cemetery above Lyle. A white pickup truck served as the hearse. A caravan of vehicles bounced out of Cloudville's potholed yard and followed Bonneville pool, then wound up the hill to the Indian cemetery. There was no emerald lawn and no elaborate headstones. The mounded dirt graves were decorated with plastic and clay toys, flowers and cheap souvenirs.

Spino's grave had been dug in the frozen ground and lined with plywood. Several men lowered the pine coffin and it was covered with tule reed mats. Elder Louie Charles led the group in additional Yakima songs. As the last warbling wail died away, one by one the Yakimas grasped a handful of dirt and threw it on top of the reed mats, saying their good-byes. The hiss and rattle of the thrown dirt became a hypnotic rhythm. After everyone had passed, Spino's brothers began shoveling on the remaining dirt.

Berner and I went back to Seattle and produced an epilogue for our series that appeared in the following Sunday's paper. Included was a speech by the Duwamish chief Sealth, or Seattle, the man the city was named after. The words were said to Isaac Stevens when it became clear that the newcomers were demanding most of the tribe's Puget Sound land. They were likely embellished by white translators, but the meaning is presumably intact:

"There is little in common between us," Chief Seattle told the new governor. "To us the ashes of our ancestors are sacred and their resting place is hallowed ground. You wander far from the graves of your ancestors, and seemingly without regret. Your religion was written upon tablets of stone by the iron finger of your God, so that you could not forget. Our religion is the traditions of our ancestors: the dreams of our old men, given them in solemn hours of night by the Great Spirit, and the visions of our sachems. Our religion is written in the hearts of our people."

I later met an Athabascan poet from Alaska named Dian Million who had lived in Portland and there had lost, in a drowning accident in the Columbia, her closest male friend. Among the native street people of Portland, she told me, intentional drownings were not uncommon; the cold, powerful river offered a quick exit.

Sometimes an alcoholic Indian would disappear. "He let the river take him," the survivors would say.

"We have a huge amount of death," she told me. "That's the primary difference between our experience and yours."

Six years after Jim Spino's funeral I was back at Cook's Landing for another death, this one of David Sohappy, Sr., aged sixty-six, his body wrapped in wool blankets. Dusk was falling, spring rain drumming on the scrap-wood roof. "It's raining now," said David Jr. "It is erasing his tracks wherever he went so he is ready to go to his Maker."

I had a scheduled meeting with the U.S. Forest Service for a trip into Hells Canyon and so missed Sohappy's final burial at White Swan. It was just as well. Berner took some leave that was owed him, left Seattle immediately after work, and drove four hours to the longhouse there, arriving at 1:00 A.M. There were about one hundred and twenty-five mourners in all. Alan watched the ceremony of drumming, dancing, and prayers that extended through that night, the next day, and into the following night until dawn. Then Sohappy's body was wrapped in an American flag for transport to the cemetery. Finally, it seemed, it was time to lay his embattled soul to decent rest.

Alan described to me what happened next. The news media were there in force. A Portland television van drove into the tribal graveyard with its diesel engine rumbling, unfolded a satellite dish from its roof, and began beaming television lights on the open grave. Only the angry shouts of David Jr. caused the news crew to back away. Next, a newspaper photographer braced himself for shooting at wide exposure in the dim light by sprawling along a nearby mounded grave, clicking upward at the mourners. People tried to ignore the sacrilege.

As the sun began to rise over the hills the natives formed a horseshoe-shaped line around the casket with its open end to the east to greet the dawn. When the shaman lifted his arms in prayer, the same photographer stepped into the opening between mourners and sunrise to take another picture, his action abruptly halting the ceremony once again. "That was *two times* the service was interrupted," Berner described in disbelief. This photographer also finally retreated—but his sunrise shot ran on the news wire. Finally, with a volley in salute from army veterans, the old man of the river was left to the earth, what Smohalla called our mother.

If the new people of the river no longer stole Comcomly's head anymore, they still were not averse to stepping into the sacred circle of the river's first people, seeking to capture David Sohappy's spirit.

Epilogue

Coyote

It was head flattening, seen on a
woman here and drawn by artist
Paul Kane, that intrigued Meredith
Gairdner. *(Stark Museum of Art)*

Nature's bill for two centuries of determined development on
the Columbia River came due in the spring of 1994. The fishery
on what had once been the world's greatest salmon river had collapsed. The man-made burden of dams, habitat destruction, and
overfishing had combined with drought and the cyclic warming
of the Pacific called El Niño that suppressed the upwelling of
ocean nutrients. Salmon spawning runs on the West Coast were
projected to be so low that fishing was severely curtailed. Native
Americans briefly threatened a protest fishery or even "war" over
regulations and heedless river construction they believed had
trampled their treaty fishing rights, but sorrowfully recognized
that no mere demonstration was going to bring the fish back.
There was a sense of trapped frustration. Society could dynamite
what it had done. It could scramble for new technological fixes. It
could meekly pray for rain.

That dry spring biologists demanded, and got, a frantic
emergency spill of reservoir water over the crest of the Snake and

Columbia River dams in hope it would flush more young salmon to the sea. Utilities pointed out that a decade of such spills had failed to produce improvement. Other biologists warned that the spill threatened to saturate the Columbia once more with nitrogen, giving fish the bends. The emergency flush dribbled away in inconclusive acrimony. Meanwhile the Bonneville Power Administration estimated that the cost of raising Columbia River salmon, researching them, and spilling water lost for hydroelectric production had reached a staggering $350 million a year, far more than the fish sold as meat. A recovery plan proposed by the National Marine Fisheries Service was criticized by environmentalists as too timid, failing to alter the basic operation of the river. Industry complained it was too costly, repeating remedies that had yet to show any cure.

The biological tragi-farce spilled into international waters. American fishermen had responded to the steady decline of the Pacific Northwest salmon run by voyaging each summer up the thousand-mile Inside Passage to Alaska. Once there they intercepted not only salmon bound for Alaskan rivers but millions intended for Canadian streams as well. Canada in turn fished endangered runs swimming down the coast of Vancouver Island back toward the Columbia. Nations had established territories in the sea in pursuit of a billion-dollar resource that now played havoc with each other's biological planning.

Canada claimed America's catch of Canadian salmon in 1994 would exceed by eight million the catch by Canada of U.S. fish. The Pacific Northwest had dammed the Columbia and its tributaries, Canadians complained, while British Columbia had left the mighty Fraser unobstructed. Now Americans were pursuing the Fraser's fish to make up for their own folly. The Atlantic cod industry had already collapsed from overfishing, throwing the Maritime Provinces into recession. Was the same thing to happen in the Pacific? In frustration, Canadian officials briefly levied a $1,500 fee on Pacific Northwest fishing boats heading through British Columbia waters to fish in Alaska.

No one pretended this made any sense. Northwest river development seemed like a ricocheting game of billiards designed only to illustrate the laws of physics. Every action in the river's tumultuous history spawned a reaction, but a reaction that in part anticipated the mysteries of quantum mechanics. The Columbia seemed to be caught in Heisenberg's Uncertainty Principle, the law postulating the ultimate unpredictability of a subatomic particle's fate. Similarly, the river's harnessing churned out unanticipated environmental complexities. No one had any glib solutions. One generation's solution had become another's dilemma. Nature was demanding humility.

Perhaps the assumptions were wrong. I talked of this book once to a former college professor of mine named Robert Keller, and he in turn revealed his intended approach to the Columbia for an upcoming history class he was teaching. During a mountain climb, Keller recounted, he discussed the river's development with Jonathan Karpoff, an economist at the University of Washington. Karpoff was asked to tick off the various interest groups embroiled in the Columbia's future and duly listed fishermen, Native American tribes, farmers, the aluminum industry, utilities, environmentalists, barge companies, recreationists, ranchers, and so on. Keller nodded, thought for a while, and then said, "You forgot one interest. Do you know what it is?"

No, Karpoff replied, thinking his tally pretty complete.

"The river's interest," Keller said.

As my former teacher recounted this, I'm sure I looked puzzled. "The river's interest," he patiently repeated. "What is the interest of the river in staying a river? What is the *right* of a river to remain a river?" All the other values were based on humans and our competing needs. None suggested that nature—the natural Columbia—might have a value outside the immediate interests of our own species. Or that such a value was perhaps as important, even more important, than the others.

Karpoff, an avid hiker and outdoor enthusiast, does not buy this idea. Humans have interests and humans have rights, he told me, but to argue that a *river* has a right "is a semantic game." It is simply a means, he thinks, to empower a view that *people* have of how a river should be used. "There is no other way to weigh value than through human benefits and costs," he said. "To pretend not is like arguing against gravity. It just is." Environmentalists may believe that the cost of developing the Columbia is too steep for its benefits, but they cannot escape the fact that the argument is about human values, not some intrinsic natural one: rights are something *we* assign, not something that salmon or rivers or rocks acquire by the mere fact of their existence.

Karpoff, in fact, used the development of the Columbia as a lesson in cost-benefit analysis for his business administration students. Most agreed with his analysis. His experience has been that even though students don't necessarily like damming the Columbia, they usually conclude that hydropower representatives have the stronger argument.

Not all, however. Some students sense a river's interest after all: that the fabric of existence no more revolves around humans than the sun revolves around the earth. One woman accepted the economic analysis until she visited Bonneville Dam, Karpoff recalled. "She was so struck with the incongruity of the dam on the river that she couldn't deal with the analysis," he said. "She told me her policy position would be based on her emotional reaction to *that* dam, across *that* river."

In the summer of 1993 I accompanied Keller and his class down the route of the Columbia, a tumultuous, exhausting journey in which the students and the people they met were by turns proud of, angry at, wistful about, and awed by what has been done to the river. We talked of an untamed Columbia none of us will ever see. We tried to imagine the world our ancestors willingly traded for this one.

In his celebratory book *Columbia,* author Earl Roberge, who canoed some of its wild Canadian stretches shortly before their damming, predicted that future generations would not lament the loss. "The fact that it is a controlled river, with much of its scenic wilderness subdued, may cause a few twinges of nostalgia for the beauty that was, but weighed against the manifold benefits provided by the controlled river it must be admitted that the changes have been beneficial to the great majority of the people whose lives it affects," he wrote.

In the comfort of a city lit by regimented water pulsing through dams a hundred miles away, it is hard to deny Roberge's argument. The Columbia is as proud and complex and irreversible a piece of human environmental transformation as can be imagined, as magnificent in its new guise as in its old. Yet it is a magnificence with an emotional hollowness, a glory that has lost its ability to startle. With our computer programs that pace the river we are like omniscient river gods, so much in control of our creation that we become bored with its predictability.

In the aboriginal dawn of the river country some early native apparently dreamed of dams, set the future in the past, and wove a story about its destruction. This Coyote story, of the hundreds or perhaps thousands told in the American West, resonates with modern power. It is a story of how Coyote brought salmon to the river people—how he outwitted the Swallow Sisters who had blocked Nch-I'Wana with a dam.

The people were starving because the fish could not ascend the Columbia and they appealed to their hero for help. Coyote was too well known to approach directly, so he craftily turned himself into a baby, was strapped onto a cradle board, and set adrift down the river. Eventually he bumped up against the dam. "Oh, look at the poor baby!" the Sisters cried, taking the infant home with them.

The next day the Swallow Sisters decided to leave the child while they went to the mountains to dig roots, and as soon as they disappeared Coyote turned back to his real form and set to work attacking the dam. When the Sisters returned he once more became a cooing baby and they did not suspect anything was awry. This went on for four days.

On the fifth day the root digging stick of the youngest sister broke, an ill omen suggesting something must be wrong. When the Sisters rushed back unexpectedly early, there was Coyote, prying away at their dam!

The Swallow Sisters attacked. Again and again they darted in angrily as Coyote dug, but he warded them off until the dam was critically weakened. Finally the barrier gave way with a roar. Its debris formed the rocks and rapids of Celilo Falls, and the cradle board a nearby outcrop. The salmon could swim by to feed the people.

The swallows still build today, but only mud nests. Their return each spring signals the return of the salmon.

No magic babies bump up against the spill gates of modern concrete dams. They are so monumental as to seem immovable, so permanent as to make us prisoners of our own logic. Talk to engineers, farmers, biologists, or fishermen, and most will sooner or later remark, with pride or wistfulness or resignation, "Well, I don't think they're ever going to take out those dams."

Some natives hold a different view. The dams may last centuries, true, but to the Columbia's tribes that is a blink of time. Sooner or later dams will fail, or become silted up, or their power will prove unnecessary. When that happens the old river will come back, and the River People will still be there to welcome the return of the Salmon People.

The irreversibility with which the Columbia River dams are regarded by the rest of us is intriguing. All were constructed in just half a century, eight of the fourteen in the 1950s and 1960s. They are hardly impregnable to change. One end of Grand Coulee has been blown off to add its Third Powerhouse. The dams *are* immovable in our imagination, however.

Should anything have been done differently? The dams are of undeniable benefit, producing energy, food, navigation, and flood control. Yet it is unlikely that the present complex would pass environmental and economic review today. Would Grand Coulee and Hells Canyon dams be allowed to choke off thousands of miles of salmon habitat without either better mitigation or modification? I doubt it. Would the Columbia Basin Project pass economic muster? To date, its second, uncompleted half has not. Would a new dam be allowed today without better provision for fish passage facilities? Certainly not. Would the Columbia be used today to lure energy-consumptive industries such as aluminum smelting and to promote electric heat? Not with quite the same enthusiasm, at least. If done over, the damming of the river would, with the benefit of today's perspective, proceed much more slowly, with greater attention to fish and water conservation. We would exhibit more caution.

Certainly the three uppermost dams on the lower Snake River, for all their value in power and navigation, would be unlikely to be built again. They proved decisive in destroying Idaho salmon runs that once represented nearly half the Columbia's total fish resource. Yes, their average power contribution of six hundred and forty-eight megawatts is significant, nearly enough to light Portland. But their generation is almost equaled by what Northwest consumers have managed to conserve in recent years, and is dwarfed by a river system generating twenty-five times as much average hydroelectric energy. "I don't think we could build those dams today," said Ted Bottiger, the Northwest Power Planning Council member.

No serious proposal has yet been made for dismantling dams of this scale. With no agency in charge of the river, none has been bold enough to even study if some of the engineering should be reversed, even though that is one of the most obvious options. Nor has any agency ever considered seriously the second most obvious solution: conceding that the Columbia has been fundamentally changed, that salmon can never thrive in an ecosystem so drastically altered, and that the huge sums being spent on Columbia salmon in what has so far seemed a futile rescue attempt would be better applied to coastal streams elsewhere in the Pacific Northwest or Alaska where fish have a realistic chance of thriving.

Ask environmentalists and biologists where to start revamping the Columbia system, however, and it is usually on the lower Snake. While deconstruction is the most drastic option, far more likely in years to come is continued tinkering with the dams and reservoirs to get salmon past them. The exact kind of tinkering remains unclear. If given billions of dollars to fix the dams, "I'm not sure what I would do next," confessed Don Bevan, head of the recovery team trying to rescue Snake River salmon.

On the Columbia River itself, Grand Coulee Dam remains too high, its power and irrigation too vital, and its reservoir too long to entertain serious thought of returning fish back to the upper watershed. Kettle Falls is drowned as effectively as the *Titanic*. Of the fourteen dams on the main river, only John Day has been closely scrutinized. Its sixty-mile reservoir is the longest that salmon still traverse, so proposals have been made to lower the water level six feet in hope its currents would quicken, urging young salmon to the sea. Yet even many fish biologists are skeptical that such a drawdown would noticeably increase the return of adult fish.

Recognizing today's second thoughts, the federal government has launched a System Operations Review of the Columbia that includes eleven federal agencies, four states, several utilities, seven tribes, twenty citizens' interest groups, a score of private individuals, and several universities. Its task is to review the conflicting uses of the river and reconcile them. No radical changes are anticipated.

And that is about the limit of our modern imagination. The dreams of natives notwithstanding, the Columbia is perceived as beyond the reach of Coyote, a necessary sacrifice to technology and civilization. "It's never going to be the way it used to be," I was told by Dick Nason, the fish and wildlife operations manager for Chelan PUD. "The environmentalists say let's put the river back the way it was. You can't. It's a people problem. There's too damn many people. They need the resource."

Yet what truly intrigues us about the Great River of the West? It is the voice of regret that permeates the expressions of human pride. It is the dream of the Columbia once again as a river, bucking and roaring and steaming with muscle, thrashing salmon leaping against its foaming tide. So if I can dream Coyote dreams for a moment, it would be about the disappearance of a different dam, The Dalles: the one that silenced Celilo Falls.

During that long, wearying classroom journey down the length of the Columbia, we stopped on a high bluff above Celilo Falls, gaining a grand view. Below was a river that has become a broad lake, flat and silent as the lid of a tomb. A Tidewater tug and barge slid past the point where the falls had been. Allowing such cargo to pass is one of the proudest achievements of American engineering.

"This is really depressing," whispered student Teresa Mitchell.

That night we sat around a campfire at Beacon Rock. Bob Keller recalled the disorienting sensation of taking one of his classes in a single day from the bottom of the Grand Canyon to the nighttime desert blaze of Las Vegas. The students traded observations of what we had seen and felt and thought, some of the women revealing they had dreamed of Coyote. We waited with amused anticipation for a comment from Jim Smith, a teacher who worked with troubled kids on the Swinomish Indian Reservation. He was perhaps the quietest person in our group and the least predictable, the oldest but the one with the most childlike ability to look at things with innocent clarity. Smith kept a certain wry equanimity toward all we saw. He talked to farmer Grady Auvil about how to cut an apple to find the star pattern inside. After a Hanford tour guide pointed to two buck deer with impressive racks of antlers resting in the shade of a tree at the nuclear reservation, he suggested, "Maybe it was one deer with two heads."

That night by the campfire Jim Smith remarked that the overlook at Celilo made him wonder what the falls must have sounded like. It made him wonder how high mist from the rapids must have climbed. "It might have reached all the way up that bluff," he said. "I wonder if it would have been moist and cool up there."

I wonder, too.

A Columbia River Chronology

25 million to 12 million years B.C.: Massive basalt flows form Columbia Plateau.

16,000 to 12,800 B.C.: Spokane floods.

9,000 B.C.: Approximate date of earliest known human habitation along the Columbia River.

1200: Bridge of Gods landslide creates Cascade Rapids, trade center well developed at The Dalles.

1775: First European smallpox plague reaches Northwest Indians. Disease returns in 1801, 1836, 1853, 1862.

Spanish captain Bruno Heceta detects the current of the Columbia but fails to discover the river.

1778: British captain James Cook explores Northwest Coast.

1788: British captain John Meares fails to find Heceta's river, calls headland Cape Disappointment.

1792: Captain Robert Gray enters the river and names it for his ship. British explore river's lower one hundred miles.

1793: Alexander Mackenzie becomes the first explorer to cross North America, reaches Pacific.

1801: French Canadian *voyageurs,* accompanying friendly Indians, first encounter the upper Columbia in Canada.

1805: Lewis and Clark descend the Columbia to the Pacific Ocean.

1807: David Thompson establishes Kootenay House on the Columbia near its source.

French invent canning, allowing later salmon canneries.

1808: Fraser River explored, found unnavigable.

1809: North West Company establishes post on Lake Pend Oreille.

1810: North West Company establishes Spokane House.

1811: Fort Astoria established by Americans, David Thompson traverses length of river.

1813: Americans sell Astoria to British, renamed Fort George.

1818: Britain and the United States agree to joint occupancy of the Oregon Country.

Fort Nez Perces built west of Walla Walla.

1819: British fur posts launch campaign to trap out Snake River country and discourage American entry.

1821: The British Crown consolidates the Hudson's Bay Company and North West Company under Bay management.

1824: Astoria is abandoned by the Hudson's Bay Company. Fort Vancouver established.

1826: Fort Colville built at Kettle Falls to replace Spokane House.

First apple seeds brought to Fort Vancouver.

1830: Chief Comcomly dies in measles epidemic.

1831: Nez Perce journey to St. Louis seeking "White Man's Book of Heaven."

1832: Nathaniel Wyeth makes unsuccessful attempt to establish a commercial fishery on Columbia. Captain Benjamin Bonneville reaches Fort Vancouver.

1834: Methodist missionary Jason Lee arrives in Oregon.

Fort Hall established in southern Idaho.

1835: Samuel Parker explores the Northwest for mission sites.

1836: Whitman, Spalding missions established.

Steamship *Beaver* arrives on Columbia from England.

1837: Whitman digs Northwest's first irrigation ditch.

1839: Jason Lee brings fifty-one Americans to Oregon as the "Great Reinforcement."

1841: Wilkes expedition explores the Northwest, concludes that the United States should press for possession of Puget Sound because the Columbia is so difficult to navigate.

1843: Wagon train of one thousand immigrants traverses Oregon Trail.

Oregon Provisional Government established.

1844: Oregon boundary question becomes U.S. presidential campaign issue, Polk wins with slogan of "Fifty-four-forty or fight."

1846: Boundary set at the Forty-ninth Parallel.

1847: Measles decimate native tribes.

Whitman Massacre, Cayuse War.

Mormons in Utah begin West's first large-scale irrigation.

1848: Oregon Territory created.

1849: Fort Vancouver made military headquarters of U.S. Army in the Northwest.

British Columbia is recognized as a Crown Colony.

1850: Steamboats *Columbia* and *Lot Whitcomb* initiate regular service on the Columbia.

1852: Settlers in present-day Washington petition Congress for separate Columbia Territory.

Ulysses S. Grant is stationed at Fort Vancouver.

1853: Washington Territory created.

1854: Gold found near Fort Colville, Washington Territory.

1855: Governor Isaac Stevens negotiates treaties, Indian war breaks out.

1856: Attack on the Cascades.

1858: Natives defeat Colonel Steptoe, are later crushed at Battle of Spokane Plains.

  Gold rush begins in Cariboo region of British Columbia.

  Era of cattle drives begins.

1859: Oregon becomes a state.

1860: John Ainsworth organizes Oregon Steam Navigation Company.

1862: Congress passes Homestead Act allowing farming of 160 acres for fee of ten dollars.

1863: Idaho Territory created from part of Washington Territory.

1864: First salmon cannery on Columbia.

  Montana Territory created from part of Idaho Territory.

  Nevada becomes a state.

1868: Northwest wheat exports begin from Columbia to world markets.

1871: Present-day Spokane is founded.

  British Columbia federates with Canada.

  First hesitant regulation of Columbia River fishing.

1872: Oregon legislature provides money for wagon road through Columbia Gorge.

1873: First Columbia obstruction dynamited by Army Corps of Engineers.

  Henry Villard creates Oregon Railway and Navigation Company.

1876: Work begins on Cascade Locks and canal.

1877: Nez Perce War, Chief Joseph defeated and exiled.

  Desert Land Act passed to promote irrigation.

1878: Defeat of Bannock marks end of Northwest Indian wars.

1879: Edison invents practical lightbulb.

  First fish wheel built on Columbia.

1880: New steamship *Columbia* with electric lights arrives in Portland.

1881: Lieutenant Thomas Symons makes survey of upper Columbia, proposes navigation improvements.

1883: Columbia salmon catch peaks, begins decline from overfishing.

  Transcontinental railroad completed to Portland and Tacoma.

1885: First paper mill in the Northwest is built on the Columbia at Camas.

Northwest's first hydropower plants built at Spokane Falls and Hailey, Idaho.

1886: Work begins on jetties at Columbia's mouth.

Canada completes transcontinental to Pacific.

1887: Work begins on Baillie-Groham Canal.

First Pacific Northwest salmon hatchery established in Oregon.

1889: Washington, Montana become states.

Railroad completed through Yakima Valley to Tacoma.

Baillie-Groham Canal completed.

World's first long-distance electric transmission line built from Willamette Falls to Portland.

Vancouver, Washington, begins region's first public power system.

1890: Idaho, Wyoming become states.

1892: Large-scale irrigation begins in Yakima Valley.

First vague proposal to irrigate central Columbia Plateau.

1893: Great Northern Railroad crosses Columbia and Cascades to Seattle.

1894: Highest recorded Columbia River flood.

Heavy logging begins in Columbia Basin.

1902: Federal Bureau of Reclamation is created to encourage irrigation.

Trail Smelter built.

1906: Last wild horse roundup in Ephrata.

1907: Sam Hill begins work on planned community at Maryhill.

First generator placed on Columbia River at Priest Rapids.

1908: First auto bridge over Columbia at Wenatchee.

1909: Minidoka Dam on Snake River marks first large-scale Bureau of Reclamation construction project.

1914: Work begins on Maryhill Mansion.

1915: Columbia River Highway completed.

The 349-foot-high Arrowrock Dam built near Boise.

1918: Wenatchee *World* publicizes idea for Grand Coulee Dam.

1919: Washington legislature authorizes study of competing irrigation proposals for Columbia Plateau.

1930: Rock Island Dam started.

Washington and Oregon allow creation of public power utilities.

1932: Army Corps of Engineers completes its master plan to build ten dams on the Columbia.

Franklin Roosevelt elected President.

1933: Bonneville Dam started, Rock Island Dam completed.

1934: Grand Coulee Dam started.

Bonneville design incorporates fish ladders.

1937: Bonneville Power Administration created.

1938: Bonneville Dam completed.

1940: Region's first aluminum plant built at Vancouver.

Maryhill Museum completed.

1941: Grand Coulee Dam completed.

Woody Guthrie writes "Roll On, Columbia."

1943: Construction of Hanford Atomic Works begins.

1947: McNary Dam started, Hanford expands.

Heavy radioactive pollution of Columbia begins.

1948: Vanport destroyed in most destructive Columbia River flood.

1952: Columbia Basin Irrigation Project begins delivering water.

1957: Celilo Falls flooded by The Dalles Dam.

1964: Columbia River Treaty between the United States and Canada approved, initiating construction of Canadian dams.

1967: Hells Canyon Dam completed, ends salmon runs to upper Snake Basin.

1968: *Sohappy* v. *Smith* case filed, decided by Judge Robert Belloni in 1969.

1974: Judge George Boldt awards up to half of salmon harvest to treaty tribes, Puget Sound decision extended to Columbia the following year.

1975: Lower Granite Dam completes barge highway to Lewiston, Idaho.

1979: Nuclear power plant construction program along river collapses.

1980: Northwest Power Planning Council created.

Eruption of Mount St. Helens.

1982: "Salmonscam" arrests of Indians made.

1983: Worst Columbia River salmon catch on record.

1987: Columbia River Gorge National Scenic Area created.

1990: Native Americans and environmentalists petition to place Snake River salmon stocks on endangered species list.

Oregon senator Mark Hatfield calls salmon summit but cannot forge agreement among competing interests.

1992: Army Corps of Engineers experimentally lowers reservoirs on Snake River to help salmon.

American Rivers Council lists Columbia the most endangered river in America.

1994: Spending to save declining Columbia River salmon is estimated as high as $350 million per year.

Runs are so poor that coastal salmon fishing is shut down from California to Canada, curtailed in Columbia.

MAJOR DAMS OF THE COLUMBIA BASIN
(LISTED BY DATE OF COMPLETION)

COLUMBIA RIVER DAMS

Rock Island Dam
Operated by Chelan County Public Utility District
Completed 1933 by Puget Sound Power & Light
River mile 453.4
622-megawatt generating capacity

Bonneville Dam
Operated by Army Corps of Engineers
Completed in 1938
River mile 146.1
1,050-megawatt generating capacity

Grand Coulee Dam
Operated by Bureau of Reclamation
Completed in 1941
River mile 596.6
6,180-megawatt generating capacity

McNary Dam
Operated by Army Corps of Engineers
Completed in 1957
River mile 292
980-megawatt generating capacity

The Dalles Dam
Operated by Army Corps of Engineers
Completed in 1960
River mile 191.5
1,780-megawatt generating capacity

Priest Rapids Dam
Operated by Grant County Public Utility District
Completed in 1961

River mile 397.1
788.5-megawatt generating capacity

Rocky Reach Dam
Operated by Chelan County Public Utility District
Completed in 1961
River mile 473.7
1,213-megawatt generating capacity

Chief Joseph Dam
Operated by Army Corps of Engineers
Completed in 1961
River mile 545.1
2,069-megawatt generating capacity

Wanapum Dam
Operated by Grant County Public Utility District
Completed in 1964
River mile 415.8
831-megawatt generating capacity

Wells Dam
Operated by Douglas County Public Utility District
Completed in 1967
River mile 515.1
774-megawatt generating capacity

Keenleyside Dam (Canada)
Operated by B.C. Hydro
Completed in 1968
River mile 770
Flood control only

John Day Dam
Operated by Army Corps of Engineers
Completed in 1971
River mile 215.6
2,160-megawatt generating capacity

Mica Dam (Canada)
Operated by B.C. Hydro

Completed in 1973
River mile 956
1,736-megawatt generating capacity

Revelstoke Dam (Canada)
Operated by B.C. Hydro
Completed in 1984
River mile 882
1,843-megawatt generating capacity

LOWER SNAKE RIVER DAMS

Ice Harbor Dam
Operated by Army Corps of Engineers
Completed in 1962
603-megawatt generating capacity

Lower Monumental Dam
Operated by Army Corps of Engineers
Completed in 1970
810-megawatt generating capacity

Little Goose Dam
Operated by Army Corps of Engineers
Completed in 1970
810-megawatt generating capacity

Lower Granite Dam
Operated by Army Corps of Engineers
Completed in 1975
810-megawatt generating capacity

MIDDLE SNAKE RIVER DAMS

Brownlee Dam
Operated by Idaho Power Company
Completed in 1959
675-megawatt generating capacity

Oxbow Dam
Operated by Idaho Power Company
Completed in 1961
220-megawatt generating capacity

Hells Canyon Dam
Operated by Idaho Power Company
Completed in 1967
450-megawatt generating capacity

UPPER SNAKE RIVER DAMS

Minidoka Dam
Operated by Bureau of Reclamation
Completed in 1909
16-megawatt generating capacity

Palisades Dam
Operated by Bureau of Reclamation
Completed in 1957
164-megawatt generating capacity

MAJOR TRIBUTARY DAMS

Hungry Horse Dam
Operated by Bureau of Reclamation
South Fork of Flathead River
Completed in 1952
428-megawatt generating capacity

Albeni Falls
Operated by Army Corps of Engineers
Pend Oreille River
Completed in 1955
43-megawatt generating capacity

Duncan Dam
Operated by B.C. Hydro
Duncan River (Canada)

Completed in 1967
Flood control only

Dworshak Dam
Operated by Army Corps of Engineers
North Fork of Clearwater River
Completed in 1973
400-megawatt generating capacity

Libby Dam
Operated by Army Corps of Engineers
Kootenay River
Completed in 1975
525-megawatt generating capacity

BIBLIOGRAPHY

This book is based on written sources, personal observation, and interviews. Most of those interviewed are quoted in the main text or cited in the acknowledgments. Following is a selected bibliography of written sources:

BOOKS

Allaby, Michael. *Water: Its Global Nature.* Facts on File, 1992.

Albro, Martin. *James J. Hill and the Opening of the Northwest.* Oxford University Press, 1976.

Allen, John Elliot. *The Magnificent Gateway.* Timber Press, 1979.

Allen, John Elliot, Marjorie Burns, and Sam C. Sargent. *Cataclysms on the Columbia.* Timber Press, 1986.

Allen, John Logan. *Lewis and Clark and the Image of the American Northwest.* University of Illinois Press, 1975.

Allen, Opal Sweazea. *Narcissa Whitman: A Historical Biography.* Binfords & Mort, 1959.

Alt, David D., and Donald W. Hyndman. *Roadside Geology of Washington.* Mountain Press Publishing Co., 1984.

———. *Roadside Geology of Oregon.* Mountain Press Publishing Co., 1978.

———. *Roadside Geology of Idaho.* Mountain Press, 1989.

American Friends Service Committee. *Uncommon Controversy.* University of Washington Press, 1970.

Baillie-Groham, W. A. *Fifteen Years Sport and Life in the Hunting Grounds of Western America and British Columbia.* Horace Cox, London, 1900.

Basque, Garnet. *West Kootenay: The Pioneer Years.* Sunfire Publications, Langley, B.C., 1990.

Binns, Archie. *You Rolling River.* Charles Scribner's Sons, 1947.

Blonk, Hu. *Behind the By-Line.* Self-published, 1992.

Brown, Bruce. *Mountain in the Clouds: A Search for the Wild Salmon.* Macmillan, 1982.

Chance, David H. *People of the Falls.* Kettle Falls Historical Center, 1986.

Chasan, Daniel Jack. *The Fall of the House of WPPSS.* Sasquatch Press, 1985.

Clark, Thomas H., and Colin W. Stearn. *The Geologic Evolution of North America.* Ronald Press, 1968.

Cohen, Jay. *Treaties on Trial: The Continuing Controversy over Northwest Indian Fishing Rights.* University of Washington Press, 1986.

Cook, Warren L. *Flood Tide of Empire; Spain and the Pacific Northwest, 1543–1819.* Yale University Press, 1973.

Cox, Ross. *Adventures on the Columbia River.* Binfords & Mort., 1831.

Cullen, Allan. *Rivers in Harness.* Chilton Books, 1962.

Czaya, Eberhard. *Rivers of the World.* Van Nostrand Reinhold Co., 1981.

Devoto, Bernard, ed. *The Journals of Lewis & Clark.* Houghton Mifflin Co., 1953.

Dick, Wesley Arden. *Visions of Abundance—The Public Power Crusade in the Pacific Northwest in the Era of J. D. Ross and the New Deal.* Doctoral dissertation, University of Washington, 1973.

Dickman, Howard Leigh. *James Jerome Hill and the Agricultural Development of the Northwest.* Oxford University Press, 1976.

Downs, Vaughn. *The Mightiest of Them All; Memories of Grand Coulee Dam.* Ye Galleon Press, 1986.

Dryden, Cecil. *Up the Columbia for Furs.* Caxton Printers, Caldwell, Idaho, 1949.

Easterbrook, Don J., and David A. Rahm. *Landforms of Washington.* Western Washington University Dept. of Geology, 1970.

Echeveria, John, with Pope Barrow and Richard Roos-Collins. *Rivers at Risk: The Concerned Citizens Guide to Hydropower.* Island Press, 1989.

Edmondson, W. T. *The Uses of Ecology—Lake Washington and Beyond.* University of Washington Press, 1991.

Egan, Timothy. *The Good Rain.* Knopf, 1991.

Erickson, Edith E., and Eddy Ng. *From Sojourner to Citizen: Chinese of the Inland Empire.* Self-published, 1989.

Fagan, Brian M. *The Great Journey: The Peopling of Ancient America.* Thames and Hudson, 1987.

Foote, Mary Halleck. *The Desert and the Sown.* Houghton Mifflin & Co., 1902.

Franchere, Gabriel. *Adventure at Astoria, 1810–1814.* 1854. Reissued by University of Oklahoma Press, 1978.

Freeman, Lewis Ransome. *Down the Columbia.* Dodd Mead & Co., 1921.

French, Herbert. *Of Rivers and the Sea*. G.P. Putnam, 1970.

Gerber, Michele. *On the Home Front: The Cold War Legacy of the Hanford Nuclear Site*. University of Nebraska Press, 1992.

Gibbs, James A. *Pacific Graveyard*. Binfords & Mort, 1950.

Gibson, James. *Farming the Frontier: The Agricultural Opening of the Oregon Country*. University of British Columbia Press, 1985.

Gilbert, Bil. *The Trailblazers*. Time-Life, 1973.

Goetzmann, William H. *Looking at the Land of Promise: Pioneer Images of the Pacific Northwest*. Washington State University Press, 1988.

Goudie, Andrew. *The Human Impact on the Natural Environment*. MIT Press, 1986.

Gould, Stephen J. *The Mismeasure of Man*. W.W. Norton, 1981.

Groot, C., and L. Margolis. *Pacific Salmon Life Histories*. University of British Columbia Press, 1971.

Guthrie, Woody. *Roll on, Columbia—The Columbia River Songs* (book and record). Bonneville Power Administration, 1987.

Hess, Karl. *Visions Upon the Land—Man and Nature on the Western Range*. Island Press, 1992.

Hildebrand, Lorraine Barker. *Straw Hats, Sandals and Steel*. Washington State American Revolution Bicentennial Commission, 1977.

Holbrook, Stewart Hall. *The Columbia*. Rinehart and Co., 1956.

———. *James J. Hill: A Great Life in Brief*. Knopf, 1955.

Howay, Frederic. *Voyages of the "Columbia" to the Northwest Coast*. Oregon Historical Society Press, 1990.

Hughes, Thomas P. *Networks of Power*. Johns Hopkins University Press, 1983.

Hunn, Eugene S. *Nch'i-Wana, the Big River: Mid-Columbia Indians and Their Land*. University of Washington Press, 1991.

Hunt, Cynthia, and Robert M. Garrels. *Water: The Web of Life*. W.W. Norton, 1972.

Irving, Washington. *The Fur Traders of the Columbia River*. (Includes the texts of "Astoria" and "The Adventures of Captain Bonneville.") Reprint, Knickerbocker Press, 1903.

Jeffrey, Julie Roy. *Converting the West: A Biography of Narcissa Whitman*. University of Oklahoma Press, 1991.

Johansen, Dorothy O., and Charles Gates. *Empire of the Columbia: A History of the Pacific Northwest*. Harper & Row, 1967.

Josephy, Alvin M. *Nez Perce Indians and the Opening of the Northwest*. University of Nebraska Press, 1979.

Keyser, James D. *Indian Rock Art of the Columbia Plateau.* University of Washington Press, 1992.

King, Philip B. *The Evolution of North America.* Princeton University Press, 1977.

Kipling, Rudyard. *American Notes—Rudyard Kipling's West.* Brown & Co., 1899.

Klein, Joe. *Woody Guthrie: A Life.* Knopf, 1980.

Lancaster, Samuel Christopher. *The Columbia: America's Great Highway Through the Cascade Mountains.* J.K. Gill, 1915.

———. *Romance of the Gateway Through the Cascade Range.* 1929. J.K. Gill, 1929.

Lang, William L. *A Columbia River Reader.* Washington State Historical Society, 1992.

League of Women Voters of Idaho. *The Great River of the West— The Columbia.* Koke-Chapman Co., 1959.

Lee, Kai N. *Compass and Gyroscope: Integrating Science and Politics for the Environment.* Island Press, 1993.

Lee, Kai N., with Donna Lee Klemka and Marion E. Marts. *Electric Power and the Future of the Pacific Northwest.* University of Washington Press, 1980.

Lesley, Craig. *River Song.* Houghton Mifflin, 1989.

Lorraine, Madison Johnson. *The Columbia Unveiled.* Los Angeles Times-Mirror Press, 1924.

Lowitt, Richard. *The New Deal and the West.* Indiana University Press, 1984.

Lucia, Ellis. *This Land Around Us—A Treasury of Pacific Northwest writing.* Doubleday & Co., 1969.

Lyman, William Denison. *The Columbia River, Its History, Its Myths, Its Scenery, Its Commerce.* Putnam, 1918.

Martin, Russell. *A Story That Stands Like a Dam.* Henry Holt, 1989.

McCoy, Keith. *The Mount Adams Country, Forgotten Corner of the Columbia River Gorge.* Pahto Publications, 1987.

McDonald, Lucille. *Coast Country: A History of Southwest Washington.* Binfords & Mort, 1966.

McGregor, Alexander Campbell. *Counting Sheep—From Open Range to Agribusiness on the Columbia Plateau.* University of Washington Press, 1982.

McKee, Bates. *Cascadia—The Geologic Evolution of the Pacific Northwest.* McGraw-Hill, 1972.

McKinney, Sam. *Reach of Tide, Ring of History: A Columbia River Voyage.* Oregon Historical Society Press, 1987.

McPhee, John. *Basin and Range.* Farrar-Straus-Giroux, 1980.

——. *Rising from the Plains.* Farrar-Straus-Giroux, 1986.

Meany, Edmond S. *Origin of Washington Geographic Names.* University of Washington Press, 1923.

Meinig, D. W. *The Great Columbia Plain.* University of Washington Press, 1968.

Mills, Randall. *Sternwheelers Up Columbia.* Pacific Books, 1947.

——. *Railroads Down the Valley—Some Short Lines of the Oregon Country.* Pacific Books, 1950.

Morgan, Murray C. *The Dam.* Viking Press, 1954.

——. *The Columbia: Powerhouse of the West.* Superior Publishing, 1949.

Morrison, Dorothy Nafus. *The Eagle and the Fort—The Story of John McLoughlin.* Oregon Historical Society, 1979.

Moyle, Peter B. *Fish: An Enthusiast's Guide.* University of California Press, 1993.

Nash, Gerald. *The American West Transformed: The Impact of the Second World War.* University of Nebraska Press, 1990.

Netboy, Anthony. *The Columbia River Salmon and Steelhead Trout: Their Fight for Survival.* University of Washington Press, 1980.

Neuberger, Richard L. *Our Promised Land.* University of Idaho Press, 1938.

Newman, Peter C. *Caesars of the Wilderness—The Story of the Hudson's Bay Co.* Penguin, 1987.

Nokes, J. Richard. *Columbia's River—The Voyages of Robert Gray, 1787–1793.* Washington State Historical Society, 1992.

Norwood, Gus. *Columbia River Power for the People.* Bonneville Power Administration, 1981.

Nuffield, Edward. *The Pacific Northwest: Its Discovery and Early Exploration by Sea, Land and River.* Hancock House, Surrey, B.C., 1990.

O'Neil, Paul. *The Rivermen.* Time-Life, 1975.

Palmer, Tim. *The Snake River, Window to the West.* Island Press, 1991.

——. *Endangered Rivers and the Conservation Movement.* University of California Press, 1986.

Parker, Samuel. *Exploring Tour Beyond the Rocky Mountains, 1835–37.* Wiley & Putnam, 1844.

Peterson, Keith, and Mary Reed. *Controversy, Conflicts and Compromise: A History of the Lower Snake River Development.* Army Corps of Engineers, 1992.

Phillips, James W. *Washington State Place Names.* University of Washington Press, 1971.

Pielou, E. C. *After the Ice Age—The Return of Life to Glaciated North America.* University of Chicago Press, 1991.

Pitzer, Paul. *Visions, Plans and Realities—A History of the Columbia River Project.* Doctoral dissertation, University of Oregon, 1990. (Scheduled to be published by Washington State University Press.)

Ponting, Clive. *A Green History of the World—The Environment and the Collapse of Great Civilizations.* St. Martin's Press, 1991.

Pringle, Laurence. *Rivers and Lakes.* Time-Life, 1985.

Raban, Jonathan. *Old Glory—An American Voyage.* Simon & Schuster, 1981.

Ramsey, Jarold. *Coyote Was Going There: Indian Literature of the Oregon Country.* University of Washington Press, 1977.

Redfern, Ron. *The Making of a Continent.* Times Books, 1983.

Reisner, Marc. *Cadillac Desert.* Viking Penguin, 1986.

Reiter, Joan Swallow. *The Women.* Time-Life, 1978.

Relander, Click. *Drummers and Dreamers.* Caxton Printers, 1986.

Rhodes, Richard. *The Making of the Atomic Bomb.* Simon & Schuster, 1986.

Richards, Kent. *Isaac I. Stevens, Young Man in a Hurry.* Brigham Young University Press, 1979.

Roberge, Earl. *Columbia, Great River of the West.* Chronicle Books, 1985.

Roe, JoAnn. *The Columbia River: A Historical Travel Guide.* Fulcrum Publishing, 1992.

Ronda, James P. *Lewis and Clark Among the Indians.* University of Nebraska Press, 1984.

———. *Astoria and Empire.* University of Nebraska Press, 1990.

Roos, John F. *Restoring Fraser River Salmon.* Pacific Salmon Commission, 1992.

Ross, Alexander. *Adventures of the First Settlers on the Oregon or Columbia River.* 1849. Reprint, University of Nebraska Press, 1986.

———. *The Fur Hunters of the Far West.* 1855. Reprint, University of Oklahoma Press, 1956.

Ruby, Robert H., and John A. Brown. *A Guide to the Indian Tribes of the Pacific Northwest.* University of Oklahoma Press, 1986.

———. *Indians of the Pacific Northwest.* University of Oklahoma Press, 1981.

————. *The Chinook Indians, Traders of the Lower Columbia River.* University of Oklahoma Press, 1976.

————. *Half Sun on the Columbia: A Biography of Chief Moses.* University of Oklahoma Press, 1965.

————. *The Spokane Indians, Children of the Sun.* University of Oklahoma Press, 1970.

————. *The Cayuse Indians, Imperial Tribesmen of Old Oregon.* University of Oklahoma Press, 1972.

Sandstrom, Gosta. *Man the Builder.* McGraw-Hill, 1970.

Sanger, S. L. *Hanford and the Bomb: An Oral History of World War II.* Living History Press, 1989.

Satterfield, Archie. *Moods of the Columbia.* Superior Publishing Co., 1968.

Schafer, Joseph. *A History of the Pacific Northwest.* Macmillan, 1933.

Schultz, Stewart T. *The Northwest Coast: A Natural History.* Timber Press, 1990.

Schwantes, Carlos A. *The Pacific Northwest: An Interpretive History.* University of Nebraska Press, 1989.

Schwantes, Carlos A., with Katherine Morrissey, David Nicandri, and Susan Strasser. *Washington: Images of a State's Heritage.* Merlin Publications, 1989.

Scott, David, and Edna Hanic. *East Kootenay Chronicle.* Mr. Paperback, 1979.

Seufert, Francis A. *Wheels of Fortune.* Oregon Historical Society, 1980.

Smith, Courtland. *Salmon Fisheries of the Columbia.* Oregon State University Press, 1979.

Sonneman, Toby F., with photographs by Rick Steigmeyer. *Fruit Fields in My Blood: Okie Migrants in the West.* University of Idaho Press, 1992.

Spring, Bob. *Adventuring on the Columbia.* Superior, 1956.

Springer, Vera. *Power and the Pacific Northwest—A History of the Bonneville Power Administration.* Bonneville Power Administration, 1976.

Stewart, Hilary. *Indian Fishing—Early Methods on the Northwest Coast.* University of Washington Press, 1977.

Stradling, Dale F. *The Columbia River—An Inexhaustible Resource?* Eastern Washington University, 1980.

Sundborg, George. *Hail Columbia—The Thirty-Year Struggle for Grand Coulee Dam.* Macmillan, 1954.

Suttles, Wayne, ed. *Handbook of North American Indians,* Vol. 7. *The*

Northwest Coast. Smithsonian, 1990.

Tamura, Linda. *Hood River Issei.* University of Illinois Press, 1993.

Tanner, Ogden. *The Canadians.* Time-Life, 1977.

Thompson, Erwin. *Whitman Mission.* Government Printing Office, 1964.

Tollefson, Gene. *BPA and the Struggle for Power at Cost.* BPA, 1987.

———. *Notes from the American West.* 3 volumes, unpublished.

Tuhy, John E. *Sam Hill, the Prince of Castle Nowhere.* Timber Press, 1983.

Unruh, John D. *The Plains Across—The Overland Emigrants and the Trans-Mississippi West, 1840–1860.* University of Illinois Press, 1979.

Vaughn, Thomas. *Paul Kane, the Columbia Wanderer.* Oregon Historical Society, 1971.

Viessman, Warren, and Claire Welty. *Water Management Technology and Institutions.* Harper and Row, 1985.

Waldman, Carl. *Encyclopedia of Native American Tribes.* Facts on File, 1988.

Weiss, Paul L., and William L. Newman. *The Channeled Scablands of Eastern Washington: The Geographic Story of the Spokane Flood.* Eastern Washington University Press, 1989.

Wendt, Herbert. *The Romance of Water.* Hill and Wang, 1969.

Wheeler, Keith. *The Railroaders.* Time-Life, 1973.

White, Gilbert F., ed. *Environmental Effects of Complex River Development.* Westview Press, 1977.

White, Richard. *It's Your Misfortune and None of My Own: A History of the American West.* University of Oklahoma Press, 1991.

Wilkinson, Charles F. *Crossing the Next Meridian: Land, Water and the Future of the West.* Island Press, 1992.

Williams, Albert N. *The Water and the Power.* Duell, Sloan and Pearce, 1951.

Williams, Chuck. *Bridge of the Gods, Mountains of Fire: A Return to the Columbia Gorge.* Friends of the Earth, Elephant Mountain Arts, 1980.

Wing, Robert C. *A Century of Service—The Puget Power Story.* Puget Sound Power and Light Co., 1987.

Winther, Oscar Osborne. *The Great Northwest.* Knopf, 1955.

Woodcock, George. *The Dukhobors.* Oxford University Press, 1968.

Worster, Dan. *Rivers of Empire: Water, Aridity and the Growth of the American West.* Oxford University Press, 1985.

Yorath, C. J. *Where Terranes Collide.* Orca Books, 1990.

DOCUMENTS, STUDIES, ARTICLES

American Rivers. Statements, background on endangered rivers, April 20, 1993.

Anderson, James Jay. "Diverting Migrating Fish Past Turbines." *Northwest Environmental Journal,* University of Washington, 1988.

Army Corps of Engineers. *The Columbia.* 1951.

———. Review Report on the Columbia River and Its Tributaries. October 1, 1948.

———. *Reservoir Control Center Guidance Memorandum.* January 1972.

———. *Columbia River Salmon Mitigation Analysis System Configuration Study.* November 1992.

———. *Lower Granite and Little Goose Projects 1992 Reservoir Drawdown Test Draft Report.* October 1992.

———. *The Columbia River and Its Tributaries.* March 20, 1950.

Army Corps of Engineers and Bonneville Power Administration. *Biological Issues Pertaining to Smolt Migration and Reservoir Draw-down in the Snake and Columbia Rivers,* with Special Reference to Salmon Species Petitioned for Listing Under the Endangered Species Act, August 30, 1991.

Army Corps of Engineers, Bonneville Power Administration, and Bureau of Reclamation. *Columbia River Salmon Flow Measures Options Analysis Environmental Impact Statement.* Two volumes. January 1992.

———. *Final Environmental Impact Statement on Interim Columbia and Snake Rivers Flow Improvement Measures for Salmon.* March 1993.

Bagnall, Gerald. *Improvement of the Mouth of the Columbia River.* Army Corps of Engineers, date unknown.

Banks, Frank A. "Why Develop More Power, Why Irrigate More Land?" Speech to the Washington Public Utility District Commissioner's Association, Coulee Dam, May 26, 1945.

Barron, James C., and Gary Thorgaard. *Salmon and the Columbia River System.* Washington State University, April 1991.

Battelle Pacific Northwest Laboratory. *Hanford Site Environment Report,* 1991.

Beak Consultants Inc. *Audit of Wildlife Loss Assessments for Federal Dams on the Columbia River and Its Tributaries.*

Behrens, Greg W., and Philip J. Hansen. *Grand Coulee Dam*. Bureau of Reclamation, 1990.

Ben Johnson Associates Inc. *Report to the Office of the Governor of Idaho on Update of Power Impacts to Protect Salmon*. November 22, 1991.

Beus, Curtis E. "Can We Save Our Soil?" *Washington's Land & People* (magazine), Washington State University, Vol. 5, No. 2.

Blewett, Steve. *A History of the Washington Water Power Company, 1889 to 1989*. Washington Water Power Company, 1989.

Blumm, Michael. "The Northwest's Hydroelectric Heritage: Prologue to the Pacific Northwest Electric Power Planning and Conservation Act." Paper for Northwestern School of Law and Lewis and Clark College, 1992.

Bonneville Power Administration. *Mortality of Yearling Chinook Salmon Prior to Arrival at Lower Granite Dam on the Snake River*. October 1991.

———. *Comments to the National Marine Fisheries Service on the Status of Snake River Sockeye Salmon*. August 6, 1990.

———. *Alternative Financing Methods*. January 1992.

———. *Modeling the System: How Computers Are Used in River Planning*. October 1992.

———. *Power System Coordination: A Guide to the Pacific Northwest Coordination Agreement*. February 1993.

———. *The Hood River Conservation Project*. April 1987.

Bonneville Power Administration et al. *Columbia River System Operation Review*. 1993.

Bouck, G. R. *Comments on National Marine Fisheries Service Status Review for Snake River Sockeye Salmon*. June 4, 1991.

Boyer, David S. "Powerhouse of the Northwest." *National Geographic*, December 1974.

Brannon, Ernie. *Stanley Basin Sockeye Salmon Lakes Fish Stocking History, Fish Eradication Projects, Present Status of the Kokanee Salmon Stocks*. November 28, 1991.

Broches, Charles F., and Michael S. Spranger. "The Politics and Economics of Columbia River Water." *Proceedings of a Conference in Portland, Oregon, October 26, 1984*. University of Washington Sea Grant Marine Advisory Publication.

Bureau of Reclamation, U.S. *The Story of the Columbia Basin Project*. 1978.

———. *Columbia Basin Project*. 1981.

————. *Report on the Columbia Basin Project on the Columbia River.* 1987.

————. *Crop Production Report, Data on the Columbia Basin,* and related documents. 1991–93.

————. *Draft Environmental Impact Statement on Continued Development of the Columbia Basin Project.* September 1989.

————. Assorted pamphlets on Pacific Northwest water projects by state. 1993.

Chaney, Ed. *A Question of Balance.* Northwest Resource Information Center. November 1978.

————. *Cogeneration of Electrical Energy and Anadromous Salmon and Steelhead in the Upper Columbia River Basin.* Northwest Resource Information Center. June 1982.

Chapman, Don. *Status of Snake River Sockeye Salmon.* Don Chapman Consultants Inc., for the Pacific Northwest Utilities Conference Committee. June 26, 1990, and February 19, 1991.

————. *Status of Snake River Chinook Salmon.* Don Chapman Consultants Inc., for the Pacific Northwest Utilities Conference Committee. February 19, 1991.

Chapman, D. W., et al. *Recovery Issues for Threatened and Endangered Snake River Salmon.* 11 volumes. Bonneville Power Administration. June 1993.

Chiles, James R. "Engineers Versus the Eons, or How Long Will Our Monuments Last?" *Smithsonian,* March 1984.

Clark, Earl. "Rufus Woods, Grand Coulee Promoter." *Montana, the Magazine of Western History,* Autumn 1979.

CLE International. "The Endangered Species Act." *Selected Papers from Legal Seminar,* Seattle, September 24, 1992.

Coast Guard, U.S. *Casualty Data from Sinkings/Capsizings Near the Columbia River.* April 30, 1990.

Columbia River Gorge Commission, U.S. Forest Service. *Management Plan for the Columbia River Gorge National Scenic Area.* September 1992.

————. *Investing in the Partnership.* February 1993.

Columbia River Inter-Tribal Fish Commission. *Wana Chinook Tymoo* (internal magazine), Nos. 1 and 2, 1993.

————. *1992 Columbia River Fish Runs and Fisheries.* January 1993.

————. *1992 Annual Report.*

"Come All Ye Bold Northwestmen." *Quarterdeck,* Spring 1991.

Cominco. *Cominco Trail Operations Environmental Report.* 1993.

————. *A Technical Description of the Main Production Processes at Cominco's Trail, B.C. Metallurgical Operations.* May 1993.

"Constructing the First Cofferdam." *Engineering News-Record,* August 1, 1935.

Corley, Donald R. "Tests for Increasing the Return of Hatchery Trout. Alturas, Redfish, and Yellow Belly." *Lakes Fisheries Investigations.* Idaho Department of Fish and Game, February 1966.

Costello, Kenneth. "Toward Accountability and Efficiency—Reform of the Bonneville Power Administration." *Policy Insight.* Reason Foundation, April 1992.

Daniel, John. "Dance of Denial." *Sierra,* March–April 1993.

David, Andrew. "John Sherriff on the Columbia, 1792." *Pacific Northwest Quarterly,* April 1992.

Direct Service Industries. "Partners in Power, Touching Northwest Lives." *50th Anniversary Reports,* 1990.

Eisbruber, Ludwig, et al. *Alternative Actions for Restoring and Maintaining Salmonid Populations on the Columbia River System.* Pacific Northwest Extension, March 1992.

Energy, U.S. Department of. *Welcome to Hanford's B Reactor.* 1992.

————. *History of 100-B Area.* October 1989.

Fairhaven College. *The Columbia River in Northwest History—A Collaborative Class Journal.* August 1993.

Fish Passage Center. Weekly reports, 1993.

Friedman, Jack. "Yakima Indian David Sohappy Went Fishing for Salmon and Caught Five Years in Federal Prison." *People,* March 28, 1988.

Friends of the Columbia Gorge. Newsletters, 1991–93.

General Accounting Office, U.S. *Potential Economic Costs of Further Protection for Columbia River Salmon.* February 1993.

Gerber, Michelle. *Legend and Legacy: Fifty Years of Defense Production at the Hanford Site.* Westinghouse Hanford Co. September 1992.

Giorgi, Albert, and Don Chapman Consultants Inc. *Comments Regarding the Endangered Species Act Proposed Listing of Fall and Spring/Summer Chinook Salmon: Issues Pertaining to Downstream Migrants.* July 31, 1991.

————. *Flow Augmentation and Reservoir Drawdown: Strategies for Recovery of Threatened and Endangered Stocks of Salmon in the Snake River Basin.* For S.P. Cramer and Associates under contract to the Bonneville Power Administration. March 15, 1993.

"Grand Coulee Dam, the First 50 Years." Wenatchee *World*, July 8, 1983.

Grant County Public Utility District. *Comments on Hanford Reach Study*. June 1992.

———. *1991 Annual Report*.

Hamilton, Joel R., et al. *The Effect of Lower Snake River Reservoir Drawdown on Barge Transportation*. University Task Force on Salmon and the Columbia River System. 1993.

Hankel, Evelyn Leahy. "The Earth People." *Clatsop County Historical Quarterly*, Winter 1980.

———. "Mad'Su (Big Noise of Thunder)." *Clatsop County Historical Quarterly*, Summer 1981.

Harvey, A. G. "Chief Comcomly's Skull." *Oregon Historical Quarterly*, June 1939.

Hickson, R. E., and F. W. Rodolf. "History of the Columbia River Jetties." *Proceedings of the International Conference on Coastal Engineering*, Long Beach, California, 1950.

Hilborn, Ray, and Steven Hare. *Hatchery and Wild Fish Production of Anadromous Salmon in the Columbia River Basin*. University of Washington School of Fisheries, September 1992.

Huppert, Daniel, David Fluharty, and Elizabeth Kenney. *Economic Effects of Management Measures Within the Range of Potential Critical Habitat for Snake River Endangered and Threatened Salmon Species*. School of Marine Affairs, University of Washington, June 4, 1992.

Hydrosphere Resource Consultants. *Water Supplies to Promote Juvenile Anadromous Fish Migration in the Snake River Basin*. Boulder, Colorado. January 1991.

Idaho Department of Fish and Game. *Sockeye of Stanley Basin Summary*. July 13, 1990.

Idaho Governor's Office. *National Treasure Threatened with Imminent Extinction* (brochure). 1992.

Idaho Power Company. *75 Proud Years*. 1991.

Interior Department, U.S. *The Endangered Species Program*. September 1990.

Jaske, Robert T., and J. B. Goebel. "Effects of Dam Construction on the Temperatures of the Columbia River." *Journal of the American Water Works Association*, August 1967.

Jolly, Carol, and Judith Leckrone. "Managing Lake Roosevelt—an International Challenge." American Water Resources Association Symposium, June 1993.

Jordan, Mabel. "The Kootenay Reclamation and Colonization Scheme and William Adolph Baillie-Groham." *British Columbia Historical Quarterly*, July–October 1956.

Kay, Dave. "Renewed Interest in Baillie-Groham Canal." *B.C. Historical News*, February 1967.

Keefe, Tom. *A Brief History of the Wanapums*. Undated.

Kelly, Christine, with John Gabrielson, John Malek, and Gretchen Hayslip. *Columbia River Basin Water Quality Summary Report: An Ecosystem Assessment*. U.S. Environmental Protection Agency, June 26, 1992.

Kidbey, Harold, and John Oliver. *Erosion and Secretion Along Clatsop Spit*. Army Corps of Engineers, 1962.

Langhe, Erwin F. "Science, Skulls and Sacrilege." *Pacific Discovery* magazine, May–June 1956.

Lazar, Jim. Speech to Washington Rural Electric Cooperatives Association, July 14, 1992.

———. *BPA Rate Subsidies and Preferences*. Briefing paper. December 22, 1993.

———. *Aluminum Industry Myths and Facts Regarding Electricity Costs*. May 1982.

League of Women Voters of Idaho, Montana, Oregon and Washington. *The Great River of the West: The Columbia River*. September 1959.

Lichatowich, James, et al. "Biologists Who Care—a Streamside Talk with the Authors." *Trout*, Winter 1992.

"The Living Landscape: Wild Salmon as Natural Capital." *Wilderness*, August 1993.

Lumley, Paul, with Robert McClure and Mike Matylewich. *1992 Columbia River Fish Runs and Fisheries*. Columbia River Inter-Tribal Fish Commission, January 4, 1993.

"Making Aggregate at Grand Coulee." *Engineering News-Record*, August 1, 1935.

Mitchell, Bruce. "Rufus Woods and the Development of Central Washington." Wenatchee *World*, June 6, 1950.

Moore, C. F. "The Lower Columbia River." *The Military Engineer*, Vol. 31, No. 175.

Mullen, Jay. "Atomic Operations and the Hanford Credibility Gap." Atomic West Symposium paper, University of Washington, September 26, 1992.

Nehlsen, Willa, Jack E. Williams, and James A. Lichatowich. "Pacific Salmon at the Crossroads—Stocks at Risk from California, Oregon, Idaho and Washington." *Fisheries*, March–April 1991.

Nelson, Elmer. "Columbia River Basin Flood." *Monthly Weather Review*, January 1949.

Neuberger, Richard L. "The Biggest Thing on Earth." *Harper's*, February 1937.

Newton, Tim: "An Overview of the Columbia River Treaty." *Columbia River Treaty Seminars*, April 1991.

Northwest Policy Center. *Northwest Portrait*. University of Washington, 1992.

Northwest Power Planning Council. *Northwest Conservation and Electric Power Plan*. 2 vols. 1991.

———. *Salmon and Steelhead Losses in the Columbia Basin*. 3 vols. 1987.

———. *Strategy for Salmon*. 1992.

———. *Strategy for Salmon Progress Review*. April 9, 1993.

———. *The Green Book—Tracking Pacific Northwest Electric Utility Conservation Achievements, 1978-91*.

———. *Information on Water Quality and Quantity Contained in the Salmon and Steelhead Subbasin Plans*. September 17, 1992.

———. *Annual Report, 1992*.

———. *Genetics and Salmon Production*. February 11, 1992.

Nusrala, Mary Anne. *Search for Survival: Columbia River Salmon*. Oregon State University Extension Service, 1992.

Oregon Department of Fish and Wildlife. *All Species Review of Columbia River Fish Management Plan*, 1991.

Pacific Builder and Engineer. Grand Coulee Powerhouse Special Issue, December 18, 1970.

Pacific Northwest Generating Cooperative. "Fish Experts Say More Science Needed." *Status Report*, November 1993.

Pacific Northwest Utilities Conference Committee. *Salmon Currents—The Battle Over Barges*. April 15, 1993.

People's Power League. *Bonneville Power to Our Home at Cost*. 1937.

Peterson, Arthur. *Economic Development of the Columbia Basin Project Compared with a Neighboring Dryland Area*. Washington State University, January 1966.

Pitzer, Paul C. "A Farm in a Day." *Pacific Northwest Quarterly*, January 1981.

Richards, Jack, and Darryll Olsen. *Columbia River Salmon Production Compared to Other West Coast Production Areas*. Army Corps of Engineers, April 1993.

River Watch. *Columbia River—Troubled Waters.* Detailed map with text. Northwest Environmental Advocates, Portland, Oregon, 1993.

"Robert Gray and Columbia's River, May 1792." *Quarterdeck,* Spring 1992.

Rubin, Rick. "Masts over Portland—The Wheat Fleet." *The Great Waterway,* Columbia-Snake River Marketing Group, 1993.

Saboe, Carroll W. *The Big Fiver: Some Facts and Figures on the Nation's Largest Rivers.* U.S. Geological Survey, undated.

Schuyler, Philip. "Moving to Hanford." *New Yorker,* October 14 and 21, 1991.

Schwiebert, Ernest. *Columbia River Salmon and Steelhead.* Proceedings of a symposium held in Vancouver, Washington, on March 5–6, 1976. American Fisheries Society, 1977.

Seely, R. K. *Construction of Grand Coulee Dam.* U.S. Bureau of Reclamation, April 1971.

Simenstad, Charles A., et al. "Historical Changes in the Columbia River Estuary." *Progressive Oceanography,* Vol. 25, pp. 299–352, 1990.

Smith, Robert David. "A Life on the Columbia." *Clatsoop County Historical Society Quarterly,* Summer 1987.

Sohappy, David. "David Sohappy—His Own Story." Briefing Paper, September 3, 1986.

Spranger, Michael, and Randall S. Anderson. *Columbia River Salmon.* Washington Sea Grant, 1988.

Statler, Oliver. "Forbidden Shores." *Winds* (magazine of Japan Airlines), January 1990.

Steele, Karen Dorn. "Hanford: America's Nuclear Graveyard." *Bulletin of Atomic Scientists,* October 1989.

"Ten Months' Construction Progress." *Engineering News-Record,* August 1, 1935.

Tidewater Barge Lines. *Tidewater: A History of Commitment, 1932–1992.* Company briefing paper.

Tollefson, Gene. "Just Who Was Bonneville?" *BPA Circuit,* July 1992.

U.S. Geological Survey. *Largest Rivers in the United States.* 1992.

Van Arsdol, Ted. "First Water 40 Years Ago." *Franklin Flyer,* April 1988.

Vaughan, Thomas. "River of the West." *American History Illustrated,* May–June 1992.

Volkman, John M. "Making Room: The Endangered Species Act

and the Columbia River." *Environment*, May 1992.

Waples, Robin. *Summary of Possible Ways to Characterize Juvenile Onchorhynchus nerka Outmigrants from Redfish Lake, Idaho.* National Marine Fisheries Service, April 1992.

Waples, Robin, et al. "Status Review for Snake River Sockeye." NOAA Technical Memorandum, April 1991.

Warren, Brad. "Barging Ahead." *Workboat Magazine*, July–August 1992.

Washington Department of Fisheries. *Status Report: Columbia River Fish Runs and Fisheries, 1938–91.* July 1992.

Washington State Fisheries Board Hearing. Transcript, May 24, 1924.

Washington State University. *Benefits and Costs of Irrigation Development in Washington.* October 1976.

Washington Water Power. *Company History.* Undated internal publication.

Weitkamp, Don, and Bob Sullivan. "Biological Risks Associated with a John Day Reservoir Drawdown." *Parametrix*, April 1993.

Western Construction, December 1969. "How to Shorten Grand Coulee Dam."

Whittlesey, Norman K. "Should We Finish the Columbia Basin Project?" *Farm Forum*, Spokane, January 1984.

———. *Energy Tradeoffs and Economic Feasibility of Irrigation Development in the Pacific Northwest.* Washington State University Bulletin 0896, 1981.

Whittlesey, Norman K., with Paul W. Barkley, Leroy L. Blakeslee, Walter R. Butcher, Joel R. Hamilton, and Philip Wandschneider. *Measuring the Benefits and Costs of the Columbia Basin Project.* Budget Committee, Washington State Legislature, September 1984.

Williams, Chuck. *Gorge Winds* (periodical of Columbia Gorge Coalition), 1990–93.

Williams, Maynard Owen. "The Columbia Turns on the Power." *National Geographic*, June 1941.

Williams, Paul C. *An Informal History of the Public Utility Districts in Washington and Their Role in Development of the Columbia River.* February 1975.

Winter, Oscar Osburn. "The British in North America." *Pacific Northwest Quarterly*, October 1967.

Woodruff, R. K., and R. W. Hanf, *Hanford Site Environmental Report*

for Calendar Year 1991. U.S. Department of Energy, June 1992.
Woods, Rufus. "The 23 Years' Battle for Grand Coulee Dam." Wenatchee *Daily World*, special section, 1944.
Yakima Indian Nation. *Summary of Fisheries*. 1992.

Index